Passing Performances

TRIANGULATIONS
Lesbian/Gay/Queer ▲ Theater/Drama/Performance

Passing Performances

Queer Readings of Leading Players in American Theater History

EDITED BY

Robert A. Schanke and Kim Marra

Foreword by Jill Dolan

Ann Arbor

THE UNIVERSITY OF MICHIGAN PRESS

Copyright © by the University of Michigan 1998
All rights reserved
Published in the United States of America by
The University of Michigan Press
Manufactured in the United States of America
⊗ Printed on acid-free paper

2001   2000   1999   4   3   2

A CIP catalog record for this book is available from the British Library.

Library of Congress Cataloging-in-Publication Data

Passing performances : queer readings of leading players in
    American theater history / edited by Robert A. Schanke and Kim
    Marra.
        p.   cm. — (Triangulations)
    Includes bibliographical references (p.   ) and index.
    ISBN 0-472-09681-8 (acid-free paper)
    ISBN 0-472-06681-1 (pbk. : acid-free paper)
    1. Gay actors—United States—Biography.   I. Schanke, Robert A.,
1940–   II. Marra, Kim, 1957–   III. Series.
PN2286.5 .P37   1998
792'.028'08664—dc21
    [B]   98-19710
                                                  CIP

For our partners,
Jack C. Barnhart
and Meredith Alexander,
whose love and companionship
animate our lives and our work

Acknowledgments

From first proposal to publication, this book has been five years in the making. Many people have helped us bring it to fruition.

We owe an enormous debt to our editor at the University of Michigan Press, LeAnn Fields, without whose vision, persistence, and savvy we would not have come this far. She encouraged us not only to develop this book, but to see it as part of a project of larger scope. For her continued willingness to take risks and navigate challenges, we thank her and look forward to the next phase of our collaboration.

Jill Dolan, coeditor of Michigan's "Triangulations" series, has supported this project since its inception. She has been a teacher to many of us, and her scholarship has profoundly influenced our own. Her guidance in helping us clarify the book's critical frameworks proved particularly instrumental to its completion.

We extend deep gratitude to our contributors, who kept their faith in us through a long, often arduous process involving numerous rounds of revision. Billy J. Harbin, with whom we are also developing a biographical encyclopedia in concert with this book, has shared many of the challenges and rewards with us, and we especially thank him for his dedication, hard work, and good cheer.

On our respective campuses, several colleagues have sustained us with their continued enthusiasm, wise counsel, and willingness to read and comment on drafts of various parts of the project: at Central College, Margaret Fitch, Mary Jo Sodd, and Treva Reimer; at the University of Iowa, Meredith Alexander, Art Borreca, Corey Creekmur, Jane Desmond, Kevin Kopelson, Teresa Mangum, and Judith Pascoe.

Numerous institutions gave permission to use photographs and other archival material. They are credited where appropriate in the individual essays. A revised version of Kim Marra's essay, "A Lesbian Marriage of Cultural Consequence: Elisabeth Marbury and Elsie de Wolfe, 1886–1933," which was originally published in *Theatre Annual* 47 (1994): 71–96, appears here with the consent of the College of William and Mary.

Finally, we thank our families, who have supported our life choices which this book makes even more public. And we cherish the new immediate family that has formed between us and our partners through our years of collaboration.

Foreword

Jill Dolan

Passing Performances: Queer Readings of Leading Players in American Theater History arrives at an auspicious moment in American culture. In 1997, comedian Ellen DeGeneres graced the cover of *Time* magazine with her wry confession, "Yep, I'm Gay," and performed her personal and professional outing in front of millions of television viewers as her eponymous character, Ellen Morgan, recognized and began to celebrate her lesbian sexuality. By the next season, of course, ABC had canceled the show, suggesting that the show's concerns had become too sectarian. Even Chastity Bono, who was at that time a spokesperson for GLAAD (Gay and Lesbian Alliance Against Defamation), was cited saying that the show had become "too gay." Although Bono said her remarks were taken out of context, the show became a lightning rod both within and outside the gay and lesbian community for determinations about the "proper" representation of gay content in a mainstream forum.

DeGeneres's partner, actor Anne Heche, caused perhaps an even greater media distraction when she accompanied DeGeneres on her public coming-out tours, since Heche had previously been identified as heterosexual. Much was made of her upcoming starring role alongside Harrison Ford in *Six Days, Seven Nights,* but Heche kept her contract to perform in the summer 1998 blockbuster. She managed to garner respectable reviews, ones that tacitly admitted that despite the doubts and anxieties, it seemed a self-declared lesbian could act like a straight woman after all. All the musing over this performance was absurd for those who know, as *Passing Performances* proves, that gay and lesbian performers have been acting straight in popular entertainment, without detection, for quite some time.

These cultural events provide a poignant backdrop to the historical, biographical, and theoretical accounts of performers collected in *Passing Performances.* Why does it matter, positively or negatively, to know the sexual practices or preferences of current and former celebrities in American theater, film, and television? Most popular magazines obsess over the romantic involvement of the stars they cover and have become more and more willing to treat gay and lesbian stars (the few who are out) equally in their prurient coverage of these performers' sexual and domestic entanglements. Many gay and lesbian journalists and scholars are committed to unearthing the subcultural knowledge (either through gossip, oral history, or archival research) necessary to determine a performer's sexual desires and proclivities. These searches offer much pleasurable validation and illumination for gay/lesbian/queer spectators and readers, and they provide an important corrective to presumptions that popular performers are invariably heterosexual.

Passing Performances looks through the annals of American theater history, reading the lives and relationships of many of its most well-known figures through the lens of contemporary queer theory and gay and lesbian studies. The collection doesn't presume to examine a "gay aesthetic" in theater history, nor to analyze plays and performances of the period through a "camp sensibility." Instead, by offering these historical/ biographical studies, *Passing Performances* provides a foundation for future work in the field, including more extensive theoretical treatments and book-length critical biographies that take full account of the sexual histories of these important players. As editors Robert A. Schanke and Kim Marra suggest in their introduction, sexuality is a historical force of filiation and collaboration, rather than a private choice without public consequence. Unearthing new knowledge through new readings of sexual practices and inclinations gives us valuable information about professional loyalties and commitments and about the transmission of knowledge of theater as an industry driven by people with complicated passions, desires, and social networks.

The notorious, primary relationship of gays and lesbians with theater has always been anecdotal. Those of us who teach in university or college theater departments, or who have worked in professional, university, or community theater, know firsthand that gays and lesbians find community in theater work and that the liberal traditions of the field tend to shield us from the kind of homophobic judgments that other, more conventional professions sometimes authorize. Despite such a relatively safe space, very few of the most public figures in contemporary theater have declared their sexual preferences or romantic affiliations publicly. Instead, subcultural networks of knowledge, a range of ubiquitous and persuasive "open secrets," have proliferated around theater's history and its present. *Passing Performances* begins the process of uncovering stories only murmured, of bringing to light, if not to voice, the same-sex relationships that fueled some of the most foundational theater work in American history. This present volume addresses the lives of actors, directors, and producers; a second volume, which will concentrate on designers and people who worked in other aspects of theater, is now in process.

This recovery project is long overdue. *Passing Performances* offers parallels to feminist scholarship that uncovered hidden troves of knowledge about women's lives and marks its debt to historical projects in gay and lesbian studies by Martha Vicinus, Martin Duberman, Lillian Faderman, and George Chauncey. Yet *Passing Performances* stakes its claim when some commentators are arguing against identity politics in the social movement and in gay/lesbian/queer studies, suggesting a move away from sectarian declarations of visibility's equation with power. Queer theory has further destabilized claims to authenticating statements of subjectivity, casting suspicion on intellectual and community projects that would look for evidence to shore up unassailable assignments of sexual "orientation." Why invest in ascertaining whether a performer was or is "gay," if that designation no longer resonates as permanent or perhaps even meaningful? And what, still, are the politics of "outing"?

Passing Performances works within these theoretical and political instabilities, admitting to "homosexuality" as a historical and changing category, one that applies differently across the many case studies collected in this volume. The authors bring with them a healthy skepticism about what constitutes knowledge of same-sex desire while simultaneously insisting on the importance of the quest for such information, however tenuous or conjectured. How can a scholar prove desire or genital contact? the editors and authors here ask. Knowing that we can't doesn't derail the necessity that we read from the perspective of desire, or from the queer perspective of non-conforming sexual practices and relational affiliations. These terminological and historical challenges motivate the work, compelling its precision even among its doubts.

The discourse of "passing," which has recently become a forceful critical trope, bears a double meaning when those passing are performers. The multiple public and private performances detailed in these case studies bring new facets to critical studies of identity as "performative." As Schanke and Marra insist, historical icons of the theater shape people's self-conceptions in deep and lasting ways. *Passing Performances*, then, is a prideful volume, one that takes intellectual and political risks to begin the process of naming important figures whose historical moments or personal choices forced them to reconfigure their private desires for public consumption. By recovering those desires and by authorizing them as a driving force in American theatrical creativity, *Passing Performances* offers important historical examples to future generations of American theater-makers. Learning our history anew allows us to cast a more hopeful, inclusive eye on our collective future.

The series Triangulations: Lesbian/Gay/Queer Theater/Drama/Performance focuses on theater, drama, and performance in all its interdisciplinary and historical variety and in all its professional and community manifestations. The series is committed to a triangulated notion of lesbian/gay/queer as well as to tracing the lines between theater/drama/ performance. We assume the most generous possible definition of performance, from the dramatic literature staged in theater buildings to the rituals of daily life that assume a performance quality (such as commitment ceremonies or memorial services) to the performative dimension of sex, sexuality, gender, race, and other identity categories. At the same time, we remain committed to scholarship about work that is specifically theatrical in reception and intent, from work at various lesbian and gay theaters and performance spaces to work by activist groups around the country, who use theatrical spectacle to political effect. Triangulations embraces traditional historical scholarship as well as high theoretical work in queer studies, emphasizing grounded materialist discourse. *Passing Performances* is a welcome addition to our list.

Contents

MANAGING HOMOPHOBIA

COLD WAR MANEUVERS

Introduction

Robert A. Schanke and Kim Marra

Only in America—Disney's America at any rate—can the act of a TV sitcom heroine declaring her lesbianism be turned into a media epic that plays out over seven months, generating a striptease of publicity that in a simpler age would be beyond the imagination of even P. T. Barnum, if not Gypsy Rose Lee herself. . . . Though there are some two dozen gay characters on other network shows, "Ellen" is the first with a gay lead. . . . it remains to be seen how many doors it will open. Who in Hollywood will have the guts to hire Ms. DeGeneres, or any out gay actor, to play a straight lead in a TV series?
— Frank Rich, *New York Times*

[I]t's all starting to feel like a Jackie Collins novel. I hired her [Anne Heche] because she was great. When she auditioned I wasn't aware of her homosexuality. I don't think she is a homosexual, by the way. I think she is probably bisexual. She's gone out with all kinds of guys. . . . I think it will do the movie some harm, and that makes me nervous.
— Ivan Reitman, producer of *Six Days, Seven Nights*

Amid the recent media sensation surrounding the on- and off-screen love life of Ellen DeGeneres, Sheila James Kuehl, who played Zeida Gilroy in the popular 1960s sitcom *The Many Loves of Dobie Gillis,* recalled her own experiences as a closeted lesbian in Hollywood. At the age of twenty-one, she was promised her own spin-off show. "People were high on it. We thought it would really go. But all of a sudden there was a great silence and it sank like a stone. A couple of weeks later, the director told me that the president of CBS thought I was a little butch." Her television career was over. Commenting on DeGeneres's coming out thirty-five years later, Kuehl asserted: "Even in 1997, I think it is an act of courage."[1]

The lesbian and gay rights movement began in 1969 with the infamous police raid and ensuing riots at the Stonewall Inn, a gay bar in Greenwich Village.[2] Yet it is still a traumatic decision and an enormous risk for a public figure like DeGeneres to make an open declaration of her sexual orientation, to acknowledge to the world what has clearly been one of the defining facets of her life and her comedy. DeGeneres's Emmy award for the writing of the coming-out episode, a commendation by Vice President Al Gore for forcing Americans to "look at sexual orientation in a more open light," and higher ratings for the series in fall 1997 rewarded her pioneering efforts but did not remove anxieties surrounding them. Homophobia resounded in the "Adult Content" warnings slapped on the show for displays of affection between lovers that would have been accepted without qualifications in a heterosexual framework.[3] By spring 1998, ABC-TV had canceled *Ellen* and aired in its time slot a new, strikingly heterosexual and male-dominated sitcom, *Two Guys, a Girl, and a Pizza Place.*

This book deals with a number of DeGeneres's predecessors in the 150 years before Stonewall who worked primarily in the theater, as opposed to television or film, but whose status as highly visible cultural icons of wide public influence was in many ways analogous to hers. Unlike DeGeneres, however, these figures were unable to "come out" because the risks were too great or because the categories of what is out and what is in, what is gay, what is straight, did not pertain or were differently drawn. Still, same-sex sexual desires significantly shaped their personal and professional affiliations and artistic sensibilities. In this volume, fourteen essays by American theater historians analyze the workings of these desires in the careers of noted actors, directors, producers, and agents.

Even though concepts of sexuality and "outness" apply differently to many of our subjects than to Ellen DeGeneres, our project has been, and will no doubt continue to be, seen in the current, highly controversial terms of "outing." This became quite obvious in August 1996 when the National Archive of the Lesbian and Gay Community Services Center of New York City sponsored a panel discussion as part of their ongoing "InQueery?!" lecture series that they called "Straight Acting: Closeted Stars of American Theater." Eight contributors to this volume engaged in a lively exchange with a standing-room-only audience, which included pioneering gay authors Jonathan Ned Katz and Kaier Curtin, for nearly three hours.[4] Several people verbalized their appreciation of the project. "We gays and lesbians need this book," they cheered. "These are our heroes." The praise was not unanimous, however. Afterward, a gay couple employed in publishing objected vehemently: "This is ridiculous! Alfred Lunt and Lynn Fontanne were great actors! Why do we have to know about their sex lives?" They insisted there was no reason, absolutely no value in learning about the sexual orientation of the stars and departed in disgust. One fired off the parting line, "I don't want to know that Lynn Fontanne slept with another woman!"

These objections reflect fear that reputations of cherished icons will be tarnished and the value of their art negated, attitudes rooted in homophobia that continues to permeate the theater world as well as the larger society. Fergus (Tad) Currie, who served as assistant national executive secretary/central regional director of Actors' Equity from 1986 to 1996 and is now professor of theater and chair at Illinois State University, observed in his professional experience

> actors afraid to reveal their sexual identity for fear of losing employment; actors who, having "come out" were at best tolerated, and in the worst cases made to feel like second class citizens; producers who, for a variety of reasons including their own homophobia refused to hire openly gay or lesbian actors. . . . Many gays and lesbians in the entertainment industry feel forced to remain in the closet, thus robbing them not only of their identity but also placing them under pressures that are counterproductive to a creative life.[5]

We argue that knowledge of the role of same-sex sexual desire in historical figures' theatrical careers is central to understanding their contributions and essential both to writing a fuller and more accurate account of history and to changing current attitudes. Indeed, not to write this history is to be complicit in what has been called "inning," the perpetuation of systematic denials that foster the climate of shame and risk surrounding same-sex eroticism within and without the theater.[6]

The rationales for our argument and the reasons this knowledge matters are manifold. As Martin Duberman, George Chauncey, Martha Vicinus, and other historians of sexuality have powerfully demonstrated, this facet of humanity cannot be relegated to a discreet realm of the private and ignored in assessments of people's public activities.[7] Sexuality permeates people's beliefs, actions, and social relations; it is not only a question of whom they sexually desire but how they see, and function in, the world. We want to examine how larger societal and cultural attitudes shaped our subjects' sense of sexual difference in their respective periods, and the interplay of their on-and offstage lives in this context; how their sexuality affected their choices of intimates, professional associates, the kind of work they did, and how they performed it; how shared understandings with people of like persuasion both enabled and inhibited their collaborations; how they and their associates exploited as well as suffered from modes of discrimination and oppression. Far from irrelevant, these questions, in acknowledging sexuality as a historical force, inquire into the very fabric of the past.

Moreover, the knowledge we seek to produce doesn't just add to but transforms the record. Pulitzer Prize–winning historian Barbara Tuchman calls biography "the prism of history."[8] When acknowledged, the facet of sexuality, considered along with other facets of identity, such as gender, race, ethnicity, and class, changes the shape of the whole and vastly complicates what we see looking through it. Reading the career of the nineteenth-century macho icon Edwin Forrest in light of his longtime, erotically charged intimacy with ardent fan James Oakes alters conventional assumptions about the construction of American manliness and the nature of audience-performer interactions in the largely working-class male world of the Bowery. Likewise, learning that the career of turn-of-the-century fashion and decor maven Elsie de Wolfe was enabled by the love of another powerful woman indicates that female same-sex eroticism was inscribed in the very fashioning of virtuous womanhood and suggests multiple layers to the modeling de Wolfe provided for her largely female following. Knowing that Alfred Lunt and Lynn Fontanne, consummate stars of heteronormativity in the 1920s and 1930s, sustained their partnership through mutual understanding of each other's same-sex liaisons confounds conventional assumptions about sexual compatibility in marriage. This information prompts a reexamination of these figures' careers and the social and cultural dynamics surrounding their performances.

Ultimately what this knowledge affects is not just understanding of the past but understanding of human identity and historical processes in the present. As women and racial minorities throughout the twentieth century have shown, reclaiming one's history from systems of repression is an essential act of self-enunciation that inspires and sustains ongoing struggles for equality. For the last three decades, it has been vital to the lesbian and gay rights movement that such recovery work involve people whose contributions are well known but whose sexual proclivities have been kept "hidden from history."[9] Acknowledging and analyzing the sexualities of famous people both fills gaps and corrects distortions in their individual histories and debunks negative stereotypes oppressive to all members of the gay and lesbian community. In demonstrating the specificity and diversity of sexualities through time, historical recovery work counters constructions of a monolithic, unchanging "homosexuality" that stigmatizes and denies people their individual differences and individual rights.

The recovery work of this collection builds on the contributions of other scholars and addresses lacunae in the still small field of gay and lesbian theater studies. Research in the history of sexuality grounds the methodology and provides crucial material about the larger sociocultural context within which we read our respective moments of theater history.[10] The work of some of these historians—notably Martha Vicinus, George Chauncey, Lillian Faderman, Eric Garber, and Esther Newton—directly intersects the world of the theater.[11] Of the scholars centered in the theater who do gay and lesbian studies work, relatively few are theater historians, and fewer still are American theater historians. Kaier Curtin's pioneering *"We Can Always Call Them Bulgarians"* (1987) and Nicholas de Jongh's more recent *Not in Front of the Audience* (1992), which divides its focus between New York and London, usefully set the twentieth-century theatrical context. Rather than focusing on the relationships between individual subjects' lives and work, as this book does, however, they survey productions of plays featuring representations of homosexuality and lesbianism. Laurence Senelick's work is exemplary in its examination of the interplay of gender and sexuality in performers' careers.[12] Where he deals with figures of the American popular theater, our project primarily concerns "legitimate" New York theater icons. Robert A. Schanke's biography of Eva Le Gallienne (1992) and James V. Hatch's of Owen Dodson (1993) offer rigorous scholarly treatments of the issues of homosexuality and lesbianism in their subjects' lives.[13] Drawing on some of that research, this book gathers under one cover a variety of shorter case studies on a range of individuals covering 150 years of American theater history.

The majority of scholars currently working in lesbian and gay theater studies specialize more in the areas of theory and criticism than theater history. While many focus largely on contemporary theater, their perspectives have informed how we read theater history. In her engagements with postmodern theory, Sue-Ellen Case's insistence on the agency of a lesbian subject positioned both inside and outside ideology and able to change the conditions of her existence continues to be inspirational. Jill Dolan's paradigmatic theorizations of feminist spectatorship and the dynamics of lesbian desire in various kinds of performances have been especially important to this project. How Stacy Wolf has continued these and other queries in exploring the "use value" of Cold War–era American musicals in shaping lesbian subjectivity has also enriched our understandings of theatrical reception. John Clum and David Savran provide leading readings of gay male sexuality in modern American drama and theater. Theoretical and critical analyses of the intersections of sexuality and gender with race, ethnicity, and class by Kate Davy, David Román, and Jennifer

Brody have pushed us to consider, for example, how Adah Isaacs
Menken's purported Jewishness and Alla Nazimova's Russian émigré
status made their sexual "deviance" more visible and threatening, how
Charlotte Cushman and Elisabeth Marbury were insulated by their ties to
upper-middle-class WASP society, how Joe Cino's Italian Americanness
informed his sense of self and the camp aesthetics he developed Off-Off-
Broadway.[14]

Recent theoretical and historical work raises key questions about the
ways knowledge of historical figures' same-sex sexual desires is produced, what constitutes that knowledge, and what its current ramifications are. A central question concerns how we as coeditors and contributors to this volume position ourselves in relation to our recovery projects.
We are using a rubric of "queer readings" within which we can both
retain the historical specificity and political agency of our respective identities and embrace the multiplicities, fluidities, and contradictions contained in contemporary notions of queerness. One can identify as lesbian,
gay, bisexual, transgender, or straight, as the contributors to this volume
variously do, and perform queer interventions. As Dolan stated in her
keynote address at "Queer Theater: A Conference with Performances,"
"To be queer is not who you are, it's what you do, it's your relation to
dominant power, and your relation to marginality, as a place of empowerment."[15] When we factor same-sex eroticism into the complex
network of forces determining our subjects' careers, we and our contributors are doing queer theater history, working from various identity positions and rereading the past in ways that challenge the normalizing presumptions of heterosexuality.

If doing queer theater history involves affixing labels to our subjects'
sexualities, the onus is on each of us to clarify the problematics of that
recuperative gesture. Key questions to pose include these: What were the
salient conceptual frameworks of sexual normalcy and deviance within
which our subjects functioned? How and to what extent did they identify
their desires and behavior as transgressive? What were the terms for
sexual deviance of their time, and how did they relate to those terms?
Historians of sexuality have shown that the terms *homosexual* and *heterosexual* were not coined until the 1890s and were relatively obscure medical concepts that did not enter common circulation until the early decades
of the twentieth century. The more popular terms *gay* and *lesbian* were in
common subcultural usage in the decades prior to World War II, but even
as many in the subculture embraced these terms as more affirming alterna-
tives to the then pathologized *homosexual,* others vehemently eschewed

them because of their connection to perversion and scandal. As terms used without as well as within subcultural circles, *gay* and *lesbian* gained widespread currency only in the last third of the twentieth century. Common usage of the term gay to refer to both men and women who sexually desire members of their own sex is problematic because it subsumes women into a male universal. Similarly, as lesbian theorists remind us, the term *homoerotic* primarily connotes male desire.[16] While many people of all sexes have reappropriated the term *queer* as a militant gesture of pride, its long history as an extreme pejorative still makes it difficult for some people to use, to describe either themselves or their predecessors. The essayists in this collection variously negotiate these terminological problems. How we do so is crucial to how we recover and relate ourselves to our subjects.

Even more vexed than the issue of what to call our subjects is the question of evidence. How do we know they desired members of the same sex? Most people's sexual desires—straight or queer—have not been conclusively documented with direct forms of proof, like eyewitness accounts and explicit photographs. Moreover, an individual's sexual behavior and desire may neither coincide nor remain consistent. The standard of "hard" evidence is elusive for different-sex desire as well, but biographers have not traditionally been faced with having to prove heterosexual subjects' sexuality; it is simply presumed, automatically buttressed less by facts than by hegemonic assumptions. Historically, many subjects never stated their subaltern desires publicly; often these subjects vehemently eschewed any imputations of sexual abnormality. Revelatory letters or photographs, if they ever existed, have likely been destroyed or kept hidden from researchers to protect reputations.

What, then, is the proof, if there is no self-identification, if there are no extant letters or diaries, if interviews with friends and colleagues are impossible or inconclusive? Neil Miller recently pointed out that "to insist on evidence of genital sex or the unearthing of some lost 'coming out' manifesto to prove that someone was gay or lesbian sets up a standard of proof that cannot be met."[17] Absence of such evidence neither proves nor disproves the existence of the desire. In fact, in John D'Emilio's words, "absence" of or "inaccuracies" in evidence may register "ways misinformation is purposely used to deflect attention away from 'who one is' or 'who one is not.' "[18]

To recover our subjects' subaltern desires and their historical impact, we have had to build circumstantial cases in which all evidence is relative and most is ersatz. The process is one of reading multiple signs, including those of absence, relative to historically contingent sign systems. Dolan's argument that the "signs of sexuality are inherently performative"[19] enables us to read our subjects' erotically charged behaviors both on and offstage as performances. For most of our subjects, these were "passing" performances, ones that enabled them to circulate as acceptable in mainstream culture while registering signs of subaltern desire in strategies of self-concealment and subversion of dominant role expectations. In these performances, the primary register of sexual identification is gender; that is, sexual deviance is often expressed through coded manipulation of gender stereotypes. Additionally, there are signs of concealment and erasure deployed by family and friends, the media, public opinion, and the scholarly community. Where possible, we have tried to find evidence of direct expressions of subaltern desire, in subjects' private papers if accessible, or in documented printed accounts by close associates. As noted, however, this kind of evidence is very rare because of the obvious risks involved in creating such documentation. Often what has remained is an ephemeral oral history handed down through generations within subcultural theatrical circles and recoverable through interviews.

In gathering this evidence and reading performances of sexuality, we cannot dismiss the value of gossip. As Edith Becker, Michelle Citron, Julia Lesage, and B. Ruby Rich have argued, gossip provides "official unrecorded history": "Long denigrated in our culture, gossip nevertheless serves a crucial purpose in the survival of subcultural identity within an oppressive society. If oral history is the history of those denied control of the printed record, gossip is the history of those who cannot even speak in their own first-person voice."[20] Of course, neither a piece of gossip nor any other single piece of evidence, such as cross-dressing, can be conclusive on its own. A circumstantial case about the workings of subaltern desire in a particular theatrical career must be built through an accretion of signs. Each sign must be read in relation to the others, and in relation to the subject's own level of consciousness about the meaning of her or his behavior within the larger framework of material and ideological circumstances that define prevailing standards of normalcy and deviance.

Vexed and elusive as it is, this evidence is vital to our project because of the highly influential and complex ways historical icons shape the self-conceptions of people across the social spectrum, both in their own time and now. The ramifications are both personal and political. While those of us who identify as gay and lesbian have always projected fantasies of desire and identification onto putatively heterosexual stars, it can be immensely validating, not to mention arousing, to know that these fantasies are not pure projection, that, in the face of our continuing degradation, widely worshiped icons were at least in some measure like us. For those who identify as straight, evidence of the role of same-sex sexual desire in star performers' careers can be profoundly disorienting. Certainly it increases awareness of the constructed, contingent, and shifting nature of all sexualities, including their own. For gays, lesbians, and straights, it can change how we consume cultural products—Mary Martin's rendition of "I'm Gonna Wash That Man Right Outta My Hair" may never sound the same. In the political realm, straight America cannot simply say to those who desire differently, "Why don't they just keep it to themselves." As the examples of Forrest, de Wolfe, the Lunts, Martin, and others in this book indicate, desire for persons of the same as well as opposite sex has been deeply implicated in the production of icons that shape dominant cultural expectations of us all; who "we" are is part of who "they" are. Charting the diversity of sexual practices and sexual identities through time clarifies how "straight," "gay," "lesbian," "bisexual," "transgender," and "queer" are distinct but symbiotic formations, and none is monolithic or transcendently "natural."

This research has particular political ramifications for the institution of the theater, which has long borne the reputation of being a haven for homosexuality. The actual dynamics that constitute that "haven" and by which people with subaltern sexual desires have sought and operated in it until recently have been largely repressed in historical accounts and still warrant further study. Nicholas de Jongh relates the modern association between homosexuality and the theater to the Puritans, who demonized the profoundly spectacular, sensual, and shifting presence of the actor's body in public performance, linking it to prostitution and the worst of all carnal sins, sodomy.[21] As modern theater capitalists cleaved to bourgeois morality and pushed the institution toward greater respectability, the dangers of revealing this allegedly sodomitical center became more acute, while the possibilities of doing so became more tantalizing.

The primary means of negotiating this minefield—and the major source of theater's allure for those marginalized on the basis of sexual deviance—has been public performance, with its distinctive potentialities for both self-concealment and self-revelation. One has special license ostensibly to become something other, which affords the protections of a mask; at the same time, one is expected to call upon one's innermost resources—"give one's all"—to enliven the role for the audience. Thus, no matter how elaborate the role playing, one is always extraordinarily vulnerable and exposed on stage. The essays in this volume explore this ambiguity, at once the greatest promise and the greatest terror the stage holds for people who spend so much of their lives hiding who they are, and for whom those very skills—of dissembling, learning what passes, speaking and acting in codes—mastered from an early age have fitted them for a theatrical career.

If, historically, the theater has been a designated arena where people are given special license to perform a range of identities, it is also the place where the art of performance has been the most regulated by conventions. Among those conventions that queer practitioners have been the most expert at manipulating are those that allow the representation of otherwise socially transgressive behavior. In this sense, the highly conventional theater has been, to use Laurence Senelick's phrase, "a safe-house for unconventional behavior."[22] Even when direct representations of same-sex eroticism were strategically avoided or strictly forbidden, subaltern desires could be smuggled in through other kinds of transgression, such as extreme heterosexual passion, criminality, gender-bending, derisive wit and ridicule, comic irony, and stylistic excess, which have been the stock-in-trade of theatrical entertainment. Such smuggling helps explain, for example, the extraordinary success of Charlotte Cushman's Romeo, Alla Nazimova's Hedda Gabler, and Monty Woolley's Sheridan Whiteside. We wish to explore the multiple ways our subjects exploited the safe-house where representations of certain social transgressions were permitted and aesthetic distance allowed both performers and audiences to indulge in multiple readings without relinquishing claims to acceptability.

These explorations involve consideration of the peculiarly American exigencies placed upon both theater and sexuality that are tied to the persistent strains of Puritanism in white, middle-class culture. The formation of modern sexual identities coincided with the formation of American national identity on principles of supreme purity and progress. The United States was to be the New Eden where Humanity could begin again, unsullied by the sinful degeneracies that were thought to have corrupted the Old World, and attain unprecedented heights of civilization. Categories of hetero- and homosexuality arose in conjunction with other categories of gender, race, ethnicity, and class formed to further the project of nationhood. Because of dominant cultural anxieties about the relatively new status of American identity, these category boundaries were especially rigid and compulsively enforced in major social institutions and public discourse. In making the theater respectable, leading U.S. theater capitalists turned it into a showcase for exemplary American manhood and womanhood.

Given the sexism as well as heterosexism endemic to expectations and representations of American nationhood, the ramifications of on- and offstage role playing have been different for women than men. While injunctions of good character weighed heavily on both sexes, the construct of the New Eden hinged most pivotally on women's moral purity. Thus, the whole issue of female sexuality has been even more vexed in the United States than elsewhere in Anglo-European culture, a dynamic that has rendered female-female eroticism alternately more invisible and more insidious and demonic. For women in the theater, this has presented special performance challenges and opportunities that variously impacted our subjects. Essays inquire, for example, into how American obsessions about ideal womanhood enabled the highly personal and professional partnership of Elisabeth Marbury and Elsie de Wolfe but vilified the far more ambiguous relationship between Nance O'Neil and Lizzie Borden. Actresses uninsulated by strong ties to respectable bourgeois society could be branded as lesbian just for taking the "masculine" step of entering a public profession.

If gender and sexual role expectations have become less restrictive for women in twentieth-century American theater and society, the reverse may be true for men. Erotically charged male bonding seems to have been a fairly open interaction surrounding Forrest's performances of American manliness at the Bowery Theatre in the antebellum period. After the public scandal of his divorce from socialite Catherine Sinclair, he did not hide the fact that his most constant and intimate companion was another man. By the 1920s and 1930s, Alfred Lunt and Guthrie McClintic assiduously maintained bearded marriages in order to further their careers. Even post-Stonewall, male actors' fear of violating heterosexist standards of American manliness prevails. England's Ian McKellan, the first openly gay actor to be knighted, observed that "there's not one [publicly acknowledged homosexual leading actor] in your country. Not one. It's odd, isn't it?"[23] Lesbian therapist and author Betty Berzon explains that "men's roles are much more rigidly defined in this society than women's, so sometimes women can make changes that men can't." Michelangelo Signorile maintains that for most heterosexual men gay men having sex with each other is more threatening than lesbian women having sex with each other. "To many men," he insists, "the next step after the idea of having sex is those men coming after them. . . . On some level for them [straight men] there's something erotic about lesbians and something very scary about gay men." In *The Advocate* essay entitled "The Amazing Invisible Men of Show Business," author John Gallagher concludes,

> While coming out of the closet may pose a greater threat to men
> than to women, staying in offers advantages to men that it does not
> offer to women. If the decision makers are all straight men, a gay
> man who keeps his mouth shut will look like he belongs to the same
> club. . . . Forced to confront sexism, lesbians may decide to confront
> the closet as well.[24]

The different and changing stakes for men versus women involved in
being identified with same-sex desire are prominent among the specific
dynamics by which American theater has functioned as a "haven for
homosexuality." Taking such factors into account renders a fuller record
and helps dissipate oppressive and distorting generalizations about both
the institution and its practitioners.

The fourteen essays are arranged in four chronological groupings to
illuminate how same-sex sexual desire impacted leading players in various
theatrical occupations relative to changing concepts of sexual normalcy
and deviance. "Tests of 'True Love' " includes Edwin Forrest, Charlotte
Cushman, and Adah Isaacs Menken, whose personal lives and careers
traded on the same-sex erotics of "true love" in the antebellum period;[25]
"Intimations of Inversion" covers Elisabeth Marbury, Elsie de Wolfe, Elsie
Janis, Nance O'Neil, and Alla Nazimova, whose intimate same-sex relations were variously interpreted around the turn of the century when the
concepts of homo- and heterosexuality began to enter popular discourse,
and homosexuals were imaged as "inverts"; "Managing Homophobia"
examines the "lavender marriages" of Alfred Lunt and Lynn Fontanne and
Guthrie McClintic and Katharine Cornell, the lesbian collaborations of
Margaret Webster and Cheryl Crawford, and the queer comic antics of
Monty Woolley, which negotiated codified constructions of homosexual
perversion in the post-Freudian inter-war years; and "Cold War Maneu-
vers" involve the on- and offstage performances of Mary Martin and Joe
Cino, who resisted the paranoid enforcements of heterosexual normality
in the McCarthy era. Illustrations accompany each essay, and the volume is
indexed to facilitate tracking of subjects' intersecting careers.

While the careers of our subjects span the decades from the 1820s to
the 1960s, the volume is not intended to be comprehensive but rather is
offered as a sampling of case studies. Many gaps remain. Some essays
undertaken for this volume that were to extend, for example, the work of
Eric Garber and others on the lesbian and gay subculture of the Harlem
Renaissance regrettably fell through because of authors' difficulties with
evidence. Neither were we able, for some of the same reasons, to main-

tain a more equitable balance between male and female subjects. Some of these gaps and imbalances will be redressed in a second volume of essays on pre-Stonewall theatrical writers, critics, and designers and in a biographical encyclopedia covering well over a hundred figures from the full range of theatrical occupations in the same period. We hope that many more scholars will further the project of analyzing same-sex sexual desire as a significant force in leading players' lives and aesthetics and in the making of theater history.

NOTES

1. Frank Rich, "The 'Ellen' Striptease," *New York Times,* April 10, 1997. See also Bruce Handy, "Roll Over, Ward Cleaver," *Time,* April 14, 1997, 78–85; Bruce Handy, "He Called Me Ellen DeGenerate," interview with Ellen DeGeneres, *Time,* April 14, 1997, 86; Jeffrey Wells, "Mr. Showbiz Exclusive: Anne + Ellen = Trouble?" News Archive, <ABCNews.com> (April 25, 1997).

2. Even though subcultures of people who desired members of the same sex had been active throughout the twentieth century and earlier, the Stonewall riots dramatically heightened their visibility and thus mark the popularly recognized beginning of the contemporary lesbian and gay rights movement. Important twentieth-century precursors to the contemporary movement were the Mattachine Society and the Daughters of Bilitis.

3. "Gore Praises 'Ellen' for Effect on U.S.," *Des Moines Register,* October 17, 1997; "Is 'Ellen' Out of Favor," *New York,* September 22, 1997, 11; "Ellen DeGeneres: Out and About, She's Reshaping TV's Take on Sexual Identity," *People,* Double Issue, December 29, 1997, and January 5, 1998, 56–57.

4. Jonathan Ned Katz has authored *Gay American History: Lesbians and Gay Men in the U.S.A.* (New York: Thomas Crowell, 1976; rev. ed., New York: Meridian, 1992); *Gay/Lesbian Almanac: A New Documentary* (New York: Harper and Row, 1983); and *The Invention of Heterosexuality* (New York: Penguin Books, 1996). Kaier Curtin wrote *"We Can Always Call Them Bulgarians": The Emergence of Lesbians and Gay Men on the American Stage* (Boston: Alyson Publications, 1987).

5. Fergus (Tad) Currie, interview by Robert A. Schanke, July 31, 1997.

6. For a discussion of the concept of "inning," see Larry Gross, *Contested Closets: The Politics and Ethics of Outing* (Minneapolis: University of Minnesota Press, 1993). Choreographer and director Tommy Tune discusses how he has been the victim of "inning" in his memoir, *Footnotes* (New York: Simon and Schuster, 1997).

7. Martin Duberman, Martha Vicinus, and George Chauncey Jr., eds., *Hidden from History: Reclaiming the Gay and Lesbian Past* (New York: Penguin, 1989).

8. Barbara W. Tuchman, *Practicing History: Selected Essays* (New York: Knopf, 1981), 73–74, 80.

9. See Duberman, Vicinus, and Chauncey, *Hidden from History*.

10. In addition to Duberman, Vicinus, and Chauncey, *Hidden from History*, we are also especially indebted to the work gathered in Kathy Peiss and Christina Simmons, eds., *Passion and Power: Sexuality in History* (Philadelphia: Temple University Press, 1989).

11. See, for example, Martha Vicinus, " 'They Wonder to Which Sex I Belong': The Historical Roots of the Modern Lesbian Identity," in *The Lesbian and Gay Studies Reader*, ed. Henry Abelove, Michèle Ana Barale, and David M. Halperin (New York: Routledge, 1993), 432–52; George Chauncey, *Gay New York: Gender, Urban Culture, and the Making of the Gay Male World, 1890–1940* (New York: Basic Books, 1994); Lillian Faderman, *Surpassing the Love of Men: Romantic Friendship and Love between Women from the Renaissance to the Present* (New York: Morrow, 1981), and *Odd Girls and Twilight Lovers: A History of Lesbian Life in Twentieth-Century America* (New York: Penguin, 1991); Eric Garber, "A Spectacle in Color: The Lesbian and Gay Subculture of Jazz Age Harlem," in Duberman, Vicinus, and Chauncey, *Hidden from History*, 318–31; Esther Newton, *Cherry Grove, Fire Island: Sixty Years in America's First Gay and Lesbian Town* (Boston: Beacon, 1993).

12. See, for example, Laurence Senelick's "Lady and the Tramp: Drag Differentials in the Progressive Era," in *Gender in Performance: The Presentation of Difference in the Performing Arts*, ed. Senelick (Hanover, NH: University Press of New England, 1992), 260–45, and "Boys and Girls Together: Subcultural Origins of Glamour Drag and Male Impersonation on the Nineteenth-Century Stage," in *Crossing the Stage: Controversies on Cross-Dressing*, ed. Lesley Ferris (New York: Routledge, 1993), 80–95.

13. Robert A. Schanke, *Shattered Applause: The Lives of Eva Le Gallienne* (Carbondale: Southern Illinois University Press, 1992); James V. Hatch, *Sorrow Is the Only Faithful One: The Life of Owen Dodson* (Urbana: University of Illinois Press, 1993).

14. See, for example, Sue-Ellen Case, "Toward a Butch-Femme Aesthetic," in Abelove, Barale, and Halperin *Gay and Lesbian Reader*, 294–306, "Performing Lesbian in the Space of Technology, Part I," *Theatre Journal* 47 (March 1995): 1–18, and "Performing Lesbian in the Space of Technology, Part I," *Theatre Journal* 47 (October 1995): 329–43; Jill Dolan, *The Feminist Spectator as Critic* (1988; reprint, Ann Arbor: University of Michigan Press, 1991), and *Presence and Desire: Essays on Gender, Sexuality, and Performance* (Ann Arbor: University of Michigan Press, 1993); Stacy Wolf, "The Queer Pleasures of Mary Martin and Broadway: *The Sound of Music* as a Lesbian Musical," *Modern Drama* 39 (spring 1996): 51–63, and " 'Never Gonna Be a Man/Catch if You Can/I Won't Grow Up': A Lesbian Account of Mary Martin as Peter Pan," *Theatre Journal* 49 (1997): 493–509; John Clum, *Acting Gay: Male Homosexuality in Modern Drama* (New York: Columbia University Press, 1992); David Savran, *Communists, Cowboys, and Queers: The Politics of Masculinity in the Work of Arthur Miller and Tennessee Williams* (Minneapolis: University of Minnesota Press, 1992); Kate Davy, "Outing Whiteness: A Feminist/Lesbian Project," *Theatre Journal* 47 (May 1995): 189–205; David Romàn, "Teatro Viva! Latino Performance and the Politics of AIDS in Los Angeles," in *Etiendes? Queer Read-*

ings, Hispanic Writings, ed. Emilie L. Bergmann and Paul Julian Smith (Durham, NC: Duke University Press, 1995); and Jennifer Brody, "Hyphen-Nations," in *Cruising the Performative: Interventions into the Representation of Ethnicity, Nationality, and Sexuality* (Bloomington: Indiana University Press, 1995).

15. "Queer Theatre: A Conference with Performances," Center for Gay and Lesbian Studies, New York, April 27–29, 1995.

16. The terms *homo-* and *heterosexuality* first appeared in print in the United States in the early 1890s as the theories of German sexologists, most influentially those of Richard von Krafft-Ebing, entered English-language medical discourse. See, for example, Katz, *The Invention of Heterosexuality,* 19–21. As Chauncey demonstrates, the medical profession did not "invent" homo- and heterosexuality; rather, doctors coined these terms in response to preexisting social phenomena. Well before the medical publications, people were self-identifying as "queer," "fairy," and "Sapphic" and did not just internalize but resisted the pathology the sexologists imposed upon them. See George Chauncey, "From Sexual Inversion to Homosexuality: The Changing Medical Conceptualization of Female Deviance," in Peiss and Simmons, *Passion and Power,* 109.

17. Neil Miller, *Out of the Past: Gay and Lesbian History from 1869 to the Present* (New York: Vintage, 1995), xx.

18. John D'Emilio, oral presentation at the Lesbian and Gay History Conference, City University of New York Graduate Center, October 6–7, 1995.

19. Jill Dolan, "Breaking the Code: Musings on Lesbian Sexuality and the Performer," in *Presence and Desire,* 139.

20. Edith Becker, Michelle Citron, Julia Lesage, and B. Ruby Rich, "Lesbians and Film," in *Out in Culture: Gay, Lesbian, and Queer Essays on Popular Culture,* ed. Corey K. Creekmur and Alexander Doty (Durham, NC: Duke University Press, 1995), 31.

21. Nicholas de Jongh, *Not in Front of the Audience: Homosexuality on Stage* (New York: Routledge, 1992), 5–6.

22. Senelick, *Gender in Performance,* xi, 39.

23. Otis Stuart, "The World's Most Famous Gay Actor," *QW,* June 21, 1992, 34.

24. All quotations in this paragraph are found in John Gallagher, "The Amazing Invisible Men of Show Business," *Advocate,* May 13, 1997, 26–32.

25. Given the early-nineteenth-century medical view of the human body as a closed-energy system whose productive force lust could readily dissipate, middle-class culture evolved the concept of true love, which separated passion from sensuality, defining the former as moral and spiritual and the latter as immoral and carnal. Significantly, the concern about potentially destructive sensuality was focused primarily on the act of intercourse. This conceptual framework defined sexual transgression chiefly in terms of base and insincere "false love" and nonprocreative and/or extramarital coitus. As Katz points out, "The early 19c middle-class fixation on penis-vagina coitus implied that numerous pleasurable acts not involving the 'penetration' of this specific female part by this specific male part were not thought of as prohibited, or even as 'sexual' " (*The Invention of Heterosexuality,* 44–47).

Tests of "True Love"

"My Noble Spartacus"

Edwin Forrest and Masculinity on the Nineteenth-Century Stage

Ginger Strand

Edwin Forrest (1806–72) owes his reputation to his status as American theater history's first native-born, native-trained star. Famous for his emotional interpretations of Shakespeare—especially the roles of Othello, Macbeth, and Lear—Forrest is also remembered as an early benefactor of American drama, which he fostered through a series of competitions for American playwrights. The prizewinning plays, including John Augustus Stone's *Metamora*, which played in repertory with his Shakespearean roles, allowed Forrest to dominate the American stage from 1835 to 1855, making more money than any American actor before him and helping to institutionalize the star system on American stages.[1]

But Forrest's legacy lingers more compellingly, if more intangibly, in the enduring image of him as representative man: a brawny, melodramatic tragedian turned hero for the working classes; a self-made man who created for himself, from a repertoire of Shakespearean monarchs and historical populists, an on- and offstage persona that embodied the mid–nineteenth century's interdependent virtues of entrepreneurial self-reliance and masculine vigor. He was, according to Walter Meserve, "essentially melodramatic: strong, direct, and representative of masculine America."[2] Bruce McConachie refines the equation, describing Forrest as representative of the mid–nineteenth century's "yeoman ideology of manly honor, republican independence, and hero worship," a construct that can also be seen in popular representations of Andrew Jackson.[3] From his own time to ours, Forrest has been constructed as a paragon of nineteenth-century masculinity.

But the particularities of this construction—what it has included and what it has suppressed—have much to tell us about the last century's changing conceptions of sexuality and masculinity. And much of it comes as a surprise. Forrest may have been "representative of masculine

America," but his sexuality is by no means straightforward. And his hypermasculine persona, on further investigation, can be seen as based not on the suppression of feminine characteristics, but rather on their incorporation. This reading is not one that needed a century to be possible. Even while creating Forrest's "manly" image, contemporary commentators acknowledged the radical sexual inclusiveness that underlay the actor's public and private lives.

Born and raised in Philadelphia, the young Forrest was apprenticed as a clerk to an importing house but nursed an unquenchable ambition for the stage. As a child, his official biographer, William R. Alger, informs us, Forrest "was thin, pale, and had a slight forward stoop of the chest and shoulders," with "a quick pulse, a nervous habit, a sensitive brain and skin," and a tendency to cry easily. Aware of these limitations, the boy created for himself a strict regimen of gymnastics and wrestling, based on that of circus performers, which ensured that by the time he was seventeen, he was "as fine a specimen of a manly youth as one might wish to see."4 It seems, then, that he was drawn to the stage as a means of creating the vigorous masculine identity that eluded him as a child. Having done so, his "Herculean" physique, along with his resounding, emotional voice, was one of his greatest assets as an actor. Working his way through the stage ranks, first with sporadic parts in his hometown, then grueling stock actor work, he made his New York debut at the newly built Bowery Theatre in 1826—a theater whose trajectory was similar to his own. After his first night, his managers promptly voided his contract for twenty-eight dollars a week and wrote a new one giving him forty. From that point on, he was acknowledged to be one of the leading actors of his age.

Forrest's rise to stardom was concurrent with sweeping changes in urban life being wrought by skyrocketing immigration and the shift in the theater business that followed. If Forrest's stage personality embodied the ascendant Jacksonian values of strength, freedom, common sense, and self-creation, his tremendous success had as much to do with the creation of an audience desirous of a hero with those traits. This audience, increasingly working class although still predominantly male, instigated a transition in both the way the theater business was conducted and the kinds of plays that were popular. McConachie describes this transition as a shift from "elite paternalism"—a paternalistically administered theater business that favored fairy-tale melodramas starring benevolent father-figures—to the period of "yeoman independence," in which stars and stock companies offered a more heterogeneous audience heroic melodramas featuring heroes for the people.[5]

The "people" were increasingly aware of themselves as such, and growing more and more self-conscious about their desires and requirements for heroes, as evidenced by the segregation of theater audiences along the lines of class. Beginning in the 1820s, and continuing into the 1830s, working-class audiences abandoned the "fashionable" theaters in favor of houses like the Bowery and the Chatham that catered to an audience of "mechanics."[6] Regularly denounced in the press for their tumultuous and uncouth behavior, these audiences increasingly became the show itself, as their move onto the stage in later "local color" dramas proves.[7] And they loved Forrest as one of themselves.

Forrest's New York debut was undertaken at a theater that Moody explains was intended to be fashionable, although "[i]n later years it became known as the democratic playhouse."[8] Walt Whitman's reminiscences of the Bowery Theatre demonstrate the specifically masculine, working-class appeal that Forrest and his audience confirmed for each other.

> Recalling from that period the occasion of either Forrest or Booth, any good night at the old Bowery, pack'd from ceiling to pit with its audience mainly of alert, well-dress'd, full-blooded young and middle-aged men, the best average of American-born mechanics— the emotional nature of the whole mass arous'd by the power and magnetism of as mighty mimes as ever trod the stage—the whole crowded auditorium, and what seeth'd in it, and flush'd from its faces and eyes, to me as much a part of the show as any—bursting forth in one of those long-kept-up tempests of hand-clapping peculiar to the Bowery—no dainty kid-glove business, but electric force and muscle from perhaps 2,000 full-sinew'd men . . . [9]

Forrest chose his roles carefully to appeal to this audience, even selecting from among Shakespeare's heroes. The non-Shakespearean plays in his repertoire all cast him as patriot and populist. John Banim's *Damon and Pythias* was perhaps the most popular of Forrest's non-Shakespearean roles outside the prize plays. In it, Forrest portrayed Damon, the ancient Greek democrat whose refusal to acknowledge the tyrant Dionysus leads to his imprisonment and death sentence and gives his beloved friend Pythias the chance to offer to die for him. The play focuses on the passionately loyal relationship between the two men. Banim's play was one of the most widely disseminated versions of a narrative that had broad popular appeal: in mid-nineteenth-century America, the phrase *Damon and Pythias* was often used to refer to an intensely loyal friendship between two men.

But Forrest found his best roles in the prize plays written specifically for him. The successful star began his play contests in 1828, requesting an American play in which "the hero or principal character shall be an aboriginal of this country."[10] The first winning play was John Augustus Stone's *Metamora; or, the Last of the Wampanoags,* a heavily sentimental depiction of the doomed noble savage who refuses to submit to the white man's tyranny. The play included a romantic subplot and plenty of thrilling action, and it was an immediate hit, as was Forrest's idea for the play contests, which constructed him as both charitable and patriotic. His motives were hardly lacking in self-interest, however. The actor bought the prizewinning plays outright and performed them, allowing the authors no further rights while creating a tremendous popular reputation for himself. Several plays subsequently became nineteenth-century American stage classics. Besides Stone's *Metamora,* Robert Montgomery Bird's *The Gladiator,* and Robert T. Conrad's *Jack Cade* were the most successful prize plays.

The contests provided a means by which Forrest could acquire exactly the kinds of roles he wanted to shape his public persona as patriotic democrat and opponent of oppression. In fact, all of the plays gave him the same role: that of the natural man, honest, unquestionably loyal, courageous, and self-reliant. In *The Gladiator,* he played Spartacus, leader of the Roman slave uprising that begins when he refuses to combat his own brother. As Jack Cade in Conrad's play of that name, he reversed the common idea of the fourteenth-century English insurrectionary leader as an odious leveler, remaking him as what Alger calls "an avenging patriot, who felt the wrongs of the downtrodden masses and animated them to assert their rights."[11]

McConachie shows that each of these plays follows a four-part formula, in which a hero in search of a utopia for himself and his people is thwarted, first by the oppression of aristocratic rulers, then by the betrayal of his own people, until he must become a martyr to his cause.[12] Even the less stageworthy prize plays provided this role for Forrest. Robert Penn Smith's *Caius Marius* cast its title figure, a Roman general found in Plutarch, as a fervent democrat battling aristocratic tyranny. Bird's *Oralloossa, Son of the Incas,* invented a son for Itahualpa the Inca, executed by Pizarro, in order to tell a tale of individual freedom struggling against tyrannical oppression. Only in Bird's *The Broker of Bogota* did

Edwin Forrest as Spartacus

*(Courtesy Billy Rose Theatre Collection, The New York Public Library
for the Performing Arts, Astor, Lenox and Tilden Foundations.)*

Forrest diverge from the role, playing a father whose happiness is ruined by his own rigid authoritarianism. While Forrest, for once, played the conservative role, the play's overall antiauthoritarian message is clear.

These plays gave Forrest a chance to display his physical and emotional prowess in a variety of idealized masculine character-types: soldier, gladiator, statesman, chieftain. They involved elaborate costuming, whose historicizing provided an excuse to foreground Forrest's physical features. And they foregrounded a populist politics that was seen as part of his specifically masculine ethos. Alger declares that the manly ideal permeates all of his roles.

> This imperial self-reliance and instinctive honesty, this unperverted and unterrified personality poised in the grandest natural virtues of humanity is the key note and common chord to the whole range of his conceptions. Fearless faithful manhood penetrates them all as the great elevating principle that makes the harmonies of one essential ideal.[13]

Forrest's ideal excludes one audience as efficiently as it addresses its particular fans. In the reminiscence quoted above, Whitman notes that while both Booth and Forrest thrilled the masculine, working-class audience, "both these great actors and their performances were taboo'd by 'polite society' in New York and Boston at the time—probably as being too robustuous."[14] Certainly "polite" critics did object to what Whitman calls the "robustuous" style of these actors. For Forrest, though, the taboo became much more rigorous after his two public scandals: the 1849 Astor Place riot, and his divorce from Catherine Sinclair.

In the Astor Place riot, at least twenty-two men died when the militia were called out to quell crowds disrupting a performance of *Macbeth* by English actor William Macready.[15] Although the ostensible reason for the riot was the performance's competition with Forrest's simultaneous enactment of the role, the rivalry between the two stars was long-standing. Like the split from his English wife, the rivalry with Macready demonstrated Forrest's equation of Englishness, aristocratic oppression, and femininity. Bad feeling heated up when Forrest hissed Macready publicly during a performance of *Hamlet* in Edinburgh. In a letter to the editor of the *London Times,* Forrest explained that he had used this "salutary and wholesome corrective of the abuses of the stage" because he objected to a "fancy dance" Macready had inserted after Hamlet's line "I must be idle."[16] Throughout the rivalry, Forrest labeled Macready as outdated, aristocratic, and effete, and his battle cry was gladly taken up by nativists and members of the Know-Nothing Party, who demanded "America for Americans" and sparked the riot by posting flyers proclaiming, "WORKING MEN: SHALL AMERICANS OR ENGLISH RULE IN THIS CITY?"[17]

For Forrest the issue of anti-English sentiment was mingled with his own domestic unhappiness. Henry Wikoff, Forrest's traveling companion during his 1835–36 trip abroad, relates that Forrest's fears about marrying Sinclair centered on her status as an Englishwoman.[18] Although he took advantage of his bachelorhood—his diary of this trip is well stocked with accounts of his trips to brothels and prostitutes, often reporting on two or three sexual encounters in an evening—the actor was, according to Wikoff, deeply committed to the establishment of domesticity.[19] Immediately upon completing his grand tour, Forrest played a brief engagement in New York and Philadelphia, then returned to Great Britain for a professional engagement. He returned in the autumn of 1837 with Catherine Sinclair as his wife.

By all accounts, the marriage was a disaster. Although there seem to have been a few happy years, Forrest carried on an extramarital sex life, and Catherine was depressed and exhausted from bearing four children, all of whom died at birth or within a few days afterward. Acquaintances reported on a vast difference in temperaments: Catherine sociable, Forrest private, with some claiming that Forrest felt self-conscious about the literary, urbane circle that Catherine drew around herself. Forrest's friend James Rees attributes much of their difference of temperament to nationality, asserting, "If Mr. Forrest had established in his household certain rules, and taught his wife the difference between English and American habits, much of the evil, arising out of their misunderstanding, might have been obviated."[20] But there also is some truth to assertions by Catherine's supporters that Forrest resented her superior social position. Writing to her from Baltimore, for instance, he recounts that a "grand democratic procession" had passed in front of the theater, "with cheers for your humble servant. You will I am sure be gratified to hear this in spite of your *pretended* aristocracy."[21]

When the split came, it was bitter and public. Each accused the other of infidelities, and the intimate details revealed in court were printed in newspaper columns. Catherine was granted a divorce; Forrest was found guilty of having committed adultery with actress Josephine Clifton, a brawny, athletic woman with, in one reporter's account, "a bust finely developed, a physiognomy indicative of great firmness of character and a mind rather of a masculine turn."[22] Biographer Richard Moody, speculating on how such a woman could possibly have interested the actor, concludes, "Perhaps Forrest was weary of femininity."[23]

If he wasn't weary before his divorce, he certainly became so afterward. Outraged at the verdict, Forrest immediately embroiled himself in a lifelong series of appeals, refusing to pay the substantial alimony legislated by the court. His letters from this point on become virulently misogynist, insisting that all women are "swindlers," referring to Sinclair as a "whore," and asserting that marriage is the "invention of the devil."[24] All these comments appear in letters to James Oakes, Forrest's constant companion and closest intimate from his divorce until his death.

James Oakes, proprietor of Boston's Old Salt Store, met Forrest backstage after a performance of *Damon and Pythias* in 1827. It was the young actor's Boston debut. The two became fast friends, and after Forrest's divorce, they spent nearly all of their free time together. They traveled together, spent summers and holidays at one another's home, and corresponded frequently when apart. Their letters are filled with passionate assertions of affection and devotion. Oakes often began his letters "My noble Spartacus"; Forrest continually thanks Oakes for his endless tokens of love and devotion. Forrest reports to Oakes on every detail of his life: his engagements, his financial successes and fears, his erratic health, and his intermittent depression. Oakes seemed concerned with all of it and always willing to offer assistance: "Command my services to the fullest extent, in anything and in everything," he signs once, "For I am, from top to bottom, inside and out, and all through, forever yours."[25]

The two often exchanged portraits of themselves; Alger relates that Forrest's Philadelphia mansion displayed portraits of Oakes in the entry, the dining room, the picture gallery, and the library. As they grew older and each suffered from a variety of health complaints, the few weeks they spent together each summer seemed insufficient. After an illness, Forrest assures Oakes that he is healthy: "No, I think we both of us have vitality enough to enjoy many years yet of happiness, even in this vale of tears," he writes sentimentally. "But then, we must inhabit it together, for

'When true hearts lie withered,
And false ones are gone,
Oh, who would inhabit
This blank world alone?' "[26]

Upon leaving for his California tour, Forrest pleaded with Oakes to join him, promising to pay all his friend's expenses and assuring him that "it would make me the happiest man in the world."[27] The two of them frequently referred to a fantasy they shared of moving together to Cuba, which Forrest expected would join the Union before long. "I think with you, we ought not to live so much asunder," Forrest writes to Oakes in 1868, "our time is now dwindled to a span, and why should we not see *together* the declining sun go brightly down upon the evening of our days. What a blessed thing to realize that dream of Cuba—I named it to you when last I saw you."[28] Two years later, Oakes retired from his business, closing the Old Salt Store, and sending his wife to live with one of their daughters while he himself stayed with his sister for a while. Forrest congratulates him on the move, declaring, "I look forward with a loving impatience to the end of my professional engagements this season that I may repair to Philadelphia there to make a settlement of such comforting means as shall make the residue of your life glide on in ceaseless ease."[29]

Forrest did leave Oakes an annuity of twenty-five hundred dollars a year in his will, and certainly his friend deserved it. In Forrest's final days, Oakes was with him for all of his professional engagements, helping him onto the stage and taking care of him after his performances. Writing to one of Forrest's earliest biographers, Oakes gives a touching account of Forrest's final performance and his own role in it.

> The last time Forrest acted was Tuesday evening, April 3rd, 1872, at the *Globe Theatre,* this city; the play was *Richelieu,* on which night he was very ill, and I was with him behind the scenes during the entire performance; and I very much feared he would not be able to get through the play. I led him from his dressing room, with the assistance of his dresser, to the wing, where I had a chair placed for him to sit in, waiting for his cue, during the three last acts, and he was so weak that he was unable to raise himself from the chair, and he would say to me: "Oakes, lift me up, and let me go on!" I would put my arms around his body, and raise him to his feet, when he would in a quick and nervous tone say: "*Steady me, steady me;* get me before the audience, my friend, and I will finish the play, but it may be the last!" Alas! it *was* the *last* time he acted. From the theatre, after the play, I accompanied him to his hotel, where a physician had been summoned, and remained with him day and night without taking my clothes off, until the 24th of April, 1872, *twenty-one days and nights,* as the physician said his life depended more upon nursing than the skill of his physician, and advised that two trained hospital nurses be procured to take charge of him. Forrest looked earnestly into the face of the physician and said: "I want my friend Oakes to take care of me. If careful nursing will save

my life, he will save it." For nearly the whole of this time his life
seemed to hang upon a thread.[30]

Forrest had pneumonia. He recovered and returned to Philadelphia,
where Oakes spent the summer with him. In the fall of 1872 he embarked
upon a reading tour but again became worn down. When he returned
home to recuperate, he died. Daniel Dougherty, a friend of Forrest's,
immediately sent a telegram to Oakes in Boston saying simply, "Forrest
died this morning; nothing will be done until you arrive."[31] The primacy
of Oakes's intimacy was never disputed; this acknowledgment of it seems
especially significant in our own time.

In another letter to Harrison, Oakes writes of Forrest,

> After he had recovered [from the pneumonia in Boston], he said to
> me: "Oakes, you have saved my life this time, and I hope that God,
> in His Great mercy and goodness, may grant that you may be with
> me at my last hour, and with your own friendly hands close my
> eyes!" But, alas! it was not so ordained. Dear, dear, old friend, he
> died alone!! But, my dear Harrison, why, what is death but life in
> other forms of being? . . . There is no such thing as death. What's
> called so is but the beginning of new existence,—a fresh segment in
> the eternal round of change. It is in *God's Justice,* that those who
> sincerely love each other here shall meet in a brighter, happier sphere
> on the "other side!"[32]

When Oakes arrived to bury Forrest, their mutual friend James Rees
relates, "His emotion, his tears, were those of a man true to one with
whom, for years, he had been so intimately associated."[33]

What are we to make of this relationship? In the life of a man so
immovably centered on masculine ideals of courage, independence, and
physical daring, the touching devotion and care stand out. Forrest,
Oakes, and the earliest biographers are not at all self-conscious about
using words like *love, passion,* and *romance* to describe the two men's
feelings for one another. In the introduction to his biography, Alger declares that Oakes was "the sworn bosom friend of Edwin Forrest. He
regarded him with an admiration and love romantic if not idolatrous."[34]
The biographer relates that "whenever they met, after a long separation,
as soon as they were alone together they threw their arms around each
other in fond embrace with mutual kisses, after the manner of lovers in
our land or of friends in more tropical and demonstrative climes."[35] For
his own part, Oakes declares to sculptor Thomas Ball, whom he had
commissioned to make a statue of Forrest: "For more than forty years I

have known this man with an intimacy not common among men. Indeed, our friendship has been more like the devotion of a man to the woman he loves than the relations usually subsisting between men."[36]

In another letter, Forrest relates to Oakes an interesting conversation he has had with Lillie Swindlehurst, his leading lady on all of his later tours. "I am glad you are pleased with Lillie," he writes to Oakes, "who in a letter which I got from her yesterday asks if *we* are married as you told her— which *is* the Woman."[37] Moody mentions this letter in his biography, but mistakenly assumed the "we" refers to Swindlehurst and Forrest, claiming that "Miss Lillie had written asking if she and Forrest were to be married. Oakes straightened her out on this matter, and Forrest forgave her womanly indiscretion."[38] Even without the question "which is the Woman," it's grammatically clear that the "we" referred to here is Forrest and Oakes. Oakes, presumably, had told Swindlehurst that he and Forrest were married, and she (in innocence? in spite? in play?) had written to ask which of them was the woman. Apparently Oakes suggested a response, because in his next letter, Forrest writes: "Thanks dear friend. I shall tell Lillie *not Lottie,* as you have it, that either of us is quite likely to *turn to* a Woman, when it is desirable. Married or Single—Eh!"[39]

As many astute critics have warned us, we must be on guard against reading too much into texts that play by different rules, or placing historical subjects into categories—such as gay or bisexual—that did not even exist at the time those subjects lived. And it is now a truism that before the invention of the category of "homosexual," passionate relationships between members of the same sex were not subject to the rigorous external and internal censorship that forces friends to demonstrate that they are not lovers, once the possibility they might be becomes thinkable. As Robert K. Martin argues,

> [I]t is obvious that the boundaries between permissible and impermissible forms of expression of male friendship were drawn very differently in mid-nineteenth-century America than they are now. It is possible that a strict interdiction against full genital sexuality . . . at the same time allowed for a much fuller expression of male friendship, since that in no way threatened to spill over into genitality.[40]

At the same time, the critic finds herself in a bind, for there is an equally distressing danger in refusing to see gay desire. As James Creech has expressed it: "One must be very prudent in attributing homosexual content to what are only stock effusions in nineteenth-century writing; but just as obviously, one must be careful not to mistake for mere rhetoric the intensely sexual longings which can be smuggled into expression using the very same language as a cover."[41]

The unembarrassed ease with which contemporary commentators remarked on the relationship between Oakes and Forrest certainly suggests that their love for one another in no way violated social or sexual norms of the period. In fact, Forrest's relationship with Oakes was seen to be a sign of his masculinity. Early biographer Lawrence Barrett refers to the relationship as one of "manly affection,"[42] while Alger appends an entire chapter on friendship to his biography, arguing that love between men is the highest form of relationship possible.

> [W]hen two men, two of these intellectual and sentient microcosms, meet, so adjusted as mutually to reflect each other with all their contents and possibilities in sympathetic communion, their life is perfected, their destiny is fulfilled, since the infinite Unity of Being is revealed in each made piquant with the bewitching relish of foreign individuality.[43]

Alger seems to have been planning a book on male friendship before he began Forrest's biography. In an 1869 letter to Oakes, Forrest suggests Alger consult Herman Grimm's recent biography of the artist Michelangelo for a look at "the beautiful friendship" between the aging artist and his "young votary Cavalieri."[44] On the pages Forrest references, Alger would have found a short description of what looks more like an older man's obsession for a young boy, including a description of drawings Michelangelo made for Cavalieri of the rape of Ganymede and a "children's bacchanal," as well as two sonnets written by the artist for his student.[45]

The relationship between Forrest and Oakes drew upon a lively nineteenth-century culture of male friendship that provided not only sanction, but affirmation. This cultural phenomenon has been less well documented than the complementary culture of love "surpassing the love of men" between nineteenth-century women.[46] But even from the evidence of contemporary responses to Forrest and Oakes's relationship, it seems clear that love between men was readily understood within a ready-made context of male devotion. The frequent reference to literary-historical models—Damon and Pythias, Jonathan and David—suggest the extent to which such relationships were understood to be part of a tradition.

Furthermore, this culture of male friendship seems to have sanctioned physical expressions of intimacy. In a brief analysis of a late-nineteenth-century diary describing a passionate friendship between two heterosexual men, Martin Duberman hazards the assertion that "some nineteenth-century men were (contrary to the traditional view) remarkable full and unself-conscious in physically expressing affection for each other."[47] At the same time, however, he points out the unusual nature of the diary, comparing it to the plethora of texts pertaining to women's relationships, and citing it as the "only evidence that has yet come to light (so far as I know) of comparable passion between heterosexual men of the period."[48] Questions surely remain about how much the private correspondence between Oakes and Forrest was a continuation of their public relationship, and how much it used that public relationship as a cover.

Alger openly acknowledges the physical intimacy of the two men, but, typically, relates it to a cultural form of otherness—the habits of "more tropical and demonstrative climes." Later biographers can only see physical intimacy and deep love for a man as a sign of effeminacy, and they downplay the relationship accordingly. The only biographer to address the question of whether the men were lovers, Richard Moody, dismisses the idea because in his eyes it is disallowed by Forrest's virility. "Except for the extravagant expressions of their affection," he declares, "there are no grounds for believing that their relationship was unnatural [*sic*]. Their letters are filled with virile observations on the sexual proficiency of various females. Forrest simply needed the genuine and enduring friendship that he found with a man like Oakes."[49]

For the early biographers, Forrest's relationship with Oakes was a sign of masculinity; for Moody it can only be a sign of femininity. Moody simply points to the fact that the men exchanged information about women as though it thoroughly undermines any attempt to ascribe homosexual content to the relationship. Forrest himself is perhaps the slyest commentator on this tendency: in his quip about being likely to "turn to a Woman," he conflates an assumed femininity with a bragging assertion of his virility. What is surprising in the comment is the playfulness with which Forrest treats the suggestion that the relationship did include genitality, and the unconcerned way in which he connects that possibility with heterosexual exploits.

Moody ignores this revealing comment. In both of the twentieth-century biographies of Forrest, many stories that set the tone of the relationship are dropped, ostensibly because they are only "hearsay," or "reminiscence"; Alger and Barrett, for instance, both mention an occasion on which Oakes was made to dress up in a silk bathrobe and wig and perform lawn chores for Forrest before breakfast.[50] Neither Moses nor Moody repeats this story.[51] And while Alger devotes nearly an entire chapter to delineating the "happy league of unselfish love and faithful service"[52] between the two men, Moses mentions the friendship only in passing, and Moody discusses it for two pages only to eliminate the possibility that it might have been sexual. "Certainly in the mid-twentieth century," he declares, "two men would shy from expressing their affection so openly."[53]

Interestingly, Moody's anxiety about Forrest's sexuality adheres to more than Forrest's relationship with Oakes. While performing in his early stock-actor capacity in New Orleans, Forrest became friends with Push-ma-ta-ha, a Choctaw chief who fostered the actor's interest in Native Americans. In July 1825, entangled in an unfortunate quarrel (over a woman) with his manager, and threatened with the possibility of a duel, Forrest decided it would be politic to leave New Orleans for the summer. He spent two months with Chief Push-ma-ta-ha and his tribe. Alger relates a story that happened one night, as Push-ma-ta-ha and Forrest were lying on the ground before a fire outside the village.

> Like an artist, or like an antique Greek, Forrest had a keen delight in the naked form of man. . . . Push-ma-ta-ha, then twenty-four years old, brought up from his birth in the open air and in almost incessant action of sport and command, was from head to foot a faultless model of a human being. Forrest asked him to strip himself and walk to and fro before him between the moonlight and the firelight, that he might feast his eyes and his soul on so complete a physical type of what man should be. The young chief, without a word, cast aside his Choctaw garb and stepped forth with dainty tread, a living statue of Apollo in glowing bronze.[54]

Moody repeats Alger's account, but adds that this is a story Forrest "might have hesitated to repeat today."[55] Again, the most recent biographer expresses a deep-felt concern that Forrest's sexuality will be "misunderstood" in a more gay-affirmative era.

In spite of his clear discomfort with homosexuality, Moody's comments unintentionally point to an interesting fact in their suggestion that today, in our own more tolerant era, many emotionally compelling aspects of Forrest's life are more likely than ever to be suppressed. It is in our own time, in fact, and not his own, that Forrest's love for Oakes dare not speak its name. This is true in more than the conservative sense that Moody's comments imply. The biographer's point, presumably, is that in our own, "oversexualized" era, Forrest's simple, friendly love for his companion would inevitably be misinterpreted as sexual. But in the wake of the construction of gay and lesbian studies as an academic category, and that category's need to conform to clear standards of historical and interpretive rigor, something quite different has occurred. The historical evidence being as vague and ambiguous as it is, Forrest is just as likely to be excluded as an object of interest for gay and lesbian history by definitions that proclaim sex—and a circumscribed notion of how to define sex—as the standard by which gay identity is measured. If sexual identities were defined as much by the practices of respect, devotion, love, and lifelong care as by the practices of genital contact, Edwin Forrest would be clearly and incontrovertibly defined as gay. Were he a woman, in fact, this identification might be easier to make: Lillian Faderman has made an influential argument for the inclusion of nongenital love relationships between women in the category "lesbian," which she defines as "a relationship in which two women's strongest emotions and affections are directed towards each other."[56] Why, then, limit the definition of male homosexuality to a practice more specific? The ongoing perpetuation of gender stereotypes surely contributes to the fact that Forrest must be described as a bundle of "contradictions": sexually involved with many different women, "married"—as he himself admits—to a man.

Discussing the wide range of possibilities for male relationships in the nineteenth-century, Robert Martin has commented, "The very range of these possibilities may suggest the extent to which the categories that we now take for granted, such as an absolute split between homo- and heterosexual based on genital behavior, were nascent and fluid. Their emergence provided a greater sense of identity for some, but simultaneously meant a loss of possibility for others."[57] Forrest's sexuality with respect to his relationship with Oakes clearly fits into one of these myriad categories, a category not very easy to delineate after the late-nineteenth-century codifications of sexuality in which, as Foucault put it, "the homosexual was now a species."[58]

Given how readily Forrest's intense relationship with Oakes was acknowledged by his contemporaries, it seems likely that Forrest's contemporaries had no concerns or anxieties about it, and it seems logical to attribute this to the wider parameters for expressions of male friendship in the nineteenth century. But there is still the question of whether Forrest's sexual ambiguity was noticed at all by his contemporaries. The answer is at best elusive. If the early biographers were not anxious about Forrest's relationship with Oakes, they were often driven to make assertions about his masculinity that can only be described as hyperbolic, even—it is tempting to say—defensive. In particular, the fact that at least one of Forrest's early performances was in a female role—as a replacement for an absent ingenue—apparently required much rationalization. Writing some reminiscences in 1857, while Forrest still lived, James Rees mentions two female roles and gives an account of the actor's appearance.

> Once more let us turn to the Apollo. It was here Forrest played *Lady Anne*, in the tragedy of "Douglass," to Charles S. Porter's *Young Norval;* he also played *Rosolia*, the beautiful and romantic heroine of the drama entitled "The Robbers of Calabria," to Mr. Porter's *Rudolph*. Forrest's dress on that occasion was not marked by that artistical taste which has since been such a prominent feature in his impersonation of character. It was one we shall never forget. He wore thick, heavy shoes, coarse woolen stockings, and a short, white dress, reaching with some difficulty to his knees; on his head he wore a bright red scarf, intended to represent a sort of fashionable, or rather unfashionable, head-dress. Every time allusions were made to the beauty and the symmetry of her form, and the matchless excellence which is only to be found in the object of our affections, and which *Rudolph* delights to utter, the audience—and it was numerous—laughed most heartily; and well they might, for it was the most comical thing we ever witnessed in the theatrical way. This, we think, was in 1817.
>
> On one occasion Forrest disputed their right to criticize his dress, averring that if silence was not observed he would march off the stage. This had the desired effect—silence was most strictly observed.[59]

Seventeen years later, in his biography, Rees alters the story, dropping the reference to Forrest as Lady Anne, and replacing Forrest's threat to stop performing with an account of a "pugnacious boy" in the pit who comments aloud on Forrest's appearance and is rewarded by having the actor step forward and threaten, "I'll whip you when the play is over." "This silenced the boy," Rees assures us, "and the play went on."[60] Told in this way, the story works much harder to subvert the feminine implications of Forrest's cross-dressing with assertions of his masculine efficacy.

Barrett also feels compelled in the telling of this story to frustrate any tendencies to see Forrest as feminized by his costume.

> In the habiliments of the weaker sex, adorned for the play by unskillful hands, in such garments as could be collected hastily and secretly from several sources, which covered a figure always the reverse of feminine, and were worn in a manner far removed from the dainty grace belonging to such robes, our hero came from behind the scenes

for his *début;* no doubt with a palpitation of heart suitable to his disguise, but in no other way belonging to his *rôle.*[61]

While not suggesting any real defensiveness on the part of the contemporary commentators, these remarks show a level of conscious design going into the representation of Forrest as a paragon of masculinity. Understanding this image as a consciously created one on the part of Forrest and his contemporaries makes it possible to look at masculine ideals themselves in a new light. And one of the most important sources for those ideals will surely be the plays themselves. The dramatic vehicles created for the actor might well be reread for what they tell us about how Forrest was perceived by those around him.

To suggest how things might look different, then, I want to close with a brief discussion of Forrest's phenomenally successful vehicle *The Gladiator,* by Robert Montgomery Bird. This play was one of the biggest moneymakers in Forrest's repertoire, holding the stage for forty years, and being the first play in English to reach a thousand performances during the lifetime of its author.[62] The second of Bird's plays to win Forrest's prize and the first subsequently to be produced (*Pelopidas* won in 1830 but was never performed), *The Gladiator* was written expressly for Forrest's contest—and for Forrest to perform. In writing it, Bird shows not only a thorough knowledge of the ideals Forrest's public persona embodied, but an interest in exploring those ideals in relation to Forrest's status as theatrical spectacle—a position that can be used to stand for a sexual ambiguity Bird may or may not have perceived in the man himself.

Not only designed for Forrest, *The Gladiator* is, in a sense, about him as well. Bird's play tells the story of Spartacus, a Thracian gladiator and leader of the Roman slave uprising. Using source material from Plutarch and Appian, Bird shaped a play that proclaims itself a populist manifesto and can be read, in its excoriation of slavery, as abolitionist.[63] The appeal for the playwright lay in the character of Spartacus, a man who could be remade for Forrest as a heroic man-of-the-people. But he is also, when the play opens, a slave, and this threat to his masculine potency and self-determination is figured by Bird through his spectacularity.

Since Laura Mulvey's influential "Visual Pleasure and Narrative Cinema" laid the groundwork, feminist film theory has associated the position of spectacle with femininity, and the position of spectator with masculinity.[64] Since then, a plethora of critics has sought to elaborate what happens when the position of spectator is occupied by a female subject,[65]

and a smaller, but still significant, number have addressed the idea of the
male as spectacle.[66] While argument rages over whether the spectating
woman is necessarily male-identified, the spectacular male is almost universally understood to be feminized.

Even if this formulation strikes one as somewhat simplistic, it is clearly
operative in Bird's text. In the play's opening scenes, Spartacus loses his
masculine privilege not only by virtue of being a slave, but also by the
spectacularity forced upon him. His first appearance on stage is prefaced
by a conversation between two slaveowners, Bracchius, who unknowingly
owns the wife and son of Spartacus, and Lentulus, who owns Spartacus
himself. As Spartacus is brought on, Bracchius mistakes him for his own
"troop of women and children":[67] all slaves, male or female, look alike to
the master class. Once arrived, Spartacus is widely admired for his muscu-
lar physique, called "A Hercules, a Mars" (244)," metaphorical titles
recalling those applied to Forrest. But Spartacus refuses to play along,
instead taunting his captors. Describing the scene where he was captured,
he tells how he believes his wife and child to be dead, since he looked back
and saw his home on fire with no one outside it. At that, he tells his
audience, "I was a man no more" (245).

It's difficult not to see in this depiction an image of Forrest himself.
Like Forrest, Spartacus combines a spectacular physique with a moody,
unbending personality, presenting both to a largely admiring crowd.
"Well I am here, among these beasts of Rome, a spectacle," he says (251).
But his unmanning lies not only in his loss of freedom, but also in the
sentimental attachments that keep him from regaining it. Eventually,
Spartacus agrees to fight in the gladiator contests in exchange for the
enfranchisement of his wife and son. Although this leads to the slave
rebellion, his sentimental attachments ultimately prove his downfall. He
quarrels with his brother, Phasarius, over a captive woman whom he
pities, causing Phasarius to defect with most of the army. Senona,
Spartacus's wife, reassures the captive Julia by telling her that the heart of
Spartacus "beneath his bloody mail / Can melt to pity quickly as thine
own" (261). Indeed, Spartacus's pity proves fatal. Outnumbered after
most of his army defects, he is unable to give up on his traitorous brother
and escape while he has the chance. Instead, he stays to help Phasarius,
bringing on his own death as well as those of his wife and son.

Bird thus constructs an extremely masculine character whose feminine capacity for sympathy is both his downfall and his exemplary quality. Was there a subtle comment about Forrest worked into this text? Was
Bird using the sexual ambiguity of Forrest to reconfigure his era's ideals

of masculine action and self-reliance? And if so, how does this shed light on our inherited notions of what those ideals were about? Lesbian and gay history cannot simply dispense with these questions. Simply enrolling Forrest as one of its subjects does not even begin to answer them. But it allows the questions to be asked, which moves us toward a broader, more complex understanding of the nineteenth-century's constructions of sexuality, gender, and democracy. And it gives us a more multidimensional look at a personality whose forceful self-creation embodied many contradictions inherent in those ideals and, in doing so, made its mark on the history of the American stage.

NOTES

I am grateful for a Mellon Fellowship in the Columbia Society of Fellows, which provided invaluable time in which to conduct this research.

1. For an excellent account of Forrest's role in transforming audience responses to stars, see chapter 3 of Bruce McConachie, *Melodramatic Formations: American Theatre and Society, 1820–1870* (Iowa City: University of Iowa Press, 1992), 69–90.

2. Walter Meserve, *Heralds of Promise: The Drama of the American People in the Age of Jackson, 1829–1849* (New York: Greenwood Press, 1986), 29. Interestingly, Meserve is here describing Forrest and his contemporary, Charlotte Cushman.

3. McConachie, *Melodramatic Formations*, 68.

4. William R. Alger, *Life of Edwin Forrest*, vol. 1 (Philadelphia: J. B. Lippincott, 1877), 96.

5. McConachie, *Melodramatic Formations*, 65–68.

6. See Mary C. Henderson, *The City and the Theatre* (Clifton, NJ: James T. White, 1973), 62. In *Theater Culture in America, 1825–1860* (Cambridge: Cambridge University Press, 1997), Rosemarie Bank points out that the evidence for class segregation in the theaters is by no means conclusive. However, it is clear from contemporary accounts that a perception of the theaters as divided by class operated in the 1830s and 1840s.

7. For an invigorating account of these dramas, see Luc Sante, *Low Life: Lures and Snares of Old New York* (New York: Vintage Books, 1991), 71–90. Bank also discusses the historical contexts and meanings of these plays in *Theater Culture in America*, 75–119.

8. Richard Moody, *Edwin Forrest: First Star of the American Stage* (New York: Knopf, 1960), 66.

9. Walt Whitman, *Complete Prose Works* (Boston: Small, Maynard, 1898), 429.

10. *Critic*, November 22, 1828.

11. Alger, *Life of Edwin Forrest*, vol. 1, 360.

12. McConachie, *Melodramatic Formations*, 104.

13. Quoted in ibid., 88.

14. Whitman, *Complete Prose Works,* 429.

15. For a complete account, see Richard Moody, *The Astor Place Riot* (Bloomington: Indiana University Press, 1958).

16. Quoted in Alger, *Life of Edwin Forrest,* vol. 1, 411.

17. Moody, *Edwin Forrest,* 273.

18. Henry Wikoff, *Reminiscences of an Idler* (New York: Fords, Howard and Hulbert, 1880), 196.

19. Ibid., 215–16.

20. James Rees ["Colley Cibber," pseud.], *The Life of Edwin Forrest* (Philadelphia: T. B. Peterson and Brothers, 1874), 347.

21. Quoted in Moody, *Edwin Forrest,* 190.

22. Quoted in ibid., 201.

23. Ibid.

24. Edwin Forrest, letters to James Oakes, CO721, Manuscripts Division, Department of Rare Books and Special Collections, Princeton University Libraries; folder 1, June 20, 1857; folder 5, February 24, 1867; folder 3, November 24, 1865. Published with permission of Princeton University Libraries. I would like to thank the archivists, especially Margaret Sherry, at Princeton.

25. Quoted in Alger, *Life of Edwin Forrest,* vol. 2, 626.

26. Forrest, letters to Oakes, folder 3, August 24, 1865.

27. Forrest, letters to Oakes, folder 4, February 27, 1866.

28. Forrest, letters to Oakes, folder 6, April 14, 1868.

29. Forrest, letters to Oakes, folder 8, November 29, 1870.

30. May 11, 1873; quoted in Gabriel Harrison, *Edwin Forrest* (Brooklyn, 1889), 181. This rare early biography is available in the Harvard Theatre Collection; I would like to thank the librarians there, in particular Michael Dumas, for their help.

31. Quoted in Alger, *Life of Edwin Forrest,* vol. 2, 834.

32. May 12, 1873; quoted in Harrison, *Edwin Forrest,* 182.

33. Rees, *Life of Edwin Forrest,* 487.

34. Alger, *Life of Edwin Forrest,* vol. 1, 15.

35. Ibid. vol. 1.

36. Quoted in ibid., vol. 2, 632.

37. Forrest, letters to Oakes, folder 4, March 29, 1866.

38. Moody, *Edwin Forrest,* 358.

39. Forrest, letters to Oakes, folder 4, April 3, 1866.

40. Robert K. Martin, "Knights-Errant and Gothic Seducers: The Representation of Male Friendship in Mid-Nineteenth-Century America," in *Hidden from History: Reclaiming the Gay and Lesbian Past,* ed. Martin Duberman, Martha Vicinus, and George Chauncey Jr. (New York: Penguin, 1990), 180.

41. James Creech, *Closet Writing/Gay Reading: The Case of Melville's "Pierre"* (Chicago: University of Chicago Press, 1993), 65.

42. Lawrence Barrett, *Edwin Forrest* (Boston: J. R. Osgood, 1881), 76.

43. Alger, *Life of Edwin Forrest,* vol. 2, 608.

44. Forrest, letters to Oakes, folder 7, May 24, 1869.

45. Herman Grimm, *Life of Michael Angelo,* trans. Fanny Elizabeth Bunnet, 2 vols. (Boston: Little, Brown, 1865), 2:392–94.

46. Two central texts documenting female relationships are Lillian Faderman's *Surpassing the Love of Men: Romantic Friendship and Love between Women from the Renaissance to the Present* (New York: Morrow, 1981), and Carroll Smith-Rosenberg's "The Female World of Love and Ritual: Relations between Women in Nineteenth-Century America," *Signs* 1, no. 1 (autumn 1975): 19–27.

47. Martin Duberman, "Intimacy without Orgasm," in *About Time: Exploring the Gay Past* (New York: Meridian, 1991), 65.

48. Ibid., 67.

49. Moody, *Edwin Forrest,* 345.

50. Alger, *Life of Edwin Forrest,* vol. 2, 628.

51. See Moody, *Edwin Forrest;* and Montrose Moses, *The Fabulous Forrest: The Record of an American Actor* (Boston: Little, Brown, 1929).

52. Alger, *Life of Edwin Forrest,* vol. 2, 619.

53. Moody, *Edwin Forrest,* 345.

54. Alger, *Life of Edwin Forrest,* vol. 1, 138–39.

55. Moody, *Edwin Forrest,* 47.

56. Faderman asserts "that women's love relationships have seldom been limited to one area of expression, that love between women has been primarily a sexual phenomenon only in male fantasy literature" (*Surpassing Love of Men,* 17–18). Although more recent feminists might find Faderman's claim somewhat essentialist in its ascription of well-rounded, loving relationships primarily to women and, by implication, genital sexuality primarily to men, acknowledging love between men that is not primarily sexual might help circumvent the unhappy gender politics of consigning lesbians to the closet once more in the arena of overtly sexual expression.

57. Martin, "Knights-Errant," 182.

58. Michel Foucault, *The History of Sexuality: An Introduction,* trans. Robert Hurley (New York: Random House, 1978), 43.

59. *Sunday Mercury,* January 24, 1857.

60. Rees, *Life of Edwin Forrest,* 50.

61. Barrett, *Edwin Forrest* 11.

62. Meserve, *Heralds of Promise,* 60.

63. Although early on Bird claimed that if the play "were produced in a slave state, the managers, players, and perhaps myself in the bargain would be rewarded with the Penitentiary," he was wrong. McConachie points out that "like other Jacksonians, southerners understood the rhetoric of slavery and freedom as referring to the traditional rights of white people" (*Melodramatic Formations,* 117).

64. First published in *Screen* 16 (autumn 1975), "Visual Pleasure and Narrative Cinema" has been widely anthologized and is republished in Mulvey's *Visual and Other Pleasures* (Bloomington: Indiana University Press, 1989).

65. A short list would begin with Mulvey's own "Afterthoughts on 'Visual Pleasure and Narrative Cinema' Inspired by King Vidor's *Duel in the Sun,*" in *Visual and Other Pleasures; E. Ann Kaplan's "Is the Gaze Male?" in *Women and*

Film: Both Sides of the Camera (New York: Methuen, 1983); and Mary Ann Doane, "Film and the Masquerade: Theorizing the Female Spectator," *Screen* 23 (September–October 1982): 74–87. Fuller treatment and consideration of the lesbian spectator are given in Jill Dolan, *The Feminist Spectator as Critic* (Ann Arbor: University of Michigan Press, 1988).

66.   See, for instance, the essays in the collection *Screening the Male: Exploring Masculinities in Hollywood Cinema,* ed. Joan Mellen, Steven Cohen, and Ina Rae Hark (London: Routledge, 1993).

67.   Robert Montgomery Bird, *The Gladiator,* in *Dramas from the American Theatre, 1762–1909,* ed. Richard Moody (New York: Houghton Mifflin, 1969), 244. Subsequent references are given parenthetically in the text.

"Such a Romeo as We Had Never Ventured to Hope For"

Charlotte Cushman

Denise A. Walen

Eulogized as a woman of noble character, and greatly respected by the upper-class society she so diligently cultivated away from the stage, Charlotte Cushman (1816–76) was, nevertheless, a figure who resisted the traditional female role assigned many women in mid-nineteenth-century United States society.[1] She was shrewd, energetic, and possessed of a natural and substantial mimetic talent. Surprisingly, Cushman achieved her fame not through the presentation of conventionally successful female characters such as dainty ingenues or lovely tragic heroines. Rather, the roles at which she excelled and that propelled her to the apex of popular and theatrical acclaim were strong, powerful, occasionally disreputable women often lacking feminine charms, or her roles that came from a vast array of complex and challenging male characters.

Cushman received extensive praise for her performances as Shakespeare's Lady Macbeth and Queen Katherine, along with Nancy in the adaptation of Charles Dickens's *Oliver Twist,* and Meg Merrilies from *Guy Mannering.* Cushman's signature roles represent heroic women expressing powerful emotions, with uncommon or unnatural wisdom, who meet tragic ends.[2] Cushman seems to have been drawn to theater by the performance dynamics that allowed women to subvert dominant constructions of womanhood. After Cushman established her prominence, she narrowed her repertoire and increasingly performed only in those plays that had engineered her popularity.

Cushman's portrayal of Shakespeare's Romeo was one of the parts both critically acclaimed and popularly applauded that became one of her standard characterizations. In fact, Cushman's performance of Romeo

Charlotte Cushman's Romeo appeared very masculine to the London audiences who saw her performance in 1845.

(Courtesy Illustrated London News *Picture Library.)*

during the London season of 1845–46 marks a turning point in her career, for it was during that season, and particularly as that hero, that London audiences and critics first acknowledged the considerable extent of her artistic abilities. Known throughout her career as an accomplished performer of "breeches roles," Cushman performed over forty different male characters.[3] Many actresses of the period performed in male roles, but few presented the range of artistic characters undertaken by Cushman. Even fewer still could claim the popular or critical renown lavished upon Cushman's replication of adolescent male love.[4]

However, if Cushman was such an accomplished tragic actress, gaining immense personal distinction in roles like Lady Macbeth, Meg Merrilies, and Queen Katherine, why did she insist on performing any male role? Where especially did the desire originate to play Romeo? And most important, how could this woman so successfully represent the ardent, anguished hero of Shakespeare's tragedy to a nineteenth-century audience so that she, more than any male actor of the age, was to be associated with the character? The prestige of Cushman's Romeo is rendered even more curious when compared to the mixed reviews accorded her portrayal of Hamlet, a seemingly more appropriate cross-dressing vehicle for actresses.[5]

The analysis and interpretation of Cushman's Romeo and her acquisition of male roles lacks an examination of sexuality as it might intersect and affect gender performativity.[6] Opaque allusions to Cushman's sexuality occur in the writings of biographers Lisa Merrill and Joseph Leach, and both writers demonstrate anxiety about identifying Cushman as lesbian.[7] More recently, Faye Dudden considers the possibility that Cushman's performance appealed to a burgeoning, though still unconscious, lesbian audience, but she refrains from exploring the connection between Cushman's own sexuality and her presentation of a romantic male lead.[8] I argue that Cushman's sexuality is related to her desire and ability for cross-gender performance in presenting Romeo. The theater afforded Cushman a space in which she, through the character of Romeo, could become a desiring subject. Cushman's sexuality led her to a performance of gender that would allow her to express desire for another woman. Cushman's behavior and the desire she exhibited toward other women was redolent with same-sex eroticism. Today, such behavior would be termed lesbian. However, while I do not subscribe to the myopically limiting constructionist theories of sexuality that deny homosexual existence before the late nineteenth century, I acknowledge that some of the evidence regarding Cushman's sexuality is challenging in its appeal to anachronism. Accordingly, I begin by establishing the historical context of her performance, identifying the critical parameters that formed Cushman's success as Romeo. Following revisionist historical paradigms, I then examine her affectional relationships with women and their connections to her extraordinary realization of this canonical male role. An analysis of sexuality as a determining factor in performance provides substantial explanation for Cushman's success and popularity in portraying Romeo. Without an investigation of sexuality, comprehension of Cushman's decision to perform this and other socially transgressive roles, as well as understanding her success in these roles, is severely limited.[9]

The mid–nineteenth century, while not best known for its drama, was known for its star actors, and though it would be impossible to offer a general description of nineteenth-century theater in the United States, since a multiplicity of theatrical entertainments existed, it is possible to situate Cushman within the specific tradition to which she belonged. The theater of the middle and upper middle class, as distinct from theater and variety entertainments favored by working-class audiences, primarily offered revivals of Shakespeare with major stars performing the marquee roles that returned to more canonical editions after the centuries-old adaptations of Nahum Tate and Colley Cibber.[10] As the essays in Judith Fisher and Stephen Watt's anthology *When They Weren't Doing Shakespeare* reveal, the legitimate theater might also produce native "American" plays like *Metamora* and those supported by Edwin Forrest's play competition, plays coming out of romanticism like *Monte Cristo,* nautical and military spectacles, sophisticated comedies of elite society like Anna Cora Mowatt's *Fashion,* and, of course, the ever popular melodrama.[11] These various dramatic forms provided an appropriate deviation from Shakespeare while serving to complement Shakespearean plays. By the 1850s aristocrats of the nouveaux riches, the likes of the Astors and the Vanderbilts, had abandoned the theater in favor of opera. Plays that were performed for a cultured New York audience at midcentury were imported from London or mimicked English forms since true style, for this audience, conformed to a European model.[12]

Cushman's triumph in London during 1845 legitimized her entrance to star status upon her return to the States in 1849. From that point on she belonged to the system of star actors who could travel to various cities and to Europe, contracted to play one of a number of signature roles in several different Shakespeare plays and a few melodramas. Cushman's status in the star system was enough of a pedigree to have her accepted, or at least tolerated, by the elite of Newport, Rhode Island, society, were she built a summer house near the end of her life.

In comparison with two other figures from the nineteenth century in this volume, Cushman was a paragon of virtue off the stage as well as a star on it. Unlike Edwin Forrest, who cultivated the image of American masculinity and became, as Ginger Strand says, "a charismatic hero of the working-classes," Cushman followed the pattern set by Forrest's rival William Macready, whose competition with Forrest erupted as much along class lines as nationality during the Astor Place riot. And, though

Adah Isaacs Menken performed a repertoire very similar to Cushman's, her cultivation of a Bohemian lifestyle is far from the careful respectability with which Cushman surrounded herself. The scandals and shocking behavior that seemed to follow both Forrest and Menken were avoided by Cushman. Despite Cushman's acquisition of a male-desiring position on stage as Romeo, anxiety concerning her performance and her life did not emerge until well after her death.

Cushman first essayed the part of Romeo while working as a stock player in New York early in her career.[13] The critic of the New York *Courier,* though not glowing in his praise, had this to say about Cushman's portrayal.

> Her personal appearance, voice and manner are singularly adapted to the performance of juvenile male characters; and a casual observer would have found some difficulty, on Saturday evening, in realizing the fact that Romeo was played by a girl not yet out of her teens.[14]

Cushman continued to perform the role during her early years of acting in the United States. After 1839, when her sister Susan also began an acting career, they performed the play together on occasion, Susan playing Juliet to Charlotte's Romeo.[15] Contemporary critics and biographers found in Susan a useful rationale to excuse Charlotte's performance of male roles, especially Romeo. The critic of London's *Athenaeum* was willing to accept Cushman as Romeo, seeing "sisterly affection" motivating her choice of the play as Susan's introduction to the London stage.[16] In all other respects, this misogynist critic was opposed to women playing tragic heroes. Another critic reasoned that Cushman had to take the male lead to provide Susan the heroine's part, since no plays existed with two strong female roles.[17] Similar arguments are made by Cushman's early biographers, Emma Stebbins and Clara Erskine Clement, who maintain Cushman was averse to playing male characters.[18] However, Cushman's performances of so many male roles, with such skill and vitality, tend to contradict their revisionist moralizing.[19] The vigor and comparability of these critical and biographical arguments belie a general social discomfort with women playing men on the legitimate stage.

Cushman's supreme achievement as Romeo came in her London performance of 1845. She had traveled to England in hopes of acquiring a reputation reserved for English actresses and had made a great hit with London audiences as Bianca in Henry Hart Milman's play *Fazio.* She continued to amaze London in several other roles, among them Meg

Merrilies. Then, on December 30, 1845, she performed Romeo with her sister Susan as Juliet at the Haymarket Theatre. Eloquent praise flowed inexhaustibly from the English critics and created a demand that extended the show's run indefinitely. The *Illustrated London News* proclaimed, "At the Haymarket, the rush to see Miss Cushman as Romeo continues; and on the nights when this gifted actress performs, every available corner is occupied."[20] The *Times* wrote, "It is enough to say that the Romeo of Miss Cushman is far superior to any Romeo that has been seen for years. . . . For a long time Romeo has been a convention. Miss Cushman's Romeo is a creative, a living, breathing, animated, ardent, human being."[21] She was electrifying, and, far from being a passing curiosity, her Romeo became a highly regarded cultural event.[22]

By far the most laudatory comments on the performance come from the dramatist James Sheridan Knowles.

> I witnessed with astonishment the Romeo of Miss Cushman. Unanimous and lavish as were the encomiums of the London press, I was not prepared for such a triumph of pure genius. You recollect, perhaps, Kean's third act of Othello. Did you ever expect to see anything like it again? I never did, and yet I saw as great a thing last Wednesday night in Romeo's scene with the Friar . . . ! My heart and mind are so full of this extraordinary, most extraordinary performance, that I know not where to stop or how to go on.[23]

Panegyric responses for Cushman were no less profound across the ocean. On returning to New York for the 1849–50 season, Cushman played Romeo to packed audiences at the Astor Place Opera House. "It was a prodigiously fine performance throughout," wrote the *New York Post* critic, "and was very much applauded."[24] She included the part in her engagement of 1858 and was christened by the reviewer in *Porter's Spirit of the Times* as "Charlotte the Magnificent."[25] As late as 1860, when at a stout forty-four Cushman was beyond looking the part, her Romeo dazzled audiences. The reviewer of the *New York Times* thought even then that "Romeo is, perhaps, the most difficult character to represent in the whole range of the drama, and we know no one now who can play the part but Miss Cushman." Even in middle age she presented "the love of a young, glowing, unreflecting Italian, rich in passion and tenderness, and yet in its hottest glow chastened with delicacy—a love not of mere sensuality, but of sensuality spiritualized by imagination."[26] These comments, though complimentary, also suggest a possible concern with her portrayal. By sanctifying the passion of Cushman's Romeo, the reviewer elevates it above the simply carnal, alleviating potential criticism of indecorous female sexual expression.

The authority of Cushman's performance was concentrated in her ability to present the character of Romeo with extraordinary veracity. Knowles was astounded by the verisimilitude of the characterization, commenting that "there is no trick in Miss Cushman's performance; no thought, no interest, no feeling, seems to actuate her, except what might be looked for in Romeo himself were Romeo reality."[27] The portrayal was even more amazing because of the gender disparity between the role and the actress. Cushman's depiction of masculine gender behavior differentiated her performance of Romeo from other actresses' pursuits of male roles.[28] Lamenting that "a pair of handsome legs has oftener been the instigation to 'get up' in Romeo than any impression of intellectual capacity to do justice to the part," a female reviewer asserted that such was not true with Cushman.[29] This performance was more than a convention designed to lure male audiences into the theater with the promise of an actress in revealing male attire. Cushman, aided by her tall body, a strong face, and expressive compelling voice, used bold, commanding movements during the performance to represent a masculine character. Her Romeo was considered passionate, exhibiting a violence of emotion not usually seen in nineteenth-century Romeos, but her performance was tempered by a lightness in places, like her gentle condescension toward the nurse.[30] Male actors, apparently in an attempt not to appear effeminate by an outward display of emotion, or to incur censure from demonstrating lustful vigor, tended to play the part with a decorous formality that left the audience cold. The balcony scene and the pronunciation of banishment in Friar Lawrence's cell were considered two of her finest scenes. In the last act she uttered her lines with an "agonized, distracted look"; and "the almost frantic expression of the face, the deadly determination" of her character, made one viewer believe "that Romeo himself stood before us."[31]

Cushman's performance was masculinized to the point that her female gender was rendered invisible in the audience's reception of the play.[32] "We have never seen the character better played," wrote the *Illustrated London News:* "In her bursts of anger or despair we altogether lost sight of the woman: every feminine characteristic was entirely thrown aside in her powerful interpretation of the *role.*"[33] The critic of the *Athenaeum* thought Cushman's characterization of Romeo was "one of the most extraordinary pieces of acting, perhaps, ever exhibited by a woman. Masculine in deportment—artistic in conception—complete in execution. . . . What there was of the woman just served to indicate juvenility, and no more."[34] Cushman's ability to perform male gender elevated her cross-dressing from the novel to the respectable. Hers was considered the quintessential rendition of the character during the period. Contemporaries Noah Ludlow and William T. W. Ball believed Cushman's Romeo surpassed any male actor's attempt at the part.[35]

Cushman's Romeo was especially unprecedented for the intense passion displayed in her scenes with Juliet. "Never was courtship more fervent," wrote the *Athenaeum,* "more apparently sincere, more reverential, and yet more impetuously passionate, than that which on the silent air of night ascended to Juliet's window."[36] Cushman's Romeo was "no fine speech-maker, no stage-lover, no victim to maudlin sentiment," declared the *Times,* "but an impetuous youth, whose whole soul was absorbed in one strong emotion."[37] Even Cushman's fellow actors remarked on the palpable desire evident in her characterization. Westland Marston considered the performance a distinguished victory for Cushman and remarked that "as a lover, the ardor of her devotion exceeded that of any male actor I have ever seen in the part."[38] Cushman not only performed male gender behavior through physical gestures of body and voice, she also replicated male desire and passion. The eroticism of her Romeo transcended Cushman's ability to signify male through the physical control of her body. The interiority of the desire motivating her physical gestures was perceptible to the spectators as well.

The vigorous passion portrayed in her performance intimates the ambiguity of sexual expression when complicated by gender performance. John Coleman felt Cushman's "amorous endearments were of so erotic a character that no man would have dared to indulge in them *coram publico.*"[39] Given the Victorian expectation of what Nancy Cott calls female "passionlessness," Coleman's statement implies that on some level Cushman's gender was identifiable to the audience, who accepted amorous displays between white bourgeois women as normative.[40] A male actor would have been expected to check his desire on stage, lest he be accused of lewd conduct. Cushman, conversely, could display desire for another woman on stage with impunity, since an ideology constructed her gender as sexually passive, even if the reality was quite different.

However, given the overt masculinization of the depiction noted by other reviewers, Cushman's performance stretched the limits of society's reception of gender schematics and sexual expression. Like Coleman, Ball alludes to the ambiguity between gender and sexual desire. In his comments that Cushman presented the best Romeo of the age, he argued that this was so "because as a woman she knew what love was, and as a woman knew how love should be made. She wooed Juliet as she herself would be wooed."[41] This, according to Ball, made her Romeo more passionate. He implies that Cushman's gender gave her insight to female desire. Ball's remarks not only suggest that Cushman's gender gave her insight into another woman's needs, but that underneath dominant cultural presuppositions about female passionlessness, sexual desire between women was possible.

Social anxieties surrounding the prospects of female desire were evident in the few negative criticisms Cushman received. Early in her career she performed the part at the Walnut Theater in Philadelphia with George Vandenhoff playing Mercutio. Vandenhoff felt that Cushman had "unsexed" herself. He called the performance a "hybrid," complaining that Cushman appeared as both sexes and that her "passion [was] equally epicene in form."[42] This combination, according to Vandenhoff, was a "monstrous anomaly." Vandenhoff's comments are edged with a rhetoric that foreshadows the sexologists' discussions of female same-sex eroticisms. These sexologists defined women who performed masculine gendered behavior and wore mannish clothes as "inverts"; since they had perverted "natural" gender presentation. That Cushman had unsexed herself was echoed by critics and fellow actors, even if they ultimately applauded Cushman's portrayal (even Vandenhoff found the performance "effective").[43]

The opposition to Cushman's portrayal of Romeo issued predominantly from the belief that by performing the role of a male character she was denying her femininity. The impropriety of this cross-dressing and gender inversion elicited apprehension, which was intensified by a fear of sexual reversal. While some critics invoked the popular culture's aversion to cross-dressing or questioned Cushman's unsexing herself, the critic of the *Athenaeum* is solicitous of Cushman's gender stability.[44] He apparently believed that the performance of male roles like Romeo would destroy or subvert Cushman's femininity and that the male gender of her characters would be incorporated into her personality, constructing a male identity. Since he already assumed Cushman possessed a masculine mind, one must wonder if the transformation to which he referred was physical in nature. The criticism directed at Cushman's Romeo is not artistic in nature, but rather is grounded in cultural assumptions of appropriate gender behavior. Individuals who objected to Cushman's Romeo complained not that she acted badly, but conversely that in performance she so realistically presented the character that she unsexed herself in the role.

Cushman's accomplishment as Romeo, and it was an accomplishment whether it subsequently engendered approbation or censure, may be attributed to her artistic expressions of her sexuality. In (re)claiming Cushman's sexuality and its impact upon her career choices, an examination of the shift in societal acceptance of affectional behavior between women is important. Following theories presented by Lillian Faderman in *Surpassing the Love of Men,* Merrill discusses the shift in public perception regarding Cushman. Merrill explains that the sexologists altered society's impression of Cushman.[45] Initially recognized as a morally responsible, virtuous, and sexually chaste member of society during her lifetime, despite her less than reputable career choice, Cushman's reputation became questionable nearly forty years after her death. The discursive rhetoric of men like Karl Westphal, Havelock Ellis, and Richard von Krafft-Ebing, when applied retrospectively to Cushman, posits her behavior firmly near aberration. Focusing more on social manifestations than sexual behavior, Krafft-Ebing identified gender inversion as characteristic of lesbianism.[46] In *Psychopathia Sexualis* he suggested,

> Careful observation among the ladies of large cities soon convinces one that homosexuality is by no means a rarity. Uranism may nearly always be suspected in females wearing their hair short, or who dress in the fashion of men, or pursue the sports and pastimes of their male acquaintances; also in opera singers and actresses, who appear in male attire on the stage by preference.[47]

According to Merrill, theater scholars came to view Cushman with anxiety after the general public accepted the sexologists' pathologizing situations of gender inversion as sexually unhealthy.[48] At the time of her death in 1876 she was enormously popular and greatly respected, but her memory was obscured with the passage of time and the potential, after 1910 or so, to identify her behavior as lesbian.

The identification of the lesbian by the early sexologists in the late nineteenth century categorized and defined, indeed constructed to some extent, the modern notion of lesbianism. However, the sexologists named behavior that existed previous to their observations and distorted it to fit their theories. Unfortunately, they chose to stigmatize and criminalize the actions of women who loved women. Faderman traces what she views as this progression from society's acceptance of romantic friendships to the condemnation of lesbianism.[49] Though the construct of lesbian did not emerge into popular consciousness until after the turn of the twentieth century, the behavior of women like Cushman formed the basis for the early construction of the identity.

Writings of scholars such as Faderman and Carrol Smith-Rosenberg
lead to a revisionist interpretation of female affectional behavior that,
though not lesbian in all the modern connotations of that word, provide an
identification and comprehension of erotic alliances between women.
Smith-Rosenberg's work suggests that although homosexuality and lesbianism became pathologized, earlier cultures, especially nineteenth-century
middle-class society in the United States, displayed acquiescence with a
broad range of same-sex erotic behavior, including emotional and sensual
attachments between women.⁵⁰ Rejecting a focus on genital contact between women, she is able to demonstrate an expansive register of affectional preferences that were all women-centered. Faderman also defines
lesbianism from an emotional and social context with little emphasis on
sexual circumstances.⁵¹ This definition issues from her finding that the
sexologists cited many cases between women that involved no genital
contact in their establishment of a lesbian identity.

To recuperate Cushman's sexuality as a meaningful historical determinant that affected not only her character choices but her popular reception,
it is necessary to look both at issues of gender inversion and affectional
preference. Cushman's gender inversion was a performative extension of
her same-sex erotic desire that found expression in cross-dressing and
lesbian behavior. Cushman remembers her childhood in Boston as follows:

> I was born a tomboy. My earliest recollections are of dolls' heads
> ruthlessly cracked open to see what they were thinking about; I was
> possessed with the idea that dolls could and did think. I had no
> faculty for making dolls' clothes. But their furniture I could make
> skillfully. I could do anything with tools. Climbing trees was an
> absolute passion.⁵²

Cushman's assumption of socially defined male behavior extended into
adulthood. At the age of twenty she was supporting her family financially
and would continue to support many of them throughout her life. By her
early thirties she had adopted a tailored style of dress that was decidedly
masculine.⁵³ And while she never married, she set herself up as the head
of any household she established, whether in the United States, England,
or as the center of an expatriate group of female artists in Rome.⁵⁴ She
also experienced strong physical attraction to women, as evidenced by
her reaction to a woman she met at a dinner party in England.

> The loveliest woman I ever looked upon . . . such eyes, such hair,
> such eyebrows, mouth, nose, chin . . . I never saw in my life be-
> fore. . . . What a lucky thing I am not of the other sex, for a heavy

mortgage would have been made upon her from this hour. As it was, it almost deprived me of appetite for my dinner.[55]

During her lifetime, Cushman became involved in several intimate relationships with women. She met Rosalie Sully while acting in stock companies early in Boston. The two corresponded when Cushman traveled to England, and at one time Cushman hoped to send for Sully.[56] Cushman apparently gave the woman a ring and bracelet when the two pledged their love for each other.[57] When Cushman sailed to England for the first time in 1844, she filled her diary with long, affecting entries expressing her misery at leaving Sully. Part of one entry reads, "I verily believe if I had her by me at this moment I could press the breath out of her body. I never loved her half as dearly as I think I do at this moment. . . . She haunts me."[58] Unfortunately, Sully died before Cushman's triumphant return to the States; however, two simple entries in Cushman's diary before she sailed for England are of interest for the sexual potential possible in the literal behavior indicated. The first entry states simply, "Caught in the rain. Slept with Rose," and the second again acknowledges her having slept with Sully.[59] Cushman then had two further romantic relationships with women. One, the poet Eliza Cook, wrote poems to Cushman and became a constant companion.[60] The other, Matilda Hays, became Cushman's acting partner for a time and played the female lead to Cushman's Romeo on occasion. Cushman's attachment to Hays, which lasted nearly ten years, caused a considerable stir among her acquaintances. Elizabeth Barrett Browning was dismayed at what she perceived to be a "female marriage." Browning wrote that Cushman and "Miss Hays have made vows of celibacy and of eternal attachment to each other—they live together, dress alike."[61]

Cushman's most prominent relationship was with sculptor Emma Stebbins. Cushman was forty when she met Stebbins in Rome, having retired there in 1857. They lived together for the last twenty years of Cushman's life—Stebbins silently supporting Cushman's acting, and Cushman vocally supporting Stebbins's sculpture. This relationship was complicated, however, by a passionately emotional attachment Cushman maintained with a young woman who would become her daughter-in-law.

In 1858, less than a year after meeting Stebbins, Cushman returned to the United States with her new companion. While acting, she stopped in St. Louis to meet Wyman Crow, a man Harriet Hosmer had recommended as a sound financial advisor. Crow's daughter, Emma, idolized Cushman, and the two became intimate correspondents. Through Cushman's letters to Emma Crow, an image of intense passion and eroticism, as well as jealousy and tension, emerges among Cushman, Stebbins, and Crow.[62] These letters reveal Cushman's fervor toward Crow and Stebbins, they imply sexual contact, and they show Cushman's regard for propriety that forestalled any sense of scandal in her life. Cushman's sexuality, interpreted through her writings to Crow, can be termed gynophilic, if not specifically lesbian. She addresses Crow as her "little lover," "child lover," and calls her "darling" and "dear" while signing herself "your loving Mistress," "faithful lady lover," or most frequently "loving lady." Though Stebbins remained Cushman's primary life partner, Crow enjoyed a complex, passionately intimate relationship with Cushman.

Two months after meeting Crow, who was only half Cushman's age, Cushman returned to St. Louis exclusively to visit with this young woman. In the letter announcing her return, Cushman gently admonished Crow for wanting to sleep with her at Cushman's hotel.[63] Several months later, upon her return to England, Cushman alluded to sleepless nights spent with Crow and how much she missed the younger woman. At the end of the letter, Cushman asked Crow to burn all her correspondence, lest someone see her letters, or else she would be less passionately obvious in her writing.[64] Cushman balanced her desire for Crow with her own sense of strict decorum, which, in an age known for its passionate female friendships, appears too self-conscious. On some level, Cushman was concerned that the desire she demonstrated for Crow was inconsistent with her society's concept of acceptable affectional relationships.

Within two years, Crow had been introduced to Cushman's adopted son, Ned. Ned and Crow, encouraged by Cushman, became romantically connected, which did nothing to curtail the emotion between the two women. In a note that Cushman sent to Crow that was enclosed in a longer letter from Ned, she wrote

> to tell you that you live fondly in my thoughts dearest places—that I long for you—want you—as perhaps you do your dearest. That no human being exercises so peculiar a power as you do over me & that I am not *whole* without you. Does *that* make you happy darling? Are you now content that I go about the world *un*whole?[65]

Within two months of this note, arrangements had been made for Crow to visit Cushman in England. In the letter announcing this visit Cushman imagined "when the time comes for us to be separated no more!" But, she again delicately deflected an invitation from Crow to sleep together in London because "elements are discordant & I like harmony so much that I shall wait a little for my pleasures." Apparently, Stebbins provided the conflicting note. Cushman closed this letter writing "that I love you fondly, dearly truly & shall do so while I live—that I long for you . . . & that I am restless and anxious to see you & hear you & feel your arms around me."[66]

The visit was brief, lasting only a week. The letter that accompanied Crow's departure displayed not only Cushman's feelings for Crow, but the inevitable jealousy occasioned by the intimate triangle.

> I had a sweet day with you on Monday and the occasional opportunities of a love word with you was very sweet to my heart. Still it hardly compensated for the hurried parting. I was so sorry you should have come all the way to our carriage for a last kiss & then that I should have been thrust all the way over to the other side so that I could not get at you. . . . but dear one—first or last kisses scarcely matter—We love each other very very dearly and fondly. We know how dear we are to each other & an embrace more or less matters little—when we are so surrounded with hungry greedy eyes. Aunt Emma got a little pang of jealousy as she saw me holding your hand on the boat & . . . was so positively disagreeable, she was so dreadfully envious & jealous, that she could not talk all the day & sulked like a fool. . . . I very soon settled Aunt Emma, who is as sweet as a summer morning. She knows how dearly I love her & allows me to smooth her ruffled plumes.[67]

Cushman's relationship with Crow continued to disrupt her harmony, for not only was Stebbins jealous of Crow, but the same feeling was expressed of Crow regarding Stebbins. At least three times over a period of several years Cushman wrote in letters to Crow about Stebbins, attempting to suppress criticism of her life partner.[68] The remainder of the letter above also explained how Ned fit into this triangular relationship.

After discussing Stebbins's jealousy, Cushman wrote of her anxiety about Crow and of her plan for the two of them to "be *together* as much as I thought would be happiest for us." An arrangement for Crow and Ned to marry had already been contracted, and Cushman referred in the letter to a conversation she had with Crow about Ned's future after their marriage. According to Cushman, Ned had very little sense for business, and she argued that if the two women were to be together successfully Cushman could obtain for him a foreign consulship from her friend Senator Seward. Since Cushman feared Ned's financial ability as a businessman, which would hinder the couple's ability to travel, she decided that foreign service would be a more suitable profession. Cushman ended her argument saying, "If you wish to be with me it will be better [for Ned] to have the consulship." Cushman and Crow conspired to marry Ned to

Crow and arrange his life so the two women would seldom be separated. If Ned ever felt concern over the relationship between his aunt and his wife, he left no mention of it. However, a very curious letter from Cushman to Crow insinuates some conflict within the family and displays Cushman's apprehension regarding Ned.

Cushman's letter is in response to "the dearest letter you have ever written to me!" Alluding to some family disagreement, Cushman tried to comfort Crow and then continued,

> When I received dear Ned's letter the other day I felt that you were not yet out of danger. That I might still be writing for "foreign eyes" who would not understand all that I might say to you. All that my heart & soul ached to say. . . . Should I who love you best in all the world (yes—it is true, no one can love you as unselfishly, as nobly, as adoringly, . . . as I do—therefore I do Ned no worry when I say I love you better than any one else can. Better even than he does. Not better perhaps than he can & will when he is as old as I am, has felt & suffered & lived as long & as much as I have, but still better than he, or any one else can—now?)[69]

Near the middle of this very long letter Cushman began to discuss her relationship with Matilda Hays and the arduous years of that commitment. She shifted then to a discussion of Stebbins and the contentment enjoyed through her new relationship. Cushman ended the letter, "I kiss you—I love you & I chain you to my heart in agony of love."

In many of her letters to Crow, Cushman attached some passionate words of affection, even if the preponderance of the letter is devoted to mundane family discussions. She also sent off short love notes dedicated entirely to expressing her desire. One such note ends, "I love you my precious ever *so* dearly, so constantly: think of you so fondly, so tenderly— want you so much—that I think you must feel it, even at the long distance we are apart. We are one are we not? my darling."[70] Another note reads,

> My own *dear* dear! Bless you my own darling for all your dear love for me & the pretty expression which you use in telling me of it. I love you—as you *would have me!* Can I say more? Do you want me to say more? If I were near you I would show you how much, how intensely I love you, but at this long distance words acquire a consequence within, which would not appear even if heard—do you understand me—my precious—& will you have faith even though "words are so little." If you will—you do—& I will wait until the 30th of March to show you how *much* there is in my words—which *written* seem to fail to express their full meaning to you—but which

> if read by other eyes might assume gigantic importance appalling to
> you to me to Ned to your father & mother to everybody.[71]

Again, Cushman's concern regarding the public's perception of her letters is intriguing. In an age that accepted excessive rhetorical expressions of emotion between romantic friends, her anxiety suggests a degree of awareness that the nature of her passion was transgressive.

These psychosexual aspects of Cushman's desire translated on the stage into her portrayal of Romeo, not only in her presentation of masculine gendered behavior, but in the fact that the love object of her character was a woman. Cushman's sexuality allowed her to personally identify with the character of the young male lover passionately desirous of a female love object. That her performance appeared so realistic, so truthful to men like Knowles, is attributable to her ability to feel desire and react passionately toward another woman. Signs of Cushman's desire, applauded by certain critics as emblematic of her acting ability, and conversely condemned by other critics as a token of her abandoned femininity, were clearly readable by her viewing audience. Her sexuality accounts for her success in the role inasmuch as the passion and eroticism that made the performance popular and critically successful originated in her sexuality.

Ultimately, this stage portrayal becomes a device that afforded Cushman the position of a desiring subject, which she could not claim as a woman in her particular nineteenth century culture. Through her portrayal of Romeo, the actress could present on stage a primary component of her own subjectivity. The theatrical space of representation allowed Cushman to become a desiring gynophilic subject through the character of Romeo. The performative aspect of theater expanded the confines of gender for Cushman so that a female body, though marked with the gender sign *woman,* could, in the representation of the gender sign *boy,* exhibit its desire for another female body in a public space. The capacity of performance in the theatrical space to confuse gender provided the potential for Cushman to explore public expressions of passion. Cushman's sexuality led her to play Romeo because the part allowed her to exhibit desire for another woman on stage, which was not possible in non-cross-dressed roles of the nineteenth century, nor was it possible to the same extent in public displays of affection. The theater, as a performative space, allowed Cushman to transgress cultural assumptions of normative sexual expression, which apparently made Cushman uneasy, according to her letters. Though in her life off the stage Cushman was cautious of the sexual personae the public might see, she, probably unconsciously, found on stage the security of representative space in which to explore, express, and play with her desire.

Significantly, Cushman was not as popularly successful in portraying other male romantic leads. What quality in the figurative character of Romeo allowed the audience to receive this portrayal favorably? The obvious answer is the patriarchal stereotype of the juvenile male, conflated in Cushman's depiction with the female performer. The character of Romeo exhibits certain qualities that the dominant nineteenth-century culture would have termed feminine. Anne Russell, in her article "Gender, Passion, and Performance in Nineteenth-Century Women Romeos," concludes that Romeo was a viable and appropriate vehicle for actresses since the qualities associated with the character—imprudence, excess emotion, inefficacy, and even youth—emasculated Romeo to the point that he was not a desirable character for actors.[72] Russell discusses the nineteenth-century perception of Romeo and the often contradictory comments concerning actresses who attempted the role. Actresses were applauded for their presentation of emotion as Romeo that actors either did not or could not replicate; however, an excess of passion might bring censure from the critics who would complain, as they did about Cushman, that the actress had unsexed herself. No comment of transgressive sexuality was ever expressed by the critics, as they avoided discussing the female Romeo in relation to her Juliet. In researching the phenomenon of female Romeos, Russell found that they do not appear until after the 1830s, and while popular in the 1850s and 1860s, by the end of the nineteenth century the female Romeo had been eclipsed in popularity as a choice for actresses by the female Hamlet. This shift is not surprising since the growing consciousness of lesbianism, encouraged by the sexologists while they denigrated the identity, would have rendered an audience culpable in the enjoyment of love scenes between a female Romeo and her Juliet, while the representation of Hamlet, more easily made asexual in performance, is devoid of such anxiety. Russell also found that the occurrence of female Romeos was far more prevalent in the United States than London. As an emotional, immature male, Romeo was an inappropriate character for actors who were either embarrassed to or incapable of performing the role. Women, it was thought in the nineteenth century, inherently possessed those qualities, by virtue of their sex, which enabled them to depict the impetuous, emotional, immature, and therefore effeminate Romeo.

The theater critic of *John Bull* described the part of Romeo exactly in these terms of its effeminacy when reviewing an early performance of Cushman's. "Of all the male persons of the drama that we can think of," he wrote, "Romeo, without being in the least *effeminate* (we hope our readers will find the distinction intelligible) is the most *feminine.*" Since Cushman "has more of the force and energy of the other sex than of the softness and grace which belong to her own," Romeo is a part in which "she is peculiarly qualified to succeed."[73] Some years later, the critic of the *New York Post* reiterated this idea. "The part of Romeo," he reflected, "is remarkably well adapted to the little more than feminine and little less than masculine qualities of Miss Cushman."[74] Similarly, the critic of the *New York Times* wrote in 1860 that "there is in the delicacy and gentleness of Romeo's character something which requires a woman to represent it and unfits almost every man for its personation."[75] Audiences, then, received Cushman's sexually gendered portrayal of Romeo as a logical, if unconscious, extension of the gender ambiguity in the character.

Cushman's sexuality was the necessary ingredient that, combined with the sexual ambiguity of the role and the potential of performance to confuse gender representations, made her portrayal of Romeo not only possible but popular and critically successful. Social and theatrical trends supplied a favorable environment in which many actresses could perform male characters. Public sentiment had been transformed by these elements to accept a female Romeo. However, if the actress had not been Charlotte Cushman, the role would never have been so propitiously received. Cushman's sexuality made her such a definitive Romeo. Cushman impressed critics and her audience with the verisimilitude of her presentation of masculine passion and desire. Cushman's lesbian sexuality provided the stimulus and inspiration requisite to display an unfeigned portrayal of her character's desire for a young woman. She played the part so well because the gendered expression of her own sexuality paralleled the nineteenth century's conception of Romeo's gender in a way that no heterosexual actor or actress could have duplicated.

NOTES

1. The quotation in the title refers to Cushman's performance of Romeo in London during the 1845–46 theater season. See Emma Stebbins, *Charlotte Cushman: Her Letters and Memories of Her Life* (Boston, 1878), 61. See Faye E. Dudden, *Women in the American Theatre: Actresses and Audiences, 1790–1870* (New Haven, CT: Yale University Press, 1994), 82–85, who discusses Cushman's desire to enter upper-class society. See Stebbins, 287–303, for eulogies.

2. Dudden, *Women in American Theatre*, 86–92, discusses the psychological configurations of several of Cushman's more famous portrayals, provides biographical data on Cushman, and explains Cushman's adaptability to such roles.

3. See Susan S. Cole, "Charlotte Cushman," in *Notable Women in the American Theatre: A Biographical Dictionary*, ed. Alice M. Robinson, Vera Mowry Roberts, and Milly S. Barranger (Westport, CT: Greenwood Press, 1989), 186; and Lawrence Barrett, *Charlotte Cushman: A Lecture*, Publications of the Dunlap Society, No. 9 (New York, 1889), 29–34.

4. Yvonne Shafer, "Women in Male Roles: Charlotte Cushman and Others," in *Women in American Theatre*, ed. Helen Krich Chinoy and Linda Walsh Jenkins (New York: Theater Communications Group, 1987), 74–81.

5. Joseph Leach, *Bright Particular Star: The Life and Times of Charlotte Cushman* (New Haven, CT: Yale University Press, 1970), 241, 306; and Shafer, "Women in Male Roles," 78.

6. For discussions of Cushman in masculine roles see Lisa Merrill, "Charlotte Cushman: American Actress on the Vanguard of New Roles for Women," Ph.D. diss., New York University, 1984, 107–12; and Shafer, "Women in Male Roles," 75, 79.

7. Homosexual inferences are also possible from Shafer's "Women in Male Roles," 74–81. I will use the word *lesbian* to identify Cushman's behavior and her desire, a desire that even within the conventional bonding of female friends of the nineteenth century reveals a transgressive eroticism.

8. Dudden, *Women in American Theatre*, 92–103.

9. Cushman's sexuality becomes a significant determinant in analyzing not only her choice of roles, but her decisions on and off the stage. For example, exploring sexuality would probably reveal significant factors in her decision to retire to Italy. I have chosen to focus narrowly on Cushman's performance of Romeo to demonstrate the richness sexuality affords in analytical research of theatrical subjects.

10. For a discussion of working-class theater see Bruce A. McConachie and Daniel Freeman, eds., *Theatre for Working-Class Audiences in the United States, 1830–1980* (Westport, CT: Greenwood Press, 1985), 3–86. On the difficulty of using class as a determinant of audience composition see Rosemarie Bank, *Theatre Culture in America, 1825–1860* (Cambridge: Cambridge University Press, 1997), 1–8, 50–59, and 109–11.

11. Judith L. Fisher and Stephen Watt, eds., *When They Weren't Doing Shakespeare: Essays on Nineteenth-Century British and American Theatre* (Athens: University of Georgia Press, 1989).

12. Tice L. Miller, "The Image of Fashionable Society in American Comedy, 1840–1870," in Fisher and Watt, *When They Weren't Doing*, 244.

13. For conflicting dates and places see Leach, *Bright Particular Star*, 64–66; Barrett, *Charlotte Cushman*, 37; George C. Odell, *Annals of the New York Stage*, vol. 4 (New York: AMS Press, 1928), 147–48; and Joseph N. Ireland, *Records of the New York Stage, from 1750 to 1860*, vol. 2 (1866–67; reprint, New York: Burt Franklin, 1968), 160.

14. Quoted in Odell, *Annals*, 147.

15. The incestuous implications of this performance require a separate and much larger study.

16. "Haymarket," *Athenaeum,* January 3, 1846, 19. Odell was no fan, either, of actresses performing male characters (*Annals,* 147).

17. Mary Howitt, "The Miss Cushmans," *People's Journal,* July 18, 1846, 48.

18. Stebbins, *Charlotte Cushman,* 59; and Clara Erskine Clement, *Charlotte Cushman* (Boston, 1882), 44–45.

19. One later commentator believes Cushman used Susan as a convenient excuse to play male roles. See Elizabeth M. Puknat, "Romeo Was a Lady: Charlotte Cushman's London Triumph," *Theatre Annual* 51 (1951): 59–69.

20. *Illustrated London News,* January 17, 1846, 42.

21. *London Times,* December 30, 1845, 5.

22. *Theatrical Journal,* January 3, 1846, 4, and February 14, 1846, 55.

23. *Spirit of the Times,* July 4, 1846, 228, reprinted from a letter Knowles had sent to a friend in Liverpool.

24. *New York Post,* May 14, 1850, n.p.

25. "Theatricals in Boston," *Porter's Spirit of the Times,* June 12, 1858, 229.

26. "Amusements," *New York Times,* November 16, 1860, 5. Cushman was nearing the end of a hugely successful two-month engagement at the Winter Garden.

27. *Spirit of the Times,* 228.

28. Tracy Davis posits the theory that the historical figure of the cross-dressed actress was incapable of, or not allowed to, realistically mimic male behavior but was constructed to signify her own femininity. Cushman was an exception that helped prove the rule. See Tracy Davis, "Questions for a Feminist Methodology in Theater History," in *Interpreting the Theatrical Past: Essays in the Historiography of Performance,* ed. Thomas Postlewait and Bruce A. McConachie (Iowa City: University of Iowa Press, 1989), 75. Laurence Senelick presents a similar argument, also stating that on the rare occasions when actresses did impersonate masculine behavior such performances were duly noted by the critics. See "The Evolution of the Male Impersonator on the Nineteenth-Century Popular Stage," *Essays in Theater* 1, no. 1 (1982): 33.

29. "Theatricals in Boston," 229.

30. Puknat, "Romeo Was a Lady," 66–67.

31. George William Bell, essay, May 20, 1876, Papers of Charlotte Cushman, Library of Congress, vol. 9, 2661, 2675–77 (hereafter cited as CCP).

32. Howitt, "The Miss Cushmans," 48, thought Cushman possessed a strong masculine nature from which she embodied male gender characteristics.

33. "Haymarket Theater," *Illustrated London News,* January 3, 1846, 9.

34. "Haymarket," 19.

35. See Clement, *Charlotte Cushman,* 176; and Noah M. Ludlow, *Dramatic Life as I Found It* (1880; reprint, New York: Benjamin Blom, 1966), 316.

36. "Haymarket," 19.

37. *London Times,* 5.

38. Westland Marston, *Our Recent Actors,* vol. 2 (Boston: Roberts Brothers, 1888), 76.

39. John Coleman, *Fifty Years of an Actor's Life,* vol. 2 (New York: James Pott, 1904), 363.

40. Nancy F. Cott, "Passionlessness: An Interpretation of Victorian Sexual Ideology, 1790–1850," in *A Heritage of Her Own: Toward a New Social History of Women,* ed. Nancy F. Cott and Elizabeth H. Plech (New York: Simon and Schuster, 1979).

41. Clement, *Charlotte Cushman,* 176.

42. George Vandenhoff, *Leaves from an Actor's Note-Book* (New York: D. Appleton, 1860), 217.

43. See *Spirit of the Times,* 228, and W. T. Ball's comments in Clement, *Charlotte Cushman,* 177.

44. See "Haymarket," 19. The critic of the *New York Times* maintains that society does not enjoy seeing women play male roles, though he goes on to praise Cushman's Romeo ("Amusements," 5) Besides Vandenhoff, Ball also objected to "the needlessness of the lady's [Cushman] unsexing herself" (Clement, *Charlotte Cushman,* 177).

45. Merrill, "Charlotte Cushman," 163–84.

46. See Carroll Smith-Rosenberg, "Discourses of Sexuality and Subjectivity: The New Woman, 1870–1936," in *Hidden from History: Reclaiming the Gay and Lesbian Past,* ed. Martin Duberman, Martha Vicinus, and George Chauncey Jr., (New York: Penguin, 1989), 269–70.

47. Richard von Krafft-Ebing, *Psychopathia Sexualis,* 12th ed., trans. F. J. Rebman (1886; reprint, New York: Paperback Library, 1966), 761.

48. Merrill, "Charlotte Cushman," 163–84.

49. Lillian Faderman, *Surpassing the Love of Men: Romantic Friendship and Love between Women from the Renaissance to the Present* (New York: Morrow, 1981), 231–77.

50. Carroll Smith-Rosenberg, "The Female World of Love and Ritual: Relations between Women in Nineteenth-Century America," in *Disorderly Conduct: Visions of Gender in Victorian America* (New York: Oxford University Press, 1985), 74–76.

51. Faderman, *Surpassing Love of Men,* 17–18.

52. Quoted in Stebbins, *Charlotte Cushman,* 13.

53. Coleman, *Fifty Years,* 361–62. Coleman implies that this manner of dress prompted speculation about Cushman's sexuality. However, he is writing some sixty years after the fact and presumably has been influenced by the sexologists' theories.

54. See Sara Foose Parrott, "Networking in Italy: Charlotte Cushman and 'The White Marmorean Flock,' " *Women's Studies* 14 (1988): 305–38.

55. Cushman, diary, January 11, 1845, Columbia University, Rare Book and Manuscript Library.

56. Another diary entry reads, "Shall I ever make sufficient money to have her [Sully] with me always? Oh dear, oh dear, how I hope it, how I sigh for it" (Cushman, diary, October 31, 1844).

57. Rosalie Sully to Cushman, May 11, 1845 (CCP, vol. 14, 3970), alludes to the bracelet and ring.

58. Cushman, diary, November 3, 1844.

59. Cushman, diary, August 19, 1844 and September 14, 1844.

60. Cook's poems promise undying love. See CCP, vol. 10, 2971–75.

61. As quoted in Leach, *Bright Particular Star*, 210.

62. Cushman destroyed all the letters that Crow wrote to her. She told Crow early in their correspondence,

> Your letters shall be destroyed as soon as I have mastered the contents—but it will be of good to you to have a loving heart to confide all your feelings—your desires, your wishes, your hopes your dreams. Write to me freely without fear. My letters are quite safe from observation, & you may make all your confessions frankly to me. (June 30, 1858)

See CCP, vol. 1, 69. In a later letter of June 29, 1861, Cushman explained that her letters to Sully and Cook had been destroyed and that she was never separated long enough from either Hays or Stebbins for her letters to be of much interest (CCP, vol. 1, 275–76). Even so, Cushman wrote to Crow weekly, sometimes more often, and these letters supply a great deal of information about Cushman's emotional attachments.

63. Letter to Emma Crow, dated March 31, 1858, CCP, vol. 1, 60.

64. Letter to Emma Crow, June 20, 1858, CCP, vol. 1, 85. On June 29, 1861, Cushman asked Crow, by then Emma Crow Cushman, to "forgo the love words" that Crow wrote to her so that their letters might stand as a record of Cushman's own history "which might meet *any* eye" (CCP, vol. 1, 275–76).

65. Letter to Emma Crow, April 5, 1860, CCP, vol. 1, 141.

66. Letter to Emma Crow, June 12, 1860, CCP, vol. 1, 157.

67. Letter to Emma Crow, June 20, 1860, CCP, vol. 1, 161.

68. Letters to Emma Crow dated July 26, 1861, May 7, 1862, and May 11, 1865. See CCP, vol. 1, 298; vol. 2, 48; and vol. 3, 788.

69. Letter to Emma Crow, May 24, 1862, CCP, vol. 2, 457.

70. Letter to Emma Crow, October 13, 1860, CCP, vol. 1, 194.

71. Letter to Emma Crow, February 26, 1861, CCP, vol. 1, 240.

72. Anne Russell, "Gender, Passion, and Performance in Nineteenth-Century Women Romeos," *Essays in Theatre* 11, no. 2 (1993): 153–67. Russell alludes to the potential of deconstructing sex/gender systems that the cross-dressed actress as Romeo offers; however she provides no substantial critique of sexuality.

73. "Theaters and Music," *John Bull,* January 3, 1846, 12.

74. *New York Post,* n.p.

75. "Amusements," 5.

Bohemian on Horseback

Adah Isaacs Menken

Noreen Barnes-McLain

The second edition of the *Oxford English Dictionary* defines the word *bohemian* as "a gipsy of society; one who either cuts himself off, or is by his habits cut off, from society for which he is otherwise fitted; especially an artist, literary man, or actor, who leads a free, vagabond, or irregular life." This connotation of the word was accepted as early as 1848 and appears in William Thackeray's *Vanity Fair.*

The free-and-easy Adah Isaacs Menken (1835–69) was a notorious performer (and poet) best known for her seemingly "naked" wild ride while strapped to the back of a real horse in the sensational stage play *Mazeppa.* Although not the first woman to play the male leading role, she certainly was the most famous. Menken, more of an entertainment personality than an acting talent, possessed shimmering eyes and a spectacular figure and embraced the flamboyant image of the nineteenth-century bohemian artist throughout her short life. With an audacious and assured calculation, she cultivated both an enigmatic biography and sexuality, encouraging conjecture about her past and speculation about her current involvements. The sexual orientation of her literary associations and social alliances added to speculation about her personal life, and, although she married four times, she also seems to have possessed a passion for women that may have exceeded mere gastronomic companionship.

A "Queer" Historiographic Approach to Menken

There is evidence that Menken had intimate relationships with several women. Lillian Faderman suggests that evidence of her same-sex eroticism is found in her poetry. Her letters to friends also suggest an unusually strong attachment to writer Aurore Dudevant, better known as George Sand, whom Menken idolized. Sand had been called a "damned

Lesbian" by Alfred de Vigny, and Victor Hugo had observed that she could not decide to which gender she really belonged.[1] Otto Weininger, in *Sex and Character,* included Sand in his list of "highly gifted women and girls" whom he described as "partly bisexual, partly homo-sexual, who reveal their maleness by their preference for either women or for woman-ish men."[2] Mario Praz wrote that it was thanks to her that "the vice of Lesbianism became extremely popular."[3] Menken emulated this popular figure who became the paradigm for the transvestite lesbian, the eloquent feminist who refused "to be hampered by women's clothes and to take the passive role in her various relationships with the effeminate men who became her lovers."[4]

Sand and Menken, both short-haired and cigar-smoking, shared a predilection for men's sartorial accouterments during their frequent public dining excursions in Paris. Despite a thirty-year age difference, several of their contemporaries certainly *thought* theirs was an erotic relationship, not merely literary. This behavior, Faderman points out, "was disturbing even to the most enlightened French, who preferred not to be confused about sex roles."[5]

Menken's life must be reviewed, then, in the context of what would have been considered "lesbian" in the late nineteenth century, with the understanding that sexual orientation is not always coincident with, or reflected by, sexual behavior. Leila J. Rupp has observed, "we have no simple answer to the question, asked of a variety of historical figures: Was she a lesbian?"[6] Although Rupp's exceptional study, " 'Imagine My Surprise': Women's Relationships in Mid-Twentieth Century America," addresses the scrutiny of the lives of women of a more recent era, the historiographic questions she identifies are applicable to the deliberations that any of us undertake: "We are faced with a choice between labeling women lesbians who might have violently rejected the notion or glossing over the significance of women's relationships by considering them asexual and Victorian" (398). She notes that while "it is enormously important not to read into these relationships what we want to find, or what we think we should find," that we also "cannot dismiss what little evidence we have as insufficient when it is all we have" (407).

Is it, then, a case of "guilt by association" for Menken? What can and cannot be read into her writing, particularly her poetry? What kinds of passion might she have been expressing for Sand and other women? Did Menken, who deliberately constructed ambiguity and mystery about her biography, encourage speculation about her sexuality as well? What do we make of the well-known offstage gender slippage, including smoking cigars, dressing in male clothing, frequenting gambling establishments and brothels—the very active bohemian life merged with the uncanny ability to upstage her contemporaries? Her most successful stage roles were those that simultaneously blurred and revealed her sexuality, exposing more of her body than perhaps any other female performer had in a legitimate venue, while ostensibly essaying male characters.

How did these performances, then, affect the public perspective of her personal life? What was the real function of her multiple marriages and affairs? What of the alliances with men such as Walt Whitman and those fascinated by sexual ambiguity and cross-dressing, such as Swinburne?

For the theater historian, several issues come into play when conducting this kind of inquiry, including the ethics of outing (even of a deceased person), and the question of where historical research ends and tabloid journalism begins. Recent applications of historiographic methods have raised questions of the means and rationales for investigating the sexual lives of theatrical personalities. The information that might be gleaned from a "queer" reading of letters or even a reconstruction of choices made by the artist in a particular performance may significantly revise and enhance the present-day scholar's reception of the artist's work. However, we must be careful of the lens through which we view a person's sexual activity and/or proclivity—and ask why we do it. How we conduct our research will determine whether the reading of contemporary queerness into the activities of others, the rereading of their biographies (and, very often, a reading into what is omitted or obscured) is spurious speculation or a valid reclamation project. More than reinforcing our own sense of value as gay, lesbian, and bisexual people today, a queer reading of Menken's performances in terms of the cultural conventions of the times can illuminate the complexities of her historical contributions, particularly her playing of cross-gender roles.

Menken's birth date has generally been accepted as June 15, 1835, although the year is followed by a question mark in some biographical accounts. The facts of her early life are unreliable, contradictory, and as mercurial as Menken was herself. Her curriculum vitae was, upon occasion, expediently revised to accommodate a mutating public image. She was probably born near New Orleans as Ada (she did not add the *h* until her first marriage) Bertha Theodore. Though she encouraged the myth that she was the daughter of a Presbyterian minister, she was really of Jewish parentage. Her father died when she was several years old, and her mother remarried a man named Josephs, who died when she was a teenager. It was to support her mother that Adah probably began her work as a teacher, but her theatrical debut soon followed her tutorial one. It also proved to be more lucrative, although throughout her life she attempted, unsuccessfully, other artistic endeavors. Claudia D. Johnson has remarked, "The different names she is assumed to have had and the conflicting stories of her background before she entered the stage would fill a volume."[7]

Adah and her sister Josephine made their stage debut in dancing roles in 1853 at New Orleans's French Opera House, then toured Mexico, Texas, and Cuba. From about the ages of nineteen to twenty-one, Adah studied and taught languages (virtually every source on Menken notes her impressive command of Hebrew, Spanish, French, and German) and embarked on her second career as a poet. Some time between 1856 and 1858, Adah married Alexander Isaac Menken in Texas, with whom she lived only a brief time, but whose name she retained for the remainder of her career, with a slight variation, adding *s* to *Isaac*.

In *Mazeppa*, his biography of Menken, Wolf Mankowitz calls attention to a pamphlet titled *The Life and Remarkable Career of Adah Isaacs Menken*, published shortly after her death, and usually dismissed by scholars as unverifiable, unbelievable, and most likely an attempt to cash in on the sudden death of the young and demotic performer. It is comprised almost entirely of what he calls "(t)he tallest of Adah Menken's Texas-style tales . . . her often recounted Ned Buntline–style dime Western version of her capture by Indians." Despite what he acknowledges as its "typically Western obviously mendacious quality" he does believe that the story, which she supposedly told to "Mr. Wm. Wallis of the Arch Street Theatre, while he was on a visit to Paris," shows some truth about Menken and Texas of the 1850s.[8] It is a firsthand narrative of being ambushed by Indians while out riding with a small party of both men and women. The frequently serialized captivity narratives, particularly those of women who had the misfortune (or, as often perceived, poor judgment) to be held by Native American tribes against their will, were extremely popular and often lurid embellishments of true adventures.

Menken's posthumous oral history is one such account. Gifted with fluency in a handful of languages, Adah's ability to speak Spanish eased her communication with the Indians, particularly with Laurelack, a maiden who was also—as she found herself—an intended bride of one of her captors. The young Native American woman helped Menken (at the time still Miss Theodore) escape but was shot by the Texas Rangers. The story is an illustration of Menken's bravado laced with the romanticism of a transgressive bond established between young women of clashing cultures.

Menken later paid a tribute to the "sister" who lost her life in a poem titled "A Memory." In the published narrative of the event, the first exchange between the two women is as follows:

"Thy sister is named Bertha Theodore," I said in Spanish, "and although I have seen you but once I already love you!"

"My white sister has my pity."

"And pity in a woman amounts to love," I quickly added.

"My sister is right," Laurelack answered, "and my pity has thus soon become a love!"[9]

Menken's farewell poem to Laurelack includes the lines:

On many hours like this we met
And, as my lips did fondly greet her
I blessed her Love's amulet;
Earth hath no treasure dearer, sweeter.

Although, in the poem, the Indian maiden's eyes are "not born for love," Menken wrote,

Yet when on me their tender beams
Are turned, beneath love's wild control,
Each soft sad orb of beauty seems
To look through mine into my soul.[10]

Mankowitz notes that the poem has "been said to contain strongly homosexual elements," but maintains his position that "in the complex erotic history of Adah Menken, there is not one close relationship with a woman recorded,"[11] although his biography includes accounts (even if without a great deal of documentation) of Adah's friendships with a few women.

Lillian Faderman cautions that in nineteenth-century fiction, it was quite common to reveal "intense emotional bonds" between women, and that female friends frequently exhibited "their emotions in front of any third party without the least suggestion that there is any reason to hide such emotions."[12] Faderman calls Menken "one of the most scandalous figures in her day and undoubtedly not a stranger to lesbian sex" and cites proof for this in her poetry (275). This is the one central example of evidence employed by the historian, yet it must be pointed out that Faderman does the very thing for which she takes others to task—excerpting only part of a document, out of context, to support this claim.

These writings, says Faderman, suggest "dimensions of lesbian intimacy which never appeared in aesthete-decadent poetry, but which we would expect to have existed knowing the lives of so many nineteenth century women who loved women" (275). She illustrates her points with some lines from another of Menken's poems, *Answer Me*.

> Speak to me tenderly,
> Think of me lovingly.
> Let your soft hands smooth back my hair. . . .
> Let my lonely life creep into your warm bosom, knowing no other
>   rest but this.
> Let me question you, while sweet faith and trust are folding their
>   white robes around me. . . .
> the Storm struggles with the Darkness.[13]

Faderman points out that, in terms of how women expressed themselves on paper, what was considered quite routine in the nineteenth century, "our century saw as perverse" (174). She cites the censoring of Emily Dickinson's letters to Sue Gilbert and compares the edited texts with their original versions to illustrate Dickinson's affection for the woman who would become her brother's wife. But in trying to make a case for Adah Isaacs Menken's "lesbian intimacy," Faderman, later in her text, omits lines from this poem, leading the reader to a lesbian rendition through a kind of elliptical extrapolation. The omitted lines serve to shift focus, for the original context of this third stanza is quite different.

> Speak to me tenderly. .
> Think of me lovingly.
> Let your soft hands smooth back my hair.
> Take my cold, tear-stained face up to yours.
> Let my lonely life creep into your warm bosom, knowing no other
>   rest but this.
> Let me question you, while sweet Faith and Trust are folding their
>   white robes around me.
> Thus I am purified, even to your love, that came like John the
>   Baptist in the Wilderness of Sin.
> You read the starry heavens, and lead me forth.
> But tell me if, in this world's Judea, there comes never quiet when
>   once the heart awakes?
> Why must it ever hush Love back?
> Must it only labor, strive, and ache?
> Has it no reward but this?

Has it no inheritance but to bear—and break?
Answer me—
Oh, answer me![14]

Scholars are necessarily selective when trying to back up their theses, but what might be read as a sexual desire shifts to a more spiritual one when John the Baptist, the Wilderness of Sin, and Judea claim their original positions in the text. The nature of the passions expressed in the poem thus may be more ambiguous than Faderman's reading implies, although Menken's use of irony and expressive metaphor in this and other works could provide additional reinforcement for lesbian interpretation. The researcher yearns to happen upon the one document, letter, poem—any concrete evidence—to confirm her queer suspicions, but caution certainly needs to be employed in reviewing Menken's own writing, in particular the posthumously published poems of *Infelicia,* as well as the writing about her.

Blurred Sexuality Both Onstage and Off

Although Menken's poetic writings and her sporadic literary aspirations earned her cachet among New York's bohemian clientele, it was her command of the spectacle of her body on stage and its preservation in the new visual art of photography that earned the audacious young performer widest notoriety. Her exhibitionism confounded sexual and gender categories while igniting and destroying four marriages, all of which seemed to have served her professional advancement. They were short, tempestuous, and, in varying degrees, reversals of the orthodox parts men and women were expected to play.

Adah made her acting debut in New Orleans in 1858, where Alexander Isaac Menken began to promote his wife's career. She appeared in *The Lady of Lyons,* followed by *Fazio, The Soldier's Daughter,* and *A Lesson for Husbands.* Adah was praised not only for her beauty and grace, but for the range she displayed in these dramatic and comic pieces. After a stint in Nashville, where she first essayed Shakespeare's Lady Macbeth opposite James E. Murdoch, she embarked on a successful run at Wood's Theatre, in her husband's hometown of Cincinnati. She was warmly received by the local Jewish community, particularly for her performance in *The Jewess.*[15] Then in Dayton, Ohio, she attempted her own cross-gender rendition of Jack Sheppard's life, her first excursion into male roles, which would quickly prove to be her most popular characters. There, a postperformance outing led to the first of many scandals throughout her career—Adah accepted the dinner invitation of members of the Dayton Light Guards, who bestowed upon her the honorary title of Captain, which she thought particularly suitable given her newfound "specialisation in male parts."[16] Her husband was appalled, and this began the disintegration of their marriage, even though Adah undertook dramatic readings instead of stage performance for a short time.

After a divorce granted by a rabbi, Adah returned to the stage in 1859, this time making her first appearance in New York as the Widow Cheerly in *The Soldier's Daughter*. Later that year she married boxer John Heenan; however, she did not realize that she had not been *legally* divorced from her first husband. A series of misfortunes followed, including a public scandal over the legality of the marriage, the deaths of an infant son and her mother, and before long Adah and John's separation in 1860 and divorce in 1862. As this marriage was disintegrating, Menken made her historical first ride as Mazeppa in the equestrian spectacle of that name, igniting her career, and quite literally catapulting her into international fame.

This success and notoriety led to a series of "Protean comedy" roles, in which the masculine sailor's uniform in *Black-Eyed Susan* and military dress in *The French Spy* actually served to reveal her shapely body. In 1863, Menken married for a third time, to writer Robert Henry Newell. They divorced in 1865. She was well into a pregnancy when she married James Paul Barclay, in the following year. Throughout her last several marriages, Menken had spent a good deal of time traveling and performing, from San Francisco to London and Paris, entertaining and becoming acquainted with the leading writers and artists of the day. Her final marriage was no exception, as she again left her husband just a few days after the wedding to go to Paris. It was there that she gave birth to a son, met George Sand and Alexandre Dumas *père*, and, in August 1868, died at the age of thirty-three. She was buried in Paris.

In 1861, when she was in her midtwenties, Menken took on the role of Cassimir, or Mazeppa, in the melodrama based on Lord Byron's poem. She became identified with this role, her most popular during the remaining seven years of her life. Other parts she assumed in other plays were often variations of what I call the "strip, then ride a horse" theme. What are the sexual implications of playing a young man who is sent to death lashed to the back of a horse because of love for a woman? The exposure of her very female form in a flesh-colored body suit gave her the semblance of nudity, and this gender-bending spectacle proved to be provocative, daring, occasionally injurious, but always financially rewarding.

Of the "novelty" of cross-gender performance during the Victorian era, Tracy C. Davis points out that "men could parody sexless women, and women could glorify what they could not suppress. In the latter case, neither convincing impersonation nor sexual ambiguity was possible."[17] Davis notes that the actress's impersonation of a heroic young man was one that emphasized rather than obscured her gender.

> Her face, "symmetry," and contoured silhouette marked her gender; prints and drawings of cross-dressed actresses from the 1830s to 50s usually show unmistakable anatomization, observing feminine curvature as faithfully as the camera later did in portrait photography. (114)

This latter art is exactly what Menken manipulated for publicity purposes in the 1860s, with the photographic transmission of her image as a full-figured female in male stage dress (or lack of it). I believe that this is exactly the kind of strategy considered by Jennifer Terry in "Theorizing Deviant Historiography," in her discussion of the characteristics of Foucault's "effective history," particularly that of tracing "the conditions whereby marginal subjects apprehend possibilities for expression and self-representation in a field of contest."[18] Menken is one of these deviant subjects who assumed the position that Terry would suggest is "resistant and excessive to the very discourses from which they emerge" (57).

Menken utilized *cartes de visite* in promoting herself from early in her career, anxious that her image be both pervious and popular. The eccentric photographer Napoleon Sarony, equally at home in the unconventional world of bohemia, was critical to the creation of Menken's public image. She approached him in 1865, dissatisfied with other photographic efforts to capture her Mazeppa. Menken thought that she needed to have greater control over her visual representation, and they agreed that she would do two sets of poses, one arranged by herself, and the second of which would be under the photographer's direction. Over one hundred negatives later, Sarony sought her out at the Birmingham theater where she was performing, photographs in hand. According to his account,

> I gave her those of her own posing first. Her exclamation was: "they are perfectly horrible. I shall never have another photograph taken of myself as Mazeppa as long as I live." Then I presented the photographs of my own posing. She threw her arms around me

Adah Isaacs Menken was fond of frequenting gambling
establishments and brothels in male attire.

(Courtesy San Francisco Performing Arts Library and Museum.)

and exclaimed: "Oh, you dear, delightful, little man, I am going to kiss you for that," and she did.[19]

Icons know how to manipulate and exploit an obfuscated sexuality, are savvy about what will pique public interest. Like the postmodern pop star Madonna's flirtation with a pansexual appeal, Menken traded on her following of both genders, whether rough Nevada miners, the London ladies who flocked to see the "classically" clad American, or the young American women with the nineteenth-century's version of celebrity crush. She was one of the first personalities to appreciate the value of—and exploit—not just the photo opportunity, but the use of a short name as well. She became known simply as "The Menken" when touring in California.

The ability to anticipate and cater to popular tastes ensures and sustains a star's success, and Menken's sense of timing served her well in this regard, at least for a few years. Not only was *Mazeppa* a clever diversion at the height of war, but Menken also possessed the chutzpah to counter the midcentury "reforms" of the theater by offering such an exhibition on the stage while many managers were eliminating the third-tier havens for prostitutes and banning tobacco and alcohol from their playhouses.

Claudia D. Johnson summarizes Adah's career as that of appearances

> either in plays of very low quality or in entertainments that could in no way be classified as drama. The Protean Comedy entertainment, an evening of poses of different historical characters, was one of her specialties. . . . She also did burlesques and impersonations of such people as Charlotte Cushman, Edwin Forrest and Edwin Booth. Good taste was rarely a hindrance. She did not hesitate to burlesque Lola Montez just after the death of that unfortunate woman.[20]

Mark Twain, however, was not as taken with Menken as other male writers were and was actually quite critical of what Thomas Schirer calls Menken's "substitution of sexual illusion for acting ability."[21] Twain lambasted her unmotivated cavorting in *Mazeppa,* referred to her as "that manly young female," and wrote of her acting in *The French Spy,*

> [A]s this spy is a frisky Frenchman, and as dumb as an oyster, Miss Menken's extravagant gesticulations do not seem so overdone in it as they do in *Mazeppa*. She don't talk well, and as she goes on her shape and her acting, the character of a fidgety "dummy" is peculiarly suited to her line of business. She plays the Spy, without words, with more feeling than she does Mazeppa with them.[22]

Notices frequently compared her to a number of Greek goddesses, and a typical evaluation of her work recalled that "She was a thorough Bohemian, possessed wonderful beauty of frame and form, and with these, accomplished triumphs which her indifferent stage ability would never have achieved. She was a rattle-brained, good-natured adventuress."[23] One writer put it that "on stage she gave the illusion of great beauty."[24]

Menken's most notorious friendship with another woman was with George Sand. The flamboyant French writer, known for her many affairs with effeminate men and robust women, did not particularly *like* women but did make several exceptions, primarily for actresses. There is documentation of an affair with actress Marie Dorval early in her life. However, the mercurial Sand later changed her mind, writing that actresses were dangerous, untrustworthy, and to be avoided in intimate relationships. If Sand and Menken were romantically involved, it was an extremely brief affair. Sand did become godmother to Adah's son; he was named, in part after Sand's real name, Dudevant, and Sand supported the child after Adah's death (until he also died, a short time later).

No correspondence between the two women seems to have survived, and Sand's own letters to others include only a few references to seeing the young performer on stage and meeting her. In January 1867 Sand wrote to her son that she had seen the American horsewoman perform in *Les Pirates de la Savane* and had found her to be attractive and friendly.[25] Adah, on the other hand, whom Samuel Edwards notes was "usually circumspect in her language," referred to Sand as "my darling George" in letters to friends and once gushed that "she so infuses me with the spirit of life that I cannot bear to spend an evening apart from her."[26]

Albert Auster cites the importance of their brief friendship, as it indicated a link "between women of the theater and literature."[27] He notes that Sand was a "close and influential friend" of Menken's, and that the relationship pointed "to a delicate network of literary and dramatic connections which brought feminists and actresses together . . . although these ties are too filled with elements of '*la vie bohème*' to have had much of an impact on society at large" (19).

Edwards, in his biography of Sand, provides the most encouragement for a lesbian reading of what he calls their "curious" relationship.

> For more than a generation Parisians had expected the worst of George Sand, and her association with Adah Menken raised eyebrows anew. Whether there was more to their friendship than met the eye is a question that has never been answered. But it appears

possible that contemporaries of the two women may have been right.[28]

Another woman with whom Menken might have been romantically linked is her friend Ada Clare, writer and actress. Clare (born Jane McElheny) had acquired the title "Queen of Bohemia" (noted editor and occasional escort Henry Clapp was bohemia's acknowledged "king") or, as mutual friend Walt Whitman dubbed her, the "New Woman." Clare encouraged Menken's writing and excelled at it herself. She was a popular, well-published cultural observer and journalist for the *Saturday Press*. Hindered by a weak voice, she was much less successful as an actress, although she persisted in periodically taking stabs at the stage. Whitman would recall Clare's "gay, easy, sunny, free, loose but not *ungood* life."[29]

One curious incident that stands out involving the two women is noted in the biographical literature on Mark Twain in the West in the 1860s. When Menken toured California, Clare was part of her entourage, and Menken paid considerably more attention to her female companion than to her husband of the moment, Robert Henry Newell, who was the editor of the *New York Sunday Mercury*, and who wrote under the name Orpheus C. Kerr. After her smashing success in San Francisco, George Williams III described Menken's arrival in Virginia City, Nevada, "with her poor, ignored husband" Kerr "trailing behind her along with a company of actors, friend Ada Clare and a pack of dogs."[30] Menken and Clare invited Mark Twain and local journalist Dan De Quille to a dinner party. Menken was seeking response to her writing, and Clare was considering a vehicle in which she could return to the stage. Both men were uncomfortable with the behavior of the two women, who doted upon the dozen or so dogs that gathered about the table. De Quille noted that "the pair" fed the dogs alcohol-soaked sugar cubes throughout the meal.[31] Menken's husband, who was not invited to join the group, sulked and paced in the hallway outside Adah's rooms, until Twain could stand it no longer and, in an attempt to kick a canine after a nip on his leg, instead booted Menken directly on a painful corn and sent her flying away from the table. The dinner party broke up shortly after that, and Twain, who had been tolerating Menken's behavior because of her husband's position, saw his hopes of finding an East Coast publishing venue vanish. Twain later wrote of Menken that "she has a passion for connecting herself with distinguished people, and then discarding them as soon as the world has grown reconciled to the novelty of it and stopped talking about it."[32] The notoriety of these women, who are usually mentioned in connection with each other, combined with Clare's scandalous lack of shame in bearing a child out of wedlock, their membership in the country's best-known literary circles, and the supposed proclivities of subcultural bohemia of the time, generated many questions about their sexual desires.

More confounding perhaps than her relationships with Sand and Clare was Adah's so-called affair with British poet Algernon Swinburne. It's possible that she was another one of his "whipping ladies" and that theirs was neither a traditionally hetero—nor a conventionally sexual—relationship. Thus, the kind of mistress she may have been to the masochistic Swinburne was probably not what polite society imagined, and certainly was one in which conventional gender roles were transgressed. Donald Thomas observes that Swinburne was probably not very sexually active.

> [M]ental excitement of suggestion and stimulus was more to him . . . than the physical excitement of sexual fulfilment. Mary Gordon, playing a boy in a birch-obsessed school, even at a distance and by correspondence, was more desirable than Mary Gordon as a wife or sexual partner. The splendid and violent Dolores, by turns an aggressive and submissive animal, held more excitement than all the tangible physical qualities of Adah Isaacs Menken could offer.[33]

Thus it was primarily erotic trope and fetish that captivated the poet, as well as a "preoccupation with lesbianism, where the man is involved only as observer and not as actor" (228).

Of their relationship Menken certainly had control, from initiating it to breaking it off after the poet had been sufficiently flattered and she had begun to tire of Swinburne's sadomasochism. Well known was her complaint to Dante Gabriel Rossetti that "I can't make him understand that biting's no use!"[34] What is perhaps more intriguing is the account of her first visit to the poet, noted in Julian Field's *Things I Shouldn't Tell*. Field refers to Menken as a "handsome boyish-looking American lady" who met Swinburne after reading his work, and who loved the poems so much that she journeyed from Paris "just to love the poet."[35] It is not only in her aggressiveness in landing on his doorstep in the middle of the night, but this description of Menken as "handsome" and, in particular, "boyish-looking" in which Swinburne's attraction to her might be found. His attraction may also have been linked to behavior alleged by Menken's second husband, a world heavyweight boxing champion, who left her "because she had beaten him for drinking too much."[36]

However, as Lois Adler points out, "the material involving Menken is a mass of contradictory statements, historical inaccuracies, and hearsay provided mainly by Menken herself."[37] Analysis is difficult when so much information must be gleaned from occasional references from others in Menken's life. Despite her careful manipulation of the press and a series of publicity stunts, Adah remains quite a cipher in many ways. Deliberately evasive regarding her real name, background, and other biographical facts, she constructed a mysterious past she may not have had. While she deliberately obscured her past, Menken capitalized on the transgressive acts that maintained her presence, in headlines and as a headlining performer. Hers was a life negotiating the nexus between mainstream and subculture, through a manipulation of gender cues, as an artist who was, in part, expected to do so. Marjorie Garber notes that the aesthetic subculture of bohemia has long been one in which it has been de rigueur among its habitants to embrace "a style of living that flouted convention, especially sexual convention."[38]

Words written a century and a quarter ago resonate differently now than they did then: for example, Menken was remembered as "the Amazonian actress," and one journalist characterized her as

> a queer mixture of sensuality and mentality, she led a life, the peculiarities of which seem impossible to fathom. . . . Living a life that was an open defiance of all moral law, sensual to the extreme in all her passions, she had a mind the most delicate and sensitive I've ever met with—a strange being, she met with a strange fate.[39]

Today's rereading of Menken reveals a woman who loved women as much as she did men.

NOTES

1. Lillian Faderman, *Surpassing the Love of Men: Romantic Friendship and Love between Women from the Renaissance to the Present* (New York: Morrow, 1981), 264.

2. Marjorie Garber, *Vice Versa: Bisexuality and the Eroticism of Everyday Life* (New York: Simon and Schuster, 1995), 191.

3. Quoted in Faderman, *Surpassing Love of Men,* 456.

4. Ibid., 263.

5. Ibid., 264.

6. Leila J. Rupp, " 'Imagine My Surprise': Women's Relationships in Mid-Twentieth Century America," in *Hidden from History: Reclaiming the Gay and Lesbian Past,* ed. Martin Duberman, Martha Vicinus, and George Chauncey Jr. (New York: Penguin, 1989), 396.

7. Claudia D. Johnson, *American Actress* (Chicago: Nelson-Hall, 1984), 147.

8. Wolf Mankowitz, *Mazeppa* (Briarcliff Manor, NY: Stein and Day, 1982), 41.

9. Ibid., 42.

10. Ibid., 45.

11. Ibid.

12. Faderman, *Surpassing Love of Men,* 174.

13. Quoted in ibid., 275.

14. Mankowitz, *Mazeppa,* 257. "The Storm struggles with the Darkness" is the opening line of the following stanza.

15. Ibid., 55.

16. Ibid., 56.

17. Tracy C. Davis, *Actresses as Working Women* (London: Routledge, 1991), 113.

18. Jennifer Terry, "Theorizing Deviant Historiography," *Differences* 3, no. 2 (1991): 56.

19. This account by Sarony is from *The Photo-American,* September 1884, 324, qtd. in Ben L. Bassham, *The Theatrical Photographs of Napoleon Sarony* (Kent, OH: Kent State University Press, 1978), 11.

20. Johnson, *American Actress,* 155.

21. Thomas Schirer, *Mark Twain and the Theatre* (Nuremberg, Germany: Carl, 1984), 31.

22. Mankowitz, *Mazeppa,* 120.

23. Donald Mullin, ed. *Victorian Actors and Actresses in Review* (Westport, CT: Greenwood Press, 1983), 327–28.

24. Thurman Wilkins, "Adah Isaacs Menken," in *Notable American Women, 1607–1950, a Biographical Dictionary,* ed. Edward T. James, Janet Wilson James, and Paul S. Boyer, vol. 2 (Cambridge: Harvard University Press, 1971), 527.

25. Georges Lubin, ed., *Correspondance de Georges Sand* (Paris: Garnier Freres, 1964), 20:283.

26. Samuel Edwards, *George Sand: A Biography of the First Modern, Liberated Woman* (New York: David McKay, 1972), 249.

27. Albert Auster, *Actresses and Suffragists: Women in the American Theatre, 1890–1920* (New York: Praeger, 1984), 18.

28. Edwards, *George Sand,* 248.

29. Philip Callow, *From Noon to Starry Night: A Life of Walt Whitman* (Chicago: Ivan R. Dee, 1992), 265.

30. George Williams III, *Mark Twain: His Life in Virginia City, Nevada* (Riverside, CA: Tree by the River Publishing, 1986), 164.

31. Ibid., 166–67.

32. Frederick Anderson, Michael B. Frank, and Kenneth M. Sanderson, *Mark Twain's Notebooks and Journals,* vol. 1 (Berkeley and Los Angeles: University of California Press, 1975), 326–27.

33. Donald Thomas, *Swinburne: The Poet in His World* (London: Weidenfeld and Nicolson, 1979), 228.

34. Ibid., 147.

35. Quoted in ibid.

36. Ibid.

37. Lois Adler, "Adah Isaacs Menken in *Mazeppa*," in *Women in the American Theatre*, ed. Helen Krich Chinoy and Linda Walsh Jenkins (New York: Theatre Communications Group, 1987), 82.

38. Garber, *Vice Versa*, 105.

39. *San Francisco Alta*, April 15, 1878.

Intimations of Inversion

Rebels of Their Sex

Nance O'Neil and Lizzie Borden

Jennifer Jones

Someone has pointed out to me recently that I have
nearly always interpreted the unloved woman in the
theatre, the woman crucified by the unseen, the conventional traditions.

—Nance O'Neil

Anyone familiar with the story of Lizzie Borden's life after her acquittal
in the famous double murder of Abigail and Andrew Borden has heard of
the "Boston actress." Victoria Lincoln in her biography of Lizzie, *A
Private Disgrace,* writes that Lizzie "loved the theatre, and she was particularly obsessed with the gifts and beauty of Nance O'Neil (1874–
1965), the star of the Boston stock company who specialized in tragic
roles with which Lizzie identified."[1] Nance O'Neil met Lizzie in the
summer of 1904, twelve years after Lizzie's acquittal in the murder trial
that captured the attention of the nation. In 1905, a provocative newspaper item appeared in papers across the country announcing that Lizzie
Borden was writing a play for her "warm personal friend" Nance
O'Neil.[2] Unfortunately, no record of that play is left to us, but the imagination reels at the possibilities.

Though the women's acquaintance was brief—their paths crossed for
less than two years during the height of Nance's popularity in Boston
from 1904 to 1906—Nance has become an integral part of the Borden
legend. In fact, were it not for her connection to Lizzie, she might easily
have faded into the obscurity reserved for the "almost weres" of the
theater. There is much innuendo in the Borden histories that Lizzie and
Nance were involved in a lesbian relationship. There are historiographical
problematics documenting any woman's sexuality at the turn of the century, a time when women were still configured in much public discourse as
asexual creatures.[3] The exploration becomes even more difficult when the

Nance O'Neil

*(Courtesy Billy Rose Theatre Collection, The New York Public Library
for the Performing Arts, Astor, Lenox and Tilden Foundations.)*

Lizzie Borden

(Collection of Fall River Historical Society.)

woman, or women, in question led highly public lives and were invested in keeping their private feelings hidden from societal scrutiny. Neither Lizzie nor Nance left any self-documentation of her feelings for the other in letters, diaries, or memoirs, but Lizzie, antisocial by all accounts, was clearly attracted to both Nance and the world she represented. She entertained Nance and her company at Maplecroft, her home in Fall River; she lent the actress money and even accompanied her into court when Nance was sued by a Boston theater manager.[4] Lincoln, who remembered Lizzie from her childhood in Fall River, wrote,

> There was the handful of dirty minded puritans in Fall River who saw Lizzie's association with Nance as a blatantly homosexual affair; they were the ones who whispered, and a few ancient survivors still do. I think they were wrong—in any overt sense, at least. Young Lizzie had crushes on school teachers that she talked about freely; her closer friendships had always been slightly overcharged and

demanding; she was sentimental and sexually immature. But I doubt that she was capable of any kind of love affair.[5]

Through these and other tantalizing suggestions of intimacy, Nance and Lizzie's affair lives on in the popular imagination, a rumor written into history by people like Lincoln who claim to doubt its truth. Just as important as knowing if there was a romantic friendship between these two women is understanding why the rumor of a lesbian relationship surfaced in the first place, and why it endured despite the attempt of biographers like Lincoln to refute it. Certainly, close friendships among women were common at the turn of the century. During the Victorian period intense female friendships were not only permitted, but idealized, and women's memoirs from the period suggest that "passionate love between women was not atypical."[6] Yet the relationship between Nance and Lizzie was constructed as transgressively sexual. Why? Whatever the women's true feelings for each other, for which we have no self-documentation, the constructed mythology of their lesbianism reveals a great deal about attitudes toward women who eschewed traditional lifestyles in this period.

When Nance and Lizzie met at the turn of the century the "New Woman" was emerging as a complex and disturbing figure in the societal fabric. By the turn of the century many women were advocating female suffrage, pursuing careers, eschewing marriage and motherhood, and claiming a freedom of sexuality until now reserved for men. The character of these independent women was subject to intense scrutiny and critique, and comparisons between the Old Woman and the New Woman, with her insistence on economic and legal independence, left no doubt about which woman was preferred.

> The "New Woman," as we know her today is a very unpleasant product; armed with little knowledge, she tends to be dogmatic in her views and offensive in argument. She tends to hate men, and to look upon Feminism as a revenge; she adopts mannish ways, tends to shout, to contradict, to flout principles because they are principles; she also affects a contempt for marriage which is the natural result of her hatred for men.[7]

Women who did not elect to stay in their "proper" sphere, choosing instead to pursue an education or career, were thought by many to have betrayed their natural destiny. As early as 1873, educated women were equated with criminals by Luke Owen Pike in his *History of Crime in England,* who wrote that "so far as crime is determined by external circumstances, every step made by a woman towards her independence is a step towards that precipice at the bottom of which lies a prison."[8] Pike effectively criminalized female independence by claiming the more active and energetic a woman was, the more apt she was to become a felon.

Similar rhetoric can be found in the early sexologists' definitions of lesbianism. Faderman writes that according to these definitions, a lesbian

> rejected what had long been woman's role. . . . All her emotions were inverted, turned upside down: Instead of being passive she was active, instead of loving domesticity, she sought success in the world outside, instead of making men prime in her life, she made first herself and then other women prime. . . . Love between women was metamorphosed into freakishness, and it was claimed that only those who had such an abnormality would want to change their subordinate status.[9]

Because of this, it is not surprising that Nance O'Neil and Lizzie Borden, each unorthodox, unmarried, and financially independent, was each in her own way criminalized by their culture, accused of sexual transgression and that old standby, insanity. When these "warm personal friends" were linked sexually in the public imagination, a chastisement and warning were sent to all women who stepped outside the culturally sanctioned bounds of feminine behavior and sought independence, feminine friendship, and a respect for privacy.

As an unmarried woman working in the theater, Nance O'Neil was vulnerable to intense public scrutiny. To escape public censorship Nance maintained a difficult balance throughout her career between cherishing her independence and distancing herself from the emancipatory discourse of the New Women. Until her marriage at the age of forty-two (to her British costar Alfred Hickman), Nance depicted herself as a woman who had sacrificed all personal relationships for her art; her single state was framed as a sacrifice, an abnormal condition voluntarily espoused in the pursuit of a career in the theater. In 1904, a reporter asked the thirty-year-old actress, "Are you a Miss or Mrs.?"

> "Miss" she replied, with a little laugh of lightness almost akin to coquetry. "Miss O'Neil."
> "Permanent?" I ventured.
> "What woman can say that truthfully? I say I am wedded to my art—isn't that what all artists say?—and yet, I can imagine that I am not totally heartless. Having a heart, therefore, and being a woman, I can't say definitely what its course will be to the end. At present however, it is steady."[10]

The implication in her response was that the "natural" state for a woman with a heart was being married to a man. In many interviews Nance seemed very conflicted about her status as an unmarried woman. On the one hand, she embraced her independence; on the other, she was anxious to show the public that she was subordinate to the men who managed her career. Her public persona presents a woman focused intensely on her own career, yet carefully distanced from feminist principles. When a reporter asked Nance if she was a New Woman, she replied,

> "I am not an old woman I hope," she said, with a touch of tragedy that could not have been better if she had rehearsed it.
> "Oh, I beg your pardon," I apologized. "Woman to me is an ageless being."
> "But what do you mean by 'new woman'?"
> "A voter. Do you ever have a yearning desire to vote?"
> "Never," she said emphatically. "Why does a woman want to try to be like a man? God never made her so and her femininity is her greatest charm."
> "Truly, and if it had not been for Eve's femininity we would all be happy in the Garden of Eden to-day," I ventured boldly.
> "In any event she never voted," was her very feminine answer.[11]

Pre-Lizzie

Andrea Weiss has written that "rumor and gossip constitute the unrecorded history of the gay subculture,"[12] and we have little more than rumor to connect Nance with Lizzie Borden. For while the Fall River gossips and Borden biographers were enthusiastically weaving Nance into the "Lizzie legend," Nance was carefully constructing her own legend, one in which the accused ax-murderess is noticeably absent. Nance was born, Gertrude Lamson, on October 5, 1874, in Oakland, California. Her father, George Lamson, was a prosperous man, a "pillar of the church, a man of stern Puritanical principle,"[13] who ran a successful auction house in San Francisco. Gertrude's older sister Lillian wanted to be an actress. When her father forbade her and she disobeyed his wishes, he disowned Lillian in front of his church congregation.[14] After this public cursing of their daughter, Gertrude's mother left George Lamson and took the girls to live with her in San Francisco.

After attending a girls' seminary in Oakland, Gertrude decided she too wanted to be an actress. What drew Gertrude to the stage? Perhaps rebellion against a stern and controlling father, perhaps admiration for her elder sister. In 1921, at the age of forty-seven, Nance told a reporter that she had always wanted to be an actress and had never considered any other life.

> When I was a very little girl I made up my mind to three things. First, that I would see the world. I've done it. Next, that I should be independent. And lastly, that I should have a career. I had been on the stage two days before my father discovered it. I was the quietest one of the family. Everybody was shocked. However I was perfectly determined.[15]

She implies that Gertrude Lamson was born a free spirit, set on living an independent and public life. If rejecting the traditional goal of marriage and children were part of this, well, then, so be it. Perhaps the stage allowed her to enact certain gender roles in public, while rejecting them in her personal life.

In the summer of 1893, just weeks after Lizzie Borden was found not guilty of murder, "an awkward, undeveloped girl" went to the Alcazar Theatre, then under the management of McKee Rankin, with a letter of introduction from Peter Robinson, the dramatic critic of the *San Francisco Chronicle*. "Here is a young friend of mine who wants to go on the stage. Kindly discourage her."[16]

An enormous change was taking place in the American theater between 1870 and 1900 as resident and stock companies were steadily replaced by touring groups and combination companies. In 1870 there were fifty permanent stock companies in the country. By 1887, however, that number had dropped to four. In that same period, 282 combination companies were on the road.[17]

McKee Rankin (1841–1914) was a Canadian-born actor-manager who, in his younger days, cut a dashing and romantic figure on the stage. Like most American actors at the end of the nineteenth century, Rankin spent most of his professional life on the touring circuit. His legal and marital problems were legendary, and perhaps a life on the road facilitated his escape from embarrassing financial and personal situations. He always seemed to be one step ahead of disaster; he was sued on numerous occasions, attacked viciously in the press for participating in dishonest business practices, and criticized for his mediocre talent.

Although Rankin was not a successful businessman, it is important to situate his reputation in the context of the Theatrical Syndicate's dominance of the American theater at the turn of century. He was an independent producer who did not cooperate with the Frohman brothers' monopoly. By 1896, the Syndicate controlled major playhouses throughout the country and dictated which stars and productions would have access to the best venues. A producer like Rankin, who operated outside of the Syndicate, had great difficulty finding theaters; he also found that the Syndicate-controlled newspapers were decidedly hostile.

Rankin, who would become Nance's longtime manager, hired her to play minor roles at the Alcazar. He began grooming her for a career in the theater by changing her name from Gertrude Lamson to Nance O'Neil, combining the names of Nance (Anne) Oldfield, the eighteenth-century British comedienne, and Eliza O'Neil, the famous tragic actress of the seventeenth century. Rankin kept a tight rein on his young star, and Nance was rarely seen outside his company. Completely in control of her career, Rankin chose the roles she would play, the costumes she would wear, and the places they would perform. He also adapted all of O'Neil's plays and, as her manager, dictated her every step and her every move on stage, even acting out roles to demonstrate how they should be done.[18]

Rankin began cultivating Nance in a series of tours throughout the small towns of the West and Northwest. She played in mining camps, town halls, and second-rate houses. Over a four-year period, she played more than fifty roles in a repertoire that reflected a grab bag of American theater at the end of the century: *The Danites, Under the Gas Light, Uncle Tom's Cabin, The Two Orphans, Oliver Twist, Hamlet, Trilby, East Lynne,* and *Ticket of Leave Man.*

By the close of 1897, Nance had made her New York debut, gaining positive critical notice from the New York critics for her performances at the Murray Hill Theatre in *East Lynne* and *True to Life.* Several New York critics saw great potential and predicted that soon Nance O'Neil would be one of America's foremost tragediennes. The critic for the *New York Sun* wrote,

> Where has she gained her stage experience? New York has never heard of Nance O'Neil before, but surely the art of giving such a finely graduated performance does not come by instinct alone. But wherever she hails from and whoever she may be, Miss O'Neil is an actress with a future.[19]

After such a promising debut, the New York critics were surprised when, instead of capitalizing on Nance's success, Rankin arranged for a world tour that would last nearly three years, taking Nance from Honolulu to Cairo and back again. As an independent actor-manager, Rankin had been targeted by the Theatrical Syndicate; in 1900, newspapers under the Syndicate's control accused O'Neil of sabotaging her career by remaining loyal to Rankin. Though the attacks were directed at Rankin and not primarily at Nance, it was implied that in some way her judgment was impaired, and her single state left her vulnerable to slanderous speculation about her sexual relations with her older, married manager. Articles in the Syndicate papers accused the two of having an affair; one article even printed reports of their "marriage," much to the real Mrs. Rankin's embarrassment.[20] David Beasley, in an article on the eventual split between the actress and her manager, attributes Rankin's strange decision to leave New York after Nance's initial success as a way of putting a stop to the personal attacks printed in the Syndicate-controlled papers.[21]

The world tour taken between 1900 and 1903 was central to Nance's own legend. For years she would capitalize on her successes in foreign lands and her reputation as an independent and adventurous explorer. Her company, which included the young Lionel Barrymore (who later married Rankin's daughter) and D. W. Griffith, set sail from Vancouver, headed toward Hawaii; but when they arrived in Honolulu the bubonic plague had just broken out, and the company left for Australia without ever disembarking. The tour ended three years later in London, where O'Neil's reception was far less enthusiastic than it had been in the southern hemisphere. In what was interpreted by the British press as an act of self-aggrandizement, Rankin had arranged for Nance to appear at the Adelphi Theatre in a series of roles that had been played by London's best actresses. The British critics were particularly harsh in their evaluations of her performance as Magda, a role for which Mrs. Patrick Campbell was famous. The venture was a financial disaster. On a Saturday night, the supers refused to go on for the second act until they were paid. Rankin convinced them with a promise of full payment by Monday. When the audience and supers arrived at the Adelphi Monday night, they found the theater doors locked and the posters covered over. The British theater press was outraged. A critic in London's *Era* wrote,

> We cannot help regretting that Mr. M'Kee Rankin did not better provide for possibility of the failure of Miss O'Neil's season so that the discreditable scenes which disgraced the historic Adelphi Theatre last Saturday and Monday might have been avoided.[22]

Beginning with plague and ending in a financial and critical fiasco, Nance's world tour ended. Despite the successes in Australia and Egypt, the company was bankrupt. Rankin was constantly embroiled in legal battles concerning money owed to actors, authors, and producers. In 1903, W. S. Cleveland, manager of the Cleveland Theatre in Chicago, sued O'Neil and Rankin to recover advance expenses for her performances in that city. Again, Rankin was the principal target of the attack, but this time the actress's seemingly incomprehensible loyalty to an inept manager was explained in a sensationally theatrical way. Cleveland testified that O'Neil was hypnotized by Rankin and that without his spell she was unable to act. Claiming that Nance had no talent or independent personality of her own, but rather owed her entire professional persona to the conjuring of a sinister Svengali, Cleveland told a reporter for the *Sunday American,*

> Time and again I have seen Miss O'Neil come to rehearsal when she was not under Rankin's spell. Her gait was slovenly, her eyes lusterless and she appeared indifferent to her surroundings. . . . Then Rankin would appear. One glance and the woman would be changed. The lines that she could not remember before would come to her as though she were reading her part. Her eyes would sparkle with fire, her words ring with feeling while her acting would thrill even the jaded professionals who rehearsed with her. I believe Rankin places her under his spell about half an hour before she goes on and removes it after the performance. I have seen her after the curtain dropped change as in the twinkling of an eye to a listless creature, the very antithesis of an able actress. Rankin is constantly at her side. He tries to keep other people away from her and she is rarely seen without him.[23]

Nance responded to Rankin's critics by publicly praising the firm fatherly hand with which he guided her career.

> Whatever success I have achieved has been largely due to the long, patient, careful instruction by one of the greatest stage directors of the age. . . . Through it all Mr. Rankin guided me with the firm, kind hand of a father. He gave me the advantages of his forty years of stage experience, and he taught me and encouraged me.[24]

As much as she wanted to cast Rankin in the role of the supportive father figure, in the public imagination Nance's relationship with Rankin kept slipping into the realm of the unnatural and the bizarre; either she was sexually involved with him, violating feminine decorum, or she was literally out of her mind, controlled by his hypnotic spell. In either case, she was not a stable or sensible woman. Perceptions of Nance's transgressive heterosexuality, coupled with accusations of bizarre insanity, may well have prepared the discursive soil in which the later accusations of pathological lesbianism would take root.

Some blame for these accusations may also lie in Nance's choice of repertoire, which included many independent women who refused to follow societal constraints. When she played roles such as Lady Macbeth, Elizabeth I, Magda, or Hedda Gabler, the negative reviews often gave equal criticism to the actress and to the women she essayed to represent. The tone taken in a negative review of a 1904 performance of *Hedda Gabler* in New York is typical.

> If there is meaning to Miss O'Neil's Hedda, she succeeds admirably in keeping it a secret. She makes Ibsen's "cussed" heroine simply a cheap, commonplace vulgarian, who has married for convenience and doesn't pretend to disguise the fact. She does not even make Hedda personally attractive, preferring to sacrifice beauty to a weird, anemic makeup, and fails entirely in suggesting the curious, morbid mentality of Ibsen's cowardly excuse for a woman.[25]

In November 1904 Nance played the title role in *Magda* at Daly's Theatre in New York. Magda was a central role in her early repertoire, and, aside from the London fiasco, she had usually received good reviews for her performance. This time though she was savaged by the New York critics. In the past, many critics had noted what they considered "masculine" characteristics in Nance's acting style—particularly in her gestures, voice, and emotional power. This *Magda* reviewer seems to critique Nance's claim to femininity as he attacks her ability to dress, to walk gracefully, and to make up her face.

> Her short mincing steps make every movement ungraceful. . . . she seems not to have learned how to make up her face nor is she a good dresser. She is always running about the stage in a motionless manner and seems much addicted to the waving of arms.[26]

The reviewer seems most disturbed by the title character's lack of womanly virtue; in his final paragraph he stops just short of equating Nance with the role she was playing.

> Nothing in the character of Magda awakens healthful sympathy and nothing in her conduct inspires respect. She is the paltry incarnation of perverse selfishness, and the only practical purpose that her presence can serve on the stage is to declare that some people exist only

to make trouble equally for themselves and all round them. She is the woman who is determined to have "a career," and when she has run away from home and turned "actress" and has become a mother without becoming a wife, it is her brazen boast that her spirit is emancipated. . . . No wound so deadly can be dealt as that which defaces the ideal and stains the glory of pure womanhood.[27]

It is unclear whom these reviewers are condemning, Magda and Hedda, or the woman who played them—a woman who, "determined to have a career," ran away from home and "turned actress." Nance was distressed at the negative reviews she received from the New York theater critics. In a clear reference to the popularity of foreign-born actresses such as Alla Nazimova, O'Neil told a sympathetic reporter in 1904, "I lack the indispensable qualities of success—I speak neither in a foreign tongue, nor in English with a dialect."[28]

Once again bankrupt after the failure of *Magda* in New York, Rankin borrowed money to finance a season for Nance in Boston. The Boston audiences were enchanted, and it seemed as if Nance's luck had finally turned. It was during this period that Lizzie Borden first saw Nance perform, most likely in *Macbeth* at the Colonial Theatre. It is fascinating to consider those three women in the theater that night— Nance O'Neil, Lizzie Borden, and Lady Macbeth—each a criminal of sorts, each the antithesis of domestic femininity.

Lizzie

On the night Lizzie first saw Nance O'Neil perform, twelve years had passed since her acquittal. The crime remained unsolved, and many had begun to believe that Lizzie had gotten away with murder. At the trial, Lizzie's defense was built upon, and in fact depended on, the belief that the gentlemen of the jury shared common assumptions about women and how they behave. Her attorney told the jury, "First create your monster . . . and you have created a character. But start with a woman, with a woman's love and a daughter's impulses, and your imaginings are foreign and base."[29]

In the defense attorney's essentialist criminology, no woman adhering to the gender expectations of the culture could ever be convicted of murder: If she were found innocent, she would be shown to be a reasonable woman and a dutiful wife/daughter/mother. If she were found guilty, she was labeled deviant, no longer a member of the class of women, but spawned from some depraved criminal class, the embodied antithesis of femininity.

If the jury believed the defense's representation of Lizzie as a "true woman," that is to say a woman who spent her life devoted to others, they could not find her guilty of murder. As long as they were convinced that Lizzie was both dependent upon her father and fulfilled in her daughterly love, gender ideology would outweigh the physical evidence and she would be acquitted.[30] Even the prosecutor argued, "It is hard, it is hard to *conceive* that woman can be guilty of crime."[31] In his opening remarks, he almost apologized for trying the case.

> The prisoner at the bar is a woman and a Christian woman . . . of the rank of lady, the equal of your wife or mine, of your friends and mine, of whom such things had never been suspected or dreamed of before. I hope I may never forget, nor in anything that I say here today lose sight of the terrible significance of that fact.[32]

The "terrible significance of that fact" was two-edged: On the one hand, the phrase was offered as a conciliatory gesture for the unchivalrous act of prosecuting a "lady" in public court. But on a deeper level, the terrible significance of Lizzie Borden was that if a "gentlewoman" like she could murder her father, then what was to prevent any young lady of the town from turning her anger and frustration into violence toward the patriarch? The defense attorney made the implications of finding Lizzie guilty very clear to the twelve men on the jury. "Gentlemen. To find Lizzie Borden guilty you must believe that she is a fiend. Does she look it? The prisoner at the bar is a Christian woman, the equal of your wife and mine."[33] If Lizzie was a "normal woman" *and* an ax murderer, then every man in Fall River must look to his own wife and daughter with suspicion.

The winning rhetoric of Lizzie's defense is reminiscent of the judges' reasoning in the trial of two Scottish schoolmistresses, Jane Pirie and Marianne Woods, in 1811.[34] The two women sued for libel against the grandmother of one of their students, who had informed the parents of all the girls at the school that the two mistresses were engaged in "improper and criminal conduct," of a sexual nature. As a result, every parent withdrew their daughter from the school. Pirie and Woods lost their life savings and, most important, their reputation and therefore their ability to make a living as teachers.[35] Finding for the two schoolmistresses, the judges argued that there was no indecency in the women's intimate friendship, and that it was not improper for them to embrace or even share a bed. Faderman writes,

> To have accepted that such behavior infers something sexual would have called into question the most strongly held beliefs of the era regarding women. It would have raised an issue which touched the very foundation of society, that of female venereal appetite. Not just the reputation of two women was at stake here, but the reputation of every respectable British woman. If these two British women of decent background, good Christian education, and admirable attainments, were possessed of such blatant sexual drives, was the wife of Lord Justice-Clerk Hope free from those drives?[36]

The discursive erasure of Lizzie's guilt parallels the erasure of Pirie and Woods's sexuality. For the decision-making men to find women capable of sexual desire for each other or of violent anger toward their fathers and husbands would have been to expose the "naturalness" of gendered norms of behavior for the social constructions that they were: "Surely it is preferable under such circumstances not to punish the offender but to pretend there has been no offense."[37] And that is precisely what happened in Lizzie's case; the court's desire for her to be incapable of the crime was so strong that it overshadowed the physical evidence, and she was acquitted. The case was closed, and no attempt was ever made to find the murderer.

After inheriting her father's fortune, Lizzie changed her name to Lizbeth and moved into a mansion on "the hill," which she called Maplecroft. One year after the murder, an editorial ran in the *Providence Journal:* "There is no reason now for Miss Borden's silence; let her speak! Let her spare no effort to bring this horrible case to a more satisfactory conclusion."[38] Lizzie, now Lizbeth, ignored the call for an explanation and remained silent, and the public who had rallied to her defense began to turn against her. Perhaps had she faded gracefully into obscurity, teaching Sunday school, having tea with ladies of similar quality, or even marrying, legend would not have made her the ax murderer she became. Lizzie was found innocent by a jury of twelve men because she was an upper-class woman whose own silence in the courtroom allowed her lawyers to represent her as a defenseless girl, a dutiful daughter, and a good Christian: all qualities inconsistent with a criminal nature. But in the absence of any other murder suspect, Lizzie was recriminalized when she refused to adhere to the same image that freed her. The pretentiousness of changing her name and flaunting her wealth did not sit well with her community. The relationship with Nance was too much. The rumors of a lesbian affair were a convenient and powerful way to recriminalize the woman who had been acquitted because she embodied a feminine ideal.

According to Lizzie Borden biographer Frank Spiering, the two women met at a summer hotel in Tyngsboro, Massachusetts, in August 1904 and became fast friends.[39] Certainly Nance needed a wealthy friend then. Despite her critical success, the company was, as usual, in financial straits. She and Rankin were being sued for commissions owed by two Boston theater managers—C. P. Salisbury, the manager of the Columbia Theatre,[40] and E. J. Ratcliff.[41] Lizzie had entered Nance's life just in time. According to several sources, she paid Nance's legal expenses in the lawsuits and even accompanied her into the courtroom for moral support. Nance and Lizzie's friendship put a great strain on Lizzie's relationship with her older, more puritanical sister Emma. Victoria Lincoln writes that Emma left Maplecroft forever on the night that Lizzie threw a huge party for Nance and her company.

> There were caterers, hired palm trees, an orchestra—for once Maplecroft fulfilled its intended function as Lizzie must have imagined it when she bought it, still full of faith in caresses that would never diminish and "floral offerings" that would not fade. The house blazed with lights from top to bottom and blared with music. That night, Emma left.[42]

The two sisters never spoke again after that night, but Emma's departure did not separate Lizzie from Nance. A week later, Lizzie rented a house in the resort town of Tyngsboro so that "she and Nance's company could enjoy a week-long house party." Those who had been in neighboring cottages remarked that "it was not a noticeably quiet and sober time."[43] Later, when Nance decided to buy a summer home in Tyngsboro, Lizzie helped Nance with the down payment.[44] Lincoln also notes that the reclusive Lizzie actually went to court with Nance when the actress was sued by a Boston theater manager.[45] One is left to conclude that their friendship must have been strong for Lizzie to step back into the public light of a courtroom after the intensity of her own ordeal. Yet, besides these stories, which are wrapped in the negative context of drunkenness and raucousness, there are no records of the women's daily habits or quiet moments together. Like Lizzie's silence in the courtroom, the historical silence surrounding the women's private relationship is frustrating for those who seek absolutes.

Post-Lizzie

It is unclear how or when the two women parted company, but by 1906 the bank had foreclosed on Nance's Massachusetts home and no more money was forthcoming from Lizzie.[46] Perhaps the article that reported Lizzie's playwriting aspirations had placed Nance in an awkward position and she, or Rankin, had found it wise to distance herself from someone as notorious as Lizzie Borden. A review of Nance's performance as Lady Macbeth in Boston in 1906 was very different in tone from the initial critical praise.

> Miss O'Neil's Lady Macbeth is quite worthy a place in the repertoire of an actress who is a woman of genuine talent, blemished though it undoubtedly has been, either by unskillful training, or *personal perverseness.*[47]

There is no explanation about what the actress's "personal perverseness" might be, but clearly it was not just Rankin being criticized this time. Nance had clearly alienated this reviewer in some way that was not related to her performance. Had her multiple court appearances or her relationship with the acquitted ax murderess ruined her credibility in the eyes of the Boston press? It is hard to say. In any event, her popularity was quick to fade. In November 1906 the actress, who the year before had been all the rage, held a benefit performance to raise money—it was sparsely attended.[48] Four days later she was in court facing a poor-debtor action.[49] When she left her home in Tyngsboro, she told a reporter that the New Englanders she had hoped would embrace her had turned judgmental and cold.

> Every evening when the train came bringing me home from Boston, the long street I had to walk to reach home was lined with the "blue-nosed" inhabitants. Hundreds and hundreds of them were lined up inside gates to "see that actress woman pass." And some of their audible comments did not endear them to me. So one day I gathered my pets and my belongings and moved back to the hotel in Boston. I had not studied them, while they had torn me to shreds.[50]

Nance never recaptured the popularity of her early days in Boston, and despite an attempt by the Shuberts to revitalize her career, she was eventually reduced to playing vaudeville, sharing the bill with Miss Kitty, the juggling equestrienne.[51]

In 1908, she finally split with Rankin, who by this time, according to one critic, was "so fat, he can't act for he can hardly move. . . . his voice is so covered from fat and whiskey that he is not intelligible."[52] Nance had been offered a position in David Belasco's company, and she jumped at the chance to leave her longtime manager. One father figure was quickly replaced by another. The dramatic critic of the *Chicago Examiner* interviewed Nance just after she began working for Belasco. He praised the transformation in her, which he assumed had been wrought by her new manager. The critic seems almost relieved that Nance's exuberance and power were subdued, replaced by womanly repose—Nance O'Neil had been tamed.

> Yes Nance O'Neil was changed in herself and in her acting. The great exuberance was gone. You did not feel a battery in her handshake. . . . her gestures did not make the big room appear small. . . . repose seems to have found her at last. . . . For more than fifteen years the critics said: "If only David Belasco would take Nance O'Neil in hand!" Without him she ran through the theatre a raw riot. She struck great sparks and greater dull sickening thuds.[53]

Nance's first performance with Belasco was as Odette, "the heart broken spinster," in a production of *The Lily*.[54] Thirty-five, and yet unmarried, Nance was often asked whether she identified with the spinsters she portrayed onstage. In an article entitled, "Is Life All Over for the Unmarried Woman of 35?" Nance seemed conflicted about her own position as a single woman—at one point defending her independence and integrity, but in the next sentence appearing to long for the social security of marriage.

> The question has been asked me hundreds of times. To the American mind, I judge, the idea is revolting. Why should a woman with a heart and a brain be withered in soul and body simply because she has the added gift of maturity? An unmarried woman of 35 has everything before her. She need not be ugly. Because she is 35 her face need not be pale or her eyes heavy. If she has money she can travel, see new things, and hear new sounds, if her means are small, dozens of avenues are open to her by which she can support herself. . . . But I rather believe sometimes these brave words are just words. There are a great many more "old maids" than people realize. Yes even in America. . . . all over the world there are starved lives. But in this country the heartache is smothered by smiles.[55]

Perhaps Nance felt that hers was a starved life, and that is why in 1916, at the age of forty-two, Nance married her former costar Alfred Hickman. It is unclear why she chose to marry later in her life; perhaps in the waning years of her career she craved a more orthodox existence. Or perhaps by 1916, when relations between women were becoming increasingly stigmatized, Nance wished to put rumors of her lesbian past to rest once and for all. The rumored affair with Lizzie had followed her even after she split with Rankin. In 1908 she left a Shubert tour without telling anyone in order to visit her friend Clara Bracy (a younger sister of Lydia Thompson), who had been discharged by the Shubert tour manager, Victor Harmon. Because of Nance's rumored relationship with Lizzie Borden, David Beasley suggests that Harmon suspected an illicit relationship between Nance and Mrs. Bracy. In a letter dated December 23, 1908, Harmon wrote,

> I feel quite sure that her main reason for going on to New York was just to see Mrs. Bracy who was discharged from the Company, and I have seen enough since I have been with the Company to show me that Mrs. Bracy is a bad old Cat.[56]

Hickman was central to Nance's career in the later years. Though never her manager, he was her professional collaborator and her director. Denying rumors of separation in 1925, Nance referred to Hickman as "the dearest and best of pals and collaborators,"[57] But some evidence of disappointment in marriage can be read in the essay she penned for *Theatre* magazine in 1920, after four years of wedlock.

> Domestic convenience, which has held so many unloved women in the biting chains of their imprisoned souls, seems a great price to pay for very little. . . . tradition has made women cowardly. Still, the freedom of all the Magdas of the world has been worthwhile, if only to enlarge the scope of a woman's emotional conquest of her own soul.[58]

Nance's essay, entitled "The Unloved Woman on the Stage," articulates an intensely feminist resistance to the gender conventions of her age, a resistance that seems provocatively absent in her historical persona. Though Nance's friendship with Lizzie had ended long before Nance composed this essay, it is easy to hear the traces of their emotional connection in the actress's words.

> In the course of events that engulf the heart of any woman who is an alert rebel of her sex (and what modern woman is not), there are all sorts of difficulties that no one understands but herself. The women who have gone deep into the swamps of feeling, because the invisible chart of their soul has led them there, are among the unloved

women. For a woman to be unloved in the sense of the highest virtue that love means to her is to sacrifice herself. If she does this, and she is a valiant rebel against the forces that bind her, some day the storm that has been brewing in her silent, patient soul, bursts, uproots the commonplace things in her life, and leaves a barren waste about her. . . . Often in women who live out their destinies in the small places into which they have been driven, there is a storm that broods but never bursts. Few women realize the joy of real liberty, not merely the freedom of time and place, but the greater freedom of supreme faith in their own feeling. They distrust their emotion and so confuse their lives. Foreseeing this I wrote in my first diary this defiant rule of life: *"Better an outlaw than not free."*[59]

Was Nance thinking of Lizzie when she wrote those words? Is the impassioned force of her rhetoric fueled by anger or regret at the way public opinion pathologized her relationship with Lizzie and drove them apart? Both Lizzie Borden and Nance O'Neil were subject to constant public scrutiny and made aware daily of how they differed from the women around them. Forced into seclusion on the one hand, and the spotlight on the other, they relied on the facade of submission—to father, or manager, or husband—to smooth their way in a world that deeply distrusted their independence. For a brief moment their lives crossed; an odd pair, but perhaps they recognized something of themselves in each other.

Lizzie and Nance were indeed outlaws, yet I doubt they were ever free.

NOTES

1. Victoria Lincoln, *A Private Disgrace: Lizzie Borden by Daylight* (New York: G. Putnam and Sons, 1967), 307.

2. Frank Spiering, *Lizzie* (New York: Random House, 1984), 208. Spiering does not provide a source for this clipping, but a similar article entitled "Lizzie Borden, Who With Her Sister was Acquitted of Murder, is Now an Author," dated June 5, 1905, can be found in the file on Nance O'Neil, Billy Rose Theatre Collection, Lincoln Center Library for the Performing Arts, New York Public Library. The author and newspaper are unidentified.

3. Lillian Faderman, *Surpassing the Love of Men: Romantic Friendship and Love between Women from the Renaissance to the Present* (New York: Morrow, 1981), 147–56.

4. Victoria Lincoln, "Whatever Became of Lizzie Borden?" *Playbill*, October 11, 1967, 16.

5. Ibid.

6. Faderman, *Surpassing Love of Men,* 161.

7. W. L. George, *The Intelligence of Woman* (Boston: Little, Brown, 1920), 87.

8. Luke Owen Pike, *A History of Crime in England* (London: Smith, Elder, 1876), 2:527.

9. Faderman, *Surpassing Love of Men,* 240.

10. "Back to Broadway: Nance O'Neil," undated, unidentified New York newspaper article, File on Nance O'Neil, Harvard Theatre Collection.

11. Ibid.

12. Andrea Weiss, " 'A Queer Feeling When I Look at You': Hollywood Stars and Lesbian Spectatorship in the 1930s," in *Multiple Voices in Feminist Film Criticism,* ed. Diane Carson, Linda Dittmar, and Janice R. Welsch (Minneapolis: University of Minnesota Press, 1994), 330.

13. "Is Nance O'Neil Another Trilby?" *Hawaiian Star,* December 26, 1903, File on Nance O'Neil, Harvard Theatre Collection.

14. Ibid.

15. Untitled article, Nance O'Neil File, Billy Rose Theatre Collection.

16. Charlotte Porter, "Boston Discovers Miss Nance O'Neil," *Critic,* June 1904, 529.

17. Oscar Brockett, *A History of the Theatre,* 5th ed. (Boston: Allyn and Bacon, 1987), 524–25.

18. David Beasley, "The Nance O'Neil Company and the Shuberts in 1908," *Passing Show* (newsletter of the Shubert Archive), 15, no. 1 (spring 1992): 2.

19. Spiering, *Lizzie,* 204.

20. Untitled article, *San Francisco Evening Post,* February 25, 1899, Nance O'Neil File, Billy Rose Theatre Collection.

21. Beasley, "Nance O'Neil Company," 2.

22. "The M'Kee Rankin Fiasco," *Era,* September 27, 1902, File on Nance O'Neil, Harvard Theatre Collection.

23. "Trilby and Svengali in Real Life: Miss Nance O'Neil Acts Under Mc-Kee Rankin's Hypnotic Spell," *Chicago Sunday American,* December 13, 1903, 1, File on Nance O'Neil, Harvard Theatre Collection.

24. "How Nance O'Neil Learned to Act," unnamed newspaper, February 25, 1904, File on Nance O'Neil, Harvard Theatre Collection.

25. Review of *Hedda Gabler, New York Evening Journal,* November 25, 1904, n.p.

26. W.W., "Miss O'Neil at Daly's Theatre," *New York Daily Tribune,* November 22, 1904, File on Nance O'Neil, Harvard Theatre Collection.

27. Ibid.

28. Untitled article dated December 18, 1904, Nance O'Neil File, Billy Rose Theatre Collection.

29. Lincoln, *A Private Disgrace,* 281.

30. The prosecution had a legally valid case based upon circumstantial evidence.

31. Ann Jones, *Women Who Kill* (New York: Holt, Rinehart and Winston, 1980), 233.

32. Ibid., 228.

33. Agnes de Mille, *Lizzie Borden: A Dance of Death* (Boston: Little, Brown, 1968), 74.

34. This is the case that served as the basis for Lillian Hellman's *The Children's Hour.*

35. Faderman, *Surpassing Love of Men,* 147.

36. Ibid., 152.

37. Jones, *Women Who Kill,* 223.

38. Spiering, *Lizzie,* 119.

39. Ibid., 204.

40. "Seeking to Enjoin Miss Nance O'Neil: C. P. Salisbury, Late of the Columbia, Files Bill of Equity," unnamed Boston newspaper, 1904, File on Nance O'Neil, Harvard Theatre Collection.

41. Spiering, *Lizzie,* 206.

42. Lincoln, *A Private Disgrace,* 308.

43. Ibid.

44. Spiering, *Lizzie,* 206; and Lincoln, "Whatever Became?" 16.

45. Lincoln, "Whatever Became?" 16.

46. "Nance O'Neil faces Poor Debtor Action," May 26, 1906, unidentified article, File on Nance O'Neil, Harvard Theatre Collection.

47. "Tremont Theatre: Macbeth," unidentified article, File on Nance O'Neil, Harvard Theatre Collection; emphasis added.

48. "Nance O'Neil Benefit," May 22, 1906, unidentified article, File on Nance O'Neil, Harvard Theatre Collection.

49. "Nance O'Neil Faces Action."

50. Spiering, *Lizzie,* 212.

51. "Nance O'Neil's First on Vaudeville Bill," October 1907, unidentified article, File on Nance O'Neil, Harvard Theatre Collection.

52. Beasley, "Nance O'Neil Company," 5.

53. Ashton Stevens, "Nance O'Neil Wins Perfect Happiness," undated and unidentified article, File on Nance O'Neil, Harvard Theatre Collection.

54. "Nance O'Neil Dies; Tragedienne, 90," *New York Times,* February 8, 1967.

55. "Is Life All Over for the Unmarried Woman of 35?" October 23, 1910, 1, unidentified article, File on Nance O'Neil, Harvard Theatre Collection. A few months later another article appeared that focused on the actress's single state: "Old Maids Are the Most Romantically Happy People in the World Says Nance O'Neil," April 25, 1911, unidentified article, File on Nance O'Neil, Harvard Theatre Collection.

56. Beasley, "Nance O'Neil Company," 6.

57. "Nance O'Neil Longs for Lighter Roles," December 20, 1925, unidentified article, File on Nance O'Neil, Harvard Theatre Collection.

58. Nance O'Neil, "The Unloved Woman on the Stage," *Theatre* 31 (June 1920): 516.

59. Ibid.

A Lesbian Marriage
of Cultural Consequence
Elisabeth Marbury and Elsie de Wolfe, 1886–1933

Kim Marra

For nearly half a century, Elisabeth Marbury (1856–1933) and Elsie de Wolfe (1865–1950) sustained a devoted love relationship while pioneering revolutionary professions. Marbury became the first theatrical agent to represent European as well as American authors and instituted the modern royalty system. In 1911, *Metropolitan* magazine proclaimed her "the fourth estate of the dramatic world." Elsie de Wolfe was the premiere fashion doyenne on Broadway when she revolutionized the profession of interior decoration in 1905. According to Diana Vreeland, "She simply cleared out the Victoriana and let in the twentieth century."[1] As their autobiographies and supporting records attest, the inspiration, practical support, love, and companionship each partner gave the other proved instrumental in facilitating their remarkable accomplishments.

Although these pioneering lovers became as wealthy and influential as many theatrical potentates with whom they associated, like Charles Frohman, David Belasco, and the Shuberts, and innumerable stars and playwrights, the treatment of their careers in American theater historiography is comparatively nil.[2] That they were women whose primary theatrical contributions lay outside the conventionally most valued feminine role of star actress may be one reason for this historiographical gap. That they were women linked in a highly visible affectional relationship suggests additional motives for erasure: the Western positivist tendency to privilege individual over relational action in history, and homophobia that specifically stigmatizes and eradicates same-sex sexual relations from the record. As women's social historian Blanche Wiesen Cook has observed,

Homophobia, a bigotry that declares woman-loving women an evil before God or a mental disease or both, has served to erase the very aspects of our history that would have enabled us to deal healthfully with what has been for most lesbians an isolating and cruel experience. Homophobia has also erased a variety of role-models whose existence would tend to obliterate crude and dehumanizing stereotypes.[3]

From a postpositivist, lesbian feminist perspective, I seek to rectify the erasure not just by recounting Marbury and de Wolfe's many accomplishments but by foregrounding their relationship itself as an historical force. This strategy raises the historiographical problem of "lesbian" classification. When Marbury and de Wolfe began their relationship in 1886, the word *lesbian* was obscure enough that it may not even have been a part of their vocabulary. It entered wide circulation in the United States only with the popularization of sexologist theory—most influentially Freud's—in the early decades of the twentieth century. Because this introduction was so heavily freighted with pathological baggage, many female couples, especially those of Marbury and de Wolfe's generation and milieu, vehemently eschewed the label. Consequently, contemporary historians must revalue the term in order to write lesbian history. Cook asserts: "Women who love women, who choose women to nurture and support and to create a living environment in which to work creatively and independently [which Marbury and de Wolfe did for forty-seven years], are lesbians."[4]

Defining Marbury and de Wolfe's lesbianism also requires problematizing current assumptions about the centrality of sex in homosexuality. Along with Cook, Carroll Smith-Rosenberg and Lillian Faderman have shown that expressions of romantic love between women vary widely across periods and that late-twentieth-century generations, owing largely to the Freudian legacy and the so-called sexual revolution of the 1960s, tend to focus more narrowly on the sexual aspects of affectional orientation than did people of earlier eras.[5] To link experiences of female lovers across generations and render a "lesbian" history visible, Faderman provides a broad definition of the term that can incorporate Marbury and de Wolfe's case, positing as lesbian

a relationship in which two women's strongest emotions and affections are directed toward each other. Sexual contact may be a part of the relationship to a greater or lesser degree, or it may be entirely absent. By preference the two women spend most of their time together and share most aspects of their lives with each other.[6]

Significantly, Faderman's definition (like Cook's) stresses the relational aspects of sexuality. The historical importance of these aspects is also emphasized in the more recent volume, *Hidden from History: Reclaiming the Gay and Lesbian Past* (1989), in which, for example, Robert Padgug asserts that sexuality "consists of active social relations, and not simply sexual 'acts.' "[7] Active social relations include not only those of intimacy, but also those with key players in the historical subjects' various other spheres of activity. Editors Martin Duberman, Martha Vicinus, and George Chauncey Jr. extend the methodological purview of Faderman's groundbreaking work to consider more of the "complex dialectic between social conditions, ideology, and consciousness that produces sexual identities."[8] In analyzing the historical efficacy of Marbury and de Wolfe's relationship, I will attempt to delineate the particular intersection of contingencies that produced their lesbianism. Extrapolating chiefly from Faderman's and Smith-Rosenberg's studies of white, middle-class female lovers in the Progressive Era, I will elaborate the terms of their mutual devotion and joint lifestyle and then analyze how, at crucial career junctures, the relational dynamics between the two women interacted with other social relations to determine their contributions to American cultural history. Marbury and de Wolfe offer an illuminating case study of the historical and historiographical problematics of recuperating female theater practitioners from this period into the lesbian past.

The dynamics of the Marbury/de Wolfe partnership fit within the Progressive Era model of the "Boston marriage." As defined by Carroll Smith-Rosenberg and Lillian Faderman, this was a long-term, monogamous alliance of two individuals who came of age with the first generation of urban northeastern New Women. Such lovers were well pedigreed and well educated but eschewed husbands to fight for their own economic independence and professional visibility. Usually feminists, Boston marrieds, according to Smith-Rosenberg, shared commitments to radical causes without relinquishing their claims to gentility.[9]

Both Marbury and de Wolfe reportedly turned down offers of heterosexual marriage to achieve, in Marbury's words, "freedom of action and protection from unproductive demands on our time."[10] In contrast to traditional heterosexual models or same-sex relationships in which one partner dedicates herself to serving the career of the other, theirs was an alliance of professional equals akin to those of contemporaries Sarah Orne Jewett and Annie Fields, and Edith Somerville and Violet Martin.[11] Along with high achievement in their respective professions, Marbury and de Wolfe were dedicated to political activism and theatrical reform.

De Wolfe avidly campaigned for woman suffrage but kept her protest respectable by marching with high-society pillars like Alva Vanderbilt. Though initially opposed to the cause, Marbury fully exploited women's new political power by becoming a leader in the Democratic Party after 1918. Genteel reforms like the moral and socioeconomic uplift of urban youth and the working chorus girl informed Marbury–de Wolfe theatrical enterprises such as the Strand Roof Garden and the Princess musicals. Through all these endeavors, their Boston marriage provided a crucial support system, enabling them to cope with both the anxiety and exhilaration of the freedoms they claimed and the roles they pioneered.

The practical benefits of the relationship may have proved as compelling as the emotional ones. Their work took them outside the home for long hours and often to other cities and countries. Each of the four houses they shared—three successive permanent residences in Manhattan and a summer villa in France—was spatially organized and staffed with maids, cooks, and secretaries in constant readiness to meet their respective personal and professional demands. Each partner maintained her own "bedroom suite," a practice common among married couples of their era and class, but Marbury's and de Wolfe's suites both included extensive office and library space, in case one needed to rest or work in quiet while the other met with friends or associates. Separate bedrooms, in their case, were also, quite literally, for show; de Wolfe conducted interviews and photography sessions for women's magazines in her exemplary boudoir and expansive shoe closet. Their living arrangements not only facilitated meeting their many business and social obligations but enabled them to coordinate their private leisure time. Very precious, says de Wolfe, were the dinners prepared for them to eat together at home in the brief window of time between the business day and the rehearsals both attended in their various capacities five or six nights a week.[12]

De Wolfe's biographer Jane S. Smith calls the working dynamic between the two women "a clear argument for the attraction of opposites." As befit their chosen professions, Marbury was more pragmatic and matter-of-fact, de Wolfe more intuitive and artistic. In her personal appearance, Marbury cared little about conforming to dominant cultural standards of femininity. Descriptions of her physique invariably mention her large girth, dark serviceable Victorian dresses, deep commanding voice, and chain smoking. After finishing school, her first enterprise was poultry farming, and whenever possible she indulged her lifelong passion for fly-fishing. By contrast, having suffered childhood taunts of "ugliness," de Wolfe made it her lifelong passion to pursue beauty in her own

**Elisabeth Marbury and Elsie de Wolfe at home
in New York c. 1910**

(Photograph by M. E. Hewitt, in Elisabeth Marbury, My Crystal Ball
[London: Hurst and Blackett, 1924], 156.)

person and in her environment. This manifested in a preoccupation not just with maintaining dominant cultural standards of femininity but in refining and revolutionizing those standards. She dressed meticulously in the latest Parisian fashions and took great pride in her slim physique, maintained through rigorous diet and exercise.[13] For all of their differences, both partners clearly admired, profited, and learned from the strengths of the other. Marbury developed a keen sense of fashionable taste in hiring designers for shows she produced, and de Wolfe developed her business acumen to preside over one of the most profitable enterprises in corporate America. When friction arose between these two different, but equally driven, personalities, the saving grace was humor, which, asserted Marbury, "has never deserted us in all the years of our intimacy. . . . Perhaps if husbands and wives exerted it occasionally, there might be fewer divorces."[14]

As to the private, physical aspects of Marbury and de Wolfe's conjugal love life, the evidence is inconclusive. There are no explicit photographs or any record of explicit references made to third parties. No revelatory personal letters or diaries have survived.[15] But lack of evidence about the most private of relations is neither surprising nor indicative of lack of erotic activity. Faderman's and Smith-Rosenberg's research attests that assessments of female same-sex love during this period must take into account values of Boston marriages rooted in older Victorian traditions of female romantic friendship. As Smith-Rosenberg has shown, separation of the spheres according to gender in white, middle-class Victorian society fostered deep bonds between women that included physical as well as emotional intimacy.[16] However, these relations transpired within a prevailing discourse of female "passionlessness" that deemed respectable Victorian women less prone to sexual impulses than men; carnal desire was associated primarily with male needs that wives supposedly satisfied chiefly for the sake of marital duty and reproduction.[17] Such beliefs served the dominant social order by asserting that neither female sexuality nor bonds between women would jeopardize male prerogatives or heterosexual marriage.

Under the ideological veil of female "passionlessness," female romantic friends could express their affection by frank and effusive declarations of love, touching, kissing, even lying entwined in the same bed together without being accused of having carnal knowledge. In the famous 1811 Scottish case said to have inspired Lillian Hellman's *The Children's Hour,* Jane Pirie and Marianne Woods were acquitted on the belief that respectable women were incapable of committing the alleged "improper and criminal conduct." Indeed, as Faderman points out, conviction of the two women would have undermined the very fabric of middle-class patriarchal society. By Faderman's and Smith-Rosenberg's estimations, this belief system shielded generations of genteel female romantic friends until the popularization of European sexology in the early twentieth century.[18] Accordingly, during the early decades of Marbury and de Wolfe's relationship, two women of their class might engage with relative impunity in a wide variety of romantic practices ranging from platonic effusions to the most intimate physical exchanges.

Moreover, women could engage in these practices with varying degrees of consciousness about their sexual nature. According to Nancy F. Cott, some women internalized the ideologies of gender sphere separation and female passionlessness to the extent of believing that carnal motivation did not taint even their most ardent exchanges with female partners. Others plainly regarded their attractions to both men and women as sexual but invoked the ideology of female passionlessness to strategic advantage, such as to avoid pregnancy and/or to rationalize spending more time with female friends. In between these two categories were many, as Faderman observes, who viewed their female romantic friendships in a general context of noble purity and considered occasional forays into the erotic and sexual realms as "slips." Smith-Rosenberg reports that, fully aware of the passionate nature of her attachment, a woman might even openly confront a husband or suitor with intruding on her relationship with her beloved without compromising either her own or the beloved's reputation; only another man could deprive a respectable bourgeois woman of her chastity.[19] As long as female intimacy could be construed as nonthreatening to the male-dominant power structure, the social and belief systems surrounding romantic friendship and its more permanent institution in Boston marriage sustained a wide range of both homoaffectional behavior and sexual awareness among women.

What little can be gleaned about the nature of Marbury and de Wolfe's attitudes toward sex and the relationship of those attitudes toward their own romantic practices reflects these complex late Victorian circumstances. Like most New Women of their generation, they adopted a conservative stance on questions of sexual morality and focused many of their enterprises on the cultivation of social respectability and, especially, feminine virtue. This agenda is evident, for example, in their support of the dance duo Vernon and Irene Castle, whose management de Wolfe encouraged Marbury to undertake in 1913. For them, the Castles represented a morally uplifting form of dance that they promoted as an antidote to urban temptations and rising sexual libertinism. Marbury described the Castles' tango as an "evolution of the eighteenth-century minuet with no strenuous clasping of partners, no hideous gyrations of the limbs, no abnormal twistings, and no vicious angles."[20]

However, Marbury and de Wolfe's complex Victorianism also enabled them to count among their close friends and associates men and women renowned for flamboyant displays of same-sex love, most notably Oscar Wilde, Sarah Bernhardt, and Emma Calvé. Wilde became Marbury's client in 1895, and she continued to represent him throughout the ordeals of his trial and imprisonment. Because acts of male same-sex love obviously involved participants not shielded by the ideological veil of female "passionlessness," white middle-class male homosexuality was institutionally condemned as sexual and criminal earlier than acts of same-sex love between respectable women.[21] In *My Crystal Ball*, Marbury proclaimed Wilde's "a clear case of psycho-perversity" and argued that greater understanding on the part of the court should have sent him to a sanitarium and not prison. As a refuge for him after his release, she bought a house near the French villa she shared with de Wolfe, but he did not live long enough to occupy it.[22] Marbury's judgment of Wilde's behavior as pathological was consistent with dominant cultural attitudes and not necessarily hypocritical in light of her own lifestyle. Because Victorian sphere separation constructed interactions between men as discrete from those between women, any connection between Wilde's proclivities and her own could easily be overlooked. Some level of empathy, however, might be read in the fact that she kept her name associated with his and went so far as to buy him a house when another in her position, given contemporary mores, might have eschewed him.

Marbury and de Wolfe also were able to keep their relationship separate from more publicly reputed acts of female same-sex display. As Bernhardt and Calvé were frequent guests in their home and at their parties, they at least tolerated the former's pointed donning of pants and the latter's lustful pursuit of Reneé Vivien but did not align themselves with this behavior. Their descriptions of their feelings for each other indicate they deemed their love profound, genteel, and enduring beyond superficial public display. Throughout their respective autobiographies, both women refer to each other as "my beloved" and speak often of the joy and sustenance through many trials their mutual devotion provided. Perhaps because of her conversion to Catholicism following the 1898 deaths of her parents, Marbury was most prone to dwelling on the spiritual aspects of their alliance. She wrote that despite all environment and every condition, through fair weather and foul, our craft of mutual faith and mutual affection glided steadily forward, and the friendship between us, which was founded upon the rock of sympathy, of love, and above all, of respect, has withstood the strain of nearly forty years, combining in one the relations of companion and of sister. . . . it is a priceless treasure, a gift from God in very fact. It is the song without words which in the singing becomes the ladder of souls stretching from earth to heaven.[23]

Given the wide range of tolerable female romantic practices of the period, such an effusion could indicate a platonic relation, in which case it would have been readily distinguishable from Calvé's professed intentions toward Vivien. Or, Marbury and de Wolfe could have linked the physical aspects of their love so inseparably to the spiritual ones as to place their alliance in a separate category from those of their more flamboyant contemporaries.

Whatever expressions of love Marbury and de Wolfe exchanged, the two women were clearly what we would call "significant others," and their connection was publicly recognized as well as privately cherished. Dubbing them "bachelor girls," "bosom friends," or "those fair inseparables," the press avidly chronicled their joint activities, both factual and rumored.[24] In spite of their well-publicized separate bedrooms, one journalist for a New York daily circa 1904 even wrote them a bed scene. Titled "Elsie de Wolfe in a Fire Scare" and subtitled "She and Miss Elizabeth [*sic*] Marbury Hurriedly Driven from their Apartments by Flames," the piece is worth quoting at length for the complex dominant cultural attitudes it reveals toward their relationship.

Into the sanctity of the boudoirs of the Misses Elsie de Wolfe and Elizabeth [*sic*] Marbury a bold and rascally fire penetrated yesterday morning—unchaperoned.

Figuratively, it was at an early hour when the first impertinent puff of smoke arrived at the bedchamber door and, without even knocking, startled the occupants of the room into fifty-seven varieties of hysteria. Actually, it was high noon when the Misses de Wolfe and Marbury, feeling secure from the eyes of the prying world, sat bolt upright in bed, clad in garments sentenced to life imprisonment in the boudoir, and sipped of their coffee and munched at their rolls precisely as they had learned to do in that gay Paris. . . .

"Bess," remarked Miss de Wolfe, readjusting the pillows behind her back, "do you believe in dreams?"

"Well—er—that is, not exactly," replied Miss Marbury, aiming a carefully planned onslaught on a hard-shell roll, "why?"

"You see, I dreamed last night that—bend nearer, dear—that a fire broke into our rooms and"—[nonsense letters indicating whispering]

"Gracious, don't!" exclaimed Miss Marbury. "That is precisely what we are insured against. That policy—may I trouble you for the cream? Thanks. That policy is our safeguard."

Silently they munched.

"Heavens, Bess," suddenly demanded Miss de Wolfe, "don't you smell something?"

Miss Marbury, with a judgment born of long experience, glanced toward a pile of manuscripts.

"Mean them?" she asked. "Well, I wouldn't wonder!"

"No, don't you smell smo—Great Sardou! The house is afire!"[25]

Among the revealing elements of this portrayal are the construction of the boudoir as a private and chaste—if potentially hysterical—woman's sphere and the characterization of the fire as an implicitly masculine, "rascally" penetrator, suggesting that heat and passion are foreign to the space; the casting of Marbury in the appetitive, authoritative role of the husband concerned with food and the insurance policy; the reference to Parisian bohemianism; and de Wolfe's compulsion to whisper even though the two women are supposedly alone. These latter two aspects hint at more hidden and perhaps forbidden levels of shared intimacy that may impart a double entendre to Marbury's invocation of the insurance policy. The two are insured against penetrating flames of passion by virtue of their gender and bourgeois status. However, the flames nevertheless take hold, raising the full spectrum of romantic possibilities and driving the inhabitants from the established private woman's sphere into one not fully defined but unavoidably public.

Public knowledge of Marbury and de Wolfe's connection as well as their deep mutual devotion impacted a wider range of social relations that galvanized crucial developments in their respective careers. The historical role of their relationship in a variety of cultural practices is well illustrated in the launching of Marbury's theatrical agency, de Wolfe's professional acting career, de Wolfe's interior-decorating business, and the Strand Roof Garden and Princess musicals.

Marbury's managerial and de Wolfe's professional performing careers both arose from their earliest associations through amateur theatricals at swank Tuxedo Park, one of the nation's first country clubs, during its inaugural 1886–87 season. From a local blue-blood family, Marbury—

the erstwhile poultry farmer—attended by birthright and because she desired, tentatively, to become a playwright.[26] De Wolfe, a *nouvelle* seeking social prominence, attended as the featured actress in an Amateur Comedy Club farce entitled *A Cup of Tea.* Her comic backflip over a loveseat, executed in full-skirted regalia, garnered particular attention and comment from Marbury and other audience members. She and Marbury did not meet personally, however, until some time later when both were invited to a luncheon given by their mutual friend, Sarah Cooper Hewitt. Their relationship developed rapidly after this initial meeting and galvanized their respective social and theatrical interests.[27]

The culminating event of their amateur careers was the 1888 charity production of Marbury's script *Contrast,* which showcased a resplendent de Wolfe and for which Marbury lined up the supporting cast, arranged publicity, printed playbills, and secured a high-profile performance space, Daniel Frohman's Lyceum Theatre, then known as the premier "society house." The event proved a tour de force for the dynamic combination of de Wolfe's social aspirations and self-conscious fashionability and Marbury's blue-blood connections and organizational skills. Frohman was so impressed that he urged Marbury to take up theatrical management on a more permanent basis, and she forsook her chickens to incubate Frances Hodgson Burnett's dramatization of *Little Lord Fauntleroy.* De Wolfe impressed Charles as well as Daniel Frohman and was offered acting lessons from David Belasco.[28]

Though these developments were auspicious, they still involved considerable risk for the lovers, who would increasingly need each other's emotional and practical support. A pivotal early crisis befell them in France in 1890. Marbury had naively joined forces for a European tour of *Little Lord Fauntleroy* with a fast-talking Australian entrepreneur who absconded with all her savings. Left high and dry in Havre, and facing a frightening uncertain future, she conceived the idea of becoming foreign authors' American representative and rushed to join de Wolfe, who was studying drama in Paris. There, bolstered by her lover's support and encouragement, she refined her scheme and found the gumption to contact Victorien Sardou, president of the French Society of Dramatic Authors, and ask for an interview. He granted her fifteen minutes, for which she madly prepared and rehearsed with de Wolfe. When the quarter-hour came, Marbury made such an impression that she gained not only Sardou's business but that of the entire membership of his organization. In celebration, the lovers embarked on a bicycle tour of the romantic Loire Valley, about which de Wolfe would later publish an article for

Cosmopolitan detailing the châteaus they saw en route. When they returned to New York, Elisabeth Marbury Enterprises opened its first offices and sold production rights to Charles Frohman for the American premier of Sardou's *Thermidor*. Marbury also convinced Frohman to cast de Wolfe in the title role for her professional acting debut. Apart from launching her acting career, the production manifested de Wolfe's growing fondness for eighteenth-century French style, through which she would make her signature impact on American fashion and decor.[29]

The interactions around *Thermidor* situated the lovers at the hub of power relations in the burgeoning commercial theater and established a pattern for their professional collaborations. Marbury developed a close association with Frohman that continued after he spearheaded the formation of the Theatrical Syndicate in 1896, a watershed in making the theater industry big business. Marbury represented many of the authors—foreign and domestic—whose plays the Syndicate produced, and, for much of her career, her offices were located in Frohman's Empire Theatre building, the nerve center of his operations. In their personal lives, the two potentates both eschewed heterosexual marriage and cohabited with persons of the same sex (Frohman with Charles Dillingham), and both used their positions to help their companions professionally.[30]

Marbury's and Frohman's shared personal and professional interests informed the kinds of work they produced and the opportunities they created for their intimates and associates. Both supported a morally uplifting theater that reinforced the values of the monied classes and catered primarily to burgeoning audiences of female consumers. The preferred vehicles included contemporary social comedies and melodramas at whose center were exemplary female characters proffered for women's emulation. While these representations served the dominant heterosexual economy, their production, which typically turned on the fetishizing of feminine fashion and decor, allowed for the circulation of subaltern desires.

Within this theatrical framework, Marbury helped de Wolfe find a niche as the "clotheshorse" in Frohman's "stable of stars." De Wolfe's emotional limitations on stage prevented her from becoming a star of the first magnitude, but she drew audiences with the Parisian fashions she imported and the costumes and sets she designed. As her reputation for arbitrating fashion and decor burgeoned, she published advice literature, such as her 1901–2 series for the *New York Evening World* entitled "How to Dress by the Best-Dressed Yankee Actress," which compounded her audience appeal.[31] Covering de Wolfe's star turn in Clyde Fitch's *The Way of the World* in 1901, society columnists chronicled the action in terms of the couture gowns and the consummate expertise with which de Wolfe wore them in each act. Lavinia Hart captured female audience rapture over the palpable sensuality of the spectacle.

> We would do away with "props" and have people act in real scenes from life—in rooms that might really be lived in, with hangings of velvet, not of paint; with statuary of marble, not of plaster; with carpets into which correctly slippered feet may sink instead of painted boards; with desks and tables that are real, not made of *papier-maché*, and with flowers not made of paper or wax, but fresh-cut and dewey, whose scent gets over the footlights and helps make a real illusion real.
>
> All this and more is given in *The Way of the World*. There never before was a play presented that reached so nearly the acme of realism.
>
> Miss de Wolfe's Mrs. Croyden is a character with whom we are all familiar, and Miss de Wolfe presents her to us just like the Mrs. Croyden on our visiting lists.[32]

This high level of realism made de Wolfe's impersonation and the decor in which she was showcased seem eminently obtainable, which raised to a fever pitch the prospect of fulfillment of consumer desire. This desire exchanged among women and across a woman's body, and not heterosexual romance, the play's ostensible focus, became the driving force of the spectacle.

The subversive operations of this dynamic are further demonstrated in another audience paroxysm of commodity fetishism captured by Hart. Before the play's opening, the columnist had aroused audience anticipation with the story of how de Wolfe endeavored to procure a unique antique tea table to set both Beatrice Croyden and her living room above the "common herd." Hart pointed out that there was only one other such tea table in existence, that owned by Queen Alexandra, and explained how de Wolfe had fallen in love with it while visiting the home of her friend the marchioness of Anglesey in Versailles. Unable to find a satisfying substitute, de Wolfe faced what Hart hyped as a potentially disastrous void in the mise-en-scène until, right before opening, the marchioness agreed to loan de Wolfe her own irreplaceable treasure. The payoff for all the trouble and anguish proved immeasurable, reported Hart.

> And the tea-table, that wonderful tea-table, pushed in on wheels by a perfectly correct butler—is a finer piece of realism to Miss de Wolfe than her whole cast. . . .

> No wonder the Matinee Girls lose track of Mrs. Croyden's flirta-
> tion when the tea-table makes its entrance! It isn't the chink of cut-
> glass as she mixes Nevill's cocktail that keeps their eyes "on the
> ball"!33

Rather than the character's desire for the man she was entertaining, the
audience followed de Wolfe's desire for the treasure, making the actress
both vehicle and object of a highly charged and eroticized female passion
for possession.

For Marbury's spectatorial pleasure, de Wolfe displayed on stage the
same ultrafeminine attributes that attracted her partner offstage. The
adulation of de Wolfe by throngs of respectable white middle-class
women validated and augmented Marbury's own regard for the actress as
well as the profitability of her theatrical enterprise. Marbury could enjoy
both the satisfaction of seeing all these other women falling at her partner's feet and the security of knowing it was her home de Wolfe would
grace after the performance.

During this phase of their professional lives, Marbury was positioned as a power broker, and de Wolfe chiefly as an object of exchange,
a pretty woman to be displayed, though she exercised more control over
the display than most leading ladies in the contemporary commercial
theater. However, when circumstances changed, Marbury used her influence to help de Wolfe attain a comparable position of power in a related
profession. Like they had done with Marbury's theatrical agency, the
lovers launched de Wolfe's pioneering interior-decorating career from
circumstances of professional crisis and cooperative inspiration and encouragement. After fourteen years, de Wolfe wearied of the limitations of
her acting career. Two embarrassing failures in the fall of 1904 (in *Cynthia* and *A Wife without a Smile*) cinched her determination to retire, but
she dreaded being unable to support herself. Pained by her partner's
shame and depression, Marbury suggested she capitalize on her greatest
talents and hire herself out to their wealthy friends to do for their homes
what she had done for the Irving Place house and so many of Frohman's
stages—remake them in the latest fashion. Coincidentally, Marbury was
on the board of the newly erected but yet undecorated Colony Club, the
first private club exclusively for women. Marbury's formidable personal
and professional support garnered the unproven de Wolfe the endorse-
ment of the board and architect Stanford White. The result was an
historic, career-making first commission.34 In a matter of months, she
went from being an actress of mediocre talent to becoming high society's

consummate professional decorative expert, and she rapidly gained business on both sides of the Atlantic. If the Colony Club made her famous, Henry Clay Frick's hiring her in 1913 to amass his world-class art collection secured her place as one of the wealthiest and most successful women of her generation.

While the pivotal Colony Club commission signaled de Wolfe's permanent departure from the acting profession, friendships with other women cultivated through the club resulted in a variety of social and theatrical collaborations. Like those of other New Women of their era and class, Marbury and de Wolfe's Boston marriage transpired within a circle of close female friends variously single, married, and same-sex partnered. Along with the ideology of female "passionlessness," this was a carryover from the Victorian period, during which rigid separation of the spheres fostered strong emotional bonds among women. Close female friendships were not seen as interfering with a married woman's relationship with her husband; on the contrary, they were viewed as complementary and valued for reinforcing sphere separation. Organizations like the Colony Club institutionalized these relations. Marbury and de Wolfe sustained close friendships with a wide array of women, many of whom were charter members of the Colony Club, including Caroline Duer, the Hewitt sisters, Alva Vanderbilt, and Anne Morgan. Like those discussed by Blanche Wiesen Cook, this network of female friends provided an invaluable support system for the pursuit of mutual personal, social, political, and business interests.[35]

Beginning in 1907, one club member, Anne Morgan, became a part of the Marbury/de Wolfe summer household in France, which prompted the moniker "Versailles Triumvirate" among their friends. Morgan yearned to escape the oppressive shadow of her father, J. P. Morgan, and looked especially to Marbury as a mentor, though she was clearly also attached to de Wolfe. She used her wealth to invest in the property, augmenting the splendor of the women's beloved villa. Unfettered by the obligations of having to earn a living, she kept Marbury and/or de Wolfe company when the other left on business or a leisure activity of which her partner was not especially fond. Thus, the dynamics of the Versailles Triumvirate, an extension of the Victorian network of close female friends, enhanced rather than threatened the primary bond between Marbury and de Wolfe. At summer's end, Morgan returned to her mother's home in New York, and Marbury and de Wolfe to their joint residence. Inspired by Marbury and de Wolfe's example, Morgan challenged patriarchal authority and pursued her own interests, which included taking a leadership role in various charities and social reforms and, eventually, finding her own primary female companion.[36]

The outbreak of World War I galvanized these female friends' shared commitment to social reform and inspired their creation of a novel entertainment enterprise, the Strand Roof Garden. In the summer of 1914, the Versailles Triumvirate was in Europe, temporarily separated for a sojourn at their respective favorite spas—de Wolfe in Germany at Baden-Baden, and Marbury and Morgan at Brides-les-Bains in Savoie, France. The declaration of war caused both parties to be detained. Communication was cut off and bank accounts frozen. For several weeks, Marbury and de Wolfe were separated and uncertain of the other's safety as the terrifying magnitude of the conflict unfolded. They were finally reunited in September and sailed safely back to New York, but this personal trauma had impressed upon them the urgency of the crisis and grave concern for the future of genteel, civilized society.[37]

The Strand Roof Garden, in the words of Anne Morgan, was conceived as "an antidote to the war." Bringing Mrs. W. K. (Anne) Vanderbilt into the partnership, the Versailles Triumvirate created a "temperance roof garden" where young men and women from the middle and working classes could "read, dance, or talk under the guidance of women of social distinction and experience." With low admission and food prices, the partners aimed to reach across what Morgan termed "caste lines" and socialize the nation's youth into fading Old World gentility. Headlines proclaimed that patrons would be "watched by the same kind of chaperones that guard the Fifth Avenue Debutantes . . . at a wonderful roof garden with a high art soda fountain designed by Elsie de Wolfe."[38] In characteristic managerial fashion, Marbury capitalized on each partner's individual talents and accomplishments in running the establishment. She described the division of labor for one of the New York daily papers.

> Miss Morgan has been placed in charge of the cafeteria because she has demonstrated both in the Brooklyn Navy Yard and in the Vacation Fund's headquarters that she can run one successfully. Mrs. Vanderbilt, as everybody knows, built and personally manages her flats in the east side, where she has a diet kitchen for tuberculosis patients, and she is interested in other movements. Miss de Wolfe has demonstrated her ability to manage a big business, and I have been in the field twenty-five years. So we think we have got together a group of women who know something about this kind of thing.[39]

Initially, low prices and the novelty of the enterprise helped make the Strand Roof Garden a success. By early 1917, however, it became apparent that the partners' "antidote to the war" ran counter to the prevailing tide of changing social values. Complaining that "Broadway and booze had formed an alliance that nothing could break," Marbury sold out to a professional cabaret manager.[40]

In their respective autobiographies, both Marbury and de Wolfe write of the war as a major rupture that irrevocably transformed their lives and, in the process, their impact on American social and theatrical history. The business partnership with Anne Vanderbilt would dissolve with the Strand Roof Garden, and the interpersonal dynamics of the Versailles Triumvirate shifted as Anne Morgan became increasingly involved in enlistment campaigns at home and relief efforts abroad. Even more profoundly, wartime tensions affected the primary bond between Marbury and de Wolfe. While Marbury's chief response to the global crisis and the personal trauma of the summer of 1914 was to remain close to home with her beloved safely beside her, de Wolfe increasingly yearned to return to France to protect their cherished villa and help tend the wounded. Neither the Strand Roof Garden nor her own business proved sufficient to override the call of duty from Versailles. Marbury biographer Strum suggests that these strains in their relationship provided a major impetus for Marbury to enter the next phase of her theatrical career, that of producer, as opposed to playbroker and agent. As producer of her own shows, observes Strum, Marbury could hire her clients as writers and performers, and, most importantly, she could hire de Wolfe to design the shows and thereby distract her from the war.[41]

Out of this relational dynamic came a revolutionary entertainment genre, the so-called intimate musical. Marbury went into partnership with F. Ray Comstock and Lee Shubert to manage the 299-seat Princess Theatre at 104 West Thirty-ninth Street. In this space, she implemented her vision of a small-scale "light opera" with a coherent script, songs organically related to the story, individualized chorus members, and domestic-scale design elements suited to de Wolfe's talents. Total expenditures for each production were not to exceed seventy-five hundred dollars, a drastic downsizing from the fifty-thousand-dollar cost of contemporary Broadway extravaganzas like the *Ziegfeld Follies*. Marbury placed de Wolfe in charge of the visual aesthetics and enlisted the team of Jerome Kern and Guy Bolton to create the book.[42]

Like the Strand Roof Garden, this Marbury/de Wolfe collaboration had a distinct moral agenda involving the proper cultivation of the nation's youth. Framed by Marbury's desire for de Wolfe, the Princess musicals extended some of the dynamics of their core bond to other women. Combatting the ill repute that often befell chorus girls, Marbury sought to protect and showcase them as young exemplars of respectable femininity with the same proprietary paternalism she had exhibited toward her own partner.[43] De Wolfe meanwhile contributed to the proper environmental conditioning of the performers through stage design, ordering to specifications from couturiers and furniture and fabric manufacturers as though the characters were her clients. The combined talents of the lovers resulted in an entertainment that eschewed the overt sensuality and ostentation associated with full-scale musicals and presented "pretty girls dressed in fashionable frocks, with an atmosphere of smartness and refinement and daintiness, with delightful and tinkly tunes and with youth as the keynote."[44]

With Marbury overseeing and de Wolfe designing, the arrangement might have re-created the theatrical collaborations of the early months of the partners' romance. As to occupying de Wolfe's focus and keeping her in New York, however, the Princess musicals were at best only temporarily successful. From 1915 to 1918, six "intimate musicals" were produced at the Princess Theatre, but Marbury and de Wolfe directly participated just in the first two. By the time the third Princess musical, *Go to It*, went into production, personal and global conflict precluded both women's participation in mounting this example of the revolutionary form they had created. De Wolfe had grown so determined to pursue the war effort in France that she schemed to do so without her partner's knowledge. When Marbury found out at the last minute, she reportedly panicked and, realizing she could not detain de Wolfe any longer, decided to accompany her rather than part in bitterness. Their departure with Anne Morgan on June 24, 1916, marked the last time the Versailles Triumvirate would make the trip together.[45] As a result, Marbury and de Wolfe missed the rehearsal period for *Go to It* and returned to New York only in time for its October 24 opening.

De Wolfe made it clear that this trip back to New York was chiefly a fund-raising venture for her war relief campaign and that she fully intended to return to France. Marbury would produce only one more show, *Love o' Mike,* another intimate musical, before she followed de Wolfe back to France in the winter of 1917. While de Wolfe worked as a nurse in the Ambrine Mission, Marbury assisted Anne Morgan with the American Fund for French Wounded.[46] The relational dynamics that had propelled Marbury and de Wolfe into their historically significant collaboration on the Princess musicals also contributed to the end of their work in this enterprise and to the end of Marbury's producing career.

Through the period of the Princess musicals, the crucial impact of the partners' Boston marriage on the course of their professional lives is demonstrable from the available evidence. After World War I, however, the role of their mutual devotion in their respective careers becomes more difficult to trace because of profound changes in the relationship itself and in its larger sociocultural context.

Though significant ties between Marbury and de Wolfe would endure, wartime experiences broke up the Versailles Triumvirate and set the partners' lives on divergent courses. Compelled by obligations to her New York–based theatrical agency, Marbury sailed home alone in May 1917. By contrast, de Wolfe's ties to France intensified. The nature of her business allowed her to run it from Europe, and, after the Armistice, she became a virtual expatriate and devotee of the postwar international party scene. Morgan, meanwhile, broadened her horizons by joining the civilian relief effort. Smith suggests it may have been in part to fill the void of separation from de Wolfe and the breakdown of the Versailles Triumvirate that Marbury turned to politics, assuming a leadership role in the Democratic Party for the next fifteen years.[47]

These developments precipitated a formal change in the partners' New York living arrangements. Since 1910, they had been renting a capacious residence on Fifty-fifth Street fully outfitted for their joint personal and professional needs. When the nonrenewable lease expired in 1920, Marbury decided to relocate to Sutton Place on Manhattan's East Side. The move inspired others in their circle of friends, including Anne Morgan and Anne Vanderbilt, to purchase property there as well, resulting in a gentrification of the then run-down neighborhood by unmarried New Women. Along with the homes of their friends, de Wolfe decorated Marbury's Sutton Place house, in which she fashioned a small "guest suite" for her own use. Meanwhile, Marbury, because of her increasing political and business ties to the American Northeast, sold her share of the Villa Trianon to Anne Morgan and bought a summer place in Maine.[48] These real-estate transactions marked the new contours of their postwar lifestyle, in which de Wolfe lived most of the year in Versailles and joined Marbury at Sutton Place for three to four months every fall.

During their limited time together, the two women apparently continued some theatrical associations. In 1923, notes Strum, "Marbury informed the Shuberts that de Wolfe had opened a new department at 677 Fifth Avenue, where she would design stage settings."[49] Although this arrangement echoes those of the prewar period, when Marbury brokered much of de Wolfe's business with the Syndicate, the terms need to be considered in light of the partners' altered relational dynamics. The two women were older—Marbury turned sixty-four in 1920, and de Wolfe fifty-five—and related to each other from the vantage point of well-established success in their respective fields. Their bond was no longer needed as a crucial support base from which to embark on new professional ventures amid economic uncertainty. Moreover, as Smith points out, de Wolfe's wartime efforts, initially undertaken against Marbury's will, had constituted a declaration of independence.[50] As a result, Marbury eventually realized that to keep de Wolfe's love, she needed to give her partner the freedom to pursue divergent interests. This postwar arrangement with the Shuberts, then, rather than a vital business connection for de Wolfe or, like the Princess musicals, a machination to control her, was more a gesture of professional courtesy indicative of residual mutual interests.

In conjunction with the shift in the partners' internal relational dynamics, a larger shift in dominant attitudes toward female same-sex love affected the sociocultural context of their association. After the turn of the century, the theories of European sexologists began infiltrating U.S. medical and intellectual circles. Richard von Krafft-Ebing and his English-speaking disciple Havelock Ellis's model of homosexuality as sexual inversion (*Studies in the Psychology of Sex: Sexual Inversion,* 1897) and Sigmund Freud's theories of sexual repression applied in essays like "The Sexual Aberrations" and "The Psychogenesis of a Case of Homosexuality in a Woman" (1920) pathologized female same-sex love. Freud's theories, in particular, became part of the popular discourse in the 1920s, as the medical establishment exploited the possibility of a psychoanalytic "cure" in service of the profit motive and patriarchal hegemony. In an era when women gained real socioeconomic and political power by winning suffrage and demonstrating their competence in formerly male professions during the war, charges of sexual perversion became a common way to derail those at the vanguard, chiefly unmarried, career-oriented, activist New Women. Female affectional alliances that had been openly accepted, even idealized, in the Victorian period became tainted and suspect, undermining a crucial support system for so many reforms and pioneering efforts.[51]

Given their high visibility and the cosmopolitan circles in which they trafficked, Marbury and de Wolfe could hardly have been insulated from this discourse. According to her memoir, de Wolfe attended at least one dinner party at which the "sexual perversions" were discussed. Too genteel, perhaps, to give specifics, Marbury refers only to her and de Wolfe's relationship having suffered "misrepresentation" and "envy."[52] Indeed, certain aspects of their public personae would have made them particularly susceptible to correlations with sexologists' profiles of pathological female behavior: their self-made wealth and power; Marbury's purported "masculinity" coupled with de Wolfe's ultrafemininity, a combination deemed paradigmatic of sexual inversion; enterprises like the Princess musicals that facilitated close contact with attractive young chorus girls; and the location of their New York residence in Sutton Place, rumored to be a dangerous, Amazonian enclave because of its gentrification by wealthy activist New Women.[53]

In her study of the impact of sexology on Marbury and de Wolfe's genteel, late-Victorian generation, Faderman observes that many women who loved women, repulsed by the stigma of invert, "fled into heterosexual marriage or developed great self-loathing or self-pity."[54] Such forces may have been a factor prompting Elsie de Wolfe, certainly a woman concerned with moral propriety and public image, at the age of sixty to marry the titled British diplomat, Sir Charles Mendl. Given her conspicuous reputation as a "bachelor girl" and her longtime alliance with Marbury, the announcement in 1926 stunned her close acquaintances and the international social world. Upon hearing the news, de Wolfe's personal French maid exclaimed, "C'est une blague!" (It's a joke!). Recalling the French civil ceremony, held sometime after the original one at the British consulate, de Wolfe wrote: "Even Charles shook with suppressed laughter when the [Versailles] mayor asked us what we intended to do with the children to be born of our marriage."[55]

That Marbury remained a significant presence in de Wolfe's life was evident when the new bride dispatched Mendl immediately after their "honeymoon," a state visit to Egypt, to employ his expert diplomatic skills at Sutton Place. He assured the enraged Marbury that he had no intention of replacing her in de Wolfe's affections, that the marriage was purely one of convenience, and that perhaps as a businesswoman she could understand the social and commercial value of such a contract.[56] A few weeks later, de Wolfe journeyed to New York for a personal reconciliation with her longtime companion, and the two continued their postwar pattern of annual fall visits in New York until Marbury's death in 1933.

These changes both within the partners' relationship itself and in the surrounding sociocultural context have fostered ignorance and/or misrepresentation of their Boston marriage and cultural contributions in historiography. Recuperating Marbury and de Wolfe into the lesbian past requires reading through the distorting and obfuscating ideologies of female passionlessness, male dominance, heterosexism, and sexologist homophobia. Such a reading reveals that for more than forty years, lesbianism was crucially operative in Marbury and de Wolfe's case, as their passionate love for each other formed the primary relational bond in both women's lives. Sustained through friendships with other female couples and activists, their Boston marriage became the center of extensive networks of social relations that inspired, enabled, and directed their talents and ambitions. Beginning with their joint amateur theatrical ventures of the 1880s, public knowledge of their connection heightened their media profiles and impacted their dealings with key business associates, like Charles and Daniel Frohman, David Belasco, Victorien Sardou, F. Ray Comstock, Lee Shubert, Stanford White, and the members of the Colony Club board. Thus, the dynamics of their partnership proved instrumental in their pursuit of pioneering professions and acquisition of wealth and influence; in the creation of historic edifices and artworks, like the Villa Trianon, the Colony Club, the Frick Collection, Sutton Place, and experimental performance genres, like the "temperance roof garden" and "intimate musical"; and in the course of their political activism in woman suffrage, war relief, urban reform, and the Democratic Party. The record warrants revision to acknowledge the production and force of Marbury and de Wolfe's lesbianism within the ideological contingencies and relational networks that have made theatrical and cultural history.

NOTES

1. *Metropolitan*, February 1911, p. 635; Diana Vreeland, preface to *Elsie de Wolfe: A Life in the High Style*, by Jane S. Smith (New York: Atheneum, 1982), xi.

2. Standard American theater histories, e.g., Barnard Hewitt, *Theatre U.S.A.*, or Glenn Hughes, *History of the American Theatre*, make little or no mention of Marbury and de Wolfe. Nor does Helen Krich Chinoy and Linda Walsh Jenkins's *Women in American Theatre* mention them, either individually or as a couple. *Notable Women in the American Theatre: A Biographical Dictionary*, ed. Alice M. Robinson, Vera Mowry Roberts, and Milly S. Barranger (Westport, CT: Greenwood Press, 1989), contains an article on Elisabeth Marbury by Rebecca Strum, whose dissertation, "Elisabeth Marbury, 1856–1933: Her Life and Work," New York University, 1989, is the first full-length biography. Smith's *Elsie de Wolfe* is the major full-length, historically researched biography of de Wolfe. As biographies, both of these works ultimately privilege individual over

relational contributions, and neither fully explores the complexities and historical efficacy of the women's lesbianism.

3. Blanche Wiesen Cook, "Female Support Networks and Political Activism: Lillian Wald, Crystal Eastman, Emma Goldman," in *A Heritage of Her Own: Toward a New Social History of American Women,* ed. Nancy F. Cott and Elizabeth H. Pleck (New York: Simon and Schuster, 1979), 416.

4. Ibid., 419–20; see also Lillian Faderman, "Nineteenth-Century Boston Marriage as a Possible Lesson for Today," in *Boston Marriages: Romantic but Asexual Relationships among Contemporary Lesbians,* ed. Esther D. Rothblum and Kathleen A. Brehony (Amherst: University of Massachusetts Press, 1993), 40.

5. Carroll Smith-Rosenberg, "The Female World of Love and Ritual: Relations between Women in Nineteenth-Century America," in *Disorderly Conduct: Visions of Gender in Victorian America* (New York: Oxford University Press, 1985), 53–76; Lillian Faderman, *Surpassing the Love of Men: Romantic Friendship and Love between Women from the Renaissance to the Present* (London: Women's Press, 1985), 15–20.

6. Faderman, *Surpassing Love of Men,* 17–18.

7. Robert Padgug, "Sexual Matters: Rethinking Sexuality in History," in *Hidden from History: Reclaiming the Gay and Lesbian Past,* ed. Martin Duberman, Martha Vicinus, and George Chauncey Jr. (New York: Penguin, 1989), 58.

8. Duberman, Vicinus, and Chauncey, introduction to *Hidden from History,* 3–4.

9. Carroll Smith-Rosenberg, "The New Woman as Androgyne: Social Disorder and Gender Crisis," in *Disorderly Conduct,* 245; Faderman, *Surpassing Love of Men,* 190.

10. Elisabeth Marbury, *My Crystal Ball* (London: Hurst and Blackett, 1924), 58.

11. Faderman, *Surpassing Love of Men,* 197–98, 205–8.

12. Elsie de Wolfe, *After All* (New York: Harper, 1935; rpt. New York: Arno, 1974), 96–97. See also unmarked newspaper clipping, Elsie de Wolfe Scrapbook, Robinson-Locke Collection of Theatre Scrapbooks (RLCTS), series 1, vol. 151, n.p., Billy Rose Theatre Collection, Lincoln Center Library for the Performing Arts, New York Public Library.

13. See Smith, *Elsie de Wolfe,* 24–29; Strum, "Elisabeth Marbury," 27–28; de Wolfe, *After All,* 1–12, 253–78; Marbury, *My Crystal Ball,* 14–15; and Elisabeth Marbury biographical sketch, TMs, Elizabeth Marbury Personality Folder, Theatre Collection, Museum of the City of New York.

14. Marbury, *My Crystal Ball,* 58.

15. Strum, "Elisabeth Marbury," 29–30.

16. Smith-Rosenberg, "Female World," 53–76; see also Faderman, *Surpassing Love of Men,* 145–230.

17. Nancy F. Cott, "Passionlessness: An Interpretation of Victorian Sexual Ideology, 1790–1850," in Cott and Pleck, *Heritage of Her Own,* 162–81.

18. See Faderman, *Surpassing Love of Men,* 152–53; Lillian Faderman, *Odd Girls and Twilight Lovers: A History of Lesbian Life in Twentieth-Century America* (New York: Penguin, 1991), 4; and Smith-Rosenberg, "New Woman as Androgyne," 273–75.

19. Smith-Rosenberg, "Female World," 58; Faderman, *Odd Girls,* 32; Cott, "Passionlessness," 173–75.

20. Elisabeth Marbury, introduction to *Modern Dancing,* by Vernon Castle and Irene Castle (New York: Harper, 1914), 20.

21. Faderman, *Surpassing Love of Men,* 153–54.

22. Marbury, *My Crystal Ball,* 96; Strum, "Elisabeth Marbury," 101, 128.

23. Marbury, *My Crystal Ball,* 283–84.

24. See, for example, the miscellaneous clippings in the Elsie de Wolfe Scrapbook, RLCTS, vol. 152, p. 75.

25. "Elsie de Wolfe in a Fire Scare," unnamed newspaper clipping, c. 1904, Elsie de Wolfe Scrapbook, RLCTS, vol. 152, p. 75.

26. For an overview of Marbury's fleeting playwriting career, see Strum, "Elisabeth Marbury," 46–53.

27. Smith, *Elsie de Wolfe,* 21–27.

28. Smith, *Elsie de Wolfe,* 41; Strum, "Elisabeth Marbury," 48–50.

29. See Marbury, *My Crystal Ball,* 63–66; Smith, *Elsie de Wolfe,* 35; Strum, "Elisabeth Marbury," 53–68. De Wolfe's article, "Chateaux in Touraine," appeared in *Cosmopolitan,* February 1891.

30. For more on Frohman and Dillingham, see Isaac F. Marcosson and Daniel Frohman, *Charles Frohman: Manager and Man* (New York: Harper, 1916), 360–84.

31. For more on de Wolfe's role as "clotheshorse," see Kim Marra, "Elsie de Wolfe *circa* 1901: The Dynamics of Prescriptive Feminine Performance in American Theater and Society," *Theatre Survey* 35, no. 1 (May 1994): 100–120.

32. Lavinia Hart, "*The Way of the World* Justifies Its Title," unidentified newspaper clipping, November 17, 1901, RLCTS, series 1, vol. 151, p. 34.

33. Hart, "Justifies Its Title."

34. Smith, *Elsie de Wolfe,* 88–89, 95, 102.

35. Cook, "Female Support Networks," 412–44. See also Smith-Rosenberg, "Female World," 53–76.

36. Smith, *Elsie de Wolfe,* 120, 190–191.

37. Ibid., 170–75.

38. See de Wolfe Clippings, RLCTS, series 2, vol. 123, pp. 40, 52–53, 56.

39. Marbury quoted in untitled clipping, de Wolfe Clippings, RLCTS, series 2, vol. 123, p. 6.

40. Marbury, *My Crystal Ball,* 233; Strum, "Elisabeth Marbury," 171–74.

41. See Smith, *Elsie de Wolfe,* 176–77; Strum, "Elisabeth Marbury," 198.

42. For a detailed account of Marbury's career as producer and the history of the Princess musicals, see Strum, "Elisabeth Marbury," 198–257.

43. Marbury, "My Girls—As I Know Them," *Harper's Bazaar,* August 1917, n.p., in Marbury Clipping File, Billy Rose Theatre Collection.

44. See Strum, "Elisabeth Marbury," 205; and "New Style of Entertainment," *New York Mirror,* February 3, 1917.

45. Smith, *Elsie de Wolfe,* 184–87.

46. Strum, "Elisabeth Marbury," 188, 241–46, 252.

47. Smith, *Elsie de Wolfe,* 190–97. See also the Marbury obituaries from the major New York papers in the Elisabeth Marbury Personality Folder.

48. Strum, "Elisabeth Marbury," 266–71, 285–86; de Wolfe, *After All,* 202.

49. Strum, "Elisabeth Marbury," 277.

50. Smith, *Elsie de Wolfe,* 196.

51. See Faderman, *Surpassing Love of Men,* 238, 314; and Smith-Rosenberg, "New Woman as Androgyne," 269–81.

52. De Wolfe, *After All,* 251; Marbury, *My Crystal Ball,* 283–84.

53. On inversion, see Smith-Rosenberg, "New Woman as Androgyne," 280. On the spread of negative lesbian stereotypes in contemporary mass literature, see Faderman, *Surpassing Love of Men,* 323–27. See also *Gossip,* November 13, 1921, for a contemporary account of the reputation of Sutton Place.

54. Faderman, *Surpassing Love of Men,* 252.

55. See miscellaneous clippings in the Elsie de Wolfe Scrapbook from the Players' Collection, Billy Rose Theatre Collection; and de Wolfe, *After All,* 211–16.

56. Smith, *Elsie de Wolfe,* 221–27.

Alla Nazimova

"The Witch of Makeup"

Robert A. Schanke

"All lying comes from fear—we are afraid of someone, of some situation or of some thing, and we lie—to escape from it."[1] The interview was with Alla Nazimova (1878–1945), explaining her character's penchant for deception in Pearl Buck's *The Good Earth,* which had just opened at the Theatre Guild in 1932. Nazimova could have been describing herself. A few years earlier she had wept to her sister, "My life has no relationship with my inner life. . . . I am alone. . . . Why did I find myself in circumstances which I had to hide?"[2]

A childhood victim of extreme physical and sexual abuse, she was forever driven to hide from the harsh realities of life. As a teenager, she lived with a family in Odessa and became infatuated with two older girls who belonged to an amateur dramatic society. She listened to them rehearse, observed them applying their makeup, and imagined herself playing the roles, fantasizing different reflections in a mirror. Performance became her means of escape. "I often wonder if the smug bourgeois who envy us know that we go to art to forget," she confessed, "and that we work hard because the more we work the more we forget."[3]

The youngest of three children, Adelaida Leventon was born on June 4, 1879, in Yalta. When her father insisted that she disguise her name rather than disgrace him publicly in a violin recital she was scheduled to perform at the age of ten, she assumed the surname Nazimova, which was the name of a heroine in a Russian novel, *Children of the Streets.*

At the age of seventeen, she moved to Moscow, where she entered the Philharmonic School and studied acting under Vladimir Nemirovich-Danchenko. Among the older students were Olga Knipper, later to become Anton Chekhov's wife, Ivan Moskvin, and Vsevolod Meyerhold. When Danchenko joined forces with Constantin Stanislavsky in 1898 to form the Moscow Art Theatre, Nazimova became one of the apprentice extras, making her professional debut as a peasant girl in *Tsar Fyodor,* playing a flower seller in *The Merchant of Venice* and a housemaid in *The Seagull*.[4]

After leaving the Moscow Art Theatre in 1899 she began acting in the provinces, where she married a penniless actor, Sergius de Golovin.[5] A year later she met Paul Orlenev, a handsome, fiery actor, who became her lover. They toured Russia with Evgeny Chirikov's *The Jew*, known in this country as *The Chosen People*. But when the pro-Jewish play was censored and they feared possible arrest, she and Orlenev fled with their company to Berlin, to London, and then to America.

Beginning March 22, 1905, they reveled in a year of headlines with their performances in New York, Chicago, and Boston. Though the media lauded an intriguing duo they believed to be married, the unmarried couple offered no correction. After all, this might hopefully serve as a convenient cover for their sinful alliance. Serving as their press agent, translator, and manager was the anarchist, feminist, and advocate of free love and free speech Emma Goldman. One performance of Ibsen's *Ghosts* was offered as a special benefit to raise money for her new political magazine, *Mother Earth*.[6]

Nazimova must have been excited when she arrived and saw the trends in the New York theater. Although sentimental plays such as David Belasco's *Madame Butterfly* and musical extravaganzas such as Victor Herbert's *Babes in Toyland* continued in popularity, the new drama of ideas was finding a growing public. Arthur Wing Pinero's play *Iris* was dubbed by the critics as a "Drama of Dirt," yet it had attracted large crowds. In 1903, Arnold Daly starred in George Bernard Shaw's *Candida*, predicted to fail, but developed into a hit with 133 performances. The native American play that drew the most attention at this time was William Vaughn Moody's *The Great Divide*. Often called the first modern American drama, the story is of the great divide that separates the refined, "Old World" culture from the rugged impulses of the frontier.

The thousands of new immigrants streaming to New York had created an audience for foreign plays. In 1904 alone, four actresses—Mrs. Fiske, Nance O'Neil, Mary Shaw, and Blanche Bates—presented their version of *Hedda Gabler* either in New York or on tour. At one point O'Neil and Mrs. Fiske were playing the role at the same time on Broadway at theaters only four blocks apart. Just as theatergoers formerly had compared Edwin Booth's and Edwin Forrest's Hamlet, so they began to compare Ibsen actresses. Since the Orlenev company was the first Russian company to play New York, Nazimova felt confident of support from the large Russian population.

Sensing that New York audiences were unusually cosmopolitan and broad-minded, she was stunned to learn of the provincial attitudes that America had about sexual diversity. In her native Russia, the laws clearly condemned anal intercourse between men, homosexual rape, and seduction of minors, but were seldom enforced. Not only were many statesmen and artists known for their homoerotic desires, but after the 1905 Bolshevik revolution, "there appeared gay and lesbian poets, fiction writers, and artists who saw in the new freedom of expression a chance to depict their lifestyles in an honest and affirmative manner."[7] America was quite different. Women who loved women were labeled "sexual perverts" and "degenerates" and were refused insurance since they were known to commit suicide, encounter violent assaults, and succumb to alcohol and drugs. Postcards and magazine illustrations portrayed negative images of women who wore mannish clothes. They were considered threats to traditional femininity.[8]

The epitome of American womanhood was the Gibson Girl. Intensely feminine and with demure demeanor, she radiated elegance and refinement. Her bridled corsets squeezed her into an hourglass shape, an elegant silhouette, and sexual restraint. Nazimova was told that even the usually tolerant New York audiences had been outraged when they had seen a woman carried by her lover through a bedroom door in a production of *Sapho*. And the papers reported daily about *Mrs. Warren's Profession*. The play dealt with prostitution, and the cast and director were even threatened with imprisonment. Only days before her first matinee with the Orlenev company, a group of religious leaders protested the lecture series being given by Russian playwright Maxim Gorky and demanded that the woman who was posing as his wife be deported. Clearly, Nazimova knew she must keep her public image beyond reproach; no one must know that she was a bisexual and living with a man who was not really her true husband. But there was still another fear that forced her to lie and made her situation somewhat different from other actresses such as Nance O'Neil—she could be deported as an undesirable alien.

Despite her confusion with American attitudes, when Orlenev and the company returned to Russia to escape creditors, Nazimova remained in New York. Championing her decision and promising her future patronage was the influential editor of *Century* magazine, Richard Watson Gilder. A published poet as well as social and political reformer, he promised to feature Nazimova in his magazine, and, perhaps more important, he guaranteed that his staff would prepare new plays for her. Accepted into his social circles, Nazimova met J. P. Morgan, Andrew Carnegie, Grover Cleveland, Teddy Roosevelt, Rudyard Kipling, and Mark Twain.

Just before Orlenev sailed, she signed a five-year contract with Lee Shubert. Encouraged by Henry Miller, Margaret Anglin, and Elisabeth Marbury, Shubert agreed to star her in plays in English. She would "not be required to act in any play unsuitable to her personality" and would receive fifty dollars per week for six months while she learned English. During the 1906–7 season she would be billed as a star with lead dressing room and no name advertised above hers, and would receive one hundred dollars per week plus 20 percent of all net profits. By the fourth year she would receive $350 per week, plus 30 percent.[9]

The Shubert contract, if nothing else, convinced Nazimova to leave the Orlenev company. When the Shubert brothers moved their producing company to New York City around 1905, they already owned or controlled several theaters in the country and had begun to purchase theaters in New York. This young organization was challenging the authority of the Theatrical Syndicate, a ruthless and box-office-driven monopoly that planned, coordinated, and administered theater across the country from a central office. The Shuberts gained support by at least appearing to champion the cause of actors and a better quality of drama. To land a contract with the Shuberts meant security and a promising future.

In November 1906 Nazimova opened in the title role of *Hedda Gabler*. Two months later, she added *A Doll's House* and in September 1907 *The Master Builder*. Dozens of articles appeared in major publications, poets penned tributes, and artists painted her portrait.[10] Just six months before she began her Ibsen series, the playwright died, thrusting his name in newspapers throughout the world and prompting a reevaluation of his work. Two major American literary critics, William Dean Howells and James Gibbons Huneker, published widely read eulogies. Whether it was merely coincidental or whether the Shuberts intentionally sought to exploit Ibsen's death, it certainly brought attention to their new star. Nazimova's fame reached such heights that in 1910 the Shuberts remodeled their Thirty-ninth Street Theatre and renamed it Nazimova's 39th Street Theatre.

She fascinated critics with her ability to transform herself physically into widely diverse characters. Her patrician Hedda had a long and aristocratic face with her hair drawn up into a semi-Hellenic pyramid. Her lips were straight and cruel; her eyebrows "slanted in languid ennui." The long, sharp lines gave a look of severity. But for Nora she shortened her eyebrows, rounded her eyes, tipped her nose saucily in the air, and painted her lips so they were full and slightly puckered. She wanted to eliminate personality acting, in which actresses presented themselves in various roles rather than representing the characters in the script. The actor "should be a creature of clay, of putty," she argued, "capable of being molded into another form, another shape."[11] Is it any wonder Nazimova became known as "the witch of makeup?"[12]

She hid behind masks in her private life as well and warned her sister, "Do not confide . . . about anything. . . . I am a mystery for the Americans and that is my biggest advertisement."[13] "One must always be at a pitch and 'acting,' " she confided. "Nazimova doesn't live except in the imagination of the public."[14] Nazimova submerged herself so completely in her roles that even family members "wondered *where* was the real Alla! She in her private life actually became the character of her current play." She admitted finding pleasure in disguise, in "living by proxy."[15]

The Shuberts were aware of her bisexuality and of her rumored liaisons with Laurette Taylor and Constance Collier.[16] Her stage manager, A. H. Canby, analyzes her androgyny: "She is certainly amenable to reason if you discuss matters with her at the proper time. At such a time she acts with the fairness of a man, but if she is peevish over other matters she is just like any other fool woman and will make a fool woman's mistakes."[17] To create a "neurotic fascination" for the new Shubert star, Canby insisted she remove her boyish mustache so she would not be identified as a "Mannish Lesbian." As they toured, Canby was concerned that it was not the men who rushed to meet her:

> The women . . . were enthusiastic about her. . . . She is keeping herself very exclusive and this intensifies the desire of the curious to meet her. [At the hotel, the] ladies' entrance was always crowded with women waiting for her to return from the theatre. It is much better that she should be exclusive and meet no one if possible. They regard her as a mystery. And there are other damned good reasons besides this one.[18]

Canby warned her that she must be discreet with her sexual pursuits.

Trying to dismantle the rumors, the Shuberts created an image of a dangerous, seductive siren. The roles they gave her to perform were more than just the strong-willed women of Ibsen; they were "invariably those of soul-racked and nerve-shaken women," women of "temperamental extremes."[19] In *The Comet* by Owen Johnson she played a glamorous, world-weary femme fatale who falls in love with the son of a man who betrayed her years earlier. In one scene her black dress fell from her arms like the wings of a bird, and her arms when outstretched gave the impression of a vampire. Although Brandon Tynan's *The Passion Flower* seemed nothing more than an amateurish reworking of *A Doll's House,* the production created a stir. In every act there was a great vase of purple passion flowers, and in her first entrance Nazimova wore a gown of soft violet. These colors—known as symbols of mystery and decadence— were also traditional symbols of lesbianism. The Shuberts were indeed living up to their contractual agreement of offering her plays "suitable to her personality."

At the end of her five-year contract with the Shuberts, even after they had named a theater in her honor, Nazimova announced on February 3, 1911, "I am anxious not to continue beyond the legal 25 weeks" of the contract.[20] Dozens of letters in the Shubert Archive reveal her distaste for the plays and her demands for rewrites. She objected to the shoddy sets, the one-night stands, the drunken stagehands, as well as the Shuberts' belittling references to her as their "little pony" and their "little Russian." Her tour ended on March 11, and by the following September she was under contract to Charles Frohman, a member of the Theatrical Syndicate and a successful star-maker whose contract lists included Ethel Barrymore, Maude Adams, Billie Burke, and William Gillette.

Her decision shocked the Shuberts. They had offered her a new contract that would have increased her salary and given her one-third of the profits. She had appeared overjoyed. When Lee Shubert asked if she were considering a different management, "she was vehement in her denial."

> She spoke with great earnestness, leaning forward as she did so and looking straight into my eyes, with tears in hers as she did so. . . . After the truth had been published in the papers, Nazimova wrote me a very tearful letter trying to justify, or explain, the deception. Shall I say that the explanation was entirely feminine?[21]

Once again her acting was convincing.

Although she objected to the image of femme fatale the Shuberts had created for her, she had few complaints with the box office that now followed under the Frohman-Syndicate banner. She toured for two years as the bizarre, temperamental exotic in *Bella Donna*, a play based on an adventuress who tries to poison her husband.[22] Nazimova performed as if she were a "serpent woman," gliding and creeping across the stage, her head moving "with the swaying, bending nod of the cobra." When finally coiled, she struck "with a swift flash of venomous fangs."[23] Theatergoers found her fiery personality, lurid acting, and sinuous beauty electrifying.

Though her reputation soared, her fame had turned to infamy. She had become so frustrated over the direction of her career that she decided to break her contract.[24] She wanted to be considered a great classic actress, but instead she had become a bizarre exotic, a novelty who had lost the respect of the critics. "I need something great and to stay in New York—to put me back where I was when I played Ibsen—something I can throw myself into," she explained, "and which will give me back my self-respect."[25]

Because she had embraced the subversive image so completely and had become notorious in the Broadway establishment as androgynous, producers were blinded to her potential. After a year of failing to sign a contract with any Broadway producer, in early 1915 she decided to become her own manager. It was a vaudeville act, and although this was an embarrassing setback for a serious actress, she at least had the opportunity of playing something other than a vamp.

The one-act play she chose to present was Marion Craig Wentworth's timely antiwar drama, *War Brides*. According to *Theatre* magazine, her acting of a young mother whose husband and brothers have been killed in a senseless war "was never more natural, earnest and fiery."[26] It was so successful that she played it on the Orpheum vaudeville circuit for over a year. Recognizing the box office value, Lewis J. Selznick produced a film version of *War Brides* and paid her thirty thousand dollars for thirty days' work, with a bonus of one thousand dollars for each day production went over schedule. The film was a bonanza, returning to Selznick more than three hundred thousand dollars in profits.[27]

Her costar in *War Brides* was Charles Bryant, a handsome Englishman who had been her male lead in *Bella Donna*. For the next fourteen years rumors buzzed that the two were married. Nazimova offered conflicting stories—that she and Bryant were married during rehearsals of *Bella Donna,* or in Europe, or in New England. The wedding date bounced from 1911 to 1913, and back again.

It was a curious relationship. When she was asked to define her ideal husband, she purred, "A man who is tolerant." "Love is far more than a kiss and an embrace. It means sacrifice. I tell you many a man has loved who has never demanded a kiss." "Charles is the acme of kindness, charm, consolation," she swooned. "There is no one better as a man in the world and he loves me as no one else ever loved me. I am like in a dream all the time and ask myself often if it is I—Alla?" Quite a contrast to a few months later when she wrote to her sister, "I am driving him out, so he [will] be more with men. Don't like his becoming a regular husband." Years later, cameraman Paul Ivano confirmed that "everyone assumed they were married, but with Alla preferring her women friends . . . I doubt whether they even had an affair."[28]

Bryant was clearly not a "regular husband," but rather another cover like Orlenev whom she hoped would conceal her private life. Her liaisons with women were beginning to threaten her deception. One of her romances was with actress Nila Mack. A native of Kansas, Mack first met Nazimova when she played her sister in both the vaudeville tour and film of *War Brides*. As she struggled to put together the film adaptation, Nazimova wrote, "I wish you were here to help me with your cool soothing hands! Well, good dear girl, . . . believe me I am very fond of you." And in another letter she joked, "Toodles [Nazimova's dog] is happy and still without kids. I wonder if she is one of us?! Poor thing! . . . A good kiss to yourself."[29] Mack went on to act in other Nazimova productions but in the 1930s began to write, direct, and produce *Let's Pretend*, a nationwide, award-winning children's radio program that dramatized fairy tales.

Certainly Nazimova's most threatening romance was with the eccentric Mercedes de Acosta. Reptilian in appearance, with her pale white face, black hair, and thin red lips, de Acosta made a bold statement by sporting mannish pants, pointed shoes trimmed with big buckles, tricorn hat, and cape. She had a thirst for knowledge and reading, and she was acquainted with many people in the arts—Augustin Daly, Ada Rehan, Jeanne Eagels, Sarah Bernhardt, Ethel Barrymore. She had met Toscanini and Caruso. As a child she had traveled extensively in Europe and had lived an aristocratic, cultured life.

Thrilled by Nazimova's Broadway performance in *War Brides*, de Acosta "could dream of nothing but meeting her." A few weeks later she witnessed Nazimova's performance at a special Madison Square Garden benefit: "As the band struck up the Imperial Anthem she waved the Russian flag as a great spotlight played over her. Then the music changed to a wild Cossack strain and . . . she ran . . . around the arena, leaping into the air every few steps." When they met in Nazimova's dressing room a few minutes later, de Acosta felt that Nazimova "seemed tiny and more like a naughty little boy. We took to each other instantly." But Nazimova began the relationship with deception. "My family were Spanish Jews who immigrated to Russia," she began. "My actual name is Lavendera, but when I began to study for the theatre with Nemirovich Danchenko I took the name of Nazimova from the Russian word *zima*—meaning winter."[30] None of it was true!

Although the two women had much in common, there was at least one major difference: de Acosta, always blunt, flaunted her sexuality. "I never cared a fig what anyone thought. As long as I feel 'right' within myself," she wrote, "society's opinion never influences me for a second."[31] A relationship could hardly last with a woman like Nazimova, who preferred a disguise, and de Acosta later moved on to liaisons with Eva Le Gallienne, Greta Garbo, and Marlene Dietrich.

Nazimova, on the other hand, moved to Hollywood. In 1918, she signed an extraordinary film contract with Metro Pictures Corporation. It supposedly granted her a special production unit as well as approval of stories, directors, and casts. Although it allowed her to complete her Ibsen season in New York, she was restricted from acting any Ibsen or Chekhov on screen. With a guarantee of thirteen thousand dollars per week with raises, it made her one of the first Hollywood superstars. Her fame reached such heights that comedienne Violet Dale added an impersonation of Nazimova to her popular vaudeville act, and a star with her name was added to the Hollywood Walk of Fame.[32]

She was delighted with what Hollywood had to offer. She now had financial security and also the freedom to pursue more aggressively her sexual interests. She signed a ninety-nine-year lease on a spectacular mansion on Sunset Boulevard for fifty thousand dollars. Christened the Garden of Alla, its four acres were landscaped with cedars, roses, and palms. Semitropical flowers and fruit trees bordered a lily pond and a sixty-five-foot illuminated swimming pool in the shape of the Black Sea. The drawing room of the main house was infamous for its lamps veiled in mauve and black, lavender divans, violet velour draperies, and oriental incense.

Protected by her bogus marriage to Charles Bryant, Nazimova quickly became the doyenne of the lesbian community. Sometimes she would entertain galas at Mary's, a lesbian bar she owned on Sunset Strip.[33] More often, however, she would hold "sewing circles" at her home, away from the prying eyes of journalists and the curious public. She enjoyed entertaining not only the biggest names in the entertainment industry, but also "the best dressed and best undressed in the land."[34] She appeared at parties wearing lavish green and gold Chinese costumes. Once she wore a long piece of flame-colored charmeuse wound around her body and caught up at one shoulder with a piece of

Russian lace, and she flicked white Egyptian ashes from her long, ebony cigarette holder.

According to her sister, she liked to invite attractive, intelligent, young Hollywood ingenues, "usually of a somewhat masculine type." "She would take up with one 'pet' and that person would be for a short time exclusively hers. . . . I recall her sitting like a Goddess surrounded by these adoring neophytes, usually insignificant actresses."[35] At one party a Broadway actress answered the door in the nude and with a monkey atop her head.[36] Among her intimates at these scandalous house parties were such lesbian protégées as Dolly Wilde, Jeanne Acker, June Mathis, and Natacha Rambova. Alla's entourage of young ladies became known as "Gillette Blades" because they cut both ways.[37]

The weekend soirees became so notorious that journalists began hinting of her androgyny. They wrote of her wearing clothes that made her look like a youthful Chinese boy and sporting a short hairstyle of "boyish brevity." A headline in *Photoplay* called her "A Misunderstood Woman" and noted that when she entered the room, "the effect was boyish."[38]

Shortly before moving to the Garden of Alla, she had met Eva Le Gallienne backstage after one of her Broadway performances. There was a noticeable spark between the two as they talked incessantly about their fascination with Ibsen. But the two women had more in common than Ibsen—European backgrounds, interest in music, and ambition. Although she was twenty years older, Nazimova's dark and penetrating purple eyes, raven black hair, slender and supple body, fiery personality, and soft Russian accent dazzled Le Gallienne.

Another of Nazimova's "female lovers" at the time, according to film director George Cukor, was twenty-year-old Dorothy Arzner, who was just embarking on her own film career. One fan magazine wrote that Arzner "invaded the sacred precincts of Alla Nazimova's dressing-room. And came out a full-fledged script girl" for the film *Stronger Than Death*.[39] Neither the relationship nor the employment lasted very long. Although Arzner learned much from this early pioneer in film, she objected to her mentor's ego and temperamental outbursts.

At first, Nazimova's film career seemed destined to succeed. Her premiere Metro picture, *Revelation*, was an enormous hit. Her character, a cabaret singer and prostitute who reforms after a religious experience, allowed Nazimova to play a full gamut of emotions. Her name soared to the top with such screen favorites as Mary Pickford and Norma Talmadge.

However, after appearing in three consecutive failures in 1920, her name dropped to twentieth in a popularity poll. With the headline "Another Nazimova Fiasco," a critic for the *New York Globe* charged that "her films have gone from incredibly bad to worse." He complained that she never left center screen or the heart of the spotlight.⁴⁰ After *Revelation,* she insisted on playing roles that were far too young for her. She was now forty-one. On stage it may have worked, but on screen the camera revealed what she was—a middle-aged, miscast woman. Major competition came from newcomer Pola Negri, another European actress known for exoticism and sensuality. Ironically, Negri's first Hollywood film was *Bella Donna.* Although Nazimova had thrilled audiences around the country when she originated the role on stage, Pola Negri was not only steaming, but barely twenty years old.

Intent on reversing her decline, Nazimova selected *Camille* as her next vehicle. "Why not a *Camille* of today?" read one of the film's subtitles. "Living the same story in this generation?" Aubrey Beardsley–like, curvilinear motifs dominated Natacha Rambova's art deco sets and costumes. Marguerite's Paris apartment featured low, round, wide-arched doorways leading to the foyer and dining area and semicircular glass doors opening to the bedroom. Viewers first saw Marguerite at the opera, where she wore a lizardlike gown of gold metallic fabric wound about her body and fastened at one shoulder. Her opera cape of heavy, black silk net accented with silver threads was studded with silver camellias and trimmed at the bottom with a wide band of fur. The visual effect was of a strangely cold, passionless, futuristic world.

For her leading man, Nazimova chose Rudolph Valentino, at that time virtually unknown in Hollywood. Throughout, Valentino appears suppliant rather than seductive, revealing few hints of the "Great Lover" he was to become. In her scenes with Valentino, the usually sensual Nazimova, appears aloof, cold, and sexless. Hints of lesbian affection are everywhere. Marguerite and her friend Nichette hold and caress each other. Four times they kiss on the mouth. When a man tries to break them apart, Marguerite insists, "Take your hands off. She is too good for you."

When invited to view the daily rushes of *Camille,* Eva Le Gallienne was shocked by the exotic, perverse, freakish interpretation. Le Gallienne quickly returned to New York, ended their three-year relationship, and began a romance with Nazimova's former plaything, Mercedes de Acosta. Whenever she thought of Nazimova, Le Gallienne later wrote to Mercedes, she felt physically sick, nauseated. She found Nazimova's behavior in Hollywood revolting and unbelievably repulsive.⁴¹

"What has happened to the great actress, the splendid genius, the

Alla Nazimova and Rudolph Valentino in *Camille*

(Courtesy Museum of Modern Art.)

incomparable artiste?" asked a bewildered critic for *Photoplay.* "Will the spark of genius light again?"[42] It was to be Nazimova's last picture for Metro. Her contract was canceled on April 20, 1921, and after less than three years her role as a Hollywood superstar had ended. Nazimova was devastated by the collapse of her career.

Fearful of returning to New York as a failure and desperate to continue the moral freedom she enjoyed in Hollywood, Nazimova invested all of her assets to set up her own film company. Her first production would be Ibsen's *A Doll's House.* The reviews were excellent and seemed to restore, at least temporarily, her faltering film career.[43]

With renewed confidence, she then threw caution to the wind with her second independent film. Oscar Wilde's *Salome* was a surreal, expressionistic production with an entire cast that was supposedly homosexual. Nazimova's Salome, a trim and pampered fourteen-year-old girl with a boyish figure, was framed within a composition of male homosexuals and eunuchs. Although United Artists ballyhooed the film "as an orgy of sex and sin" with hints of nudity, viewers found it rather innocuous. As one critic later observed, "Nazimova's Salome was sexless and a product of her own lesbian psyche. . . . Some of the other characters play obvious homosexuals with such an abundance of embarrassing cliches as to be ridiculous."[44]

The censors insisted that several scenes be eliminated, including one that showed a homosexual relationship between two soldiers. "This picture is in no way religious in theme or interpretation. In my judgment, it is a story of depravity and immorality made worse because of its biblical background. Sacrilegious." Labeled "degrading and unintelligent" and an example of "unimaginative stupidity," *Salome* wiped out Nazimova's savings and destroyed what was left of her credibility.[45] When questioned about her motivation for making her last few films, Nazimova declared, "I made them to please myself."[46] Unfortunately, they pleased few other people.

Hollywood in the 1920s had become a new Babylon. The culture was different; the values were different. "Oh, the parties we used to have!" Gloria Swanson later recalled. "In those days the public wanted us to live like kings and queens. So we did—and why not? We were in love with life. We were making more money than we ever dreamed existed and there was no reason to believe it would ever stop."[47] Nazimova found herself immersed in a new sexual morality and freedom that created scandals for the likes of Fatty Arbuckle and Charlie Chaplin but allowed her an openness she had never before experienced. The same woman who had for years concealed her private life so carefully now began to flaunt it. Ironically, she continued to confuse the public by maintaining her peculiar relationship with Charles Bryant.

A decade earlier, she had bowed to the will of the men around her—the Shuberts, Charles Frohman, playwrights Owen Johnson and Brandon Tynan. One historian even claimed that "Nazimova turned to female companionship because she was mishandled and abused by an assortment of scummy men."[48] But now she was under the mesmerizing influence of the dark and sultry Natacha Rambova. Men ogled her; women glared. Rambova was considered a cold-blooded, calculating opportunist. Although Nazimova called Rambova "the human iceberg," she nevertheless relied on her for both erotic gratification and advice, which eventually led to professional suicide.[49]

In another attempt to rally her career, she resurrected once again her image as a dangerous, seductive witch and returned to Broadway in *Dagmar,* a Hungarian play about a nymphomaniac Russian countess who toys with several men before she is murdered by a jealous lover. "She just vamped and vamped," charged one reviewer. "She was alluring, gorgeously picturesque and unmistakably dangerous, but there was nothing in her role to make her really interesting." Kenneth Macgowan called the play "a rank absurdity," and Alexander Woollcott quipped, "In the next scene, Nazimova will torture her Pekingese."[50] Eva Le Gallienne and Mercedes de Acosta were both astounded that Nazimova had chosen such a preposterous script. The choice was not surprising, however, since she was incredibly gullible and often accepted bad advice. In the words of critic Edward Wagenknecht, she "seemed an easy prey for charlatans."[51]

Back in Hollywood in the spring of 1923, she found herself in the middle of a sensational scandal. Natacha Rambova asked Nazimova to witness her marriage to Rudolph Valentino in Mexico. When the wedding party returned to Los Angeles, Valentino was arrested and charged with bigamy since he was not legally divorced from Jean Acker, another of Nazimova's liaisons. At the trial three weeks later, witnesses were forced to admit under oath that the wedding couple had not shared a bedroom in Mexico. One of the witnesses was Nazimova, who had been apprehended by process servers. Apparently, she feared adverse publicity might prompt her deportation as an undesirable alien, and she was discovered "swathed in veils," boarding a train for New York.[52]

Faced with financial ruin, Nazimova returned to vaudeville, starring in George Middleton's *The Unknown Lady,* originally called *Collusion.*

She boasted of eleven curtain calls at a matinee performance and nine in the evening: "They like it, am happy. Alla."⁵³ But Roman Catholic Church representatives were outraged. They claimed that the story—a married man arranging an affair with a prostitute to prove infidelity in a divorce court—was "a menace to public morals." Though she had been touring the play for eight weeks and had advance bookings for five more, Edward F. Albee, head of the vaudeville circuit, canceled the bookings and bought off her fifteen-thousand-dollar contract. Although the press and the courts ultimately allowed the play, theaters refused to book it. "Ain't it a joke?!" she cried to the author. "I feel rotten about it, but can do nothing; it's a Chinese wall. Anything will do, they say, but not this. . . . At any rate there is little ambition in me left to fight."⁵⁴

About a year later, Nazimova's pseudo-marriage came to a halt when Charles Bryant decided to marry a twenty-three-year-old society girl. Nazimova confessed to her sister,

> It's been four years since we've had sex and other relations gradually came to an end. It would seem that we are friends but no more— something lukewarm. I am no longer sorry that he's gone. We have nothing in common. My personal life is stupidly and ridiculously no joy or pain or *sense*. You must understand how I must keep up appearances.⁵⁵

His departure brought their fourteen-year "marriage" into full view. When he applied for his marriage license and confirmed that he was single, a *New York Times* reporter was prompted to charge that Nazimova and Bryant had never been legally married. A local district attorney forced Bryant to swear under oath that he had never been married to Nazimova. Shortly after the separation, she confessed, "I am a girl of 16 in the matters of the heart. Falling in love and obeying this love down to the last step of self contempt, this was [my] only way of living . . . and paying dearly every time. . . . Muddy heels from walking in mud."⁵⁶ Friends knew that she contemplated suicide.

The break with Bryant was another financial setback. In 1907, she had purchased a six-acre country estate in Port Chester, New York, which she had named Who-Torok (little hut). For nearly twenty years it had been her escape from the city and public scrutiny. When Bryant insisted that she owed him thirty-five thousand dollars, she offered to sell Who-Torok to settle the debt. But convinced that it would not sell, she finally deeded the property over to Bryant. A few months later he sold it for sixty-five thousand dollars but shared none of it with her.⁵⁷ She was now nearly destitute, though she managed to pay her bills by promoting various products such as Lux Toilet Soap and Lucky Strike cigarettes.

Another notion to cover expenses was the conversion of the Garden of Alla into a hotel. In exchange for the lease, she became a stockholder in the company, was paid a monthly sum, and was guaranteed, rent-free, an apartment above the garage as long as she lived. Twenty-five bungalows were clustered around the pool, and the new Garden of Alla opened on January 9, 1927. By the end of the year, however, the company had failed, Nazimova lost her entire investment, and the property reverted to the original owner, who resumed the luxurious resort hotel. Although she continued to live on the estate, she was forced to pay rent. Because of the traumatic turn of events, she suffered a nervous breakdown, canceled several stage appearances, and was ordered to "have absolute quiet."[58]

It had been six years since Eva Le Gallienne had turned from Nazimova in embarrassment. In the intervening years, Le Gallienne had gained national prominence as one of Broadway's leading ladies and the founder of the Civic Repertory Theatre, a repertory company specializing in the classics and in modest ticket prices. By 1928, however, audiences and critics were beginning to complain that Le Gallienne starred in too many of the productions and that the company needed to add more star names to the roster. When she now asked her former lover to join the company, the older actress was thrilled.

> Eva LeG writes me the most lovely letters. I feel so happy when I think of my future work. . . . Of being taken care of, to have someone who has eliminated all worries about plays, managers, agents—to be able to do the very things that one believes in and that no one else could even see!! And to be in my family. . . . What that means to me—to be surrounded by people of the same ideas on work and life.[59]

She could have added, "the same ideas on sex." Robert Lewis, the future director and cofounder of the Actors' Studio, who was an apprentice actor with the Civic Rep at the time, recalled that "it was a lesbian theatre. Eva lived upstairs with Jo Hutchinson, and most of the apprentice girls . . . were lesbian. So was the set designer, Gladys Calthrop. So was a considerable part of the audience." Indeed, it was so much a lesbian theater that critic George Jean Nathan dubbed it "the Le Gallienne sorority."[60]

Nazimova's portrayal of Madame Ranevsky in Chekhov's *The Cherry Orchard* was a true comeback performance. A critic for the *New York American* praised her "moving and real" performance that was filled with "subtlety of gesture and grace of movement," and the *Boston*

Transcript reported that her acting "was like a mirror, a crystal turned from angle to angle." She played her part "with a flowing rhythm that catches every evanescent mood and intonation."[61] The run was a virtual sellout.

One scene in particular suggested a new and unexpected reality in her acting. Forced to sell her family estate to pay her bills, Nazimova's Madame Ranevsky sat silently as she listened intently to the offstage sound effects of Russian peasants cutting down her treasured cherry orchard. The actress confessed that as she played the scene she imagined hearing her own creditors chopping away at the Garden of Alla and Who-Torok. The moment was very personal, very intimate.

She had spent much of her life—on and off stage—in deception and disguise. Her acting had often been described as fake. But since the Valentino-Rambova scandal—as well as the many scandals of her own—had exposed her, it was now pointless at this stage to conceal her personal life. "Sis, sis, sis!" she sighed. "Soon I will be home and will have nothing to hide or be ashamed of."[62] She now could be honest and incorporate her own life and experiences to enrich her acting. As critic Helen Ormsbee observed, the "years have added a touching humanity" to her performances.[63]

At first, Nazimova had not minded Le Gallienne's flaunting traditional custom and listing all casts alphabetically: "My name as small in print as all the others! I am still giggling!"[64] But when she was asked to return for a second season, Nazimova refused. Neither she nor Le Gallienne would explain, but a representative from the Civic said Nazimova had been "too temperamental" and had objected to billing in which Le Gallienne's name as producer preceded the alphabetical listing of the performers.[65] She may have been angry, too, when she learned that her weekly salary for the next season was to be only $250, which was $50 less than the contract offered to Jacob Ben-Ami, the Civic's leading man.

Leaving the Civic with Nazimova was her new paramour, Glesca Marshall, a young actress who had played small roles in Le Gallienne's productions of *Peter Pan* and *Katerina*. Though Nazimova had always been close to her sister Nina and to niece Lucy and nephew Val, the family always resented Marshall, calling her a "theatre hanger-on," and "a will snatcher."[66] They viewed her as "a liar, a mannish type" of lesbian they absolutely abhorred. Nazimova exploded: "I don't believe in family any more. . . . I think one should build one's family around one, of people that are *kins in spirit and tastes*." Her niece replied coolly, "It is strange that you resent our polite civility to your 'friend.' Her peculiar relationship to you demanded at least that from us, even though her personality never appealed to us."[67] Although Nazimova and her sister continued to correspond through the years, she and her niece never again communicated.

Nazimova joined the prestigious Theatre Guild in 1930 and performed to glowing reviews in *A Month in the Country, Mourning Becomes Electra,* and *The Good Earth.*[68] Plaguing her during these brighter years, however, was a frightening lawsuit against her with a fine of thirty thousand dollars for the wrongful death of a woman hit by her car.[69] To meet her expenses, in 1935 she directed and starred in her own version of *Ghosts* and in the following season revived *Hedda Gabler,* which played successfully both in New York and on national tours. Glesca Marshall served as stage manager.

Tragically and unexpectedly, Nazimova's renewed popularity was cut short. In late 1938 she underwent major surgery for breast cancer that, in her words, "hit me like a stroke of lightning and disrupted not only my health but my career."[70] Indeed, her final Broadway performance, in Karel Čapek's war-themed *Mother,* was a disappointment. Though it seemed timely in the spring of 1939, shortly before the outbreak of World War II, critics found the script "dreary and pedestrian." Playing the role of a mother who sends her only living son off to war, Nazimova "went through the motions of despair and grief, but it was an alien, Stanislavsky grief."[71] It was certainly a different reaction from what she had received during World War I with *War Brides,* another antiwar play. Even with the attraction of the young and closeted Montgomery Clift playing her son, she could not keep it running more than a month.

She returned to Hollywood. But since there was little demand for a sixty-year-old dramatic actress, she accepted small roles in such films as *Escape* (1940), *The Bridge of San Luis Rey* (1944), and *In Our Time* (1944). To help her out financially, director George Cukor, himself a closeted homosexual, created a job for her as a technical advisor on *Zaza.*

Her last years were spent in her modest apartment at the Garden of Alla. Living nearby in luxurious cottages at the palatial estate were such notables as Greta Garbo, F. Scott Fitzgerald, Orson Welles, Errol Flynn, and Dorothy Parker. "If you only knew what I went through all these last years," she wrote to her sister in 1941. Two years later, she wrote,

> But it's over, it's over now. The little apartment . . . is sunny and sweet and the few pieces of furniture I did not sell I have here and am quite comfortable. . . . I have stopped worrying about my situa-

tion. . . . We don't go out at all except once in a blue moon. . . . We have few visitors and, as usual, only for tea.[72]

The "witch of makeup" had focused so much of her life and energy on disguise and deception and evoking the image of female danger. In the end, she internalized so completely this image of an assertive seductress that it ultimately destroyed her career and self-esteem.

> I climbed very high as an artist. And the scales went rather low on the other side. . . . I found that I had undervalued the woman in me for so long, neglected her, cheapened her. . . . And the result: *There is nothing of great value left.* My work has become cheap, and the woman in me has become cheap.[73]

July 13, 1945, witnessed the passing of the legendary femme fatale. She had become a recluse, isolated in a rented apartment above the garage at her own former estate. She died nearly penniless and forgotten, except for that "theatre hanger-on," that "will snatcher," that beloved partner of seventeen years, Glesca Marshall. Though she left no great financial estate to Glesca, she bequeathed her theater memorabilia and an annuity of $60 per month. Only a few old friends came to her funeral, but none of her family.

NOTES

1. Katharine Roberts, "Artists Don't Need Ruffles," *Collier's*, December 10, 1932, 10.

2. Nazimova to her sister, November 2, 1924, Nazimova Collection, Library of Congress.

3. Quoted in Gavin Lambert, *Nazimova: A Biography* (New York: Knopf, 1997), 95. Information about the abuse she suffered as a child is recorded in her unfinished, unpublished autobiography, "A Mummer's Odyssey," located in the Alla Nazimova archive, Glesca Marshall Library, Springer Opera House, Columbus, Georgia, and it is discussed in Gavin Lambert's biography.

4. Because she was something of a mythmaker and there are many contradictions in Nazimova's stories to reporters, the information presented here about her Russian past is derived mainly from four sources: (1) a letter from Nazimova's sister to Edward T. James, July 13, 1962, Harvard Theatre Collection, (2) Lucy Olga Lewton, *Alla Nazimova: My Aunt* (Ventura, CA: Minuteman Press, 1988), (3) Jean Kling, "Biography of Alla Nazimova," an unpublished, incomplete manuscript in the Nazimova Collection of the Library of Congress, and (4) Gavin Lambert, *Nazimova*. Jean Kling was married to the son of Nazimova's nephew.

5. Although some sources indicate that she married an actor named Sergei Nazimoff while a student at the Philharmonic School and received her surname from him, this seems to be one of the many myths she created.

6. For more information about the Orlenev-Nazimova tour see Laurence Senelick, "The American Tour of Orlenev and Nazimova, 1905–1906," in *Wandering Stars: Russian Emigré Theatre, 1905–40,* ed. Laurence Senelick (Iowa City: University of Iowa Press, 1992), 1–15. Emma Goldman describes her work for Orlenev and Nazimova in her autobiography, *Living My Life: Emma Goldman,* vol. 1 (New York: Dover Publications, 1970), 373–79. Her experience served as the cornerstone for her book *The Social Significance of the Modern Drama.*

7. For a discussion of Russian attitudes toward homosexuality see Simon Karlinsky, "Russia's Gay Literature and Culture: The Impact of the October Revolution," in *Hidden from History: Reclaiming the Gay and Lesbian Past,* ed. Martin Duberman, Martha Vicinus, and George Chauncey Jr. (New York: Penguin, 1990), 347–64.

8. Jonathan Ned Katz, *Gay American History: Lesbians and Gay Men in the U.S.A.* (New York: Harper and Row, 1976), 61; Jonathan Ned Katz, *Gay/Lesbian Almanac* (New York: Harper and Row, 1983), 313–20.

9. Contract with the Shuberts, May 14, 1906, Shubert Archive.

10. Louis Untermeyer's "Nazimova as Hedda Gabler" appears in Ada Patterson's "An Interview with a Multiple Woman," *Theatre,* August 1907, 219; Sigismond de Ivanowski's portraits of her as Nora and Hedda appeared in Owen Johnson's essay, "Mme. Alla Nazimova," *Century,* June 1907, 221, 223–26.

11. Johnson, "Mme. Alla Nazimova," 222–23.

12. *Cleveland Leader,* April 20, 1908.

13. Nazimova to her sister, 1908, Nazimova Collection.

14. Nazimova to her sister, October 12, 1912, Nazimova Collection; Nazimova interview with Viola Justin, *New York Evening Mail,* n.d., Shubert Archive.

15. Lucy Lewton (Nazimova's niece) to Jean Kling, August 27, 1974, Nazimova Collection; Djuna Barnes, "Alla Nazimova," *Theatre Guild,* June 1930, 61.

16. Axel Madsen, *The Sewing Circle: Hollywood's Greatest Secret—Female Stars who Loved Other Women* (New York: Birch Lane Press, 1995), 117, 146.

17. A. H. Canby to Lee Shubert, December 29, 1908, Shubert Archive.

18. Ibid.

19. *New York Evening Star,* n.d., Shubert Archive.

20. Nazimova to Shubert, February 3, 1911, Shubert Archive.

21. Unpublished autobiography of Lee Shubert written in 1936, 272–77, Shubert Archive.

22. E. J. Symons's portrait of her in *Bella Donna* hangs in the National Portrait Gallery, Washington, D.C.

23. *Toronto World,* January 21, 1913.

24. Mary B. Mullett, "How a Dull, Fat Little Girl Became a Great Actress," *American,* April 1922, 114.

25. Nazimova to her sister, February 14, 1914, Nazimova Collection.

26. "Nazimova in *War Brides*," *Theatre*, March 1915, 116.

27. Jack Spears, *The Civil War on the Screen and Other Essays* (South Brunswick, NJ: A. S. Barnes, 1977), 125–27.

28. To add to the confusion, there were rumors that Charles Bryant was homosexual. *Toledo News Bee*, October 21, 1916; *New York World*, October 20, 1907; Nazimova to Lucy, April 14, 1913, Nazimova Collection; Nazimova to her sister, October 14, 1913, Nazimova Collection; quoted in Sheila Graham, *The Garden of Allah* (New York: Crown, 1970), 14.

29. Nazimova to Nila Mack, n.d., and July 12, 1916, Billy Rose Theatre Collection, Lincoln Center Library for the Performing Arts, New York Public Library.

30. For a discussion of their meeting see Mercedes de Acosta, *Here Lies the Heart* (New York: Reynal, 1975), 72–75.

31. Ibid., 113.

32. *New York Dramatic Mirror*, April 14, 1919.

33. Madsen, *The Sewing Circle*, 99.

34. A comment by reporter Lucius Beebe as quoted in Dan Swinton, "Garden of Allah, Once Oasis, Awaits Kismet," unmarked article, Nazimova Collection.

35. Lucy to Jean Kling, August 27, 1974, Nazimova Collection.

36. Dan Swinton, "Garden of Allah, Once Oasis, Awaits Kismet," unmarked article, Nazimova Collection.

37. Madsen, *The Sewing Circle*, xii.

38. Edwin Fredericks, "The Real Nazimova," *Photoplay*, February 1920, 55–56, 128; Herbert Howe, "A Misunderstood Woman," *Photoplay*, April 1922, 119.

39. Judith Mayne, *Directed by Dorothy Arzner* (Bloomington: Indiana University Press, 1994), 23.

40. *New York Globe*, December 6, 1920.

41. Interview by Robert A. Schanke with Anne Kaufman Schneider, May 18, 1989; Eva Le Gallienne to Mercedes de Acosta, November 7, 1922, Rosenbach Museum, Philadelphia.

42. "An Open Letter to Mme. Alla Nazimova," *Photoplay*, August 1921, 31, 94.

43. DeWitt Bodeen, "Nazimova: Her Film Career Was a Pale Reflection of Her Genius as an Actress," *Films in Review* 22 (December 1972): 594.

44. Spears, *Civil War on Screen*, 148–49; Thomas Craven, "Salome and Cinema," *New Republic*, January 24, 1933, 225–26. For more discussion of the film's homosexual subtext see William Tydeman and Steven Rice, *Wilde: "Salome"* (New York: Cambridge University Press, 1996), 159–65.

45. Vito Russo, *The Celluloid Closet* (New York: Harper and Row, 1981), 29; Craven, "Salome and Cinema," 225–26.

46. Herbert Howe, "The Dancing Salome," *Photoplay*, March 1923, 120.

47. Quoted in Kenneth Anger, *Hollywood Babylon* (New York: Dell Books, 1975), 83, 86, 101.

48. Clifford Ashby, letter to the author, August 19, 1994.

49. Spears, *Civil War on Screen*, 142.

50. *New York Evening World,* January 23, 1923; *New York Globe,* January 24, 1923; quoted in Lucy Olga Newton, *Alla Nazimova: My Aunt* (Ventura, CA: Minuteman Press, 1988), 31.

51. Edward Wagenknecht, *The Movies in the Age of Innocence* (Norman: University of Oklahoma Press, 1962), 179.

52. Spears, *Civil War on Screen,* 150.

53. Nazimova, letter to George Middleton, August 27, 1923, Nazimova Collection.

54. Nazimova, letter to Middleton, November 13, 1923, Nazimova Collection.

55. Nazimova, letter to her sister, November 2, 1924, Nazimova Collection.

56. Nazimova, letter to Lucy, September 23, 1925, Nazimova Collection.

57. Lucy, letter to Jean Kling, October 11, 1979, Nazimova Collection.

58. Unmarked newspaper clipping, Newark, NJ, Nazimova Collection.

59. Nazimova, letter to Isabel Hill, August 8, 1928, Nazimova Collection.

60. Quoted in Lambert, *Nazimova,* 305; George Jean Nathan, "The Theatre," *American Mercury,* May 1928, 122.

61. *New York American,* October 16, 1928; *Boston Transcript,* May 11, 1929; *New York Times,* October 18, 1928.

62. Nazimova, letter to her sister, May 18, 1928, Nazimova Collection.

63. Helen Ormsbee, *Backstage with Actors* (New York: Crowell, 1938), 253–54.

64. Nazimova, letter to Isabel Hill, August 8, 1928, Nazimova Collection.

65. *New York Telegram,* July 18, 1929.

66. Val Lewton became a director of horror films such as *The Cat People.* Lucy, letter to Jean Kling, October 11, 1979, Nazimova Collection.

67. Nazimova, letter to her sister, January 24, 1929; Lucy, letter to Nazimova, May 14, 1932; Lucy, letter to Jean Kling, October 11, 1979; Nazimova Collection.

68. In the chapter on Cheryl Crawford found elsewhere in this volume, author Jay Plum suggests a "lesbian friendship" existed between Nazimova and Crawford when they worked for the Theatre Guild in the 1930s.

69. *New York Daily News,* June 9, 1937.

70. Nazimova, letter to her sister, March 26, 1941, Nazimova Collection.

71. *Nation,* May 6, 1939, 539; unidentified clipping as quoted in Margaret McKerrow, "A Descriptive Study of the Acting of Alla Nazimova," Ph.D. diss., University of Michigan, 1974, 233.

72. Nazimova, letters to her sister, March 26, 1941 and February 27, 1943, Nazimova Collection.

73. Nazimova, letter to Lucy, September 23, 1925, Nazimova Collection.

Elsie Janis

"A Comfortable Goofiness"

Lee Alan Morrow

There was no eulogy. Instead, four hundred middle-aged men in old and often ill-fitting military uniforms slowly marched to the flag-draped casket, saluted, and stepped outside the chapel. In odd contrast, the pews were filled with the faces of Old Hollywood: Walter Pidgeon, Ina Claire, Clifton Webb, Pola Negri, Louise Dresser. Carmen Miranda's husband had arranged the funeral.

In the rain, as the veterans boarded rented school buses, the famous climbed into limousines. A small group of reporters stood by, hoping for a statement. Only Mary Pickford paused.

> Elsie Janis was a valiant person, a great trouper, a great soul. She was certainly one of the greatest entertainers of all time. She wanted no ostentation, no fuss. No flowers at her funeral—she'd rather the money went to charity. She was always thinking of others. She would go without things so others might have them.
>
> I remember her when she was sixteen and the rage of New York. And when she sat beside men wounded in battle in World War I. She had a beautiful career—a beautiful life.
>
> This ends the vaudevillian era.[1]

In many ways, Elsie Janis (1889–1956) did have a beautiful career. Her impersonations of celebrities, ethnic types, and, most famously, men, gave her wealth and renown. Her front-line entertainment of World War I troops made her an international favorite. Surviving the rigors of war encouraged her to fight the restrictions of her gender and empowered her to compete with men on the highest levels. Before the war, she achieved Broadway stardom at sixteen, appeared in a series of commercially successful musicals, and toured as vaudeville's highest paid headliner. After the war, she became one of the first women to direct a Broadway musical; one of the first women to write, produce, direct, and star in a motion picture; the first woman to produce a talking picture; the first woman announcer on nationwide radio. She also became a facile contributor to many areas of writing—plays, novels, poetry, songs and lyrics, a comic strip, and a newspaper gossip column.

The shape of Elsie's life and career was determined by women, most strongly by her domineering stage mother, Jennie Cockrell Bierbower, who launched Elsie as a child star and functioned as her manager for forty years. For the first half of her life, Elsie appeared to follow her mother in passive obeisance. But during World War I, when she played for the troops on the front lines, Elsie gained a maturity and a greater sense of her own power as a performer, and she began to share in making decisions that previously would have been made exclusively by Jennie. Her mother remained the primary influence in Elsie's life, however, even after Jennie's death in 1930. Throughout their long years of collaboration, the two women were primarily committed to each other in a relationship that was mutually nurturing and sustaining but, also, for Elsie, controlling and, at times, suffocating. Insofar as each formed close emotional bonds with other people, these bonds were chiefly with other women. While we cannot know for certain whether either Elsie or Jennie had or consciously desired genital sexual experiences with any of their close female associates, it is clear that they lived most of their lives in a gynocentric world of their own creation, and that homosocial bonds were the chief determinants of their professional success in the male-dominated entertainment industry and the military. This essay examines the dynamics of Elsie's homosocial world and how they enabled her unconventional career track, gender-ambivalent role identifications on and off stage, and the inspiration and opportunities she would provide to a younger generation of lesbian and gay theater and film artists.

That Elsie Jane Bierbower would go on the stage was never in doubt: it simply was to be. While pregnant in 1889, Jennie Cockrell Bierbower convinced herself that the child would be the fulfillment of her own stunted theatrical ambitions. Jennie decided that her daughter was going to be a synthesis of the great actresses of that day, having the "dramatic eloquence of Modjeska, the versatility of Maggie Mitchell, the elfin alertness of Lotta."[2] By the time Elsie was four, Jennie, the budding impresario, had groomed her for small parts in Columbus, Ohio's Valentine Stock Company. After the *Columbus Press-Post* referred to her daughter as "the child wonder,"[3] Jennie, against her husband John's wishes, committed herself to creating a life in the professional theater for "Little Elsie." Elsie remembered years later, "I think in all honesty that I should have been named co-respondent in [the] divorce of my mother and father,

for had they not disagreed over me, my future, my talent and the development of it, Mother would never have thought of looking for another
reason for leaving John and John would probably never have given her
the reason, but he did."4

Just as Jennie had been sent away to live with relatives by a step-
mother unwilling to cope with an unwanted child, Elsie's older brother
Percy was similarly banished. He had no place in Jennie's plans. John,
recognizing that he was no match for Jennie, submitted to her will and
did not contest the divorce. Divorce at the turn of the century was not a
commonplace event; it was a socially damning affair. To escape the
stigma, Jennie took to telling reporters she was a widow.

After the divorce in 1897, Jennie began to take out advertisements
announcing Elsie's availability for performances at "parlors, churches,
schools, societies, lodges and stock companies." Initially, most of her
act—with Jennie at the piano—consisted of such children's songs as
"Little Orphan Annie" and "Won't You Come to My Tea Party?" But
soon Elsie's imitations became the most popular feature. Jennie would
take Elsie to see a performer they wished to imitate. Returning home, the
two would practice together in front of mirrors, perfecting the impression
bit by bit—"Well, you know, I have four eyes. I have two eyes and
mamma has two. What my eyes don't see, mamma's do. Then sometimes
I see what mamma does not."5 Elsie made some money, but not yet
enough to free them from dependence on John's financial contributions.
Something extraordinary had to happen to lift Elsie and her career out of
the Columbus area.

When William McKinley was governor of Ohio, Elsie often was
asked to entertain the invalid Mrs. McKinley. In late 1899, with McKinley
now president, Elsie and Jennie traveled from Ohio to Washington during
the Christmas holidays in hopes of being received. On Christmas Day
Elsie entertained President and Mrs. McKinley and their guests in the Blue
Room of the White House. Dressed in a dark velvet Little Lord Fauntleroy
suit, Elsie began with a favorite song of Mrs. McKinley's, "Break the
News to Mother." That was followed by a recitation, "Cease Awhile,
Clarion; Clarion, Wild and Shrill." Elsie finished with two imitations,
Anna Held singing "Won't You Come an' Play Wiz Me?" and May Irwin
singing "If You Ain't Got No Money, You Needn't Come 'Round." After
her prepared pieces Elsie tossed off an impromptu imitation of her host.
She marched about, the likeness of the president, thrusting her hands
between the buttons of her coat, and then took on his tight-lipped smile,
rigid bearing, and the orotund tones of his voice. President McKinley

lifted Elsie upon his knee, kissed her, and proclaimed, "You are my little Ohio constituent and I am proud of you."[6] With the short slogan "Recited for the President" attached to their act, mother and daughter moved into the world of professional vaudeville.

The years 1899 to 1904 were spent in almost constant touring—split weeks in small theaters in small towns playing "continuous" vaudeville, full weeks in larger theaters in bigger towns, playing two shows a day. Their life was bounded by theaters, hotels, and railway cars and stations. Elsie performed daily—perhaps a total of forty minutes on the stage. On Sundays they traveled to the next town. The theaters were interchangeable. The dressing rooms were invariably small and either too cold or too hot, furnished with a small pitcher and bowl, and a few hooks and nails. Sometimes the room was shared with another performer and his or her trunks and traveling companions.

On Monday mornings, each performer would get a chance to speak for a few minutes with the orchestra's leader. They would go over any difficult sections or pieces of music specially timed to the performer's act. An orchestra in a large, first-class theater would consist of first and second violins, viola, cornet, clarinet, trombone, bass, piano, and drums and traps. Smaller theaters got by with piano and drums. Each vaudeville act carried its music in a variety of arrangements, suited to different configurations of instruments. (Musicians could tell when an act was first playing "the big time"—the piano part was well worn, while the music for the other instruments was brand-new.)

Jennie's days were filled tutoring Elsie and tending to the management of the business. Two weeks before arriving in a town she would send Elsie's photographs for display in the theater lobby. Travel time was given over to mending Elsie's costumes. Once in town, Jennie would impress her personality on the local newspaper's writers to secure favorable publicity. She sat through each interview with Elsie and later carefully pasted the articles in leather-bound scrapbooks. Each week Jennie would take out an advertisement in one of the New York theatrical newspapers to tout Little Elsie's latest achievements. It was important to remind New York of Elsie's existence.[7]

Whenever in New York, Jennie sought the advice of Elsie de Wolfe and her companion Elisabeth Marbury, both professional theater women, who are discussed by Kim Marra in this volume. Jennie and Elsie often attended all-women dinners hosted by the de Wolfe–Marbury duo. Such women gave her good counsel, empowering her independence by their own example. For Jennie, men, including her own relatives, were either hindrances to escape or obstacles to overcome. Whenever possible, she chose to work with women and tolerated male theater professionals only to the extent that they could offer what she believed Elsie's career needed.

The theater, for Jennie, was both refuge and salvation. It got her out of an uninteresting marriage and into a fascinating life. It enabled her to surround herself with supportive women, women who understood her own new marriage to Elsie's career. In the culture of the theater Jennie found a niche of the greater society where she could be fully herself; she realized that the Shuberts and Keith-Albee would gladly treat her as an equal in order to get Elsie's name on a contract.

The theater, for Elsie, was both a proving ground of her love for her mother and a playground for her own very high spirits. Elsie knew that she was the reason her parents divorced. And that knowledge made her feel a great need to satisfy her mother; if her mother were to reject her, to whom would she turn? Significantly, Jennie also understood that without Elsie, she would find herself alone.

Jennie's single-minded ambition and devotion to her daughter eased Elsie's arduous years of touring. Jennie decorated each hotel suite and theater dressing room with pictures of friends and family. She brought Elsie breakfast in the morning, lunch each afternoon, and supper after every performance. Skating parties were given, sleigh rides organized, moving-picture theaters bribed to remain open so that Elsie could see a film after her own performance. Jennie fought to pull Elsie from her backstage games to study other performers, fought to keep Elsie's name in the large type she believed her daughter merited, fought for extra heat in trains and dressing rooms to protect Elsie's health. During performances, Jennie watched from the wings whenever Elsie was on stage, sat with Elsie in her dressing room when she was not on stage, dressed and undressed her, put on her makeup and took it off. No matter how great the applause Elsie might receive, she would return to the wings where Jennie was always waiting and ask, "Did I please you, mamma?" During the early years, rumors passed that if Jennie was not pleased with Elsie's performance, she would be spanked. Elsie even remarked once, "My ambition is to keep just one step ahead of mother's ambition for me."[8]

As Elsie mastered her craft, Jennie came to realize that touring in vaudeville was not the fullest theatrical education for a future career on the legitimate stage. Elsie's confidence on stage was marked, and her talent as a mimic was unquestioned. A long career in vaudeville was theirs for the taking, but Jennie believed that it was on the legitimate stage of Broadway, in musical plays, that Elsie's real fortune and enduring fame would be made. So Jennie signed for Elsie to play regional tours of *The Belle of New York*, *The Fortune Teller*, and *The Little Duchess*. When Elsie opened as "Flo Berry, masquerading as the 'Little Duchess,' " she was for the first time the star of a musical-comedy company. During the final act the plot was suspended while Elsie took center stage to present her imitations. One reviewer said that the "other members of the company were forced to retire in the face of her encores" and that Elsie's performance was "a series of ovations."[9]

Vaudeville performers yearned for the legitimate stage for many reasons. The prestige of appearing as the leading player in a Broadway company greatly outshone that of being merely one act on a bill. Even the greatest vaudeville headliners spent only twenty minutes on the stage. Starring in a Broadway musical meant three hours before the public. Vaudevillians often were desperate for relief from the ennui of doing the same act some six hundred times a year.

On New Year's Eve, 1904, the tour of *The Fortune Teller* ended in St. Catherine's, Ontario. As her daughter slept, Jennie opened Elsie's diary and read that night's entry. Jennie was governor of both the public and private Elsie. In the first minutes of 1905 Jennie wrote on that diary's final page,

> And thus, dear girl, another year is ended! Would that I could always be more and more each year to you! Don't forget that Mother it was who first gave you thought and Mother it was who first taught you how to use that thought. As you grow older, you will find much that does not please you. When such times come, when you think you know more than I do, just say to yourself, "Well! If I do know more, after all, it was Mother who did most to help me!" Please, dear, Do study and elevate your thoughts and actions. I'm not much help! I'm so anxious, worried, nervous and not always reasonable, but I love you! May God's choicest blessings be yours every year. Mother.[10]

The ability of children under the age of sixteen to perform in New York was controlled by the Gerry Society—the Society for the Prevention of Cruelty to Children—headed by Commodore Elbridge T. Gerry. Jennie's efforts to arrange performances for Elsie in New York had been of limited success. Children could "recite" (thus allowing them to perform in plays) but could not sing or dance. Jennie continually tried to circumvent these strictures by scanning the audience to spot a Gerry employee and then signal Elsie how far away from mere recitation she could go.

Jennie's luck was never perfect, and she was often dragged into court on child endangerment charges. At one trial, Elsie de Wolfe presented herself as a character witness. After Jennie's acquittal, de Wolfe and Elisabeth Marbury hosted an "acquittal party," which was attended by Thomas Edison.

Elsie finally made her Broadway debut at age sixteen in *The Vanderbilt Cup*. Although Elsie had toured in vaudeville for ten years and had had her few fleeting performances in New York, she was not well known, and her performance in *The Vanderbilt Cup* captured New York's fancy. It was a colossal hit. With the average Broadway actor earning forty dollars a week, Elsie's one thousand dollars a week made her the highest-paid sixteen-year-old in the country.

The Vanderbilt Cup was one of 115 shows to open on Broadway that season. Joining it in competition for the audience were such shows as George M. Cohan's *Forty-Five Minutes from Broadway* and *George Washington, Jr.* Patrons seeking light, nonmusical entertainment could see J. M. Barrie's *Peter Pan*, starring Maude Adams or David Belasco's *The Girl of the Golden West* (made into an opera four years later by Giacomo Puccini). Those looking for more intellectually stimulating material could find it in George Bernard Shaw's *Man and Superman*.

Broadway theater managers worked to make attending a show a pleasant experience. Box offices now accepted mail orders, doormen and ushers wore evening dress, and newspaper advertisements were de rigueur. Counterweighted lines and electrical lighting made scenic effects such as those featured in *The Vanderbilt Cup* possible. The same electricity lighted the theater lobby, auditorium, and "retiring" rooms.

Broadway's newest star was eagerly sought for interviews. Jennie always sat in. One writer noted that Jennie would have made a "capital actress, for she has the plastic countenance, the mobility of expression, which is necessary to perfect dissimulation." Her determination to capitalize on free publicity was combined with loquaciousness: "If Elsie ran short on conversation, her mother ran long. She can tell you more about Elsie in twenty minutes than you would believe it possible for Elsie to have lived in twenty years."[11]

Stage mothers are a show business institution. To put their children on the stage, most had burned their bridges and could go only forward. They were ferociously protective and fiercely demanding of their child, and all of their energies were directed toward the child's career. Jennie was an obvious example. Buster Keaton, who had himself been put on stage by his parents, observed about Jennie,

I have seen stage mothers who were furious, hysterical, given to
lioness-like rages and ear-bending tantrums, but never another like
Mrs. Bierbower for do-or-die energy in putting a daughter over.
Even then, when Elsie Janis sang on the stage, Mrs. Bierbower,
watching from the wings with a hypnotized look on her face, sang
every note with her as though transported.[12]

One day, Jennie was not present when Elsie was interviewed by Forrest Arden of the *Chicago Examiner*. Elsie, for once unchaperoned,
stated,

Now, to tell the truth, when I say I want to be something more than I
am, take it that somebody's lied to you. It's mother who takes me
wherever I go. As for me, I'd rather sit about and be happy without
having to work too hard. But Mamma Svengali—that's what I name
her—rings the call bell and I have to respond.[13]

However, the balance of power in their relationship was in continual
flux, as each depended upon the other for success. To the partnership
Elsie gave her talent. That talent earned the money. In return, Jennie gave
her own very real talents for negotiation and management. While Jennie
negotiated all the contracts and arrangements, Elsie could focus chiefly
on performing and playing. To the public, Elsie was one of the most
unaffected, disarming, genuine performers on the stage; it was Jennie
who came across as the pushy, demanding one. Her conversations with
managers, producers, and reporters were peppered with phrases such as
"Elsie wants," "Elsie needs," and "Elsie feels." Eileen Lamb, Elsie's longtime maid and housekeeper, remembered an incident that revealed the
backstage dynamics of the partnership. Elsie and Jennie arrived at the
theater to be told that the star dressing room had mistakenly been given
to another performer. With the theater manager, Elsie was all smiles, but
under her breath she hissed to Jennie: "Get me that dressing room or I
won't go on." This threat was always her trump card with her mother.
Likewise, if Elsie expressed the thought that a house in the country would
be swell, Jennie had one bought and furnished before the week's end. Yet,
others of "Elsie's demands" originated with Jennie. It was Jennie who
decided what salary or billing to ask for, often without telling Elsie what
she had demanded in her name.[14] But mother and daughter both understood that each received more from the partnership than either could
have realized alone. Without Elsie, Jennie would have no means of support. Without Jennie, Elsie would have no career.

Elsie's career was founded in the school of Personality. People came to see Elsie Janis, not a great feat of Barrymore acting, not a great afternoon of Caruso singing. At this point in her career, she could sleep late, drive her new car (with chauffeur sitting beside her), play her matinee, nap, do the evening performance, dine fashionably late at the most fashionable restaurant, and entertain friends until dawn. Elsie's crowd-pleasing talents and her open, winning personality gave her the freedom to conduct her life as she pleased, as long as she stayed free of scandal.

Jennie was an ever-vigilant chaperon. She refused to allow Elsie to meet anyone who could not be introduced by a close friend or a member of the family. For all Jennie's precautions, Elsie, now lionized by the press, was constantly linked romantically with every man seen with her.

For Elsie and Jennie, career and life were as twisted as a double helix. Their mutual dependence forged them into a powerful, independent, female force in the male-dominated theater industry. This unconventional female strength and assertiveness found expression in the gender-ambivalent stage personae that became Elsie's stock-in-trade. The Broadway musicals and touring opportunities that Jennie arranged for Elsie in 1907–13 capitalized on her emerging "unfeminine" personality.

One vehicle was *The Hoyden,* a French play, the rights to which had been bought simply because of its name: "Hoyden? Tom-boy? Perfect for Elsie Janis!"[15] Producers and playwrights were learning to capitalize on Elsie's own nature. For *The Fair Co-Ed,* the renowned newspaper humorist George Ade was hired to write the book. The coed of the title was Cynthia Bright, the only girl student in the until now all-male Bingham College. At a school dance she dresses as a cadet from a nearby military academy, attracting all the Bingham students' girlfriends. After many complications, songs, dances, and, of course, interpolated imitations, Cynthia got her man.

In 1914, Elsie, the star of four extremely successful Broadway musicals and countless SRO tours in vaudeville, sailed for Europe to make her London debut—*The Passing Show of 1914*—in which she would sing three songs, perform in a series of sketches, and do her imitations. One of the songs, "Florrie Was a Flapper," was meant to be performed by Elsie as Florrie.[16] A few days into rehearsal, Elsie announced her intention to perform "Florrie Was a Flapper" in full *male* evening dress, playing a man commenting upon a girl he had known. Male impersonation was an extremely popular tradition in British music hall, descending from the "principal boy" in British pantomime. The most successful male impersonators in American vaudeville were British—Vesta Tilley, Ella Shields, and Cissie Loftus. Now, a confident young American was challenging the British, in

London, in a field they considered theirs. Elsie had certainly performed in drag on stage (e.g., *The Fair Co-Ed*), but until this time she had done her vaudeville impersonations of men in her usual female stage dress. The risky choice proved a remarkable success in London. The *Times* reported that "Miss Janis's success is instantaneous. . . . She has a quaint individuality of her own which quickly established her as a London favourite last night."[17] Night after night Elsie would be greeted at the stage door of the Palace by well-wishers who mobbed her car and, refusing to let her chauffeur drive, insisted on pushing the car in a triumphant procession to her hotel.

One evening, from out of the stage-door crowd came a low female voice calling, "Ah! Mlle. Janis. Vous étiez épatante aujourd'hui!" Thinking the girl was French, Elsie answered back in that language. The stranger ran up to the car, "Au revoir, Mlle. Janis!" "Why not ask her to come in for a cup of tea in your dressing-room?" Jennie suggested. Elsie called to the girl. She ran across the street, dodging a bus and was invited to come backstage after the upcoming Saturday matinee. When she returned Saturday, Eva Le Gallienne walked into the Janis's life.[18]

Le Gallienne felt that Elsie's performance in *The Passing Show* was "never-to-be-forgotten," and she wrote, "All London went mad over this fascinating and bewilderingly talented young American star. Her versatility, her charm, her marvelous dancing—now eccentric, now graceful— her amazing imitations took the town by storm."[19] Le Gallienne was quickly taken into the circle of friends closest to Jennie and Elsie. After the war, Elsie would repeatedly hire Le Gallienne when she was between engagements.

If Elsie contended, "I'll be a baby as long as Jennie watches over me,"[20] her twenty-eight-year adolescence ended with America's declaration of war with Germany. Jennie received permission for Elsie to become the first American woman to perform at camps outside the immediate Paris region and scheduled the tours to include a return to Paris every few days for rest. When soldiers learned that Elsie Janis was available, the Liberty Theatre Division of the War Department—the bureau in charge of entertainment for the troops—was swamped with requests. Elsie brought the essence of vaudeville: sheer entertainment, with an act that included popular songs and the newly emergent jazz. She was an oasis in the midst of visiting legislators and lecturers.

Elsie and Jennie quickly discovered that there were more troops in more places than she could ever entertain by doing only two shows a day. Hospitalized soldiers were not allowed to attend outdoor performances, so this required additional performances. Of course, once inside, there

**Elsie Janis wearing her World War I helmet,
bent in action in France**

(Collection of the author.)

were soldiers unable to be moved to a cafeteria or other central location. A passage from Elsie's diary shows how all these circumstances came together to fill the hours.

> Got up at nine, still very cold. . . . Went out to the hospital. Gave one show in the hall for about fifteen hundred men, then sang under the window for the fellows in quarantine. Went through the wards singing and telling stories. They got two hundred and sixty wounded in here before yesterday. Went to tea at officers' mess. Came home to

dinner. Went out to same hall. Gave another show to fifteen hundred, then down to the Y.M.C.A. and gave another. Home at midnight all in![21]

If such a schedule was tiring for the twenty-eight-year-old Elsie, one can only imagine the fatigue felt by the fifty-three-year-old Jennie. But even the horrible physical strain would not keep her from accompanying Elsie at every stop of the journey.

Eddie Hartman was a vaudeville critic for *Variety* when he enlisted. After one of Elsie's performances in April 1918 he sent back to the States a review of her work. As if this were a regular vaudeville performance, Hartman prefaced his review with the usual information.

Elsie Janis
Songs, Imitations, etc.
50 mins.
Full Stage
Somewhere in France, April 28 [1918]
Wherever she may go Miss Janis scores her usual knockout and from the soldiers' point of view is the biggest thing that ever came down the pike. On this specific occasion the inimitable mimic kept up a steady run of applause for one hour, interrupted only by convulsions of laughter. Miss Janis' work is one round after another of clever entertainment, so construed as to be comprehensible to the boy from the sticks as well as those from the big towns. Every one feels at home, with both general and buck private equally entertained. It is an apparently carefree Elsie that we have over here, full of the old pep so necessary and hard to keep so far from home.[22]

After hundreds of shows, Elsie knew her audience intimately, having acquired the average soldier's point of view. She knew what life in the trenches was really like and how the soldiers felt about it—because she had walked through the trenches and worn gas masks. She had seen the dangers and had witnessed her "gang" in all situations—because she had fired cannon into German-held territory. She used the slang dear to their hearts—because she had learned the ribald, "manly" words with which the soldiers addressed their enemies. Elsie understood that men who had been under fire wanted to be kidded and treated "like pals, not lauded and treated like heroes."[23] Elsie was so loved that she was given dozens of nicknames—"The Playgirl of the Western Front," "The Lady of the Smiles," and "The Sweetheart of the A.E.F."

However, Elsie's appeal to the troops was not the conventional heterosexual female/male matrix. She had never presented herself as a "sex symbol" in her career, preferring to play more in the tomboy/girl-next-door arena. Her daily "costume" while with the troops was a long dark blue skirt, white blouse, dark blue sweater, and a dark blue beret. The beginning of every performance found her sitting on the front lip of the stage and changing from her boots to shoes; she couldn't dance in boots. And when she brought soldiers from the audience up onto the stage, it was not to dance with her, but to encourage them to sing or dance solo for the enjoyment of their colleagues. Elsie appeared before these men as a beloved kid sister, not as an unattainable sex object.

By consciously unsexing herself—loose, conservative clothing, a beret covering her hair, telling "soldier" stories—Elsie kept any sexual interest the soldiers might have in her at bay. She could have presented an act that would have the men howling like wolves. Instead, she was there to make them howl with laughter—a means of maintaining both physical and emotional distance. It was this dropping of all seeming pretense that had the distinct action of camouflaging Elsie's personal life. This gal-next-door was neither female or male, simply neuter.

During the war, the relational balance between Elsie and Jennie shifted. While Jennie made all the arrangements and traveled every mile along the front with Elsie, it was Elsie who stood up on stage under the bombardment and conquered thousands of men. Her triumph over adversity and appeal to these soldiers empowered her to take more control over her career. It was a transformation noticed by many. Maurice Chevalier had known Elsie before the war. Then he had considered her "boyish."[24] After the war, when he joined Elsie in London to make his debut there with her, his feelings changed. Elsie, said Chevalier, "worked with the trained precision of a boxing champion." He came to consider Elsie "the most independent woman in show business."[25] With her increased maturity and independence, the "boy" Elsie became a "man."

After the Armistice, Elsie and Jennie returned to America to re-create their wartime entertainments, to show those who had stayed behind what had become so popular with the troops. News of Elsie's personal heroics and her unselfish performing at the front had made her a national heroine in America. Everyone now wanted to see what "their boys" had seen. An additional selling point of the show, *Elsie Janis and Her Gang,* was that the cast consisted primarily of men and women who had been overseas in the war effort. While Jennie and Elsie had always been intimately involved in the direction of their productions, now for the first time Elsie billed herself as director. Eva Le Gallienne, a cast member, remembered how Elsie conducted rehearsals.

> [Elsie would] direct in one corner of the hall a sketch, in another corner a specialty number, while in another corner she would try to initiate me into the mystery of "turns." In the meantime she would be jotting something down on a piece of paper. At the end of an hour the sketch, the specialty and the turns would be pretty well set and she would produce on the piece of paper a corking set of lyrics for the composer's latest tune. What a worker![26]

One day she stopped the chorus and roared, "Where's that fellow I told to stand on that bench?" He finally appeared from backstage.

> "Didn't I tell you to stand on that left bench?"
> He stood at attention. "Yes, sir."
> "Well, cut out the 'sir' and stay on that bench until I tell you to come down."[27]

In the second act, Le Gallienne and Elsie, dressed as a French soldier, danced a "potpourri number." It began with a fox-trot, became a tango, then a waltz, and finally ended with the then-popular Castle walk. At another point, Elsie, still dressed as the soldier, sang to four maidens (dressed to represent the Allied nations) "I Love Them All a Little Bit." What today would be camp and more than tinged with lesbian overtones was then thought by Alexander Woollcott to be a great moment "not to be forgotten in a year of theatre-going"[28]

By the midtwenties the popularity of Elsie's "gang" shows had run its course and her career stagnated. She headed the Los Angeles production of Gershwin's *Oh, Kay!*—a rare performance without interpolated imitations—but she dropped out of the show after a few months, citing "fatigue."[29] She made her Paris debut, in French, in a revue that featured a scene set on the Isle of Lesbos. Elsie did not appear in this scene, perhaps because she feared it was too risqué and would jeopardize her reputation for providing "clean entertainment." In the final number, however, Elsie did, as was now her custom, appear in male dress.

Realizing that because of her age and changing audience tastes she could no longer sustain a viable stage career, Elsie announced her retirement from performing in 1928. She settled in Beverly Hills and channeled her talents and ambitions primarily into the even more masculine-identified enterprises of writing, directing, and producing for stage and screen. She wrote music and lyrics, scripts and dialogue and, with *Paramount on Parade*, became the first woman to produce a talking picture.

**Elsie Janis as World War I soldier in one of her
"Gang" shows**

(Collection of the author.)

In late June 1930, she directed the musical numbers for Cecil B. DeMille's first musical, *Madam Satan.*

This new career path, however, was soon interrupted by Jenny's death from pneumonia in mid-July 1930. During the days that followed Jennie's funeral, Elsie began to sort through Jennie's belongings and discovered a sealed envelope containing a letter written seven months earlier on New Year's Eve.

> We have lived fifty-fifty and I leave content if you will just carry on and not grieve. I shall always be near you. I know we could not have lived as we have and not still be close to each other. Don't get hard. Love and give as we have always done. Don't weaken. You will have hard times. God tries our fortitude to make us see Him and know Him better. Right or wrong, He will be near you as I will. You should be a rich woman, dear, but we have lived without thought of riches and if you will try to be happy, I'll carry on Somewhere, Somehow! My prayers, my love and all I have is yours, Mother.[30]

Even after death, Jennie continued to be a major determinant of her daughter's life course, whether Elsie lived in concert with her mother's desires or in reaction against them. In her 1932 autobiography, *So Far, So Good,* Elsie wrote of the announcement she made after the funeral,

> I have made the decision not to marry . . . and that is only a continuation of a resolve that I made while [my mother] was alive. And now that she is gone, I do not believe that conditions are changed greatly . . . and I believe that my work will give me all the companionship that I want.[31]

Elsewhere in the autobiography, however, Elsie contradicted this credo. When published, the text began, with "For the first time in my life I have lost my sense of humor over a man!" and concluded,

> I have fallen in love with one young enough to be my son had I been as precocious in the home as in the theatre. I know that it couldn't last. I know that the joy thereof will be overbalanced by the misery, but if I am at last to marry, I don't see why I should not have the experience I would have had at seventeen with someone young and not over-experienced.

On December 31, 1931, Elsie married Gilbert Wilson. At Elsie's specific request, the "obey" clause was omitted from their vows. Wilson, sixteen years Elsie's junior, had been born in Chicago and played semi-professional football there before moving to Los Angeles hoping for a motion-picture career. When the marriage was announced, the reporters' first questions, naturally, dealt with the difference in their ages. Wilson responded, "If Mrs. Wilson were not a famous woman no one would ever guess it. I'm a lot older than she is in many ways. We do not feel there is a year's difference in our ages." Elsie's answer was more revealing.

> This being my debut on the stage of matrimony some may wonder why I took a husband 16 years younger than myself. Well, I've never had a child. Now I have a husband and he can be my child, too. . . . and I don't see why I should start in the great gamble with someone of my own age who knows all about it when I am an absolute beginner. Anyway, we are happy for the moment and sufficient unto the day is the joy thereof.[32]

Elsie also mentioned that Wilson filled the "great companionship need" that had been a part of her life since the death of Jennie.

Because of Elsie's gender-ambivalent persona and the fact that her primary emotional relationships had always been with other women, chiefly her mother, Elsie's friends were as confused as the public about this life choice. Rather than a conventional marriage, however, this union represented a complex response to Jennie's stifling influence over Elsie's life. The marriage expressly reversed the power dynamics of the mother-child relationship, placing Elsie in the dominant role. Although with far less success than Jennie, Elsie even tried to mold her "child's" career by arranging screen tests for him at Paramount and MGM. In Wilson, Elsie embraced the husband and son Jennie had rejected to devote herself to her daughter's career.

Besides these relational dynamics, there is some evidence to suggest that the marriage served as a "beard" enabling both partners to participate in the same-sex subculture of Hollywood. In 1934 Elsie was asked by Leonard Sillman to serve as production supervisor for a new revue featuring a cast of unknowns. Elsie was to provide her expertise as a variety artist, but also to help raise funds from her Hollywood friends. *The New Faces of 1934* introduced to New York audiences Imogene Coca and Henry Fonda. Also in the cast was Nancy Hamilton, Katharine Cornell's lesbian companion.[33] Elsie attended parties at which same-sex desire was not masked. At one such party she arrived, dressed in men's clothes, carrying a riding crop, and accompanied by Marilyn Miller, a major Broadway star.[34] Elsie's husband, also in New York at the time, had originally been cast in *New Faces* as a condition of Elsie's participation. She was forced to fire him two weeks before opening. He landed a spot in the chorus of Noël Coward's *Set to Music* and after that often accompanied Coward to parties.

Life had been simple while Jennie was alive. Elsie did not have to think about her career or her life. She certainly did not have to think about dating or sex. Now, on her own, Elsie bounced from job to job, from point to point on the social compass. It is not difficult to see why Elsie tried on so many different personae. After all, she was an impersonator and was probably more comfortable being anyone but her own self. It is not surprising that Elsie eventually chose nothingness: living in sexless seclusion with her housekeeper and chauffeur.

If Elsie attempted to forge new personal and professional relationships in Hollywood, her mother's memory continued to intercede. One day Elsie came into rehearsal announcing that she had the perfect opening for the show. She said she had a long talk with Jennie, and Jennie suggested beginning the show in heaven with angels looking down on the young performers. Jennie remained such a part of Elsie's life that at all script conferences Elsie always set an extra chair in the circle for her. At one point Elsie freely admitted that her life was not perfectly normal by anyone's standards. "All my life things have happened to me that made people talk—I know they say I am goofy now. Well, let me tell you, it's a very comfortable goofiness."[35]

Having been intimately involved with a show rekindled in Elsie a desire to perform. In December, Elsie was introduced in a special program as the first woman staff announcer on NBC radio. Once Elsie was allowed to read news bulletins, but listeners complained that a woman's voice was inappropriate for such serious matter. Staff announcers had to operate the switchboard that controlled on-the-air programs, check copyright credits on songs, and write department reports on various programs. Worst of all for Elsie, staff announcers were expected to remain anonymous. Within weeks Elsie left. Her only means of employment was performing, yet she was unwilling to work as anything less than a star.

A year later, on July 5, 1936, the *Tarrytown (New York) News* published a letter addressed to "My dear Boss." Following a car accident, Elsie said that she had experienced a kind of religious conversion or reawakening and had gotten the "orders" for which she had been waiting: she was auctioning everything "except the talent, personality, pep, or whatever it was that put me in the money as Little Elsie and kept me there for 30 years."[36] Elsie had come to think of God in military terms—a commander in chief issuing his inexorable orders from HQ. Divine inspiration started Elsie on a plan to devote the remainder of her life to charity. It is hard not to read into this conversion the simple idea that Elsie was merely replacing Jennie's missing guidance with that of another omnipotent being. Elsie told friends she would not have been spared if God had not had some purpose in mind. Therefore, she was devoting the rest of her life to helping other people and "making people happy."

For the next several years, Elsie worked intermittently as a Hollywood writer and attempted to return as a performer on stage and screen without lasting success. These efforts included a stint with old friend Eva Le Gallienne in *Frank Fay's Vaudeville*. Elsie's imitations served as the draw in the first act, Le Gallienne's balcony scene from *Romeo and Juliet* was the second-half draw, the "class" act. The bill also featured Smith and Dale with their "Dr. Kronkheit" sketch, a high-wire walker, and one "Maxine de Shone," a striptease artiste. The show was well received, but the audiences were small. Fay prevailed upon Elsie and Le Gallienne to accept less than their full salaries to keep the show going. The second week they got half salary, a token salary the third, and nothing for the next four weeks. The women laughed over the situation, wondering whose bank account could endure the longest. Fay wanted to tour the show, and it took solemnly delivered promises to convince Elsie and Le Gallienne to continue. After two weeks in Boston with only small cash gifts to the stars, *Frank Fay's Vaudeville* closed.

On April 19, 1941, just over a month past Elsie's fifty-second birthday, Gilbert Wilson enlisted in the United States Army. Elsie recognized the irony of the situation by saying that "having sent everybody else's husband into the 1st war, it is the least I can do to have my own go into the Army."[37] Wilson would be gone for over five years—six months and the duration. For a while after Wilson's return he and Elsie attempted to continue their life together. Elsie was fifty-two and Wilson thirty-six—she had reverted to her "old maid" habits and "snuggled back into my old groove."[38] They separated but never divorced. He never remarried.

During this war Elsie traveled every day—driven by Frank Reme, her World War I army chauffeur—to the Veterans Hospital at Sawtelle, California, where she would read to the soldiers, help them to write letters, or, especially for those veterans of World War I, tell a few jokes or even sing a song. Several times, for the benefit of the war effort, Elsie gave public performances. She appeared as a special guest on Dinah Shore's radio program—the sweetheart of the "war to end all wars" alongside one of her successors. In April 1942, Elsie joined Bob Hope and Jerry Colonna to perform before four thousand soldiers at the Long Beach,

California, naval base. Elsie Janis was singing songs for the sons of fighting fathers.

On August 16, 1949, Elsie gave her final performance. That day marked Ethel Barrymore's seventieth birthday, and ABC radio had prepared a nationwide tribute to the actress. Among those offering congratulations were Lionel and John Barrymore, the Lunts, Spencer Tracy, Cary Grant, Eleanor Roosevelt, and Presidents Truman and Hoover. Elsie contributed an imitation of the honoree.

Elsie's remaining years until her death from cancer in 1956 were spent in quiet routine. She would visit the VA hospital, spend an hour daily praying in the All Saints Episcopal Church in Beverly Hills, entertain a few friends, and write in her diary. She lived in virtual seclusion, shunning publicity, and hoped that her death would receive as little notice as her life had in recent years. However, although Elsie had not performed in decades and her career's peak was forty years past, the *New York Times* paid her due tribute on the front page. Newspapers in London and Paris also gave wide coverage to her death, which occurred just nineteen days short of her sixty-seventh birthday. She had an amazing career, touching all the forms of popular entertainment of her time, save circuses and Wild West shows. Her life had taken her all over the world and, during World War I, she had become one of the most famous women in the world. Her lasting legacy has proven not to be in her own shows, or songs or books, but in those women who followed the paths blazed by Elsie. Some women—Eva Le Gallienne and Nancy Hamilton, especially—knew firsthand of her pioneering work and followed in her path as directors and producers.

Elsie left specific instructions that the funeral be as "private and unostentatious as possible," that only close friends attend, that there be no eulogy and "No flowers! This by special request, as I hate seeing them wilted and I would like folks to send the money they would cost to some charity."[39] On Thursday, March 1 at 2:30 in the afternoon, Elsie's casket was interred in a crypt just above Jennie's in the Forest Lawn Mausoleum. The Daughters of the American Revolution later placed a plaque upon Elsie's crypt. It reads, "ELSIE JANIS, 1889–1956, 'Sweetheart of the A.E.F.' "

NOTES

1. *Los Angeles Times,* February 28, 1956, 1.
2. Elsie Janis, *So Far, So Good!* (New York: Dutton, 1932), 11.

3. "All Unconscious of the Gaze of Admiring Spectators Was This Little Danseuse," *Columbus Press-Post,* n.p., Elsie Janis Scrapbook, 1:5. The scrapbooks, hereafter cited as EJS, followed by volume and page numbers, are in the author's possession. Kept by Jennie, the volumes are numbered sequentially and cover the years 1894–1900 (vol. 1), 1901–4 (vol. 2), 1905–6 (vol. 3), 1907–11 (vol. 4), 1912–17 (vol. 5), 1918–19 (vol. 6), 1919–20 (vol. 7), and 1920–27 (vol. 8). As the clippings are closely cropped, many are difficult to identify, especially dates and page numbers.

4. Janis, *So Far, So Good!* 16.

5. Lida Rose McCabe, "Imitator of Imitators Before Footlights," unidentified newspaper (1900?), n.p., EJS 2:49.

6. " 'Little Elsie'—The Protegee of the President," unidentified newspaper (1901?), 12, EJS 1:74.

7. Jennie would soon follow suit in finding a more "adult" name—"Little Elsie" becoming "Elsie Janis," a surname derived from Elsie's middle name, Jane.

8. Unidentified newspaper (November 1899?), n.p., EJS 2:8; "Mother's Aid Means Much," unidentified newspaper (August 1926?), n.p., EJS 8:9.

9. Review of *The Little Duchess* by Reginald De Koven and Harry B. Smith, unidentified Toronto newspaper (1905?), n.p., EJS 3:62.

10. Janis, *So Far, So Good!* 35.

11. Charles N. Young, "Elsie Janis Finds Every Minute of Life Interesting," *Boston Traveler,* February 29, 1908, n.p., EJS 3:94.

12. Buster Keaton with Charles Samuels, *My Wonderful World of Slapstick* (New York: Doubleday, 1960), 15.

13. Forrest Arden, "Wee Elsie Janis Mutinies; Wants to Discard Trousers," *Chicago Examiner,* January 17, 1909, n.p., EJS 3:94.

14. Eileen Lamb, interview by the author, March 24–26, 1981.

15. "Miss Elsie Janis the 18 Year Old Star Says She Is Abundantly Satisfied with Her Quick Success in Musical Comedy and Never Intends to Inflict Upon the Public Another Juliet," *New York Herald,* January 21, 1906, 14.

16. The first incarnation of the "flapper" character on stage.

17. Review of *The Passing Show of 1914* by Herman Finck and Arthur Wimperis, *London Times,* April 21, 1914, 4b.

18. Eva Le Gallienne, *At 33* (New York: Longmans, Green, 1934), 91–93.

19. Le Gallienne, *At 33,* 91–93.

20. "Child Players Who Made Good," unidentified newspaper (April 1909?), n.p., EJS 4:48.

21. Janis, *So Far, So Good!* 188.

22. Eddie Hartman, review of Elsie Janis, *Variety,* April 28, 1918, n.p., EJS 6:21.

23. N. B. Myran, "Elsie Bids Adieu to France," *Over Here,* September 4, 1918, 81+, EJS 6:17.

24. Maurice Chevalier, *The Man in the Straw Hat* (New York: Crowell, 1949), 159.

25. Gene Ringgold and DeWitt Bodeen, *Chevalier: The Films and Career of Maurice Chevalier* (Secaucus, NJ: Citadel, 1973), 22.

26. Eva Le Gallienne, *With a Quiet Heart* (New York: Viking, 1953), 137–38.

27. "Versatility Her Forte," *Baltimore Sun*, November 10, 1919, n.p., EJS 7:4.

28. Alexander Woollcott, review of *Elsie Janis and Her Gang, New York Times*, December 2, 1919, n.p., EJS 7:16.

29. The cause of her fatigue was the much better reviews Elsie's understudy received when Elsie was forced to miss several performances due to vocal distress.

30. Janis, *So Far, So Good!* 342.

31. Ibid., 343.

32. *New York Times*, January 14, 1932, 23.

33. Hamilton and Elsie had known each other for years, as Hamilton had been the Smith College roommate of Elsie's cousin, Mary Loren Jeffrey. It had been Elsie who suggested Hamilton to Sillman.

34. Richard Hecht, interview by the author, July 22, 1983.

35. Unidentified newspaper, n.d., n.p., Clippings File, Billy Rose Theatre Collection, New York Public Library for the Performing Arts.

36. Elsie Janis, letter to the editor, *Tarrytown (New York) News*, July 5, 1936, n.p., Clippings File, Billy Rose Theatre Collection, New York Public Library for the Performing Arts.

37. *New York Times*, April 19, 1941, 8.

38. Unidentified newspaper (1949?), n.p., Clippings File, Billy Rose Theatre Collection, New York Public Library for the Performing Arts.

39. Elsie Janis, Last Will and Testament, 1955, Record Department, Los Angeles County Surrogate Court.

Managing Homophobia

Staging Heterosexuality

Alfred Lunt and Lynn Fontanne's Design for Living

Sam Abel

The husband-and-wife acting team of Alfred Lunt (1892–1977) and Lynn Fontanne (1887–1983) dominated the serious Broadway theater for the central decades of the twentieth century. From their first success as a couple in *The Guardsman* in 1924 through their 1958 production of *The Visit* their marriage was hailed as the ideal union of life and art. To the adoring critics, Lunt and Fontanne's onstage rapport reflected the offstage harmony of their marriage. Publicly, and with enthusiastic help from the press, the names Lunt and Fontanne became synonymous with artistic achievement, personal integrity, and the nobility of the acting profession. While other actors gave in to the lure of Hollywood and became the objects of public scandal, the Lunts, through their marriage on and off stage, symbolized moral purity and selfless devotion to serious theater.

But if the Lunts appeared in public as the perfect married couple, their private lives did not correspond to this idealized portrait. While Lunt and Fontanne were discreet about their lives offstage, clearly they were not an average married couple. They socialized with New York's large gay clique; both were rumored to have engaged in same-sex affairs, and some of their contemporaries have begun to confirm these rumors.[1] They were notoriously difficult people who squabbled frequently; Lunt was prone to bouts of depression.[2] He cooked; she did not. They had no children, but they virtually adopted the closeted Montgomery Clift. They played husband and wife onstage, but often in plays that disrupted normative views of heterosexuality, most notably *Design for Living,* written by Noël Coward for himself and the Lunts. Despite these deviations from heterosexual norms, however, the public belief in the sanctified image of their marriage remained intact.

According to current definitions and the available information, Alfred

Lunt and Lynn Fontanne would probably be described most accurately as bisexual. But the central issue is not whether Lunt and Fontanne were "really" gay or bisexual, or whether they engaged in specific same-sex acts. To frame the issue this way would, as recent analysis has argued, essentialize a notion of gay identity and oversimplify both the shifting social constructions of same-sex desire in the twentieth century and the Lunts' own perception of their sexual identity.[3] The more important question is why, in the eyes of the public, such a clearly nonnormative pair as the Lunts had to appear, at all costs, perfectly straight. The Lunts created their mystique of heterosexuality against the background of New York's gay subculture, both in their private lives and their stage performances. Early in their careers, in the relatively open atmosphere of gay life in New York, the Lunts evoked both "normal" and "deviant" sexuality to further their popularity. After 1930, as George Chauncey documents in *Gay New York,* gay life in the city shifted from comparative openness to intense repression, a move reflected in the Lunts' choice of roles and in their publicity. The Lunts initially used their marriage to further their careers; later, their union protected them from the public's increasing hostility to gay sexuality.

Lynn Fontanne settled in New York in 1916 at age twenty-nine; Alfred Lunt, five years her junior, arrived in 1919 at age twenty-seven. Fontanne, British by birth, began her professional career at age eighteen, and until 1915 she played small roles in London and on tour through England. In 1916 the actress-playwright couple Laurette Taylor and Hartley Manners invited her to join their company in the United States. As London during World War I offered little opportunity, she accepted and moved to New York. Interestingly, Fontanne was engaged to be married when she emigrated. The Lunts' biographer Jared Brown questions Fontanne's seriousness about the engagement, since she left her fiancé behind to pursue her career with little intention of returning.[4] (Or perhaps she left England to avoid the marriage; the issue became moot soon after, when he was killed in the war.) Fontanne remained with Taylor and Manners until 1917, when she left the company to take a leading role in a Shubert production. Lunt's professional career began in Boston in 1912 while he was a student at Emerson College. Between 1915 and 1919 he acted with a number of touring companies, including a few brief stints in New York; in 1919 he was offered the title role in Booth Tarkington's *Clarence,* and the play's success established his Broadway career. Lunt and Fontanne met in 1919; according to their biographers, they fell immediately in love, though Brown says that Laurette Taylor "stage-managed the romance."⁵ They were married in 1922, shortly after both had returned to New York from playing on the road.

Lunt and Fontanne, then, established their careers playing mainly in popular works of minimal literary pretension. Both actors came to New York with a strong desire to perform in more sophisticated drama. Fontanne had learned the classics in London, and her first encouragements in acting came from no less a personage than Ellen Terry; Lunt received a strong classical theater training in college, had traveled to Europe, and had performed in Greek tragedies in one of his early professional tours. Once they had made a name for themselves on Broadway, they worked actively to claim the title of New York's serious acting family. From 1924 to 1932, early in their careers, they associated themselves with the Theatre Guild and its reputation for drama of artistic merit; they chose for their vehicles plays either by European authors (Molnár, Shaw, Chekhov, Shakespeare, Werfel, Giraudoux, Coward, and Dürrenmatt all figured prominently), or "art" plays by American playwrights.

But before they could become the leading actors of serious drama in New York, Lunt and Fontanne had to contend with the performers who already had solid claim to the title: Broadway's "royal family," the Barrymores. The stage performances of John, Ethel, and Lionel Barrymore in the first quarter of the century offered a rare taste of serious theater for New York audiences. Their private lives offered another, equally interesting public entertainment: Ethel Barrymore's contentious marriage, and her divorce in 1923; John Barrymore's obsessive love affairs, drunkenness, and periodic breakdowns; the family's notorious egos, their wealth, and the eventual departure of the whole clan to Hollywood (all satirized by George S. Kaufman and Edna Ferber in 1927 in *The Royal Family*). Broadway audiences loved the Barrymores but loved even more to gossip about their troubled lives. Lunt and Fontanne, in setting themselves up as rivals to the Barrymores, aspired to the opposite image: a stable, happily married pair, modest in their lifestyle and retiring in their personal habits, devoted selflessly to each other and to the theater, shunning Hollywood and scandal in the service of their art. They succeeded brilliantly, and by the thirties the Lunts, not the Barrymores, were the first family of Broadway.

The Lunts' goal to claim the position of Broadway's serious acting family was abetted considerably by the shift in American playwriting that coincided with their arrival in New York. Brooks Atkinson has characterized the New York theater of the 1920s as the first time Broadway consistently offered "Theater for Adults."[6] Broadway in the teens had banked heavily on the tomfoolery of the Jerome Kern–Guy Bolton–P. G. Wodehouse Princess musicals, the lavish display of the *Ziegfeld Follies*, and the comforting domesticities offered by playwrights such as Manners, Avery Hopwood, and Owen Davis. As Kim Marra mentions in her essay on Elisabeth Marbury and Elsie de Wolfe in this volume, the Princess musicals made considerable advances in the form of the American musical comedy. Their subject matter, though, stuck firmly to romance and light-hearted intrigue, and rarely broached subjects that the audience might find troubling or controversial. But in the 1920s the parameters of Broadway theater were expanded by the alumni of George Pierce Baker's 47 Workshop—Eugene O'Neill, Sidney Howard, S. N. Behrman, Philip Barry—along with contemporaries Elmer Rice, Maxwell Anderson, George Kelly, George S. Kaufman, and Marc Connelly. Prompted by the success of the Little Theatre movement, which saw the founding of the Provincetown Players (1914), Washington Square Players (1915), and *Theatre Arts Magazine* (1916), dramatists in the 1920s began to incorporate Freudian psychology and its underlying sexual tensions in their plays. Most notable of these experiments was O'Neill's *Strange Interlude* (1928), starring Fontanne as Nina Leeds.

Broadway audiences of the twenties developed a distinctly ambivalent attitude toward this kind of sexually daring material. Audiences accepted and even encouraged images of sexual "deviance" that only a few years before would have been unthinkable. The idealized images of marriage and womanhood drawn in popular pre–World War I melodrama, and the titillating but equally idealized images presented by Ziegfeld, were replaced by the adultery and sexual obsession of *Desire under the Elms* (1924), *They Knew What They Wanted* (1924), and *Machinal* (1928) and the blatant sexual come-on of Mae West. Yet when West tried to bring her sexually explicit plays to Broadway—in particular her gay-themed *The Drag* in 1927—the theater was shut down and she and her cast arrested. Broadway audiences wanted to see sexual "deviance," but the limits of toleration for such experiments were both very real and largely unpredictable, and it was hard to know in advance when a production might be deemed to have gone too far.

Broadway's response to sexually daring material strongly parallels the same public's response to overt displays of homosexuality. The New York public was fascinated in the twenties by sexual abnormality, especially homosexuality. Greenwich Village and the Upper West Side harbored active and visible gay communities, including many men who wore drag in public; a gay subculture also flourished in Harlem. Straight couples flocked to drag balls or traveled to gay haunts to watch the passing show. But as with the same public's attitude toward racial difference, the fascination with public displays of sexual "deviance" did not always translate into tolerance. It was fashionable for wealthy people to go slumming in Harlem or to attend drag balls, but not to live in a slum or to be gay themselves. Police still raided gay establishments, newspapers printed the names of those who were arrested, and many lives and careers were still ruined as a result of the ensuing scandal.

In order for the Lunts to fulfill their dream of dominating the serious Broadway theater, they had to maintain their pristine public image. Even more than avoiding the heterosexual peccadilloes of the Barrymores, it was imperative that they steer clear of same-sex scandal, which could lead to arrest and an abrupt halt to their careers. They could, and did, perform in plays that explored the edges of sexual propriety, but they had at all costs to keep these stage roles distinct from their private lives. The task was not always easy. Even though the Lunts did their best to craft their image as Broadway's happy couple, during the twenties and thirties gossip about their private lives perpetually threatened to draw them into scandal. They maintained an intense discretion about their sexual lives (they left few traces of their sexual activity, with each other or anyone else, even in personal letters), yet rumors of same-sex affairs hovered persistently about them. Broadway gossips said that they had a marriage of convenience and that they carried on same-sex affairs in private. Rather than mentioning the Lunts by name, however, scandal mongers published statements such as the following item from 1933, a clear reference to the Lunts that appeared in the tabloid *Brevities* under the headline "Stage Stars in Queer Action":

> It's a great old world and it takes all kinds of people to make the wheels go round. This little fact concerns two of the greatest stars of the legitimate theatre and who are supposed to be happily married. The pair, however, are as queer as a couple of bugs. He is a pansy who is conducting an affair with his male secretary, while she is a lesbian and has several girls acting as her lovers. Cute, eh?[7]

But these rumors never blossomed into scandal. The mainstream press rarely mentioned the rumors, and the two early adulatory biographies of the Lunts do not acknowledge them.[8]

Jared Brown's exhaustive, though equally adulatory, biography, published after their deaths, does discuss the rumors, but only to deny them fervently. Brown's denial, however, raises more questions than it answers. He says, late in the book and after asserting the happiness of the Lunts' marriage,

> Rumors were rife: their union had begun as a "marriage of convenience," they were said to argue furiously in private; they never shared the same bed; Lunt engaged in homosexual relationships; they saw as little as possible of each other offstage. If any of these rumors had been remotely true, however, some confirmation would surely have been found; they were married for fifty-five years— ample time for the dark underside of their marriage to be seen by *some*one, at *some* time, *some*where.[9]

Brown acknowledges that the Lunts quarreled occasionally and insists that they slept in the same bed. He then softens his denial, saying that if Lunt had gay affairs, no one he interviewed could confirm the rumors. (He does not entertain the possibility that no one he spoke to was willing to confirm them, as some recent interviewees have done). He quotes one company member.

> If Lunt was homosexual, I must have been very unattractive, because he never made a pass at me. And there would have been plenty of opportunity to be surreptitious about it, to invite me out, or to do something or other to indicate that he was interested—but it never happened. And if he was having a relationship with anyone else in the company at the time, he was awfully discreet about it.[10]

Brown's evidence is hardly convincing. The fact that Lunt failed to make a pass at one unidentified actor—who presumes egotistically that Lunt would have desired him—does not support Brown's claim of unsullied heterosexuality. It is clear from all accounts that the Lunts were close, but such closeness might arise from factors other than sexual attraction, for example, a shared experience of sexual transgression. And even if they were bound by sexual attraction, that fact does not preclude other sexual interests. In fact, Brown offers a range of evidence for the "dark underside of their marriage": Lunt's erotically evocative letters to a male friend, Fontanne's close association with Laurette Taylor, the couple's intimacy with Noël Coward, their quarrels. And while Brown's biography is exhaustive, it omits or downplays information that corroborates rumors of same-sex interest. If rumor mongers were intent on showing the Lunts as desiring the same sex, Brown is equally invested in proving their heterosexuality.

For example, Brown mentions, but does not discuss, evidence suggesting that the Lunts considered their marriage as a means of self-promotion. Brown quotes Coward, who recalls a time when he, Lunt, and Fontanne, all single and largely unknown, plotted their careers: "Lynn and Alfred were to be married. That was the first plan. Then they were to become definitely idols of the public. That was the second plan. Then, all this being successfully accomplished, they were to act exclusively together. This was the third plan."[11] In other words, the Lunts' marriage was a career move, and Coward their facilitator. This story does not preclude their fondness for each other, but it suggests that the Lunts' marriage in 1922 had been inspired not by starry-eyed romance, as the biographers claim, but from career concerns, and largely for public show.[12] The Lunts made heterosexuality into a performance, perhaps the most successful one of their careers.

When Lunt and Fontanne moved to New York, the city had an active and visible gay community. Chauncey documents that homosexuality was a largely accepted part of city life from the 1890s through the 1920s and a central element of New York's bohemian culture. Unlike earlier manifestations of bohemian culture in New York, this fringe culture in the early twentieth century revolved around an explicit and often public gay sexuality. In particular, during the years of Prohibition (1919–33), Chauncey identifies what he calls the "Pansy Craze," a public fascination with homosexuality in which large crowds, gay and straight, frequented gay bars, restaurants, and drag balls. Gay life in New York centered in Greenwich Village and the theater district around Times Square, where same-sex couples and men in drag were visible on the streets and in entertainment and dining establishments. The connection between the Pansy Craze and the theater world was discussed prominently in the press, especially in tabloids such as *Broadway Brevities,* which ran a series of articles in 1924 called "Nights in Fairyland," detailing gay life in the theater district and especially among theatrical personalities.[13]

Lunt and Fontanne arrived in New York at the beginning of the Pansy Craze, and their work put them in the middle of New York's bohemian gay theater scene. Brown writes that they initially lived in a "theatrical boarding house."[14] As Chauncey records, these boarding houses were central to gay life. Young gay men and women coming to the city flocked to these transient living quarters, which offered low-cost housing, privacy, and relative anonymity. While many residents of theatrical boarding houses did, in fact, work in the theater, others came to them specifically to be with other gay people.[15] Given their living arrangements and their work in the theater during the Pansy Craze, Lunt and Fontanne could hardly have avoided an active knowledge of gay life.

More importantly—despite Brown's protestations—both Lunt and Fontanne arrived in New York with intimate same-sex relationships in their immediate past. Lunt's closest friend as a boy was Ray Weaver, who boarded for three years with Lunt's mother and stepfather. Weaver shared Lunt's interest in theater, and the two boys became close. Brown quotes Weaver: "[Lunt] never dated any girls. Neither did I. . . . We were a world unto ourselves."[16] In 1914, when Lunt was twenty-two, he traveled to Europe; in his letters to Weaver he addressed his friend as "dearest boy," "honey," and "my hero of delight." Brown admits that such emotionality is uncharacteristic of Lunt's otherwise perfunctory writing style; nevertheless, he denies the erotic implications of these letters, arguing that they reveal "only an intense emotional closeness, expressed in a florid rhetorical style typical of the period."[17]

Brown's refutation is problematic on several counts. First, as Chauncey observes, the pathological model of homosexuality and its connection with "feminine" emotionality was well established by 1914; such effusiveness was not considered masculine at this time. Second, as Chauncey also argues, if such effusions do not necessarily indicate homosexuality in the modern sense, then they also cannot be used to show heterosexuality, because the two ideas are mutually dependent.[18] If the letters do not prove that Lunt was sexually attracted to Weaver, neither can they disprove it. Brown attempts to counter this "incriminating" evidence with another letter to Weaver, intended to prove that Lunt had a sexual encounter with a woman. This letter, however, further undermines Brown's argument. Lunt describes admiringly a woman he met named Anne. He then says: "It was the privilege of the young lady to teach me a good deal & this knowledge I hope some day I may impart to you."[19] If this statement suggests that Lunt had sex with Anne, then Brown fails to draw the obvious conclusion from Lunt's subsequent remark that he intended to pass this sexual knowledge on to Weaver, presumably by equivalent means.[20]

The biographers offer another suggestive story from Lunt's pre–New York days. In 1915 he was hired by director Margaret Anglin to act minor roles in a tour of Greek tragedies. In *Electra*, Anglin asked Lunt to lead a procession of revelers that would suggest decadence. Anglin told Lunt his first attempt was too wholesome. In his second attempt, as biographer Maurice Zolotow reports,

Alfred gilded his hair and his nipples, painted his fingernails and toenails red, and draped vineleaves in his hair. He got two members of the company to be his assistant deviates. He painted *their* fingers, toes, hair, and breasts. Now he came on obviously drunk and embracing two Grecian boys.

"I am sure we shall all be arrested," Miss Anglin said, laughing. "But we will do it—though it is a bit more *fin de siècle* than I had in mind, Alfred."[21]

If Lunt had not engaged in homosexual acts, the young man from Wisconsin knew enough about sexuality between men to evoke homoerotic images, and to perform them in public.

Evidence for Fontanne's early same-sex experience is more circumstantial, primarily through her relationship with Laurette Taylor while a member of her company. The Taylor-Manners marriage was, it was rumored, a business arrangement. According to Zolotow, Taylor had affairs at home with her husband's knowledge; he does not specify the gender of her lovers. As Robert A. Schanke notes in his essay on Alla Nazimova in this volume, Taylor had relationships with women, including Nazimova.[22] Zolotow reports that Fontanne and Taylor had a close and troubled relationship, that Fontanne spent weekends at Taylor's home, and that Taylor became the dominant influence in her life. He remarks, "Laurette criticized Lynn for her 'shyness' and her 'fidelity' and said that one could not blossom into a great actress without periodic bouts of great passion to vitalize one's erotic energies."[23] Zolotow, like Brown, observes that Taylor tried to stage-manage Fontanne's relationship with Lunt and then turned bitter and jealous when it became too close.[24] In 1923, the year after the Lunts were married, Taylor broke with Fontanne, and they rarely saw each other in later years.

In 1924 the Lunts appeared in their first hit together, Molnár's *The Guardsman*, cementing their identity as a married acting pair. After this production they rarely acted apart, and not at all after 1928. But while their reputation as a couple grew, in private they associated with the city's gay social scene. The Lunts' biographers cling to the story that the couple had a limited social life in New York, especially when performing. They rarely went out, Zolotow and Brown relate, avoiding parties and seeing only a few friends for quiet evenings at home. "Never invite them for dinner during the run of a play unless it is for a Sunday dinner," Zolotow warns his readers.[25] Yet they participated, as the biographers also relate, in an active social circle, which included some of New York's most prominent gay men. Their most intimate friend was Noël Coward; they spent time with him and his circle, in New York and abroad. They were also close with Carl Van Vechten, the gay photographer associated with the gay and lesbian subculture in Harlem.[26] Other regular guests, according to Brown, included Gilbert Miller, director of the lesbian-sympathetic play *The Captive,* and the critic Alexander Woollcott.

The Lunts' relationship with Woollcott presents an intriguing enigma. The Lunts were regular visitors to Woollcott's Vermont retreat, and Woollcott was a frequent guest at the Lunts' Wisconsin home. (In 1914 Lunt purchased a house in Genesee Depot, Wisconsin, near his childhood home; as the Lunts' fame grew, "the farm" became their refuge from the New York press and a place to entertain friends in private.) Woollcott was a man of ambiguous sexuality who enjoyed putting on drag and playing "Aunt Aleck" with his friends.[27] Rumors about Woollcott's sexuality were rampant; he confided with the Lunts, but they refused to reveal his secret. Zolotow quotes Lunt:

> Those stories about Aleck being cruel. . . . Well, he was a very unhappy man. . . . I think only Lynn and I knew how brave he was. And knew why he suffered. He never talked about his problems to anyone but us. Can you see how hard it is to be charming, to be amusing, when you're in so much pain?[28]

Zolotow speculates whether this pain was physical or emotional and questions Harpo Marx's explanation that Woollcott was impotent because of the measles. Whatever the cause, the Lunts were very protective of him; when, in 1939, the *New Yorker* published a profile of Woollcott that implied he was homosexual, the Lunts canceled their subscription.[29]

Through the early years of the Lunts' career, then, they worked within New York's gay community and were intimate with many of its members. After 1929, however, gay life in the city underwent a significant shift. While police occasionally raided gay bars during the Pansy Craze, most were left in peace if they kept within clear geographical bounds. As Chauncey reports, however, in the early 1930s several newspapers, together with newly rejuvenated moral-reform societies, began to attack public manifestations of gay life. Under increased pressure, the police raided gay clubs and bars, especially in the theater district, eventually using the new liquor laws that were passed after the repeal of Prohibition in 1933.[30]

These raids not only drove gay bars underground; they also had a chilling effect on the individual expression of gay sexuality. Newspapers stepped up publication of the names of people arrested in the raids. These revelations proved disastrous for public figures and the wealthy, who often lost their careers and social positions when their sexuality became known.[31] Noël Coward, writing in his diary in 1955 in response to an antigay court ruling in England, articulates the repressive effects of such crackdowns: "for as long as these barbarous laws exist it should be remembered that homosexuality *is* a penal offense and should be considered such socially, although not morally."[32] In other words, under the threat of police raids, anyone engaging in homosexual activities must make an external show of heterosexuality to maintain a place in society.

In fact, the atmosphere of antigay repression had affected the theater well before the renewed bar raids. In 1926 Gilbert Miller opened his production of Edouard Bourdet's *The Captive,* a play dealing overtly with lesbian issues; in the same year Mae West premiered her play *Sex* and announced plans to open another play, *The Drag,* with a sympathetic view of gay men. On February 9, 1927, when *The Drag* was in tryouts in New Jersey, the police shut down *The Captive, Sex,* and a third play called *Virgin Man,* and arrested many members of the casts, including West. The motivation for the raids seems to have been West's intention of bringing *The Drag* to Broadway; the action successfully prevented West from presenting her play. These raids were covered extensively in the New York press.[33]

Following these raids, the New York State legislature, which already prohibited gay "lewdness" in public, revised the public-obscenity law to ban from the stage all plays "depicting or dealing with the subject of sex degeneracy, or sex perversion."[34] Similar measures were adopted privately in the entertainment industry. In 1931 the R.K.O vaudeville circuit disallowed the words *fairy* and *pansy* on stage; in 1934 Hollywood established the Production Code Administration to enforce the existing 1930 studio policy preventing the depiction of immorality on film.[35] The Lunts were aware of the impact of these new laws. Coward relates his early plans with the Lunts for the play that became *Design for Living;* they initially planned a play modeled on Schnitzler's *La Ronde,* with the setting an enormous bed. They dropped this plan, however, when they realized the stage business they envisioned might lead to their arrest.[36]

In spite of this growing antigay atmosphere, however, the Lunts did not shy away from controversial sexual subject matter in their stage work. On the contrary, they embraced sexually daring roles. While promoting themselves as a happily married couple, through the late 1920s and early 1930s the Lunts embarked on a series of performances, many in conjunction with Coward, that tested the boundaries of the new regulations. These performances did not depict "deviance" in the direct manner of *The Captive* and *The Drag;* instead, they discussed homosexuality and other kinds of "degeneracy" obliquely. By veiling their subject, and with the protection of their marriage, the Lunts explored issues of sexuality in ways unavailable to other performers.

These sexually daring productions occupied the Lunts' career for a decade. In 1928, Fontanne starred as Nina Leeds in the Theatre Guild's production of O'Neill's *Strange Interlude;* Lunt referred to the play as "a six-day bisexual race."[37] In the early 1930s the Lunts planned a production of *Twelfth Night* in which Lunt, playing Orsino, would have been aware of his apparent homosexual attraction to Viola/Cesario; Coward was slated to play Malvolio. According to the Lunts' friend Alan Hewitt, the production was ready to go, "but their producers of the time could not be persuaded to accept the financial risk."[38] (Brown, notably, makes no mention of this production, although he had read Hewitt's account, as he reveals in a letter to Hewitt.)[39] In 1934, Coward wrote *Point Valaine* for the Lunts, a play that Brown calls "a lurid study of sexual obsession."[40] And in 1938 the Lunts triumphed in Giraudoux's *Amphitryon 38,* a mythical story of marital infidelity with Lunt playing Jupiter; it featured a notorious scene with Jupiter in the clouds, Lunt's face emerging from a bare-bottomed plaster figure of the god.

The most daring experiment, however, was *Design for Living,* written by Coward for himself and the Lunts, which opened in New York in January 1933. Coward's play differs from Mordaunt Shairp's *The Green Bay Tree* and Lillian Hellman's *The Children's Hour,* two other plays dealing with homosexuality that appeared in New York in 1933–34. In these serious plays homosexuality is a destroyer of human lives; *Design for Living* offers a comic celebration of sexual bohemianism. In the play, Otto (Lunt) and Leo (Coward) both love Gilda (Fontanne), but they are also in love with each other. Each of the play's three acts has a scene in which two of the three lovers emerge from the bedroom: first Gilda and Leo, next Gilda and Otto, then, climactically, Leo and Otto. At the end, they vow to live together in a three-way relationship. Coward fills the play with references to Otto and Leo's love and its physical nature and includes enthusiastic defenses of those who defy sexual norms. Many critics expressed discomfort with the play's rejection of traditional marriage, but most assumed that Otto and Leo were just close friends. The gay audience members who saw the play, however, had no doubt about their true relationship.[41]

Later critics have discussed the double entendre in *Design for Living*, and Coward's skill in allowing heterosexually inclined viewers to ignore the play's homosexual content.[42] What has gone unmentioned, though, is the possibility of reading the play as autobiography. Coward wrote the play specifically for himself and the Lunts. The character Coward wrote for himself is clearly autobiographical: he is a playwright who scores a huge success with a play that the critics find scintillating but shallow. He even inscribes his first name into his character's, backward: Leo for Noël. Gilda and Otto are, like the Lunts, in the same artistic line, though Coward makes them visual artists rather than actors. Coward even dedicated the play to the trio's other sexually enigmatic associate, Alexander Woollcott.

There are several well-known photographs of the play's final scene, with the three characters erotically intertwined on a sofa. But in December 1932, a month before the play opened, the Lunts and Coward posed for a similar studio photograph, in street clothes rather than in costume. Coward sits nestled against Lunt, who rests his hand on Coward's shoulder; both men gaze longingly toward Fontanne. This intriguing photo invites the viewer to blur the lines between stage and reality and suggests that the play's bisexual triangle spills beyond the frame of fiction. It would be problematic to push this argument for autobiography too literally; there is no evidence to suggest that Coward had slept with either Lunt or Fontanne. But it seems reasonable to read the play's defense of bohemian sexuality as a reflection of the trio's own views.[43] Just as the play's homosexual content was readily apparent to gay spectators in 1933, it is plausible that Coward wanted to suggest, at least to certain audience members, that he and the Lunts were not what the press made them out to be, sexually speaking.

A fictional profile of the Lunts that appeared in 1930 in *Theatre Guild* magazine also invites readers to look beneath the surface of their marriage. This piece, which Brown again fails to mention, is titled "Lord Alfred and Lady Lynn: An Interview to Prove That Marriage is No Hindrance to Art." It is supposedly an interview of the couple, written in an ironic, overblown heroic style, by lesbian author Djuna Barnes.[44] In this mock interview, Barnes visits the Lunts in their separate dressing rooms and asks them whether being married makes their acting more convincing. Fontanne argues that she must forget her marriage while on stage; Barnes has her say, "Any life we portray in public; any lines we speak on the stage; any glance we cast in a professional capacity, must of necessity be impersonal." Lunt conversely effuses over their close relationship, to which Barnes remarks that "here is the very corpse

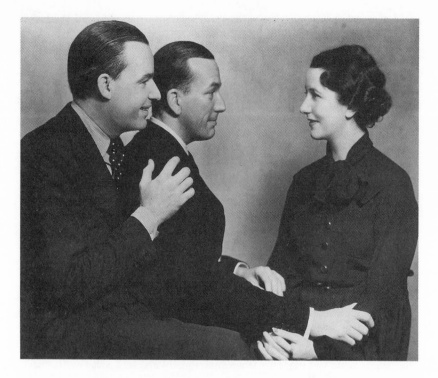

**Alfred Lunt, Noël Coward, and Lynn Fontanne,
studio photograph taken prior to the opening of
Design for Living, December 1932**

(Collection of the author.)

of discrepancy!" The actors unite and discuss how they rehearse their roles day and night, even in bed, and how they are always searching for the perfect roles; the "interview" concludes with Lunt's remark to his wife: "One of these days, my girl, you shall be a titled hussy, and I your charlatan!" The article is accompanied by a cartoon drawn by Barnes of Lunt and Fontanne, glaring unpleasantly at each other from separate single beds, framed by theatrical curtains. The ironic tone of this "interview" strongly suggests that the Lunts' marriage was as much a performance as their appearances on stage. Like *Design for Living,* it opens cracks in the idealized image, while leaving the public myth of the Lunts' marriage undisturbed.[45]

The Lunts, and the people who wrote about them, then, could play with hints of nonnormative sexuality in a period when public censure of

Alfred Lunt and Lynn Fontanne, illustration by Djuna Barnes.
"We rehearse at breakfast, at dinner, in taxi-cabs, and in bed."

(Theatre Guild, March 1930. Reprinted by permission.)

homosexuality was intensifying.[46] This freedom came about because their image as a married couple was planted so firmly in the public mind. Even Brown admits that their stage performances were sexually daring, and that their marriage allowed them to push the limits of sexual propriety on stage. Brown relates a story of an elderly audience member, uncomfortable about a particularly erotic scene; her companion, reassuring her, was overheard to say "Isn't it nice, my dear, to know that they really are married?"[47] What was important, in other words, was not that the Lunts were in fact happily married to one another, but that their audiences believed that they were.

Public life for gay men and lesbians in New York took a turn for the worse in 1939. In that year, as Chauncey reports, police stepped up their raids on gay establishments in an attempt to eliminate all visible manifestations of homosexuality before the 1939 New York World's Fair. Chauncey details the raid of the Times Square Garden and Grill, and the concern expressed by police that "fairies" were seen associating there with off-duty soldiers. Again, arrests were made, jail sentences handed out, and names published in the newspapers.[48] These raids, and the wartime atmosphere that followed, successfully drove gay life in the city underground, where it would remain for several decades.

Following the 1939 crackdown, the sexual daring of the Lunts' performances diminished considerably. This shift can certainly be attributed in part to the couple's advancing age, and consequently to the more mature and less sexually active roles available to them. But the increased antigay repression also took its toll, as demonstrated by the Lunts' relationship with the young Montgomery Clift. In April 1940 the Lunts starred as middle-aged parents in Robert Sherwood's *There Shall Be No Night;* Clift played their son. The Lunts, who had no children of their own, virtually adopted Clift, bringing him to their home and instructing him in acting and dramatic literature. Brown relates that the Lunts gave Clift a photograph of themselves signed, "From your *real* mother and father."[49] Patricia Bosworth, Clift's biographer, says that Lunt took Clift alone to the theater; at postperformance dinners at the Lunts', while Fontanne played games with the other guests, Clift and Lunt would do the dishes and have heart-to-heart talks.[50]

Brown explains that the Lunts had no children because they were too busy, and that their relationship with Clift substituted for their thwarted parental desires.[51] But the Lunts had not developed similar relationships with other young actors, and Bosworth suggests that the Lunts took interest in Clift specifically because of his homosexuality, trying to protect him from a hostile public. Bosworth reports that Clift at the time was involved with a man she identifies only as "Josh." She quotes "Josh" as saying that Lunt feared that this relationship would become public and ruin Clift's career.

> Up until a few years ago it would have been career suicide for us to have confessed our homosexuality. Now it doesn't matter. Then it was crucial to *hide everything.* I remember Monty telling me how Lunt scolded him sometimes. Lunt adored Monty, but he was afraid he was turning gay. He never said anything direct about it, but alluded to Gielgud, and then he said, "Well, y'know Noel Coward's an exception. You can't ordinarily be a pansy in the theatre and survive."[52]

Lunt's statement reflects the growing suppression of public gay life; less than a decade before he had been eager to defy sexual norms in *Design for Living.* The Lunts encouraged Clift to marry an actress named Phyllis

Thaxter so that they, too, could become an acting team.[53] In later years, when Clift began to drink, and as rumors of his sexuality spread, the Lunts broke with him, possibly to protect their own reputation.[54]

As the attacks against homosexuality increased, so did the number of high-profile articles portraying the Lunts as a happily married couple. These features created an increasingly uniform portrait of the Lunts as the ideal of American domesticity. The earliest of these articles, appearing in the 1930s, focused on the Lunts' stage work. In 1937, *Life* ran a feature about the Lunts' appearance in *Amphitryon 38*, with the statement, "Despite their stage laughter at married love, the Lunts are conspicuously happy in their married life."[55] A career retrospective appeared in the *New York Times* in 1939 commemorating the fifteenth anniversary of the couple's appearance in *The Guardsman*, with pictures of their major productions.[56]

Beginning in 1940, immediately after the antigay crackdown, the tone of these profiles changed significantly. Rather than focusing on the Lunts' stage career, these articles dealt with their domestic life, featuring images of the Lunts at home, especially on their Wisconsin farm. Rather than theatrical publications such as *Theatre Guild* magazine and *Stage*, or general-interest magazines such as *Life*, these articles appeared in home and family magazines: *Vogue, Coronet*, and *Ladies' Home Journal*. Their titles advertised the Lunts as the model married couple: "Lynn Fontanne and Alfred Lunt, of Genesee, Wisconsin"; "Mr. and Mrs. Alfred Lunt"; "Far from the Crowd: Alfred Lunt and Lynn Fontanne Take Up the Muse of Agriculture"; "Lunt and Fontanne: First Family of the Theatre."[57] These profiles portrayed the Lunts as a "normal" couple, the kind of stars (as one article emphasized) who eat corn flakes instead of caviar. A 1940 *New York Times* profile asserted hyperbolically: "Their marriage is as happy as any marriage ever has been or ever will be."[58] And the *Ladies' Home Journal* offered this question, though the author seems unaware of its irony: "Married eighteen years, still magically young, successful, in love—how do they do it? What is the Lunts' design for living?"[59]

Photography played an important part in these articles and was used by journalists to further the Lunt myth. The pictures show them living a quiet, secluded life on their Wisconsin farm. Lunt happily tends the garden and makes dinner in the well-equipped kitchen, while Fontanne sews and writes letters. Rarely do the photos show houseguests; the couple seem to live entirely by themselves. The pictures are heavily posed, looking very like the earlier pictures of the couple in their famous stage roles.

Unlike New York, in Wisconsin the Lunts could control the access of the press to their lives, and thus promote a controlled image of domestic serenity. By the start of World War II, then, the press had firmly planted in the popular mind the idea of Alfred Lunt and Lynn Fontanne as the perfect married pair, with plenty of visual documentation in high-profile family publications. This idealized image transformed into a perceived reality and became cemented in the two early biographies of the Lunts, by George Freedley and Maurice Zolotow.

In the early years of their acting careers, then, Lunt and Fontanne's marriage allowed them to experiment with sexual subjects that pushed the limits of public tolerance and permitted them to travel freely in the openly gay subculture of New York. As that subculture came increasingly under attack, they could rely on the public perception of their marriage. They used the power of the press to quell the rumors that they were homosexual and to present themselves not only as a happily married couple, but as the ideal domestic pair. Lunt and Fontanne were nothing like Ozzie and Harriet or Ward and June Cleaver, the heterosexual icons of 1950s television. But after 1940, in the public eye the Lunts came to represent the American ideal of marital bliss just as powerfully as the famous couples on television did in the 1950s. They enhanced the myth of their marriage by linking, paradoxically, the glamour of the Broadway stage to the image of idyllic domesticity. The Lunts turned normative heterosexuality into a spectacularly successful theatrical performance, a performance that continued beyond their deaths, inscribed for posterity on their joint gravestone.

> Alfred Lunt and Lynn Fontanne were universally regarded as the greatest acting team in the history of the English speaking theater. They were married for 55 years and were inseparable both on and off the stage.[60]

NOTES

1. Graham Payn, a close associate of Noël Coward and the Lunts, comments in an interview with Philip Hoare that "Lunt was 'a bit of a freelancer' sexually" (quoted in Philip Hoare, *Noël Coward: A Biography* [New York: Simon and Schuster, 1995], 96). Kaier Curtin recalls an actress named Isobel Elsom who, he says, had a close relationship with Fontanne that he presumes was sexual; she visited Fontanne regularly at the Lunts' Wisconsin home. Elsom, toward the end of her life, denied in print any knowledge of Fontanne's sexuality (Curtin, *"We Can Always Call Them Bulgarians": The Emergence of Lesbians*

and Gay Men on the American Stage [Boston: Alyson, 1987], 112), but Curtin believes she was attempting in this remark to disguise her own proclivities (Billy J. Harbin, interview with Kaier Curtin, September 4 and November 21, 1996, conveyed to the author by correspondence with Harbin). Rumors are, of course, notoriously difficult to document. Curtin reports, "Alfred Lunt and Lynn Fontanne, the illustrious husband and wife co-stars, were rumored to be discretely gay," along with the husband-wife pair Katharine Cornell and Guthrie McClintic, and others including Talullah Bankhead, Alla Nazimova, Estelle Winwood, and Eva Le Gallienne (Curtin, 57, 112). Brendan Gill, reviewing Jared Brown's biography of the Lunts, remarks, "Brown takes it for granted that it was a conventionally heterosexual marriage, and this astonished me, for I had always assumed that it was one of those 'white' marriages so common among people in the theatre. (One thinks of Cole and Linda Porter, of Katharine Cornell and Guthrie McClintic, and many others.)" Gill, "The Perfectionists," *New Yorker*, October 13, 1986, 155. Axel Madsen mentions the rumors about Fontanne in his gossipy *The Sewing Circle: Hollywood's Greatest Secret—Female Stars Who Loved Other Women* (New York: Birch Lane Press, 1995), 45.

2. The biographies of the Lunts all mention their fights and Lunt's depression. Jared Brown, in *The Fabulous Lunts: A Biography of Alfred Lunt and Lynn Fontanne* (New York: Atheneum, 1986) provides the most thorough documentation; see in particular his discussions on pp. 206, 252, 255, and 289. Evidence of the Lunts' unpleasantness is also found in letters (dated December 27, 1970, and January 6, 1971) to Alan Hewitt from Fitzroy Davis (both acted with the Lunts) in which Davis expresses his intense dislike of the Lunts and describes what he feels was their ruthless use of other people to further their own careers. The vicious tone of Davis's letters, however, may call their objectivity into question (Alan Hewitt Papers, Baker Library, Dartmouth College).

3. See George Chauncey Jr., *Gay New York: Gender, Urban Culture, and the Making of the Gay Male World, 1890–1940* (New York: Basic Books, 1994). See also essays in Martin Duberman, Martha Vicinus, and George Chauncey Jr., eds., *Hidden from History: Reclaiming the Gay and Lesbian Past* (New York: Penguin, 1989); and Michael Warner, ed., *Fear of a Queer Planet: Queer Politics and Social Theory* (Minneapolis: University of Minnesota Press, 1993).

4. Brown, *The Fabulous Lunts*, 45.

5. Ibid.

6. Brooks Atkinson, *Broadway* (New York: Macmillan, 1974), 193.

7. *Brevities*, May 15, 1933, 1. *Brevities*, sometimes published under the title *Broadway Brevities*, appeared from 1931 to 1934 and billed itself as "America's First National Tabloid Weekly." Some issues are in the collections of the New York Historical Society and the New York Public Library. The reference to the Lunts appears on p. 1; the banner headline for that issue reads "B'way Queers Brazen!" Chauncey discusses *Brevities* frequently in *Gay New York*.

8. The earliest biography is George Freedley's *The Lunts* (London: Rockliff, 1957). This was followed by Maurice Zolotow's more extensive *Stagestruck: The Romance of Alfred Lunt and Lynn Fontanne* (New York: Harcourt, Brace and World, 1965); the title indicates its emphasis on the Lunts' idealized marriage.

9. Brown, *The Fabulous Lunts,* 395.

10. Ibid., 396. Brown does not identify the speaker.

11. Ibid., 79; also in Zolotow, *Stagestruck,* 70, quoted from Coward's book *Present Indicative* (Garden City, NJ: Doubleday, 1937).

12. Brown quotes George Bugbee, Lunt's brother-in-law, as saying of the couple that they acted constantly, on stage and off (*The Fabulous Lunts,* 397).

13. Chauncey, *Gay New York,* esp. chap. 11. "Nights in Fairyland" is discussed on p. 321. Chauncey limits his analysis to New York's gay male subculture; at this time there is an equally active, though perhaps less public, lesbian subculture in the city.

14. Brown, *The Fabulous Lunts,* 94.

15. Chauncey, *Gay New York,* 302–4.

16. Brown, *The Fabulous Lunts,* 26. Brown also quotes a college classmate of Lunt's, Adaline Burchart Hoag, who testifies that while many female classmates fell in love with Lunt, he never dated them, and that he was always too busy to have time for women (25–26).

17. Ibid., 62–63.

18. Chauncey, *Gay New York,* 120–21.

19. Brown, *The Fabulous Lunts,* 63.

20. Brown says little about Lunt's later relationship with Weaver. He mentions that Weaver, who taught theater at the University of Michigan, criticized Lunt for acting in trivial comedies with Noël Coward (ibid., 210). This statement could be interpreted as motivated by jealousy, especially given the implied gay relationship between Lunt and Coward in *Design for Living.*

21. Zolotow, *Stagestruck,* 45. Brown offers a toned-down version of the story, omitting specific reference to Lunt's gilded hair and painted nipples and the equivalent decorations on his young partners (*The Fabulous Lunts,* 69).

22. Zolotow, *Stagestruck,* 25. Zolotow does not specifically mention these rumors, only implying them by his vague gender reference; Madsen asserts them as fact (*The Sewing Circle,* 25, 117–18, 136), but he provides no documentation.

23. Zolotow, *Stagestruck,* 25.

24. Ibid., 65–68, 90–91. See also Brown, *The Fabulous Lunts,* 90, 111–13.

25. Zolotow, *Stagestruck,* 132. See also Brown, *The Fabulous Lunts,* 148–49.

26. See Eric Garber, "A Spectacle in Color: The Lesbian and Gay Subculture of Jazz Age Harlem" in Duberman, Vicinus, and Chauncey, *Hidden from History,* 318–31.

27. Edwin P. Hoyt, *Alexander Woollcott: The Man Who Came to Dinner* (London: Abelard-Schuman, 1968), 255.

28. Zolotow, *Stagestruck,* 144.

29. Ibid., 150. Hoyt presents a whitewashed view of Woollcott's life in his biography. A more probing biography of Woollcott needs to be written.

30. Chauncey, *Gay New York,* 331–37.

31. Ibid., 335–49.

32. Graham Payn and Sheridan Morley, eds., *The Noël Coward Diaries* (Boston: Little, Brown, 1982), 290–91.

33. Chauncey, *Gay New York,* 311–13; Curtin, *Call Them Bulgarians,* 43–

104. Jonathan Ned Katz documents newspaper accounts of these productions in *Gay American History: Lesbians and Gay Men in the U.S.A.*, rev. ed. (New York: Meridian, 1992), 82–91.

34. Chauncey, *Gay New York*, 313.

35. Ibid., 353.

36. Quoted in Brown, *The Fabulous Lunts*, 204–5.

37. Ibid., 167.

38. Alan Hewitt, "Repertory to Residuals: Reflections on American Acting since 1900," in *The American Theatre: The Sum of Its Parts* (New York: Samuel French, 1971), 98. Critic Elliot Norton also mentions this story in an article in the *Boston Herald-Traveler*, September 2, 1972.

39. Letter from Jared Brown to Alan Hewitt, November 7, 1983, Alan Hewitt Papers.

40. Brown, *The Fabulous Lunts*, 218. Nicholas de Jongh discusses the homoeroticism of *Point Valaine* in *Not in Front of the Audience: Homosexuality on Stage* (London: Routledge, 1992), 123–24.

41. Chauncey interviews an audience member who reports that gay viewers understood the double entendre (*Gay New York*, 288 and note). Curtin documents the critical response to the play (*Call Them Bulgarians*, 170–76).

42. See Curtin's discussion (*Call Them Bulgarians*, 170–76) and John Clum's analysis in *Acting Gay: Male Homosexuality in Modern Drama* (New York: Columbia University Press, 1992), 99–104. One point they miss is Gilda's line in act 3, scene 2, describing how she left Leo and Otto and "sat in Childs weeping into glasses of milk" (Noël Coward, *Plays: Three*, London: Methuen, 1979, 120). Childs restaurants, especially in the theater district, were noted gay cruising areas (Chauncey, *Gay New York*, 166).

43. Coward suggests in his autobiography that all of the ideas he and the Lunts toyed with for this play dealt with nonnormative sexuality.

44. Djuna Barnes, "Lord Alfred and Lady Lynn: An Interview to Prove That Marriage Is No Hindrance to Art," *Theatre Guild*, March 1930, 11–12.

45. It is unclear whether the Lunts approved of this article. When it appeared, they were under contract with the Guild and so presumably could have stopped publication had they so desired. A similarly suggestive, though less ironic, fictional conversation by Sargent Armstrong appeared in *Stage*, October 1935, 29.

46. Alan Hewitt recounts that the Lunts' 1935 tour of *The Taming of the Shrew* was "a fantasy of sex in every possible combination," though he claims innocence of the sexual activity in the company at the time (Alan Hewitt, private letter, April 5, 1986, Alan Hewitt Papers).

47. Brown, *The Fabulous Lunts*, 178. Both Clum (*Acting Gay*, 100–101) and Curtin (*Call Them Bulgarians*, 175–76) also suggest that the Lunts used their marriage to get away with sexual liberties on stage.

48. Chauncey, *Gay New York*, 340–41.

49. Brown, *The Fabulous Lunts*, 290.

50. Patricia Bosworth, *Montgomery Clift: A Biography* (New York: Harcourt Brace Jovanovich, 1978), 78–79.

51. Brown, *The Fabulous Lunts*, 152.

52. Bosworth, *Montgomery Clift*, 82.

53. Ibid., 80.

54. Ibid., 276, 321. Later, as Brown reports, the Lunts developed other ties with young men. They became intimate with the young Dick Van Patten, who performed with them in the late 1940s (*The Fabulous Lunts*, 356). Brown reports that Lunt hired a series of "summer boys" to work on their Wisconsin farm; Brown emphasizes how much the Lunts enjoyed having the boys around (374).

55. "The Lunts, World's Greatest Acting Team, Again Make Fun of Married Love," *Life*, November 1, 1937, 106.

56. "Broadway's No. 1 Couple," *New York Times*, October 8, 1939, Rotogravure section.

57. Ward Morehouse, "Lynn Fontanne and Alfred Lunt, of Genesee, Wisconsin," *Vogue*, May 1940, 70–73; Alice-Leone Moats, "Mr. and Mrs. Alfred Lunt," *Ladies Home Journal*, December 1940, 14+; "Far from the Crowd: Alfred Lunt and Lynn Fontanne Take Up the Muse of Agriculture," *New York Times*, March 15, 1942, 1–2; Lawrence Lader, "Lunt and Fontanne: First Family of the Theatre," *Coronet*, June 1948, 123–32.

58. Charlotte Hughes, "Of the Lunts: On Stage and Off," *New York Times*, June 30, 1940, 1–2.

59. Moats, "Mr. and Mrs. Alfred Lunt," 14.

60. Headstone engraving as reported in undated news clippings in Alan Hewitt Papers.

Kit and Guth

A Lavender Marriage on Broadway

Lesley Ferris

The marriage of Katharine Cornell (1893–1974) and Guthrie McClintic (1893–1961), which lasted for forty years, from 1921 until McClintic's death in 1961, has been portrayed as an ideal relationship, combining the private with the public in ways that produced some of the best American theater of the period. Cornell and McClintic married the moment her Broadway career began to take off, and McClintic directed her in twenty-five plays, most of her Broadway successes, establishing them both as a formidable producing team by 1931.

When McClintic died of cancer in 1961, Cornell retired. In their biography of Cornell, Tad Mosel and Gertrude Macy suggest that "Kit could have continued acting for other managements as long as she wanted to. But with Guthrie gone, there was no point. There was no announcement of an official retirement; she simply never went back to work."[1]

So the "official" narrative of her professional life ends appropriately with Cornell as a grieving widow who eschews the career shaped and promoted by her director-husband. After his death "there was no point." Although Mosel and Macy make it clear that Cornell lived the rest of her life with another woman, Nancy Hamilton, the authors compress her years with Hamilton, from 1961–74, to a few cursory pages at the end of their book.

Tackling the books written about Cornell is much like approaching a roman à clef, a genre of novel writing that developed in seventeenth-century France. These novels were works of fiction in which actual persons are presented under fictitious names. Keys to the novels were provided later, or, in certain eighteenth-century versions, the novels were published with a useful key character list. Part of the great popularity of the roman à clef resided in the reader's figuring out who the characters were in real life and making connections between the fictionalized account and the so-called lived reality.

Unlike the seventeenth-century roman à clef, the names of the characters in the Cornell-Guthrie story require no key. We do need a key, however, to interpret the material, since an important aspect of the relationship is missing from all the standard accounts. Kit and Guth, as they were known to their friends, had a lavender marriage: a marriage of convenience and companionship while both maintained various same-sex relationships.[2]

This essay falls into two major parts. We begin by looking at the difficulty of trying to retrieve information that for the most part has been deliberately obscured or erased from history. There is a kind of dishonesty in accounts of people's lives that wilfully disregard the important aspect of their sexuality. Such dishonesty, though undoubtedly maintained in many cases out of self-censorship and fear of reprisal, misrepresents those under discussion. Of course, all forms of biography have to tackle contradictory sources, different points of view, and lack of clarity over moments long past. However, the lives of public figures who desired the same sex are more challenging because of the varieties of obfuscation facing any researcher. Accordingly, the first section of this essay focuses on the dilemma of finding and interpreting material on such figures as Katharine Cornell and Guthrie McClintic.

The second part examines the social dynamics around Cornell's performance choices during the crucial, early decades of her career. Critics of the twenties, some of whom make insinuations about her sexuality, battered away at the plays that Cornell chose, claiming they were artistically beneath her, while audiences flocked to see her play a variety of dangerous women characters. When in 1930 Cornell decided to play the role of Elizabeth Barrett Browning in *The Barretts of Wimpole Street,* the critics gasped with relief. The play was conventionally "artistic" and soothingly heterosexual; it was based on the events of one of the most celebrated love stories in English letters. Like others before her, Cornell's career choices were shaped by a dominant culture that feared independent, autonomous women, women who, according to the psychosexual mores of the times, could be classified as "deviant."

The Importance of Keying into Gossip

As Andrea Weiss so bluntly states, "Rumor and gossip constitute the unrecorded history of the gay subculture." To further her argument Weiss quotes the introduction to the 1981 lesbian and film issue of *Jump Cut:*

"If oral history is the history of those denied control of the printed record, then gossip is the history of those who cannot even speak in their own first-person voice."[3] For those of us trained in conventional research methods, this concept is undoubtedly unsettling; nonetheless, gossip has inevitably played a role in my research for this essay.

During my earliest considerations of Cornell and McClintic, I asked a theater historian if he were aware of their same-sex relationships. He replied, "Yes, of course, it was common knowledge among the New York theater crowd." But how to key into that "common knowledge?" Through questioning many people as well as relying on conventional research methods I discovered—much to my scholarly delight—a few recently published accounts. These accounts, however, rarely attribute their information to any specific source.

The fullest account is Axel Madsen's in *The Sewing Circle: Hollywood's Greatest Secret—Female Stars Who Loved Other Women.* Although the book's major focus is on the film industry, Madsen discusses Cornell's relationship with the women involved in the business. Mercedes de Acosta, a screenwriter and lover to both Garbo and Dietrich, fell in love with Katharine Cornell (according to Madsen) when Cornell was still playing secondary roles with the Washington Square Players (1916–18). In Madsen's account, Cornell introduced Mercedes to Elisabeth ("Bessie") Marbury, "the doyenne of Sapphic Broadway," who was a theater producer and agent. Since Cornell at this stage in her career had not yet married McClintic, Madsen makes a case that their marriage was a marriage of convenience from the start.[4]

Another recently published account is found in Ann Douglas's *Terrible Honesty: Mongrel Manhattan in the 1920s.* In a footnote she says that Cornell, "who played Iris March on Broadway, was one of the most gifted, beautiful actresses of the day; she specialized in fallen-women roles." Douglas describes Tad Mosel and Gertrude Macy's biography of Cornell as excellent, "though it makes no mention of Cornell's well-known lesbian orientation."[5]

According to Kaier Curtin in *"We Can Always Call Them Bulgarians,"* "Common gossip in the higher echelons of show business concerned the female attachments of Katharine Cornell, often referred to as 'The First Lady of the American Theater,' and the more blatantly gay activities of her husband, director-producer Guthrie McClintic."[6] Curtin also quotes from an interview with Isobel Elsom, an English actress who appeared in 1926 in the first play with a lesbian character written in the English language, *Sin of Sins,* which, due to its subject matter, failed in its

Chicago premiere. Elsom discusses her lack of awareness of gay people in the theater world: "One heard very little on the subject—which was simply taboo among show business gossips—except it was said that Katharine Cornell and her husband, director Guthrie McClintic, and Lynn Fontanne and her co-starring husband, Alfred Lunt, were all supposed to be gay, but I didn't know if this was so."[7]

Elsom's comment, that homosexuality was a taboo subject, is itself a kind of gossip ("it was said" that Cornell and McClintic were gay) and evokes the importance of hearsay and rumor in relation to gay and lesbian history. Furthermore, recent oral history records that Elsom's comment reveals another complicated layer. In 1996 Kaier Curtin stated that Isobel Elsom associated all her life with gay and lesbian circles. The book that Curtin published in 1987, based on research from several years earlier, deliberately masks Elsom's own personal involvement in the theatrical homosexual community. Although Curtin knew Elsom well, when he interviewed her officially for his book, she was aged and ill. She made it clear to him that proper British ladies do not speak of such matters.[8]

Patricia Meyer Spacks considers gossip to be symptomatic of oppression, but a tool that gives power to those otherwise powerless: it "embodies an alternative discourse to that of public life, and a discourse potentially challenging to public assumptions; it provides language for an alternative culture."[9] In other words, gossip is an important source to consider when looking at aspects of the gay subculture; it has provided a network of communication, a way of negotiating the monolithic dominant culture for those disenfranchised by compulsory heterosexuality.

Thus, the key to the *roman* of Guthrie and Kit, the way to understanding the dearth of information regarding their sexual lives, all those great silences that are embedded in their official histories, lies in a cautious embrace of gossip and rumor. As Weiss, writing about Hollywood stars and lesbian spectatorship in the 1930s, puts it,

> Something that, through gossip, is commonplace knowledge within the gay subculture is often completely unknown on the outside, and if not unknown, at least unspeakable. It is this insistence by the dominant culture on making homosexuality invisible and unspeakable that both require us and enable us to locate gay history in rumor, innuendo, fleeting gestures, and coded language.[10]

Heterosexual actress Elsom was not party to the taboo subject of homosexuality. She states that she was unaware of gay men or women who were working in the theater in the twenties. However, claiming not to know, she knows. Even in her case there is seepage, a mysterious conduit that transfers information from one cultural realm to another, rumor that crosses over from the gay subculture to the dominant culture. The taboo subject circulates, although it is officially "unspeakable." It is that same circulation or leakage that makes it possible for the historian to tell me that Cornell and McClintic's sexuality was "common knowledge" among theater folk.

A fascinating aspect of using gossip as a source for information is that although the general outlines appear reliable (i.e., Cornell and McClintic by all accounts were gay), the details of their lives in relation to their sexuality are vague and often contradictory.[11] For example, one important source for me was an E-mail correspondence with Lee Alan Morrow, a New York City writer whose godmother had roomed with Nancy Hamilton at Smith College. Morrow's godmother and Hamilton remained lifelong friends after college days until Hamilton's death in 1985. Morrow's godmother dined with Hamilton and Cornell after McClintic's death, and Hamilton was often called Cornell's "companion" or "lover."

I asked Morrow if he thought the Cornell-McClintic marriage was "lavender" from the beginning; his impression was that it was not. His sense, based on his godmother's comment, was that Cornell was rather naive sexually when she married McClintic. The marriage took place because of a clear attraction, career ambition (both were moving higher on the Broadway ladder), and social pressure. According to Morrow, Guthrie strayed first with his relationships with a variety of young men, and Katharine—out of a sense of loneliness and loss—began to rely more frequently on her female friends. With Guthrie's death, she could have a fully committed relationship with Hamilton.[12] Morrow's view of the marriage is in clear contrast to Madsen's. The *Sewing Circle* claims Cornell had a relationship with Mercedes de Acosta between 1916 and 1918—before her marriage to Guthrie.[13] But he gives no specific source for this important piece of gossip.

The details on Guthrie's homosexuality are even more sparse than Cornell's. As we have seen from the above, he is usually referred to in relation to Cornell. When McClintic is described by writers, he is called frail and small-boned. He was an only child whose childhood was miserable because his father was brutal and often violent. His loving, indulgent mother tried to shield the sickly youth from his father's outbursts. John K. Tillinghast says that "McClintic had always preferred women with a strong maternal streak and Miss Cornell looked after him with great devotion."[14] Lawrence Langner, the founder of the Theatre Guild, describes an early meeting between the couple: "[Cornell] attended the first Guild meetings at my home . . . where she met a pale, frail young man named Guthrie McClintic, who made a far greater impression on her than I did."[15] Later, Langner contrasts the "placid calm" of Kit Cornell with "the nervous elegance of Guthrie McClintic."[16] Guthrie characterizes himself in his biography as follows: "I was definitely not the athletic type (I am still definitely not). I was scrawny and underweight, with a mop of dark brown hair and large eyes that seemed larger because of my extreme thinness."[17] Describing a childhood anecdote in which, unlike other boys on his street, he preferred novel reading to being mesmerized by the new cars that were recently on the road, Guthrie says that his mother had "to face the fact that her one and only was 'different,' to put it mildly—a non-conformist you might say."[18] "Putting it mildly," these descriptions of McClintic's physicality belie a conventional rendering of a highly sensitive, artistic, frail, homosexual man. The violent father and doting mother further this image considerably. A final reference to Guthrie is found in a 1948 comedy of backstage life in which the director is considered swishy and effeminate. As Gerald Bordman puts it, "Although [McClintic] was a sensitive, knowing director, he was a prissy, volatile man, who was deftly parodied as Carleton Fitzgerald in Moss Hart's *Light Up the Sky*."[19]

The one major source that openly discusses his homosexuality is the Mosel and Macy biography *Leading Lady*. Of all the works written on Cornell this one has the stamp of "official, sanctioned version" written all over it since Mosel, the primary writer, gives secondary authorship to Gertrude Macy. Macy, whose relationship with Cornell began as a shipboard friendship, started to work for Cornell as a secretary. She was the stage manager for *The Barretts of Wimpole Street* and eventually moved to the position of general manager for Cornell, in charge of the box office and all financial dealings. A straightforward, quiet, and extremely efficient person, Macy was described as "shock-proof."[20] Cornell herself had said, "She runs the whole shooting match, as far as I'm concerned," and she was frequently heard to say, "May goodness and Macy follow me all the days of my life."[21] And once Macy began to work for Kit, that is exactly what she did.

Gertrude Macy is also the person who selected Tad Mosel to write the biography of Cornell. Mosel remarks that

> of all the writers she could have chosen, Miss Macy chose me to be
> the first to write the life of Katharine Cornell. For three years she has

shared with me the vast resources of her meticulous private files and the abundant riches of her tentative memory; she has been scrupulously fair in her evaluation of herself and the other characters in the tales she has told me and, more important, in allowing me my own interpretation of those tales.[22]

It seems surprising that the book, published in 1978, reveals very little—merely "innuendo, fleeting gestures, and coded language"—about Cornell's relationships with women. Macy was clearly in the know in her relationship with Kit; she worked for Cornell from 1928 until Cornell's death, handling her personal correspondence as well as business elements. She was very close to Kit and the acknowledged "second author" of her latest biography. Furthermore, Macy was responsible for bringing Cornell and Hamilton together. Gert Macy made her theatrical debut as a producer with a musical revue called *One for the Money* by Nancy Hamilton and Morgan Lewis. It was the success of this revue in the late 1930s (which featured unknown performers Gene Kelly and Keenan Wynn) that brought Nancy Hamilton into the circle of Cornell's friends.[23]

Mosel and Macy credit Nancy Hamilton with bringing laughter into Cornell's life. A comic revue writer as well as an actress, Hamilton became known for her fun-loving nature and her clever machinations in party giving.

Kit, the most reserved of party-goers, loved the originality of Nancy's gatherings, where no one was given a chance to be reserved. An unsuspecting arrival might be . . . handed a long pole with a cross-piece nailed to it and directed, drink in hand, to a trunk of old clothes to make a scarecrow.[24]

One marvelous anecdote in Mosel and Macy describes a moment during World War II when Cornell was touring *The Barretts of Wimpole Street* to troupes in the European war zone. Between August 11, 1944, and January 31, 1945, the company performed an impressive 143 times in Italy, France, and Holland. Nancy Hamilton joined the tour as wardrobe mistress, and she was also responsible for a small musical revue performed by cast members in hospital wards wherever the company toured. When the tour was in Paris, Gertrude Stein and Alice B. Toklas wanted to see the play. Performances were strictly limited to military personnel. Nancy Hamilton and Gertrude Macy supplied Stein and Toklas with GI raincoats and special visored caps, so they happily passed as military personnel with the rank of captain.[25]

The details that Macy does allow into the book are wonderfully revealing at times. Though there is meager information on Hamilton, Macy clearly has great respect and regard for her. The bravura sense of humor that seems to have infected Kit's life ends fittingly with a description that Hamilton read from Anthony Trollope on the last nights of Cornell's life. So why the silence on Cornell, on the reality of the relationship as lesbian? In contrast to this, Guthrie's homosexual "indiscretions" are openly referred to by the authors.

Guthrie's "young men" were many and his sexual relations with them seem to have been intense but short-lived, though they often stayed on with him in peripheral production assistant roles.

> If the subject of homosexuality came up in Kit's presence, she waved it away as no more than a gossipy word. In her view, love was love, whether between man and woman, man and man, or woman and woman. She discussed Guthrie's clandestine sexual activities with no one; whatever she knew of them she kept to herself. Only one thing was apparent to an outsider—that she took special pains to be pleasant and agreeable to all his young male friends, going out of her way to see that they were never excluded or slighted, inviting them to dinner . . . or to weekends . . . , often in preference to her own friends.[26]

Mosel and Macy discuss in some detail a particular man, Jimmy Vincent, who came to work for the McClintics as a factotum whose diligence, willingness, and dedication led him to stage management responsibilities. The original relationship between Guthrie and Vincent was probably sexual, but as Vincent became more involved in production work, his devotion to Cornell developed and grew while his relationship with Guthrie became filled with contempt. Vincent's complaint was

> professional and much the same as Gert's. Trying to keep a production rolling smoothly and efficiently, to get things done properly and on time, he felt he was constantly being plagued by this privileged madman's supercilious unpredictability. Whereas Kit's dedication to a production increased with every performance, no matter how long the run, Guthrie felt his responsibility ended with rehearsals.[27]

Guthrie was unwilling to do any of the things, such as notes to actors or tightening of cues, needed to keep a long-running show up to standards. Although Vincent as stage manager was delighted to be given this responsibility, Guthrie's cavalier attitude caused him profound resentment. On the 1936 tour of *The Barretts,* Guthrie joined the production on tour, became enamored with one of the young actors playing a Barrett brother, lured him to the Turkish baths after his first scene, and returned him in time for his last. Macy observed Jimmy Vincent's "professional contempt turned to black personal hatred."[28]

Perhaps Mosel and Macy tell the story of Jimmy Vincent as a memorial to Vincent, a dedicated worker who revered Cornell but whose life ended tragically in alcoholism and suicide. However, telling the story also indicates an aspect of Guthrie's life that Gert Macy, herself, found difficult to endure. It was not the homosexuality itself that she and Vincent found intolerable. It was Guthrie's lack of genuine dedication to the production (or at least a dedication comparable to Cornell's) combined with his secretiveness and lack of discretion. He was known to leave a sexual rendezvous just in time to pick up Kit after a performance, allowing her to think he had been out front watching her all evening. As people behind the scenes, whose job it was to know what was going on, both Vincent and Macy knew Guthrie's proclivities and often shielded the details from Kit.

After pages of discussion on Jimmy Vincent and Guthrie's "young men," Mosel and Macy briefly speculate on Cornell's sexual life. They argue that "Kit could hardly have lived so many years with Guthrie, sympathetically tolerating his "other" life, if she had not had a separate emotional life herself." They point out how different her "emotional attachments" were from his: first, they were not secretive, it was always quite clear whom she loved at any one moment. Second, "unlike Guthrie, she found rapport and spiritual affinity more important than physical gratification. There may have even been some sexual repression." When giving an example of "physical experience," Mosel and Macy present a man as the object of "an easy, spontaneous offering." They end their discussion with a statement that Cornell's closest relationships, often with women, "might aptly be called "passionate friendships."[29]

Where is the key to the authors' choice to discuss McClintic's homosexuality while using the coded language of "passionate friendships" for Cornell? *Passionate friendship* both says it and does not say it; it is innuendo, suggestion, rumor. Of the husband-wife team, Cornell was the "star," the most visible player, the First Lady of American Theater, and to label her lesbian was still clearly taboo. In 1978, the date of publication of the biography, lesbianism still carried with it the stain of sexual deviancy. And as Lillian Faderman so articulately points out, the "Boston marriage," a long-term relationship between two women, was an established precedent and a convenient way of describing two women who lived together as a couple. Because "it was assumed (at least by those outside the relationship) that love between women was asexual, unsullied by the evils of carnality, a sex-hating society could view it as ideal and admire, and even envy, it."[30] And so Mosel and Macy continue a long-held perception about women's relationships with other women: they can be "passionate," but the possibility of sex is cloaked in silence.

Cornell's Wanton Women of the Twenties

If her "official" biographers emphasized asexuality in depicting Cornell's private life, her early stage roles fostered a more sexually active and transgressive image. Because of their sensational, if not scandalous, subject matter, the plays that pushed Cornell into star status in the 1920s were generally viewed by theater critics as questionable vehicles for her talents and received lukewarm reviews, though her acting ability was enthusiastically received. The critical reaction, however, rarely prevented her plays from becoming financially successful. Audiences longed to see her exude a magnetic exoticism and stage charisma that established her as one of the leading actresses of the day.

Her first hit was Clemence Dane's *A Bill of Divorcement* (1921), in which she played the role of Sydney Fairfield, an excitable seventeen-year-old whose father, institutionalized since the war, suffers from shell shock. When it is revealed that the shell shock has uncovered an inherited family insanity, Sydney accepts her fate as a carrier of her father's disease and breaks her engagement, fearful of passing on the illness to the next generation.

While *Bill of Divorcement* was Cornell's first hit, running 173 performances, *The Green Hat* made her a household name. This production opened in New York in 1925, the first of many times that her name would appear in lights. The play had a twenty-nine-week run in New York, followed by eight weeks in Boston and a twenty-four-month tour as far west as Kansas City.

The reviews were far from enthusiastic, but Cornell was hailed for her consummate acting in the role of Iris March, a woman driven to promiscuity by being forcibly separated from the man she truly loves. When she meets her first "pure" love years later on the eve of his wedding, her passion for him is uncontrollable. In a moment that became famous for Cornell (and was responsible for selling thousands of green Iris March hats to her female admirers), Iris tossed her green hat on the floor as she turned out the lights to consummate her love. The defiant gesture captured a certain female zeitgeist, and Iris March became a model for aspiring young sophisticates. Despite the play's predictable ending (Iris delivers a stillborn baby in a convent, sends her now-married lover back to his wife, and recklessly drives her car to her death), the independent, freedom-seeking Iris of the tossed cloche hat was remembered and copied.

The Green Hat was based on a best-selling novel of the same name by Michael Arlen. Both Guthrie and Kit had read it. Guthrie thought it was rubbish, but Kit was immediately interested in playing Iris March if the novel were dramatized. Iris March epitomized a certain 1920s female type. As Gladys Malvern states in her 1943 biography of Cornell,

> It was the day of the flapper. The flapper was a girl whose figure was hipless, flat-chested, boyish; whose galoshes, perpetually open, flapped as she walked; whose hair was cut close to her head, shingled in the back almost like a man's; whose skirts were at the knee or slightly above it; whose hat was a small, closely fitting felt; and who smoked cigarettes from a long holder—the longer the smarter.[31]

The success of Cornell in *The Green Hat* led to many offers for her next production. She turned down O'Neill's *Strange Interlude* to take the role of Leslie Crosbie in *The Letter,* by Somerset Maugham. Whereas Iris March flagrantly took a variety of lovers, Leslie Crosbie went so far as to shoot one dead. Cornell opened the play with a pistol in her hand, firing shots at a man who stumbled across the stage and collapsed. Leslie Crosbie pleads self-defense, claiming that the man tried to rape her. The clever machinations of the plot, however, reveal that she was having an affair with the man and shot him in jealous rage.

Cornell's final role as a tainted female was in *Dishonored Lady,* a melodramatic rendering of a famous Glaswegian murder case from 1857, in which a woman callously killed her lover with poisoned cocoa to get him out of the way so that she could marry a man of wealth and respectability. In the dramatized version, with an updated New York setting, she is named Madeleine Cary, a femme fatale if there ever was one. Cary plans to put strychnine in the coffee of her Argentinean lover, a cabaret singer. While heating up the coffee on the stove, Madeleine is so sexually aroused by the proximity of her Latin lover that she decides on one last evening of passion before the murder. Like a black widow spider, she destroys her lover after sex.

The critics almost uniformly decried the low morals and objectionable sexual ambience of the piece. Several criticized Cornell for lowering herself to play such a role as Madeleine Cary. In the *New York Times,* for example, Brooks Atkinson claimed that if Cornell was to continue presenting such questionable roles she clearly placed "very little value on her art."[32] John Mason Brown in the *New York Evening Post* described the play as a "trashy chronicle of murder" and "a waste, a wicked waste, of Miss Cornell's talents."[33] In a scathing review in *Commonweal,* Richard Dana Skinner judged Cornell's role nothing but a "sentimentalized version of a degenerate," much worse than her questionable roles in *The Green Hat* or *The Letter.* Skinner questioned why Cornell allowed "her fine talents to be exploited in such fifth-rate claptrap."[34]

Although the critics' responses were enthusiastically unfavorable, the play ran a respectable sixteen weeks, with audiences thronging to see Cornell as yet another irresistibly wicked woman. Particularly disturbing to the critics was their inability to reconcile their image of who Katharine Cornell was with the disturbing roles that she played. As Mosel and Macy say, "What shocked and angered them was not that it was fifth-rate claptrap or that it was beneath her or that it was badly written or that it was a waste of time, what shocked them was that she did it so well and with such relish."[35] In other words, the fact that she did so well with these roles suggested that Cornell could not be separated from the roles she played. If she impersonated Madeleine Cary with such delight, could it mean that in her own private life she identified with this lascivious character? This anxiety of the critics points to the age-old prejudice: when it comes to theater, women are not actors, in the sense of artistic creators, but merely playing themselves on stage.[36]

Such prejudice suggested the possibility of a fearful hidden reality: that those androgynous, dangerous, promiscuous women that Cornell played were indeed very like the actress who played them. Since the woman who played these roles was known among her close friends as a woman who liked other women, the knowledge, as we have seen above, leaked from the gay subculture to certain elements of mainstream culture. Critics, in particular, often had access to this information since they befriended certain actors and snooped around the theater scene. Alexander Woollcott, one of the leading theater critics of the twenties and part of the famous Algonquin Round Table, was a closeted homosexual and undoubtedly party to the gossip of the gay subculture.[37] Although the public was unaware of the private lives of Guthrie and Katharine and believed in the matrimonial bliss of this husband-and-wife team, a certain amount of anxiety was undoubtedly prompted by Cornell's wanton women roles of the twenties and the way in which such roles fed into any potential gossip about her sex life. On the one hand, although the characters she played were heterosexual, their transgressive actions suggested a wild kind of femininity that neatly aligned itself in the public mind with another kind of transgressive activity: the sexual deviancy known as lesbianism. In the public imagination, strong women wielding pistols had a close affinity to women loving other women. After all, wasn't the Greek myth of the Amazons just such a story?

The twenties focused on sexuality in new and startling ways. The dissemination of scientific and medical "knowledge" that began in the late nineteenth century with Richard von Krafft-Ebbing (*Psychopathia Sexualis*, 1882) and Havelock Ellis (*Studies in the Psychology of Sex: Sexual Inversion*, 1897), which pathologized same-sex relationships between women, was overtaken by a fascination with Sigmund Freud. Although Freud always claimed that Americans never really understood the complexities of psychoanalysis, he nevertheless acknowledged that the country had been the first to welcome it with enthusiasm.[38] In 1920 Freud published "The Psychogenesis of a Case of Homosexuality in a Woman" and continued the Ellis/Krafft-Ebbing belief that homosexuality was undesirable and needed to be cured. So pervasive and popularized were Freud's theories that it was not necessary actually to read Freud's essays to know that love between women originated as childhood trauma and arrested development.[39]

The interest in same-sex love between women was not confined to medical debates. In 1928 two landmark novels were published: Virginia Woolf's *Orlando* and Radclyffe Hall's *The Well of Loneliness*. While Woolf could code and veil her subject matter through historical distance and literary devices, Hall set her novel in the present and openly declared the lesbian protagonist a martyr to her sexuality. Hall had hoped to present a sympathetic portrait that would alleviate the standard prejudice against lesbians through understanding their predicament. Instead, the novel was banned in England six weeks after its publication. At an obscenity hearing in 1929, the presiding judge stated, "The book can have no moral value since it seems to justify the right of the pervert to prey upon normal members of the community" and was "antisocial and offensive to public morals and decency."[40]

Broadway was not immune to such repressive measures. In 1922, while Cornell continued to play Sydney Fairchild, Sholom Asch's *The God of Vengeance* introduced one of the earliest representations of lesbians on the American stage. Asch, the first Yiddish playwright to establish a reputation outside the Jewish community, had many productions of his controversial play over a seventeen-year period, including Max Rein-hardt's 1907 production in Berlin. It had been produced several times in New York's Yiddish theaters but created havoc only in its first English-language production in New York City. During a performance on March 6, 1923, a detective appeared backstage at the Apollo Theatre to inform the theater owner, the producer, and the twelve actors that they had been indicted by a grand jury for violation of the penal code by "presenting an obscene, indecent, immoral and impure theatrical production."[41] When the case went to a jury, a guilty verdict was handed down to the company, making headline news in the New York dailies. Their conviction was the first time that a jury had found actors guilty of performing immoral material as public entertainment. The judge in his opinion asserted that "the time had come when the drama must be purified," and he applauded what he perceived would be the trial's wholesome effect on the theater of the day.[42]

The police detectives on stage for censorship purposes had reacted predictably for the period. In 1928, the same year that Katharine Cornell appeared in the role of Ellen Olenska in *The Age of Innocence,* a stage adaptation of Edith Wharton's novel, Mae West's production of *Pleasure Man* was closed on Broadway when detectives walked on stage and gagged the actors with their hands. *Pleasure Man* continued West's oppor-tunistic Broadway productions of controversial subject matter. Two years before, she had been convicted for on stage obscenity. *Pleasure Man* depicted the backstage antics of a group of female impersonators who played out a homosexual subtext with wit and double entendre. As Marybeth Hamilton states, "In 1928, New York state law forbade open stage depiction of homosexuality. Yet West managed to depict gay cul-ture's most sensational elements (and deny any sensational intent) by exploiting the link between mainstream vaudeville traditions and the female impersonation at the heart of gay style."[43]

New York City in the twenties was the center of a cultural upheaval: the Jazz Age, the age of the flapper, the core of an exciting melding of high and low art, and, as we have seen, a fascination with Freudian musings. While critics read Cornell's performances as "trashy," melodra-matic renderings that were beneath her, her audiences (particularly the women) read her performances as enacting a kind of androgynous, sexu-ally ambiguous freedom, dangerous, on the edge. Leslie Crosbie fired a pistol and got away with it. But such a transgressive act could not go unpunished. Accompanying such public acts of freedom and wanton sexual ambiguity were repressive measures that culminated in a New

York state law in 1928 that forbade any depictions of homosexuality on the stage, and in 1934 the Motion Picture Code prohibited any references to homosexuality in films. These pronouncements from the cultural thought police came none too soon for many who, instead of seeing New York as an artistic melting pot of exciting and boundary-breaking creativity, viewed the twenties as a miasma of decadence, decline, and sexual confusion. In an editorial that commented on the indictment of the actors in *The God of Vengeance,* the *New York Herald* in 1923 stated,

> This country particularly demands that its literature, its stage and its art be kept clean as American opinion has maintained them. It will not do to defend impure plays or books with the statement that they have been tolerated in this or that country of Europe. The Continental standards are not ours.[44]

While many male critics viewed Cornell's performances of the late twenties with apprehension and alarm (how can she be good at being wanton?), a parallel anxiety was invoked by critics of Hollywood: two of the film industry's most bankable stars, Marlene Dietrich and Greta Garbo—dangerously "Continental" imports—were cracking open gender boundaries with their cross-dressed performances and erotic screen personae. In *Morocco* (1930) Dietrich, dressed in a top hat and tails, suddenly turns and kisses a woman on the lips. But Garbo, who arrived in the States in 1925 and began producing films a year later, was the screen's counterpart to Cornell's stage presence.

By 1930 Garbo was a well-established Hollywood star known for her enigmatic, fascinating screen presence. The titles of some of her films in the twenties suggest her dark, mysterious allure: *The Temptress* (1926), *Flesh and the Devil* (1927), *The Mysterious Lady,* a story of espionage (1928), and two films in which she played a lovely young wife who cuckolded her older husband: *Wild Orchids* and *The Kiss* (both 1929). A connection between Cornell and Garbo was made in 1928, a film version of *The Green Hat,* now titled *A Woman of Affairs,* with Garbo in the role of Iris March. So perhaps it was not surprising when theater critics, trying to come to terms with Cornell's role as the murderous but seductive Madeleine Cary in *Dishonored Lady,* compared her to Garbo. In the *New York Mirror,* Walter Winchell, one of the few critics who praised Cornell's *Dishonored Lady,* stated,

> It is chockful of breathtaking episodes and highly explosive love encounters, all of which leave young persons, such as your reporter, terribly limp. But it is always the electrifying Katharine Cornell who

keeps you on edge, sometimes leaving you hotter than hot with her stronger-than-Garbo-appeal, and sometime leaves you cold, with her artful interpretation of a murderess.[45]

Richard Watts Jr., writing in the *New York Tribune*, described Cornell as "the Greta Garbo of the stage."

> She possesses that same inscrutable sort of fascination, and there clings to her that same aura of glamour and romantic illusiveness, that identical and fascinating combination of the strange, the sinister and the beautiful. About her there is that indefinable touch of the decadent which, allied to a certain vague eeriness and a certain very definite poetic loveliness, results in the irresistible, half fabulous quality that her colleague of the screen offers to such a valiant degree.[46]

Winchell's review suggests a curious duality, a performance that can leave you both hot and cold, and Watts continues this duality with Cornell's combination of "the sinister" and "the beautiful." Garbo's screen persona also projected a duality: a touching fragility combined with strength and control. This duality was compelling to both men and women. As Andrea Weiss states,

> The public could be teased with the possibility of lesbianism, which provoked both curiosity and titillation. Hollywood marketed the suggestion of lesbianism, not because it intentionally sought to address lesbian audiences, but because it sought to address male voyeuristic interest in lesbianism. This use of innuendo, however, worked for a range of women spectators as well, enabling them to explore their own erotic gaze without giving it a name.[47]

When innuendo got out of hand or too close to the edge, the Hollywood machine happily complied by creating the impression of a heterosexual romance, which is what MGM did for Greta Garbo by urging her to marry her costar, John Gilbert (although she put him off and never did marry). Garbo's counterpart on Broadway was already married, but, almost as if to erase those images of androgynous, dangerous, sensual women that were so popular but so criticized, Cornell staged the heterosexual romance of her career.

Just one year after the damning reviews of *Dishonored Lady* appeared, Katharine Cornell shifted dramatic gears. No longer would she tempt her critics with comparisons to the sultry, sexually ambiguous Garbo. No longer would she delight her audiences with her wanton women and feed the growing paranoia of the naysayers who saw such characters as indicative of a general decline toward degeneracy. From now on, she would present roles that were wholesome and thoroughly "artistic." Cornell's next role—in fact the dramatic character that many consider the defining role of her long career—was Elizabeth Barrett in *The Barretts of Wimpole Street*.

The play had already been rejected by at least twenty-seven producers in New York who considered it a conventional Victorian costume play based on the love story of two clean-cut poets, a work that would have no interest to the public. Even her manager from *The Green Hat* advised her against the role, believing her public would not accept her in a part in which she spent her entire stage time lying down as an invalid.[48]

The Barretts was the first play that Cornell produced herself, and it turned out to be the high point of her career in number of performances and financial success. Opening on February 9, 1931, it ran for 370 performances and then immediately toured the country. A second tour was organized in 1933, encompassing seventy-five towns and cities over a twenty-nine-week period. This was followed by the European War Zone tour, a Broadway revival in 1945 that lasted for eleven weeks, and a 1947 tour. Cornell played Elizabeth 1,019 performances in all.[49]

When the play opened on Broadway for the first time, Brooks Atkinson wrote in the *New York Times*: "After a long succession of meretricious plays it introduces us to Katharine Cornell as an actress of the first order. Here the disciplined fury that she has been squandering on catchpenny plays becomes the vibrant beauty of finely wrought character."[50]

The critics seemed to sigh with relief that Cornell performed so well in a play with a sympathetic female role who battled against her domineering patriarch of a father to win the love of her life, Robert Browning. Moreover, any threat posed by her sexual desire was diffused by her physical infirmity. And in addition to the compelling love story was the great poetry.

With *The Barretts*, Cornell had hired Ray Henderson as a press agent. Henderson, who evolved a system of interesting and press-worthy weekly releases about Cornell, helped create a persona for Cornell the artist and the lady that earned respect and dignity. From now on she was Miss Cornell. He stage-managed her interviews as well, shifting her style from the personal, expressive, spontaneous, and buoyant interviews of *The Green Hat* days to a more thoughtful, calm, and ladylike demeanor.[51] Now, Cornell's trajectory was one of "great" roles. After *The Barretts*, the role for which she received the most praise was Juliet in *Romeo and Juliet*, once again celebrating heterosexual romance. In 1923 Cornell had played a cross-dressed, swaggering Mary Fritton, the Dark Lady of the sonnets, in Clemence Dane's historically spurious *Will Shakespeare*. Mary Fritton was an alluring, raucous role, her big scene a tavern

Katharine Cornell and Basil Rathbone in *Romeo and Juliet.*
Stark Young claimed her portrayal of Juliet
"makes you believe in love."

(Courtesy John McFadden Archives.)

brawl with Shakespeare and Marlowe. Later she saves the day when the boy actor playing Juliet sprains his ankle on opening night and she steps into the part. Just eleven years later, in 1934, her Juliet was called "the foremost American Juliet of her generation."[52] The conservative thirties called for conventional couplings. To be the "First Lady of the American Theater," Katharine Cornell had to give up her tarnished, "meretricious" roles and perform only "first-rate" characters, roles that allowed her to playact her love for men on stage. Gone for ever were the dangerous, androgynous, transgressive roles of the twenties.

The Legacy of the Cautious Thirties

Historical evidence from the 1930s clearly demonstrates that this decade proceeded with greater restraint than the hedonist twenties. The moral policing of themes presented on the stage shifted discernibly, and, just as significantly, the number of productions decreased because of financial instability during the depression. The tenuous theatrical economy was debilitated further by the increased popularity in the cinema. In 1920 some fifteen hundred theaters outside New York City were available for staging plays. By 1930 only about five hundred remained, many of the theaters having been converted to movie houses.[53] With the reduction in available stages, so too the number of road shows decreased. In 1900 over three hundred theatrical road shows toured the country, while in 1933, the year Cornell took her three-show repertory on the road, there were less than twenty.

Although Cornell had been approached by Irving Thalberg to recreate her role of Elizabeth Barrett Browning for the silver screen, Kit refused the offer. Unlike other actresses of her generation—Tallulah Bankhead and Helen Hayes for example—she could never imagine herself easily moving from one medium to another. Tad Mosel speculates on why Cornell refused the Hollywood overtures.

> She did not feel she was acting for historians or nostalgia fans of the future but for audiences of the here and now, people who came into the theatre tonight, sat in their seats and waited for the curtain to go up. Not only were they the ones she wanted to reach, but she wanted to be there when they responded, she did not want to be off in another part of the world while they gazed at a second-hand image on a screen. In fact, she was not sure she could give them anything to respond to without the inducement of their presence.[54]

It was no doubt Cornell's insistence on the here and now of live theater that induced her to tour. What is a Broadway star to do when she refuses the temptations of Hollywood? She takes her productions on the road, where she can offer herself directly and in person to her public.

Although she had toured single shows many times in the past, Kit decided, along with Guthrie and her publicity manager Ray Henderson, to launch a repertory tour of three plays: *The Barretts, Candida* (a popular hit of hers from 1925), and *Romeo and Juliet.* Cornell's production company was taking great financial risks. Many people, including the theatrical press, said the road was dead. Only two celebrated actors were still touring: Eva Le Gallienne and Walter Hampden.[55] But Kit and Guth rose to the challenge and demonstrated their faith in the road, with their repertory tour of 1933–34. While Broadway itself was witnessing Maxwell Anderson's *Mary of Scotland,* the Group Theatre's production of Sidney Kingsley's *Men in White,* and a stage adaptation of Erskine Caldwell's *Tobacco Road,* the Cornell company toured seventeen thousand miles in seven months; their 225 performances played to five hundred thousand people. As Mosel states, "She set box office records wherever she went. She proved that lost, neglected, uncultivated audiences in thirty-four states would patronize the living theatre if given a chance."[56]

While Cornell's tour during the height of the depression is often credited with reviving the viability of the road, it also generated another nearly forgotten legacy more germane to our study here. In 1942 a theater novel was published entitled *Quicksilver.* The author, Fitzroy Davis, began his professional theater career in a small role in Cornell's follow-on 1935 tour of *Romeo and Juliet.* Davis delivers a fresh, perceptive, detailed account of life in a large theater company as it takes its Broadway success—*Romeo and Juliet*—on the road. From travel arrangements, to salary differentials, to housing of the lower-tier performers, to company politics, to the idiosyncrasies of provincial theaters, the book provides a panoply of detail and captures the combination of dedication, hard work, ego flashing, and chaos that went into such an enormous undertaking.

Historian Charles Shattuck, who recovered *Quicksilver,* explains in a recent essay that although the novel is just that, a fictional account, Davis, as a young, ambitious thespian, compiled a record of Cornell's production—line readings, scene sketches, and stage business—by standing in the wings and taking notes.[57] The characters in the book—the majority of them actors in the company—portray a variety of social mores, prevailing prejudices, and individual enthusiasms that filter through the company atmosphere as the itinerant players bring their culture to the provinces. The point of view of the novel is primarily that of the bit players, but the framing dynamic is the star of the tour, the leading lady of the theater, Miss Evelyn Navarre, widely assumed to be Cornell under another name.[58]

The portrait of Miss Navarre is far from flattering: she is self-centered, grasping, jealous of other actresses; she cultivates her favorites and luxuriates in her mink coats. She is also a lesbian. Her current lover-companion in the novel is the much despised Deborah, secretary of Miss Navarre, nicknamed "Madame Veto" behind her back by the company members. Greatly feared for her influence over Miss Navarre, one of the actors in the company exclaims, "God, the power that dyke has, it's criminal."[59]

The lower-tier actors reveal homophobic sentiments occasionally tempered with a live-and-let-live attitude. When one of the new actors to the Navarre company learns for the first time that the star actor playing Romeo has his lover with him, the fledgling Thespian shouts, "I'd beat him to a pulp. If there's anything that makes my stomach turn, it's that! . . . How the hell can you guys take it so casually?" And then later, "There's a superstition it's good luck to have one pansy in the company. . . . They just say that because there always is one."[60]

Quicksilver was well reviewed, highly praised for its "authentic knowledge of backstage realities," and must have been widely read, as it went into a second printing.[61] At the same time, it undoubtedly caused a scandal among the theater professionals. The reviewer in *Theatre Arts* "prophesied there would be 'bitterness out loud' among theatre folk as they 'recognize portraits among the company that Evelyn Navarre, 'the first lady of the American theatre' takes on tour in *Romeo and Juliet*."[62]

It is very difficult to speculate on Davis's intentions when writing this novel. I imagine he was stunned by its negative reception amongst theater people themselves. It did after all get him blacklisted from the profession, and as Shattuck points out, he virtually erased any reference to Katharine Cornell from his life.[63] For nestled among the extreme and hateful homophobic reactions of some of the actors are brief ambivalent insights into what it must have been like to come to terms with this long and deep-seated prejudice. For example, near the end of the novel, when the central character, Henry, a comic actor with the Navarre company, walks down Fifth Avenue after his return from the long and harrowing tour, he spots one of Hollywood's leading actresses and reflects on the longevity of her fame, her style, her beauty—and her affairs.

Even if the public learned about her affairs with one leading man
after another, they would forgive them in return for that perfect
grace. Whereas, let the whisper of just one of Miss Evvy's [Evelyn
Navarre] inverted episodes pass over the land, and the carrion
would gather to pluck out her gorgeous orbs.[64]

For a brief novelistic moment Davis's character begins to question the
heterosexual imperative. But such questioning no doubt seemed a moot
point to a theater profession that was trying to hide from that "carrion"
the very thing that Davis so openly makes public in *Quicksilver*. Davis's
novel—"the truest portrait of the stage today"—illuminates a homophobic atmosphere that necessitated lavender marriages.[65]

NOTES

1. Tad Mosel with Gertrude Macy, *Leading Lady: The World and Theatre
of Katharine Cornell* (Boston: Little, Brown, 1978), 314–15.
2. The lavender marriage seems to have come into its own in Hollywood in
the twenties, when known homosexuals and lesbians were married by the studios
as a ploy to cover up and divert attention from their same-sex relationships. These
marriages were used by studio impresarios to spin good romantic press material
with numerous photo opportunities of wedding receptions and honeymoon jaunts.
Some of the more famous include Judy Garland and Vincent Minnelli, Barbara
Stanwyck and Robert Taylor, and Charles Laughton and Elsa Lanchester.
3. Andrea Weiss, " 'A Queer Feeling When I Look at You': Hollywood
Stars and Lesbian Spectatorship in the 1930s," in *Multiple Voices in Feminist
Film Criticism*, ed. Diane Carson, Linda Dittmar, and Janice R. Welsch (Minneapolis: University of Minnesota Press, 1994), 330.
4. Axel Madsen, *The Sewing Circle: Hollywood's Greatest Secret—
Female Stars Who Loved Other Women* (New York: Birch Lane Press, 1995), 41.
5. Ann Douglas, *Terrible Honesty: Mongrel Manhattan in the 1920's*
(New York: Farrar, Straus and Giroux, 1995), 539.
6. Kaier Curtin, *"We Can Always Call Them Bulgarians": The Emergence
of Lesbians and Gay Men on the American Stage* (Boston: Alyson, 1987), 57.
7. Curtin, *Call Them Bulgarians*, 112.
8. Billy J. Harbin, interview with Kaier Curtin, November 20, 1996, conveyed through correspondence with Harbin.
9. Patricia Meyer Spacks, *Gossip* (New York: Knopf, 1985), 46.
10. Weiss, "Queer Feeling," 331.
11. Inconsistencies and contradictions are often part of "traditional" research as well. I do not mean to say otherwise, merely to suggest that with
reliance on so many nontraditional sources combined with accounts that deliberately avoid the topic, it is more difficult to piece together the shapes of the
peoples' lives who are under consideration.
12. Lee Alan Morrow, E-mail correspondence with the author, February 29,
1996, and March 19, 1996.

13. Madsen, *The Sewing Circle,* 25, 41. Although Madsen's book is compelling, it is frustrating. There are no footnotes; instead, a bibliography for each chapter provides a source for some general point, leaving the specifics blurred. In "Notes on Sources," Madsen states, "In researching *The Sewing Circle,* I believe I talked to every major living figure who knew Sapphic Hollywood. The entertainment-industry fishbowl forced homosexuals to be imaginative, to resort to sumptuous surfaces, campy disguises, and witty conspiracies" (217). Madsen goes on to list the many Hollywood people he interviewed. He also had access to the unpublished, early drafts of Mercedes de Acosta's autobiography.

14. John K. Tillinghast, "Guthrie McClintic, Director," Ph.D. diss., Indiana University, 1964, 44.

15. Lawrence Langner, *The Magic Curtain* (New York: E. P. Dutton, 1951), 101.

16. Ibid., 198.

17. Guthrie McClintic, *Me and Kit* (Boston: Little, Brown, 1955), 3–4.

18. Ibid., 4.

19. Gerald Bordman, *Oxford Companion to American Theatre,* 2d ed. (Oxford: Oxford University Press, 1992), 448.

20. Gladys Malvern, *Curtain Going Up! The Story of Katharine Cornell* (New York: Julian Messner, 1943), 153.

21. Mosel and Macy, *Leading Lady,* 221.

22. Ibid., 522.

23. Ibid., 423–24.

24. Ibid., 437.

25. Ibid., 461.

26. Ibid., 383.

27. Ibid., 384–85.

28. Ibid., 385.

29. Ibid., 386.

30. Lillian Faderman, *Surpassing The Love of Men: Romantic Friendship between Women from the Renaissance to the Present* (London: Women's Press, 1981), 203.

31. Malvern, *Curtain Going Up!* 138.

32. Brooks Atkinson, "Dishonored Lady," *New York Times,* February 5, 1930.

33. John Mason Brown, "The Play: 'Dishonored Lady.' " *New York Post,* February 5, 1930.

34. Richard Dana Skinner, "Dishonored Lady," *Commonweal,* February 19, 1930, 453.

35. Mosel and Macy, *Leading Lady,* 240.

36. For a discussion of this idea of actresses "playing the self" on stage see Lesley Ferris, *Acting Women: Images of Women in Theatre* (London: Macmillan, 1990), chaps. 3, 4, and 5.

37. Woollcott, at Carl Van Vechten's strenuous prompting, went to the second performance of *A Bill of Divorcement,* giving it an excellent review in the *New York Times,* and saving the show from an early closing. Woollcott remained a lifelong supporter of Cornell.

38. Douglas, *Terrible Honesty,* 127.

39. Faderman, *Surpassing Love of Men,* 314–15.

40. Vera Brittain, *Radclyffe Hall: A Case of Obscenity?* (New York: A. S. Barnes, 1969), 138.

41. Quoted in Curtin, *Call Them Bulgarians,* 36.

42. Quoted in ibid., 37. For a full account of the press comments and details of the script itself see chapter 1 of Curtin's book.

43. Maybeth Hamilton, " 'I'm Queen of the Bitches': Female Impersonation and Mae West's *Pleasure Man,*" in *Crossing the Stage: Controversies on Cross-Dressing,* ed. Lesley Ferris (New York: Routledge, 1993), 114.

44. Quoted in Curtin, *Call Them Bulgarians,* 37.

45. Review reprinted in Katharine Cornell, *I Wanted to Be an Actress: The Autobiography of Katharine Cornell* (New York: Random House, 1938), 253.

46. Review reprinted in ibid., 256.

47. Weiss, "Queer Feeling," 331.

48. Lucille M. Pederson, *Katharine Cornell: A Bio-Bibliography* (Westport, CT: Greenwood Press, 1994), 71.

49. Ibid., 116.

50. Review reprinted in Cornell, *I Wanted to Be,* 260.

51. Mosel and Macy, *Leading Lady,* 291.

52. Pederson, *Katharine Cornell,* 91.

53. Barnard Hewitt, *Theatre U.S.A. 1668–1957* (New York: NY McGraw Hill, 1959), 383.

54. Mosel and Macy, *Leading Lady,* 279.

55. Ibid., 322.

56. Ibid., 339.

57. This document is in the theater library at Lincoln Center Library for the Performing Arts, New York Public Library, with Davis's own note saying that he used some of his backstage observation in writing parts of his novel. See Charles Shattuck, "*Quicksilver* Revisited: A Portrait of the Stage in the 1930's," in *The American Stage: Social and Economic Issues from the Colonial Period to the Present,* ed. Ron Engle and Tice L. Miller (Cambridge: Cambridge University Press, 1993), 191.

58. As Shattuck tells it, "A friend of mine who knew Davis in later years (he died in 1980) tells me that in the early 1940s everybody assumed that he had written a thinly veiled account of the Cornell tour" ("*Quicksilver* Revisited," 191). Here is another example of the importance of gossip, as discussed at the beginning of this essay.

59. Fitzroy Davis, *Quicksilver* (New York: Harcourt, Brace, 1942), 177.

60. Ibid., 107.

61. Shattuck, "*Quicksilver* Revisited," 199.

62. Ibid., 191.

63. Ibid. Shattuck points out that the publication of the novel "seriously damaged his prospective career in professional theatre." *Quicksilver* is not mentioned in Mosel and Macy's *Leading Lady* or Pederson's bibliography, *Katharine Cornell.*

64. Davis, *Quicksilver,* 567.

65. Shattuck, "*Quicksilver* Revisited," 190.

Webster without Tears

A Daughter's Journey

Milly S. Barranger

Margaret Webster (1905–72), the only child of British actors Benjamin N. Webster III and Dame May Whitty, was the fifth generation of a distinguished theatrical family, including actors, managers, and dancing masters, to carve out an international career.[1] She established herself in the United States as a notable actress and stage director whose career reached its zenith in the 1940s on Broadway. Her journey to distinction in theater, opera, and letters was marked by triumph and failure as she wrestled with the skepticism, prejudice, and vagaries of the theater industry on two continents.

"Peggy," as family and friends called her, was born on March 15, 1905, in New York City at an address on West Fifty-eighth Street while her father, accompanied by her mother, was on tour with the William Brady–Grace George Company. As the only child of highly successful professional actors, she grew up in the glamorous world of London's West End. Her childhood companions were her parents' professional friends. These "aunts and uncles," as she called them, included Hilda Trevelyan, who played the perennial Wendy in the seasonal *Peter Pan,* Constance Collier, who played Ophelia in the John Barrymore *Hamlet,* and Jean Forbes-Robertson, who starred with her husband Johnston Forbes-Robertson in *The Passing of the Third Floor Back.*

During Peggy's early years, three strong-willed, accomplished women emerged as role models for the young girl: May Whitty, Edith Craig, and Sybil Thorndike. Described as a "petite doe-eyed beauty," May Whitty had little personal time for her daughter. Her mothering was sandwiched between professional engagements and her many committees for the war effort during World War I. Edith Craig played an enormous role in the young girl's development, since she and her bohemian companions, both male and female, lived in the redbrick Victorian multidwelling at 31 Bedford Place near Covent Garden where the Websters resided on the top

Margaret Webster rehearsing

*(Courtesy Billy Rose Theatre Collection, The New York Public Library
for the Performing Arts, Astor, Lenox and Tilden Foundations.)*

floor. Twenty-six years older than Peggy, Edith Craig was the daughter of
the renowned actress Ellen Terry and architect Edward Godwin and sister
to the famous designer Edward Gordon Craig. Her life was characterized
by exceptional devotion to her mother and by a career as a stage director
that was circumscribed by her fiery temperament and aggressive personality and by the male-dominated theatrical establishment of the day. She
was relegated to staging secondary events, such as benefits, pageants, and

charity matinees. Edith Craig was an early example for Peggy of the social and professional marginalization of women who did not aspire to stage prominence as actresses or to backstage positions as dressers and seamstresses. Edith Craig's bisexuality also represented an alternative lifestyle that would play a large role in Peggy's developing sexuality, for it became an accepted fact for the various families at 31 Bedford Place.[2]

Sybil Thorndike and May Whitty, on the other hand, were accomplished actresses whose husbands provided an emotional and professional support system both at home and on stage. Married to actor-manager Lewis T. Casson, Sybil Thorndike, a distinguished actress in classical roles and in plays by George Bernard Shaw, was the leading actress of the Casson-Thorndike company that was to provide Peggy with her professional stage debut in 1924.

Peggy's first separation from her parents' glamorous world came at the start of the zeppelin raids over London in 1916. May Whitty sent her daughter to a Christian Science boarding school, Bradley Wood House, in Devonshire. Peggy endured her "exile" with feelings of homesickness and anxiety over her mother's inability to attend her school theatricals. At war's end, Peggy transferred to the prestigious Queen Anne's School, a small public school dedicated to the education of young women of professional parents, located in Reading.

The year Peggy was to graduate the school authorities encouraged her to try for a scholarship to Oxford or Cambridge. She had excelled with an "A" certificate in literature, history, and languages, and her teachers envisioned that she would become one of the few women of the day to achieve admission to a university. They had not counted upon May Whitty's determination that her daughter should not, and would not, depart from the Webster family tradition. Arguing that Peggy could not change her mind about a stage career at age twenty-one should she decide that she was unsuited to a scholarly career, May Whitty offered Peggy a three-month sojourn in Paris followed by professional actor-training at the Etlinger Dramatic School. The Herbert Beerbohm Tree School, established in 1904, was the premiere training ground for young actors in the 1920s (it would become the Royal Academy of Dramatic Art), but it so happened that both Ben and May were teachers at the Etlinger School, and Peggy's formal journey to the stage began in 1923 under their tutelage. Forever sanguine about her career choice, Peggy said in later years that May and Ben objected "to my stage career with the usual insincerity of theatrical parents."[3]

What May Whitty could not envision (and it must be remembered that May had almost no formal education because of the Whitty family's financial difficulties that sent her to the stage to earn a living at age sixteen) was that her daughter would eventually achieve distinction as a stage director and author rather than as a preeminent actress. Peggy's "American" experience was beyond both parents' knowledge of the industry. As actors, Ben and May found career fulfillment and social distinction in the commercial theater, and at age seventy May Whitty became a film star as well. Ben's grandfather, Benjamin Nottingham Webster I, known to the theater world as "Old Ben," had been one of the most famous West End actor-managers of his day, managing both the Haymarket and Adelphi Theatres in the mid-1800s. It was not until Peggy met Lilian Baylis, the formidable manager of the Old Vic Theatre on Waterloo Road, that she would observe a woman in the powerful position of theater manager. First, however, Peggy's apprenticeship as a professional actor would occur in the crucible of the regional repertory companies.

Peggy Webster's adolescent weight problems—she was five feet, four inches tall, and weighed 140 pounds—relegated her to the secondary roles of aunts, spinsters, and chorus members. She made her professional debut in 1924 with the Casson-Thorndike company as a chorus member in *The Trojan Women*, with Sybil Thorndike playing Hecuba. The following year she toured with the company in *Saint Joan* as Sybil Thorndike's understudy. As was the custom of the time, understudies filled in as court ladies and swelled crowd scenes.

Following her twenty-first birthday and fearing a professional lifetime of crowd scenes with the Cassons, she joined the Macdona Players and toured as dowagers, servants, and an occasional ingenue in a repertory of George Bernard Shaw's plays. The following year she joined J. B. Fagan's Oxford Players and toured in plays by Shaw, Anton Chekhov, James M. Barrie, and August Strindberg. The role of Sonya, the emotionally deprived young woman doomed to spinsterhood in Chekhov's *Uncle Vanya*, was the high point of this tour. Peggy cheerfully admitted that for the privilege of playing Sonya for one week she would agree to "carry a spear for six months."4

The rhythm of Peggy's life was seemingly established. A period of intense rehearsing and performing was followed by a period of inactivity relieved only by weekly auditions and Sunday-night showcases when the theaters were otherwise dark. She also experienced the double-edged sword of many children of famous theatrical parents. While doors were opened to her that might otherwise have remained closed, the interviews and auditions were often perfunctory and ended with, "Give my love to your mother and father." Peggy also learned that some employers were reluctant to hire young talent of well-known parents because of the risk of creating professional and personal difficulties with the parents should the child not be successful.

No parental influence was exerted when in 1928 Peggy joined the slightly disheveled and unfashionable Sir Philip Ben Greet Shakespeare Company, a troupe famous for its "pastoral" tours of Shakespeare's plays. "B. G.," as Ben Greet was known to his actors, had pioneered Shakespeare at the Old Vic Theatre during World War I and had managed some early summer festivals at Stratford. Many young British actors as well as audiences owed their first experience of Shakespeare to his efforts. By the time Peggy joined his company, he was an elderly man of benevolent appearance, with a shock of white hair, bright blue eyes, and a cantankerous disposition.[5] His company, however, was a training ground for playing Shakespeare in all kinds of weather, topography, and costumes. The general idea was that the company would play out of doors (hence, "pastoral"), adapting to such existing conditions as rose gardens, soccer fields, and rain-drenched pastures. Ben Greet avoided fancy theories, modern analogies, and stage gimmicks; he trusted the lines and the actors to reach the audience and hold them enthralled. Peggy was to carry this lesson throughout her career and even into her own MarWeb Shakespeare Company that she formed in the late forties and toured into the American heartland.

Women had made great social strides during World War I, when necessity required that they undertake the jobs that three million men had left behind in England when they crossed the channel to fight in the trenches of Europe. May Whitty excelled at committee work for the many good causes and in 1917 was named a Dame Commander of the British Empire for her exceptional efforts. Nevertheless, the commercial West End theater that had been home to the Webster family for four generations had changed very little. A patriarchal system remained in place with men empowered as producers, managers, and directors. The mercurial Lilian Baylis (1874–1937) challenged the system from her domain in the Royal Victoria Theatre, whose management she inherited from her aunt, Emma Cons. The Old Vic, which had risen from a temperance hall, was by 1929, when Peggy first appeared there, a nonprofit theater whose repertoire was largely devoted to Shakespeare.

Peggy's entree to the Old Vic came through a small maid's role in an eighteenth-century comedy called *The Confederacy*. In his first season as artistic director at the Old Vic under Baylis's management, Harcourt

Williams had difficulty casting Molière's scheming maid in *The Imaginary Invalid*. He saw Peggy's performance in *The Confederacy* and offered her a seasonal contract. At age twenty-four Peggy emerged from the chaotic obscurity of pastoral touring and makeshift showcases onto the stage of the prestigious Old Vic.

In the 1929–30 season Peggy played secondary roles opposite London's newest young stars, John Gielgud and Martita Hunt, a slim, high-spirited young woman known for playing "modern" Ibsen heroines. Overshadowed by these two stars, Peggy played Lady Capulet in *Romeo and Juliet,* Nerissa in *The Merchant of Venice,* the duchess of York in *Richard II,* and Lady Macduff in *Macbeth.* Always her own severest critic, Peggy's greatest success that season, in her own estimation, was as Audrey with a putty nose and flaxen wig in *As You Like It.*

Realizing that performing with this company of rising stars—which was shortly to include Laurence Olivier, Ralph Richardson, Jessica Tandy, Edith Evans, and Charles Laughton—she would never progress beyond the minor queen in tragedy or the country maid in comedy, Peggy declined to renew her contract for a second season. "Never mind, dear, you'll be back," Lilian Baylis predicted.[6] In fact, Peggy returned to the Old Vic as Lady Macbeth in 1932 and again twenty-five years later to direct *Measure for Measure* in the 1957–58 season.

With a sense of determination but with growing disappointment that after six years of hard, devoted work her career had yet to take off, she turned to the West End for employment. In one very real sense she was returning to her parents' world—the familiar world of her childhood that she had never left, since she continued to reside at 31 Bedford Place—but it was also a world of many hard object lessons learned by women who aspired to work there. Peggy was determined to climb the mountain equipped with her repertory experience of playing Shakespeare and Shaw. She was also equipped with a remarkable voice, which was her distinguishing quality as an actress along with her sensitive readings of the texts.

As unexpected as her departure from the Old Vic was the offer of a major role in a West End production. The actor-manager Sir John Martin Harvey had announced a revival of *The Devil's Disciple* with himself as Richard Dudgeon. He cast an inexperienced ingenue, Peggy, in the role, expecting that critics and audiences would demand the return of Lady Harvey, who was then sixty-one and forcibly in retirement, to replace the less experienced actress. Contrary to the Harveys' expectations, Peggy received such critical praise that she remained in the part for the length of the play's run. However, her West End success was followed by eighteen months of work in less prominent roles, although she appeared in some twenty-two plays.

John Gielgud, from whose brightness she had fled the Old Vic, rescued her from obscurity. He was involved in a Sunday matinee performance of *Musical Chairs* along with Frank Vosper, Jessica Tandy, and director Theodore Komissarjevsky. He invited Peggy to play a role, and the production then moved to the Criterion Theatre for a run of nine months. Gielgud followed *Musical Chairs* with a production of *Richard of Bordeaux* in 1933 with himself as Richard II, Gwen Ffrangcon-Davies as Anne of Bohemia, Ben Webster as the duke of Lancaster, and Peggy as the countess of Derby. Now a popular star, Gielgud's production ran for fourteen months and was his first West End success as a director. But Peggy also made her directing debut that season with Shakespeare's *Henry VIII* for the British National Federation of Women's Institutes in Kent. This was a "pastoral" production with eight hundred women to move around in crowd scenes. The year was 1934, and Peggy had at last found her true artistic place in the theater, but it would be several more years and an ocean voyage before she would be recognized as an important director.

The contrast with Gielgud's career is a measure of the traditions and prejudices that existed in the commercial theater both in England and the United States. While he was invited by producers to direct a West End production at age twenty-eight, Peggy would not receive a similar invitation until 1937 at age thirty-two and only after a resounding success on Broadway.

Peggy's American adventure began with a transatlantic telephone call. She was playing a dour Irish cousin in *Parnell* in the West End when the stage doorman announced, "Personal call. Mr. Maurice Evans from New York."[7]

Her parents were already in New York City, where May was playing in the London transfer to Broadway of *Night Must Fall*. Peggy's friend Maurice Evans had been brought to New York to play opposite Katharine Cornell in *Romeo and Juliet* and *Saint Joan*. The Websters learned that he was interested in doing a series of classical revivals on Broadway and had an American backer by the name of Joseph Verner Reed. There are no records of May Whitty's manipulations in this matter, but Evans is reported as saying to her, "We'll do some Shakespeare and get old Peg out here too."[8]

In that fateful telephone call, Evans invited Peggy to come to the

United States and direct him in a repertory season of four plays, beginning with *Richard II,* a play not seen on Broadway since 1878. Evans's choice of Peggy Webster is highly provocative since she had no comparable directing experience in the West End, and, before telephoning Peggy at the New Theatre, he had contracted British designer David Ffolkes to design scenery and costumes.

Admittedly, Evans was faced with the very realistic dilemma that there were no directors with a Shakespearean background in New York City, and his friend Peggy had experience playing with Ben Greet's company, with Harcourt Williams at the Old Vic, and with Donald Wolfit's provincial touring company. She had also played with Gielgud in *Richard of Bordeaux* and again in his West End production of *Queen of Scots.* Evans was also aware that Peggy's career as an actress was mired in minor roles in undistinguished plays and that her personal life was unencumbered. He went so far in his memoir to say, "This was partly, I think because her mother . . . wouldn't let her plough her own furrow."9 (Since the school crisis of 1923, May Whitty continued to control and influence her daughter's career choices.) Evans also knew that if he were to engage one of the rising young male directors, such as Tyrone Guthrie or Michael Redgrave, he risked losing control of the production and possibly even the leading roles. Most persistent was Evans's conviction that he could influence Peggy's artistic choices and control the production from center stage. Into the bargain he would gain an actress to play the duchess of York, as he also proposed.

With thirty seconds left on the call, Peggy said yes to the New York venture and changed the direction of her career. The Cunard shipping line that had taken her as a child from the city of her birth to England would now return her to the United States to begin a career that would place her at the center of American stage history for the next thirty years.

The year 1937 was an eventful one in world history. In the United States Franklin Delano Roosevelt had been re-elected president the previous year; in England, the Wally Simpson–King Edward VIII affair reached the national press; Hitler and Mussolini were marching to power; Franco's fascistic forces in Spain were winning the civil war; the Japanese warlords were preparing the largest naval armada in history; and in Russia, Stalin was consolidating his power with summary executions and exiles to Siberian camps. The Evans-Webster *Richard II,* a play about abuse of power and vacillating rulers who love unwisely, opened at the St. James Theatre on Forty-fourth Street to unprecedented critical notices on February 5, 1937. Brooks Atkinson, dean of Broadway critics, admired the "infinite subtlety and burning emotion" of Evans's king and praised Peggy's "versatile and powerful staging." John Anderson of the *Evening Journal* described the event as "a brilliant spectacle, handsomely turned, deeply moving, richly imagined, superbly executed."[10]

Evans quickly abandoned his plans to produce four plays in repertory when the success of *Richard II,* which played for 171 performances, made plain the financial wisdom of playing a single production at a time. The Evans-Webster team did, indeed, stage four more Shakespeare plays on Broadway in the next decade, including *Hamlet, Macbeth, Henry IV, Part I,* and *Twelfth Night.* In effect, the three Websters settled in America with Peggy's parents relocating to Hollywood, where May Whitty embarked upon a major film career that included *The Lady Vanishes, Night Must Fall, Mrs. Miniver, The White Cliffs of Dover, Lassie Come Home, Suspicion,* and *Gaslight.*

Peggy's war years on Broadway vacillated between wildly triumphant Shakespeare productions, eccentric and even sentimental choices of undistinguished scripts to provide work for her parents and close friends, and absorption into a lesbian subculture of theater artists that would generate its own frissons in her career and personal life.

The year 1938 was significant. Peggy firmly established that her work on *Richard II* was not a onetime affair; she directed Evans as the prince in an uncut *Hamlet,* as Falstaff in *Henry IV, Part I,* and as Malvolio in *Twelfth Night* with newcomer Helen Hayes as Viola. Peggy's connection with the Theatre Guild was made, first, at the intervention of May Whitty, who encouraged her friends Alfred Lunt and Lynn Fontanne to cast her daughter as Masha in their production of *The Sea Gull* on Broadway. This was the first of three critically admired performances that Peggy gave on Broadway, including Emilia in *Othello* and the nun-detective in *The High Ground.* Then there were the unwise but understandable choices of plays to direct for her parents, friends, and companions: *Young Mr. Disraeli* for Ben Webster, *Viceroy Sarah* for May Whitty and Mady Christians, and *The Trojan Women* for May Whitty and Walter Slezak. Mady Christians, whom Peggy saw in the Orson Welles production of *Heartbreak House* and described as "blonde, distinguished, opulent . . . [with] a slight German accent" and cast as Queen Gertrude in *Hamlet,* became the first of several women whom Peggy loved and lost to other relationships or to untimely deaths by natural causes.[11]

It would be easy to argue that Peggy's marginalization to secondary roles as an actress and to undistinguished scripts as a director was directly related to her sexual orientation, which segregated her from the

Broadway power brokers. The facts, however, do not support these conclusions. Peggy Webster had never been a willowy ingenue nor a woman of fashion. She wore sensible shoes, unfashionably bobbed hair, and smoked cigarettes prodigiously. She was Audrey and Nerissa, not Rosalind and Portia. She was a supporting character actor, and these roles as written by Shakespeare, Ibsen, and Shaw were for court ladies, loyal confidantes, comedic servants, poor relatives, and emotionally starved wives. Peggy's London experience also instilled the habit of directing any and every possible script for the experience and without serious consequence at times when the West End theaters were dark. No such tradition existed in the New York theater. In the 1940s there was one way to produce a play and that was with all the expense of a commercial production. Peggy was not an independent producer-director, as Alfred Lunt and Maurice Evans had become. She was dependent upon others to throw opportunities her way. Lawrence Langner and Theresa Helburn of the Theatre Guild would bring important projects her way in the forties, and the wisdom of hindsight tells us that she should have waited for these opportunities rather than staging *Young Mr. Disraeli, The Trojan Women,* and *Therese* in New York. However, she was compelled financially and emotionally to keep working during the intervals, and she proceeded in the only way she knew how. Peggy was also idealistic and involved herself, like her mother before her, in the "good causes." In the 1940s, she joined fundraising groups in support of the Soviets in their efforts against Hitler's armies and directed a play on Broadway that was clearly sympathetic to the Soviet cause. These associations would bring her before the House Un-American Activities Committee (HUAC) in the fifties along with other notable theater people.

Despite difficulties, the 1940s were halcyon days for Peggy. Following the success of the uncut *Hamlet,* she directed, again with the Theatre Guild producing, *Twelfth Night* (with Maurice Evans and Helen Hayes), *Battle of Angels* (with Miriam Hopkins), and *Macbeth* (with Evans and Judith Anderson). What then followed was the remarkable production of *Othello* that made stage history.

The fierce defiance of stage and social conventions that was the fabric of the 1943 production of *Othello* proclaimed Peggy's independence from Maurice Evans (he declined to play Iago, saying that "stars" would not play either Iago or Desdemona) and the theatrical status quo. She was advised against casting an African-American as Othello. It took fifteen months to negotiate financing, cast, rehearse and try out the Webster-Robeson production, but on October 19, 1943, Paul Robeson became the first African-American actor to play Othello on Broadway, in a production directed by Peggy Webster. When he walked onto the stage of the Shubert Theatre with José Ferrer as Iago, Uta Hagen as Desdemona, and Peggy as Emilia, theatrical history was made. In the face of hostile predictions of doom for Peggy's decision to use an interracial cast, all fears and grievances melted away as Robeson with Othello's first words endowed the play with larger-than-life stature and perspective on human and social issues. Critics used phrases such as "unbelievably magnificent," "nothing to equal it," "consummate genius," and "one of the great events of theatre history," and the lines at the Shubert box office the next day confirmed Peggy's courage and craft.[12] With 296 performances, the production broke all box office records for a Shakespeare play.

Throughout it all, Peggy was not without her self-doubts, as her nightly letters to her mother revealed. She had been careful to defend her selection of Robeson, arguing the paramount importance of a black actor to the play's "credibility and to the validity of every character in it."[13] The fact that she had not grown up with an understanding of American society and its ingrained racial prejudices helps, in part, to explain her daring and conviction. Also, her emotional disconnection to family (nothing that she did could affect May Whitty's film career) and the lack of other emotional dependencies, which would develop soon enough, freed her independent spirit and hardened her resolve. Nevertheless, there were other pitfalls. She stumbled upon the fact that Robeson's stage presence as a performer far outweighed his technical skills as an actor. Convinced of the "unambiguous racial identity" of Shakespeare's Moor, Peggy convinced herself that Robeson's problems with speaking verse and his lack of technical skills could be overcome. Some critics expressed reservations about Robeson's "deep organ tones becoming a trifle monotonous."[14] But, the overriding importance of Robeson's *Othello* as a racial event of great importance overwhelmed the critical measurements and reduced them to insignificance.

In retrospect, *Othello* was to be the high-water mark of Peggy's career. It was also the time in her life when she was emotionally independent of her mother's control (May Whitty was otherwise engaged in Hollywood), of her lovers' needs, and of Maurice Evans's agendas. This independence was short-lived. Eva Le Gallienne, her childhood friend from summer vacations at Chiddingfold, England, who was six years her senior, reentered her life as an established actress and director at a time Peggy was being ostracized by the Robeson-Hagen-Ferrer trio from decisions regarding cast albums, costumes, and the national tour. Peggy grasped at another project and withdrew from the national tour of *Othello* and, at the urging of Le Gallienne, entered into her old friend's household and dream of establishing a national repertory theater to be called the American Repertory Theatre (ART).

This giant step away from the commercial theater thrust Peggy into a world of women producers, directors, designers, and stage managers that included her lifetime friend and now lover Eva Le Gallienne, as well as Carly Wharton, Cheryl Crawford, Rita Hassan, the Motleys, Thelma Chandler, and others. For eighteen months they struggled to create a repertory theater on Columbus Circle in New York City. Though Le Gallienne's Civic Repertory Theatre (1926–33) had failed under crushing financial constraints, she had not abandoned her dream of a national repertory theater. Le Gallienne enlisted coworkers, like Cheryl Crawford, who were successful producers and managers and shared an alternative life-style as well.

By the beginning of the 1945–46 season, the three women had launched the idea of ART with plans to open two plays in September and to add four more during the season. They believed the theater would become a self-supporting business within three years. By the time the first production opened in November 1946, prospects were good. They had sold about three hundred thousand dollars in stock, Joseph Verner Reed had contributed one hundred thousand dollars, and other well-known theater people had signed on as sponsors with over five thousand subscribers. But ART would survive less than two years. The reasons for the theater's failure have been attributed to many forces: the New York theater critics, unreasonable union demands, and play selection. Many found the choice of plays *(John Gabriel Borkman, Ghosts, Hedda Gabler, Yellow Jack)* self-serving and ill advised for the New York scene. Peggy and Le Gallienne traded roles and directing responsibilities. Peggy directed *Henry VIII* with Le Gallienne as Katharine of Aragon and also *Ghosts* with her friend as Mrs. Alving. Le Gallienne directed *John Gabriel Borkman* with herself as Ella Rentheim and Peggy as Mrs. Borkman. The most popular choice was *Alice in Wonderland* with Le Gallienne as the White Queen and Peggy as the Red Queen. The trio did everything that they could to salvage ART except abandoning, as did the Lunts a decade earlier, the idealistically classical repertoire.

The times were against them in more ways than Broadway tastes and union demands. The critics took the position that ART's management team revived plays the actors wanted to act rather than plays the public wanted to see.[15] Broadway audiences declined following the war as audiences moved to the suburbs; movies and the new invention, called television, absorbed the entertainment dollars.

Then there was an assault from the radical Right of the day. Peggy and Cheryl Crawford were the objects of invidious charges that they were Communist sympathizers. Crawford had been a cofounder of the "leftist" Group Theatre and had traveled in the Soviet Union; Peggy had directed a Soviet play on Broadway and had worked as a fundraiser for two organizations sympathetic to the Soviet war effort in the 1940s. Peggy's involvement with these "Red" organizations was rising up to haunt her and would eventually bring her before HUAC in 1953.

Finally, America's attitude toward women in the late forties was a harsh societal fact. Although eight million women had entered the workplace by 1945, at war's end this work force would be diminished, if not outright fired. With the return of the male population from Europe and the Far East, American women would again be relegated to the "domestic." The commercial theater establishment in which men were managers and producers had remained unchanged during the war years. By opening ART in New York City, the three unmarried, middle-aged women had openly challenged the establishment with a new theater devoted to classics and repertory. The fact that they were lesbians was the final count against them. Postwar America had become a land of conformity to ensure national security, justice, and common decency. Sexual conformity became a cornerstone of national security, and same-sex desire was condemned as a menace to morals and a threat to national policy.[16]

The late forties were years of immeasurable loss for Peggy. Her parents died in Hollywood. Ben Webster passed away in 1947, and May's death less than fourteen months later coincided with the demise of ART. Peggy was bereft of family (one cousin remained in London), and with May's steady advice for over forty years halted, Peggy was more alone, than she had ever been in her life.

In 1950, Peggy was named a Communist sympathizer and her career was further marginalized by the insidious charges. Besides being an elected member of the "Red" Actors' Equity Council, she was guilty of employing a known Communist, Paul Robeson, of directing a Broadway play sympathetic to the Soviet cause, and of raising funds for two international organizations that gave money to the Soviets. (Nothing was said about these activities taking place at a time when the Russians were our allies in a global war.) Peggy's name appeared in *Red Channels,* a booklet compiled by the FBI listing Communist sympathizers on Broadway and in the entertainment industry, and she was summoned to appear before

HUAC in 1953, almost eighteen months after the death of her former companion Mady Christians, who had been branded as a German emigré-turned-Communist by the House subcommittee. With her career and health destroyed by the ordeal, Mady Christians died at age fifty-one.

Having been named by fellow actor José Ferrer, Peggy, guided by attorney Louis Nizer, appeared before the McCarthy committee for over an hour and was pronounced an "Ok American" by Roy Cohn. However, her anxiety and fear over this public humiliation took its toll emotionally and financially. Grief-stricken by Mady Christians's premature death, Peggy was afraid of imprisonment for the "good causes," but her fear of exposure of her lesbian preferences, which were against the law in some states, possibly far outweighed her fright over future unemployment. Because the witch-hunts of the 1950s conflated alleged forms of degeneracy, such as Communism and homosexuality, Peggy risked standing before the Senate subcommittee not only as a traitor but also as a sexual pervert. The fear, grief, and anger that she felt that day over the injustice of the hearings was in no way alleviated by Roy Cohn's flip dismissal.

Some years later Peggy wrote in her autobiography that "no one touched the blacklist, witch-hunt pitch, without being lessened and to some degree defiled." She considered her career "undermined, if not ostensibly broken."[17] Her friend and admirer, Brooks Atkinson, summed up her situation by saying that "her Broadway career was permanently tarnished. She never again could work with the scope and exuberance of her early years on Broadway."[18]

There is, nevertheless, more to Peggy Webster's latter-day story than Red-baiting, sexual orientation, and professional isolation. The kind of theater that Peggy knew and loved was not possible in New York City in the late forties. Zelda Fichandler and others were to open Arena Stage in Washington, D.C., in 1950 and fellow-Briton Tyrone Guthrie established his successful repertory theater in Minneapolis in 1963, far from the New York critics and the theatrical unions. Other nonprofit theaters were to spread in the sixties from Baltimore to Seattle.

Moreover, Peggy was experiencing artistic difficulties as a director. She conceived of acting as the process of shaping outer form. Typically, she would tell an actor where to stand and how to speak—the hows, not the whys. This external process that she encouraged often resulted in actors skilled in outer effect and vocalization rather than inner exploration of emotion. Such practices sometimes lead Peggy to ignore the psy-

chological aspects of both Shakespeare's texts and contemporary works
that she directed. She remarked to an interviewer that she had no interest
in psychoanalytical interpretation and said, "It's walking all around the
block, that sort of fiddle-faddle."[19] At midcentury, the work of directors
Elia Kazan and Harold Clurman was preferred for its psychological insights and social emphasis. Peggy sought refuge from a changing Broadway and the blacklist at the New York City Theatre Company, where she
directed Shakespeare and Shaw: *Richard II, The Taming of the Shrew,
Richard III, The Devil's Disciple,* and *Saint Joan.*

Rudolph Bing also became an unlikely savior from artistic obscurity
and financial hardship. As the new general manager of the Metropolitan
Opera Company in 1950, Bing decided to revive the fading "dinosaur"
by hiring accomplished directors and designers to revitalize the staging at
the Met. In that first season, he contracted Alfred Lunt, Garson Kanin,
Tyrone Guthrie, and Peggy Webster—the first woman director to be
hired by the opera company. Bing invited Peggy to stage *Don Carlos,* the
first opera in his opening season, with Jussi Bjoerling, Jerome Hines, and
Robert Merrill, Peggy was reluctant to try a medium in which she had no
prior experience, but Bing argued that the effects he wanted were essentially Shakespearean and, of course, the woman who had directed eight
hundred women in Kent could stage an opera with ninety-five chorus
members and twelve principals.

Peggy staged seven operas for the Metropolitan Opera Company and
the New York City Opera over a period of ten years. The grand operatic
style with historical costumes, elaborate scenery, mannered acting, and
glorious vocalizations could have afforded Peggy a distinguished second
career and a comfortable income. She pronounced herself, nevertheless,
frustrated with the limited rehearsal hours, which she called one of the
"greatest evils of operatic staging," and turned her back on opera, declaring that she had devoted her life and skills to the legitimate theater and
that was where she belonged.[20]

Despite the twelve years left in Peggy's life and career, which she
filled with solo performances, lecture tours, term professorships, the writing of two memoirs, and acting and directing jobs in England and the
United States, she was not to reestablish herself as a major artist. She
remained marginalized by the changing theatrical establishment, by her
women companions, and by ill health that was probably a result of a
lifetime of cigarette smoking. Maurice Evans sought her out for a final
collaboration in 1962 on *The Aspern Papers* with Evans and Wendy

Hiller that ran for ninety-three performances and became Peggy's last successful Broadway production.

Although Le Gallienne remained a lifelong friend, their partnership ended with the HUAC investigation into Peggy's political activities. (Le Gallienne, a political conservative, declined to become involved in the public display or risk undue exposure to herself.) The two partners of Peggy's final years were, first, British novelist Pamela Frankau and, lastly, Bostonian Jane Brundred. Peggy met Pamela Frankau sometime in 1955, and they maintained a London residence at 55 Christchurch Hill for ten years before Frankau's death in 1967. Despite her own illness from colon cancer, Peggy maintained her lifelong habit of existing between two continents. During her last four years, she received medical attention in Boston and frequently stayed with Le Gallienne in Weston, Connecticut, and on Martha's Vineyard, where she met Jane Brundred, who died in 1969. Brundred bequeathed a small fortune to Peggy that subsequently became devalued in the decline of the stock market in the early seventies. However, Peggy used the money to pay her medical expenses and bequeathed the remainder to Pamela Frankau's first cousin, Diana Raymond, to Eva Le Gallienne, and to St. Christopher's Hospice in Sydenham, England, where she spent her final days.

Despite the disappointments, Peggy Webster sustained an active professional career for forty-five years. For thirty-two of those years she exchanged letters over two continents with Ben and May detailing her self-doubts, enthusiasms, struggles, and accomplishments, always described tentatively.[21] One by one she saw her companions and loved ones die and Le Gallienne reject her only to extend her friendship again in the last decade of her life. Upon her friend's death, Le Gallienne said in the *New York Times:* "It is rare for a woman to succeed in this difficult field. She must be quite exceptionally talented to overcome the ingrained prejudices, the skepticism, and distrust that stand in her way."[22]

It is true that Peggy's career was supported and enhanced by the Cassons, Lilian Baylis, the Lunts, Maurice Evans, Joseph Verner Reed, Lawrence Langer, Sol Hurok, and Rudolph Bing. She was awarded honorary degrees by seven American colleges and universities, elected one of Ten Outstanding Women of the Year in 1946 by the Women's National Press Club and named to the Theatre Hall of Fame in 1979. As long as she remained connected to the commercial theater as a director or actor, the work was forthcoming and satisfactory, although the HUAC investigation severely reduced her chances for employment. Inspired by Peggy's last performance as an actress on Broadway in *The High Ground,* her friend and admirer Brooks Atkinson praised her as "the ablest woman in our theatre."[23] She also directed many great actors, including Maurice Evans, Helen Hayes, Paul Robeson, Uta Hagen, José Ferrer, Flora Robson, Wendy Hiller, Eva Le Gallienne, Arnold Moss, Maureen Stapleton, Tyrone Power, Faye Emerson, Judi Dench, John Neville, Emlyn Williams, and Sybil Thorndike.

Whereas her own worth diminished in her mind when measured against the beauty, grace, and accomplishments of May Whitty, Sybil Thorndike, or Eva Le Gallienne, one of Peggy's eulogists finally got it right when she wrote that Peggy's career was more "distinguished than that of any member of the four previous generations of the Webster family that had contributed to English theatrical history."[24]

Despite the social and artistic marginalization that she experienced in her lifetime, Peggy Webster endured and succeeded as one of the few women to establish herself as a stage director both in England and the United States, as the first woman to direct Shakespeare's plays on Broadway and Verdi's operas at the Metropolitan Opera House in New York City. May Whitty's daughter, who could have been an Oxford don, followed in the family's theatrical footsteps and made an imprint on the English-speaking stage far larger than those generations of Websters that preceded her before the footlights. The fact that she did so in the thirties and forties without "proper" social connections, personal fortune, glamour, husband, or family influence speaks to her extraordinary intelligence, wit, drive, and devotion to a profession that, as she was fond of saying, required "the courage of a lion, the strength of an elephant and the hide of a rhinoceros."[25] Her strength, courage, and tenacity carried her successfully through an industry that militated against women directors and producers. May Whitty's daughter journeyed through the professional theater of her day with few competitors—a fact that remains true even fifty years later. And, she did so in a way that ran counter to established tradition, fashion, and sexual mores on two continents.

NOTES

1. Margaret Webster, *The Same Only Different: Five Generations of a Great Theatre Family* (New York: Knopf, 1969).

2. Nina Auerbach, *Ellen Terry: Player in Her Time* (New York: Norton, 1987). Auerbach writes of Ellen Terry's manipulation of her daughter's life and of Edith Craig's love affairs with men and women, namely Martin Shaw and Christopher Saint John (née Christabel Marshall). See pages 365–436.

3. *Celebrity Register, 1959* (New York: Celebrity Register, 1959), 814.

4. Webster, *The Same Only Different*, 316.

5. Ibid., 321.

6. Ibid., 345.

7. Ibid., 374.

8. Ibid., 372.

9. Maurice Evans, *All This . . . and Evans Too! A Memoir* (Columbia: University of South Carolina Press, 1987), 110.

10. *New York Times,* February 6, 1937; *New York Evening Journal,* February 6, 1937.

11. Margaret Webster, *Don't Put Your Daughter on the Stage* (New York: Knopf, 1972), 26.

12. *New York Daily News,* October 20, 1943; *New York Herald Tribune,* October 20, 1943, October 31, 1943; *New York Journal-American,* October 20, 1943, May 23, 1945; *New York Sun,* October 20, 1943; *New York Times,* August 16, 1942, October 20, 1943, October 24, 1943, May 23, 1945; *PM,* October 20, 1943; *Variety,* October 27, 1943.

13. Margaret Webster, *Shakespeare without Tears* (New York: McGraw-Hill, 1942), 178.

14. See Louis Kronenberger in *PM,* October 20, 1943; and Mary McCarthy in *Mary McCarthy's Theatre Chronicles, 1937–1962* (New York: Farrar, Straus, 1963), 73–74.

15. *New York Journal-American,* February 28, 1947.

16. Lillian Faderman, *Odd Girls and Twilight Lovers: A History of Lesbian Life in Twentieth-Century America* (New York: Penguin, 1991), 139–58.

17. Webster, *Don't Put Your Daughter,* 273.

18. Brooks Atkinson, *Broadway,* rev. ed. (New York: Macmillan, 1974), 435.

19. Barbara Heggie, "We: A Margaret Webster Profile," *New Yorker,* May 20, 1944, 36.

20. Margaret Webster, "How I Stage an Opera," *Etude,* January 1951, 57.

21. The letters of Margaret Webster are found in the Library of Congress, Washington, D.C.

22. *New York Times,* November 26, 1972.

23. *New York Times,* February 21, 1951.

24. *London Times,* November 14, 1972.

25. Webster, *The Same Only Different,* 153.

Cheryl Crawford

One Not So Naked Individual

Jay Plum

Unlike the other children in her grammar school class, Cheryl Crawford (1902–86) never learned the Pledge of Allegiance. She skipped the grade in which the recitation became part of the daily civics lesson. Desperate to fit in and too proud to admit her ignorance, she rose every morning with her classmates to recite what she thought were the words: "... pledge allegiance to the flag of the United States of America, and to the Republic for which it stands, *one naked individual,* with liberty and justice for all." For Crawford, more than providing a title for her 1977 autobiography, the metaphor of standing alone, vulnerable, and exposed against sometimes hostile forces aptly describes a theatrical career that lasted more than half a century: "Out on the barricades I was finite and vulnerable, and I had only myself to depend on. Alone against the world, one instinctively grabs for armor. What I discovered was that the reality of being one naked individual was, when I accepted it, a superior armor."[1]

Crawford was instrumental in some of the most ambitious and significant enterprises in American theater history, namely the Group Theatre, the American Repertory Theatre, the American National Theatre and Academy, and the Actors Studio. Her record numbered more than one hundred productions, among them four plays by Tennessee Williams and such musicals as *One Touch of Venus* (1943), *Brigadoon* (1947), *Paint Your Wagon* (1951), and *Brecht on Brecht* (1962). As represented in *One Naked Individual,* her career gives testament to the values of individualism, democracy, and progress that circulate as governing statements in conventional histories of the American stage as well as in traditional biographical criticism.[2]

The title plays up the enabling fiction of autobiographies as exposés of "naked" truths, allowing Crawford to construct a narrative in which her life consists of little more than a series of productions, names, and dates. "Cheryl Crawford's record as a producer is illustrious, one of our very best," Agnes de Mille claims on the dust jacket. Hers was "an extraordinary career full of work, authority, courage, and above all, belief and passion," adds Janet Flanner. "She knows the theatre the way a good cook knows the kitchen." She was "virtually unequaled in [Tennessee Williams's] experience. An honesty, a gallantry, a courage uniquely hers irradiate this book." It is for this reason that Mary Martin finds *One Naked Individual* "a perfect book": "Cheryl Crawford has met life head-on, always boldly, and she writes about it with exciting intensity. . . . She doesn't skip an emotion." Such endorsements corroborate Crawford's reputation as an exceptional individual whose knowledge of theater is translated into a candidly honest reconstruction of her life. Her knowing becomes synonymous with her being. That these statements are made by professional or personal acquaintances (i.e., people "in the know") give them a currency in which the fantasy of knowing is exchanged as truth. For Flanner, Martin, and Williams, however, being "in the know" also marked being "in the closet." Their endorsements of Crawford's biographical performance inadvertently points to the subcultural knowledge circulated through a complex network of social and professional relationships among lesbians, gays, and bisexual men and women in the American theater with which they all were familiar.

Recent interventions into autobiographical writing suggest that the rules governing the form serve bourgeois individualism through the reinscription of representative man as the universal subject. Not only does this model position the autobiographical figure outside history, ignoring the material and cultural conditions of her/his experience, it neutralizes or dismisses histories and identities that cannot be made universally representative. According to Sidonie Smith,

> When people assigned in varying ways to the cultural position of "other" speak as autobiographical subjects, they consciously and/or unconsciously negotiate the laws of genre that work to construct them as culturally recognizable subjects. These laws establish rules of inclusion and exclusion and set the terms for participation in privileged or canonical forms.[3]

In Crawford's case, the negotiation of generic expectations and personal identity is defined in terms of the values of American individualism and democracy. The relative anomaly of her gender in an otherwise male-dominated field is explained away, as is any sense of Crawford as a sexual subject.

Crawford's reluctance as well as her inability to provide details about her personal life prevents her subjectivity from being known. She fails to "be" according to the expectations of standard autobiographies. In his review of *One Naked Individual,* Christopher Lehmann-Haupt insightfully describes Crawford's "purely functional" prose as "lifeless": "She simply doesn't enjoy writing about herself. She keeps insisting that she is telling all, because the theatre has been her whole life. Yet a sense of self is missing from these pages. We seem to lack the true source of Miss Crawford's pride and pain."⁴ Crawford goes to great lengths to divorce her professional and personal lives, suggesting that her theatrical commitments left little time for things social, let alone sexual: "This is the story of my life as a producer. My private life is mentioned only in passing because that's how it was lived."⁵

Crawford's life indeed was lived "in passing" as a heterosexual. Her anomaly as a female producer (especially as a *successful* one) placed her in a highly visible position from which she constantly negotiated the boundaries between the professional and personal, the public and private. As Eve Kosofsky Sedgwick explains, "Living in and hence coming out of the closet are never matters of the purely hermetic; the personal and political geographies to be surveyed . . . are instead the more imponderable and convulsive ones of the open secret."⁶ If same-sex desire was understood during Crawford's lifetime, it was not openly discussed in the theater. Broadway occasionally exploited gay and lesbian themes for their sensationalism; for the most part, though, homosexuality was treated only in a handful of productions and then only through highly coded figures and language. Even in the forward-looking companies that Crawford helped found and build, the oppression of sexual minorities was not a subject that was addressed. As a result, Crawford's sexuality can be understood today only as a fragmentary and complicated history, partly because her "secret" has ceased circulating but, more significantly, also because of the impossibility of identifying any single activity as "proof" of a lesbian biography. Crawford's sexual identity was defined by more than acts performed in the bedroom. Her lesbianism, to paraphrase Martha Vicinus, was everywhere, even as it was nowhere.⁷

The practice of lesbian and gay history requires a revaluation of traditional rules of evidence that acknowledges the fluidity of identities as well as the rapid and sometimes conflicting changes in social attitudes regarding sexualities. Evidence of experience should not be used as evidence of difference but rather, Joan W. Scott argues, as "a way of exploring how difference is established, how it operates, how and in what ways it constitutes subjects who see and act in the world."⁸ Moving beyond an understanding of identities as constructions to an exploration of identities as constructed/constructing processes suggests strategies for locating sexuality within biographical narratives like Crawford's where it is seemingly absent. At a recent conference on lesbian and gay history at the City University of New York Graduate Center (October 6–7, 1995), historian John D'Emilio remarked that so-called inaccuracies in the personal narratives of lesbian and gay subjects should not be dismissed as evidentiary flaws. Their presence, instead, may point to ways in which misinformation is purposely used to deflect attention away from "who one is" to "who one is not," to fashion oneself according to lesbian and gay codes, or to "pass" as someone or something else.

These strategies are manifested in the silences, exaggerations, jokes, and grammatical slips found in Crawford's personal statements, including but not limited to *One Naked Individual*. Crawford's failure to write herself as a whole subject according to the generic expectations of autobiography is a "queer" act that locates her lesbianism as spatially and temporally in tandem.[9] The spatial disjuncture between an identity that is everywhere but nowhere reproduces gaps, slippages, and excesses through which Crawford can be read as other. The temporal rupture between her lived and recorded experiences (marked by her writing as well as by mine) moreover points to the constructed/constructing processes working on, through, and against the stability of Crawford's self-performances. In short, Crawford's life as "one naked individual" was more complicated than she suggests.

Leaving Normal

"How does a girl from a nice, normal Midwestern family become a Broadway producer?" Crawford claims that even she doesn't know the answer: "I'm still wondering."[10] She mentions as one possibility a touring production of *Uncle Tom's Cabin* in which the actress playing Little Eva walked into the audience to hawk souvenir pictures following her character's ascent into heaven. Young Cheryl stood on her chair and protested: "Even then I knew that the illusion must not be broken."[11] More important to Crawford than how she became a Broadway producer is how the question's utterance creates an illusion of a childhood "origin." Crawford may be fabricating a complete sense of self to mask her lesbianism, but the details of her descriptions are as revealing as the wires that flew Little Eva into the grid.

The conceit of childhood is typically evoked in autobiographical narratives to identify behavioral patterns that repeat throughout a subject's lifetime. Childhood anecdotes create an illusion of a continuous and comprehensible human experience through their seduction of factuality. Crawford returns throughout her career to her Middle American background as "proof" of her normalcy. Judy Michaelson noted in her 1964 feature on outstanding business women, for example, that Crawford "speaks with economy in the flat, low-keyed tones of the Midwesterner and occasionally her speech is dotted with such homey phrases as 'grist to the mill,' 'another kettle of fish,' 'the real McCoy.' "[12] Grace Turner similarly attributed Crawford's commercial success as a producer to her background: she knew the tastes of the average American family because she was one of them.[13]

In its phrasing, however, the question that begins Crawford's autobiography suggests an uncertainty at the same time that it assumes a continuous and comprehensible identity. The terms *nice* and *normal* are not occupied by Crawford. They are used only to describe the family from Akron, Ohio, not their eldest daughter who dreamed of adventure. Crawford characterizes her childhood self as rebellious. "There were many confrontations over the years, since [her] spirits didn't conform to the conventions of virtue" upheld by her parents.[14] She and her brothers formed a strong arm of the neighborhood gang, which Cheryl joined after they agreed that she could sit on a red velvet chair they found in an abandoned barn and rule as "king or queen."[15] She smoked straw cigarettes before moving to cigars stolen from her father. She would have preferred to smoke "Violet Murads" but feared that her parents would learn of her habit from the local grocers. She refused to eat the crusts of her bread, even though her mother told her they would make her hair curl. She learned about sex from a book her father kept stashed in the bottom of his dresser. She stole sips from her grandmother's "tonic" and father's sherry. She eventually learned from college boys how to drink bloody Marys and screwdrivers.

Crawford's refusal to conform to accepted standards of femininity invites a reading of her as a lesbian tomboy. Her narrative functions much like those in the recent collection edited by Lynne Yamaguchi and Karen Barber: "As lesbians, we may look back on our childhood tomboy years with nostalgia, but we don't look back at them as if those years spent playing in the dirt were themselves dirty, or transitory, or merely cute. As tomboys, we were 'other' then; as lesbians, we are 'other' now."[16] I don't want to dismiss Crawford's tomboyhood as a "phase," nor do I want to reinscribe it as the "origin" of her lesbianism. I am more interested in how it functions for Crawford, both as a strategy for passing and as a code for her lesbianism. On the one hand, the tomboy narrative points to the independent leadership that characterized her career. Harold Clurman recalls a satirical sketch staged by Group Theatre members in which Margaret Barker played Crawford as "a kind of female cowboy, addressing herself with laconic shrewdness to her two quixotic partners."[17] But Crawford's tomboyish behavior—as an adult and as a child, and as represented by Crawford, Barker, and others—also marks her as different or "queer."

The absence of a developed discourse on female sexuality required bourgeois women of Crawford's generation to turn to the male discourses of pornography, literature, and medicine to define themselves as sexual subjects. In the case of Crawford, who developed a fascination and familiarity with Freudian psychology, her sexuality can be explained through the language of inversion. Nineteenth-century sexologists like Richard von Krafft-Ebing, whose writings gained currency as Crawford was coming of age, believed that the female invert possessed masculine characteristics: "Even in her earliest childhood she preferred playing at soldiers and other boys' games; she was bold and tomboyish and tried even to excel her little companions of the other sex."[18] Crawford's childhood antics easily read as lesbian according to this framework, even though they fail to prove anything.

Crawford seemed conscious of her "selves" as performed identities. When asked if she ever considered a career in acting, she responded emphatically: "No thank you! Imagine trying to find out what each character you play is. I have enough trouble trying to figure myself out, and I'm still quite interested in that subject."[19] Crawford represents her subjectivity as unpossessed and still evolving. Moreover, the curious substitution of "what" for "who a character is" suggests an understanding of role playing as a conscious activity different from the view represented by proponents of Method acting with whom she collaborated. Crawford maintains that the desire for masquerade is innately human: "Actors are like other people, *only more so*."[20] Both their public and private lives are ruled by illusions. The same might be said for lesbian, gay, and bisexual theater professionals, who found theater's world of make-believe a space in which they could safely perform their sexual selves.[21] The "larger than life" nature of stage acting was conducive to the expression of queer sexualities. "Somehow [Crawford] always wanted life to be larger, more spacious, more adventurous."[22] It was not that she herself wanted to be bigger than life, but that she wanted life to be large enough to accommodate the social performance that she desired rather than the one in which she was cast according to type.

Like the role-playing games that Crawford played as a child, the tomboy narrative in *One Naked Individual* marks an experience of otherness that Crawford traces to her naming. According to Flanner's feature in the *New Yorker*, Crawford's mother named her daughter Cheryl because she thought it was a pretty name.[23] In an earlier interview with journalist Florence Ramon, Crawford explained that the name was sent to her mother from a friend living out West. Crawford confesses, however,

> When people ask me how I got my name, I tell them that I am the only child of a love match. I tell them my mother named me by combining the first two words my father ever spoke to her. One night Carl Van Vechten spent about three hours trying to figure out what the two words were. It kept getting dirtier and dirtier.[24]

The different responses to the same question point to the construction of a personal history, marking Crawford's difference as well as her reluctance to fix an origin for her identity. Judith Butler describes the unstable agency produced by repetition as the "illimitable *et cetera*" of identity politics according to which one's sense of self is not predetermined but constantly evolving and changing.[25] Crawford's responses suggest possibilities rather than answers. I cannot help wondering what adventures the young woman from Akron dreamed of. Were they of life among other Cheryls? Were they of a freedom associated with "the West" as the land of cowboys? Were they of a place where a tomboy (i.e., a "female cowboy") from the Midwest might feel at home? Were they . . . ?

Coming Out/Passing

Education was an historically significant factor in the rise of lesbianism among middle-class American women. The reputation of women's colleges during the 1920s as breeding schools for lesbianism reflects a change in social mores marked by the redefinition of women's eroticism and the declining reticence about sexuality more generally. The social awakening feared by some appealed to Crawford: "By eighteen I wanted the hell out of the tame Midwest, Akron social life, parental supervision, all of it."[26] Crawford "escaped" by enrolling as a student at Smith College, where her experiences became part of a "purple past" (26). In her senior year, she was briefly expelled and denied graduation honors for telling "exaggerated tales of sex exploits, . . . boast[ing] of low life among real bohemians, [and] incit[ing] wide-eyed innocents to follow the teachings of Nietzsche" (24). As a freshman, Crawford's "low voice and the ability to ape men, learned from [her] brothers, always won [her] male roles" (15). It also may have won her female admirers. In spite (or perhaps because) of her notoriety, at the end of her junior year Crawford was elected president of the Drama Association, defeating "a socially acceptable girl of solid, Protestant convictions" (17). Crawford "appointed [her] rival head of makeup, which seemed a harmless position to indulge her in"; the outgoing officers, however, named a faculty committee to supervise Crawford because they feared she might produce "something outlandish and dangerous to young ladies' morals" (17).

Crawford's representation of her days at Smith reflects the possibilities as well as the limitations that the emerging science of sexology afforded women. While the era between the repressive Victorian and McCarthy periods tolerated more freedom in expressing sexual desire, that tolerance applied only to a heterosexual paradigm in which women played a compliant, passive role. The association of recreational sex with prostitution among lower-class women impelled women of the middle and upper classes to legitimize their sexuality through narratives of heterosexual romance.[27] Lesbianism remained an "unnatural" act.

Lacking a discursive space in which to perform her sexual identity, Crawford cloaked her "purple past" through her chosen object of desire. Encouraged by her internship with the Provincetown Players during the summer of her junior year, Crawford moved to New York to pursue a theatrical career after her graduation from Smith in 1925: "Of course after Provincetown I wanted in live in Greenwich Village among the bohemians."[28] Crawford shared an apartment in the Village with the daughter of a family friend, claiming to have supported herself by playing poker, bootlegging, and exploiting the generosity of a "sugar daddy."

Crawford enrolled in the short-lived Theatre Guild school, beginning what she termed a "long love affair" with the company. Founded with the expressed aim of producing "plays of merit not ordinarily produced by commercial managers," the Guild built its reputation as a modern art theater through a largely European repertoire that slowly expanded to include such American dramatists as Sidney Howard, John Howard Lawson, Eugene O'Neill, and Elmer Rice. Crawford arrived at the Guild during its peak as a producing organization. Between April 1926 and October 1928, for instance, the Guild staged an unprecedented fourteen plays, providing Crawford an opportunity to work as a stagehand or stage manager on such productions as *Juarez and Maximilian* (starring Edward G. Robinson and Alfred Lunt), *Pygmalion* (starring Lynn Fontanne), Jacques Copeau's adaptation of *The Brothers Karamazov, Right You Are If You Think You Are, Mr. Pim Passes By, The Second Man* (starring Lunt and Fontanne), and *Porgy*. It was at the Guild that Crawford found a professional mentor in executive director Theresa Helburn as well as an extended family in the company at large. "Their uninhibited exuberance, their sense of fun and their ability to live 'for the day thereof' entranced [her]."²⁹ The group, among other things, often visited the speakeasies and rent parties in Harlem, a favorite haunt among Village bohemians because of its laissez-faire attitudes regarding social and sexual mores.³⁰

The way Crawford represents the announcement of her professional plans to her parents sounds vaguely like a coming-out story: "Bombs bursting in air! My father's eyes flashed, my mother's were full of tears. The response couldn't have been greater if I told them I was going to enter a brothel or a nunnery."³¹ Crawford's unconventional career choice, however, was legitimized as a romance. Michaelson described Crawford as "a woman who has a deep love affair for the theater," one that Flanner insisted had been "consecrated."³²

Crawford seemingly prided herself on being a faithful workaholic. In a publicity photograph for the Maplewood Theatre (a stock company in New Jersey where she found success as an independent producer following her resignation from the Group Theatre in 1937), Crawford posed on a park bench wearing a striped dress. Her hair is coiffed. A small dog sits at her heels. "Trying it on the dog," reads the caption, "Cheryl Crawford, in a moment of *what passes for leisure,* goes over the script of a new play that may appear on the boards of the Maplewood Theater."³³ Crawford's passing prevented the public expression of a life outside the theater, implying that her free time was occupied solely with work. Her career publicly performed the reproductive labor of an "absent" sex life.

Crawford's image as a woman married to her career deflected attention away from her romantic entanglements, notably with Dorothy Patten during their tenure with the Group Theatre. The Group Theatre's annual retreats were notorious for their "communal, al-fresco summer life."³⁴ Crawford's diary entry for June 26, 1933, suggests that there was more to her experience with the group than just work: "I was in a bad temper all day—rain, problems of financing, housing difficulties, sex."³⁵ Her relationship with Patten was well known within the company. They

practiced a "Boston marriage" when other members of the Group Theatre tried communal living. Their travels together included visits to their
family homes in Akron and Chattanooga. Patten suffered a nervous
breakdown shortly after her split with Crawford, but they renewed their
acquaintance at the Maplewood Theatre, where Patten was employed as
a playreader.[36]

Crawford presents her experience with the Group Theatre as strictly
business: "Work. Work. Work. At this time I had little or no private life.
Anxiety for the future of the Group absorbed most of my energy. There is
a spurious belief that theatre people enjoy a hot bed of sexual experience.
It ain't true. The 'casting couch' is mainly a myth."[37] But the girl from
that nice, normal Midwestern family admits that she had three experiences as a producer with "indecent exposure." The first was with a
theater owner ("besides being ancient, he was at least fifty") with whom
she was negotiating a contract for an upcoming production. He left the
room and returned with his trousers open to expose his erect penis. "Oh,
how funny you look!" she blurted out. The owner went limp. Crawford
received "an exceptionally favorable contract." The response was not as
successful when used on a "public jokester" (again "an ancient fiftyish")
who unzipped his pants in a meeting with Crawford. Her line stopped his
advances, but she was unable to persuade him to host a benefit for the
Group Theatre.

> The only other time I received an unrequested advance was during
> an evening visit from a very attractive man. Since the visit took place
> at my apartment and at my request, I'm sure he thought he was
> doing the obligatory thing. Actually, I wanted to discuss a role. (Are
> you sure of that, Cheryl?) Anyway, when I saw the equipment I was
> struck with awe. The usual response was certainly unfitting. "Good
> God!" I cried. "Put it back. It isn't possible." (61)

The anecdotes follow the disavowal of sexual activity in the theater, as
if a confession of heterosexuality has been wrung from Crawford. Her
performance, however, is marked by its excessiveness as well as its
placement within a seemingly unrelated discussion of her 1933 production of *Big Night*. Crawford's candor overshadows the claim that immediately follows the stories of indecent exposure, namely that "the major
part of what little private life [she] had did include some intermittent
love life but centered mostly on books, records, and dinners with
friends, whom [she] usually asked to bring something to read" (61). The
discussion's awkward placement in turn points to its rhetorical construc-

tion, suggesting that the "real" drama was somewhere outside the one staged by Crawford.

Drowning

After evening rehearsals for *Another Sun* (1940), Crawford and playwright Dorothy Thompson often went to a small bar next to the theater. They didn't talk much about the production. Their conversations focused on their lives as "ambitious, independent women." Crawford discovered that Thompson, whose intellect had a "masculine character" but whose "emotional side was surprisingly feminine," was insecure about her sexuality. Thompson felt attracted to other women but remained heterosexually identified.

> She confessed that she needed a man, talented, strong and tender. "Well," I said, "who doesn't and where in hell are they?" I went on to offer her the wisdom of another woman writer. When I was about twenty-seven, I had nervily asked Edna Ferber, "Miss Ferber, how does it feel to be an old maid?"
>
> "Well, Cheryl," she promptly replied, "it's rather like drowning—not bad once you stop struggling."[38]   •

Thompson found the anecdote amusing but "cold comfort." Crawford, however, took the description of Ferber's lesbianism to heart.

The theater represented a place where Crawford sought support among other lesbians and bisexual women. It was a source of pleasure for Crawford, whose descriptions of Marlene Dietrich, Lynn Fontanne, Mary Martin, and Alla Nazimova are charged with desire. Nazimova's representation in *One Naked Individual,* however, suggests that Crawford's relationships with these women went beyond infatuation. Nazimova was "a most enchanting person with sex appeal galore and a mischievous sense of humor" who, Crawford suggests in her interpretation of the following letter, suffered from loneliness.

> Cheryl, dear, I am leaving tomorrow for Columbus, Ohio. Did you really want to see me? Four weeks at the Longacre I've been waiting, so *hoping* for a kindred soul. Why are we all so small-circled? Surely we know that others are just as lonely, and yet—No, of course I can't see you now—too late. I am terribly tired, terribly discouraged and can't see farther than my nose. Perhaps someday we shall be able to have a talk, sans holidays, sans whiskey, and until dawn. Who knows? Alla.[39]

In the discussion of the letter in her autobiography, Crawford treats Nazimova's desire for friendship as symptomatic of the loneliness that accompanies stardom. But the letter also marks a possible lesbian friendship between Nazimova and Crawford. Sedgwick contends that "erotic identity, of all things, is never to be circumscribed as itself, can never not be relational, is never to be perceived or known by anyone outside of a structure of transference and countertransference."[40] If erotic identities are transferred and relational, then Nazimova's use of the plural "we" performs a shared sense of knowledge that I find "queer."

Nazimova's correspondence constitutes an intimate space where shared values can be expressed, representing a form of gossip that, as Patricia Meyer Spacks argues, is foundational to the maintenance of subcultural groups.

> The value of gossip at its highest level involves its capacity to create and intensify human connection and to enlarge self-knowledge predicated more on emotion than on thought. The philosophic position that condemns much genuinely meaningless talk also excludes the large body of conversation based on personal rather than public values—conversation that may or may not be meaningless.[41]

Nazimova's letter indeed is more about emotions than thoughts, a sense of the personal rather than the public. In effect, the letter stages a drama about friendship circles in which Crawford "becomes" lesbian.

Crawford's lesbian friendships seem to have been commonly known among her professional associates. In a 1997 interview with Mel Gussow, for example, Robert Lewis "outs" Crawford to suggest that she could not have been involved in the conception of the Actors Studio: "I'll tell you something about Cheryl. We were really not in her immediate circle. I don't think it's any secret that Cheryl was a lesbian and she had a lot of very good lesbian friends who were actors. Cheryl's lesbianism [*sic*] was very valuable. The rest of us didn't pal around with those girls—they were all society girls. I won't say we were exactly poor, but we were not on that level. We were much more on the level of the artistic world, not the society world."[42] Lewis makes no mention of his own sexual identity, recirculating gossip about Crawford's lesbianism to secure his own position within the artistic world. Crawford is cast in the role of an outsider more at home among other "society girls," although her shrewd business sense made her tolerable to her "artistic" male collaborators.

The epistemological shift in which homosexuality was no longer viewed as an immoral act but as a product of biological essentialism was

potentially liberating for lesbians of Crawford's generation. Egalitarian-
ism, which for Crawford was embodied in the figure of Walt Whitman,
proved foundational to the project of community-building among lesbians aspiring for social and economic independence from men and for the
freedom to nurture relationships with women who shared their identity.
In this light, Crawford's self-description rejects the normalizing operations of compulsory heterosexuality. Moreover, the rehearsed substitution of "one naked individual" for "one nation indivisible" positions
homosexuality against the "erotics of nationalism" manifested as the
"love of country" in the morning recitation of the Pledge of Allegiance.[43]
The metaphor of "one naked individual" finally expresses a tension in
Crawford's career between her success as an independent producer and
her desire to be part of egalitarian projects.

In 1931, Crawford abandoned the security of the Theatre Guild,
where she had been promoted to assistant to the Board of Managers, to
begin a directing career with the Group Theatre. The Guild's distinctiveness as a commercially viable art theater had begun to wane by the early
1930s. Lawrence Langner recalls that the Guild by this time had become
part of the "most affluent section of the commercial theatre" in the
United States.[44] Crawford was seduced by Harold Clurman's "Whitman-
esque moods" and "jeremiads" about the declining state of the American
theater (specifically its failure to address the social and political problems
of the day) and by Lee Strasberg's interest in creating an American version of the Stanislavsky method.[45]

Crawford mistakenly thought Clurman and Strasberg would be sympathetic to the problems confronting women directors. Early in the rehearsals for *The House of Connelly*, the two men went back on their
pledge that Crawford and Strasberg would share directing responsibilities, announcing that Strasberg alone would direct the production and
that Crawford would rehearse the scenes between the two black servants.
When Crawford objected, Clurman informed her that her ego was getting
in the way of her artistic and political commitments. After much soul-
searching, she accepted her assignment without further question. For the
next six years, Crawford suffered a self-imposed martyrdom in which she
expressed feelings of going unappreciated. Her primary responsibilities
included handling the Group Theatre's financial and business affairs,
reading new scripts, scheduling rehearsals for new plays, and planning
the summer retreats. In short, she performed the tasks that failed to
interest her male collaborators, which could include the direction of
plays.[46]

Crawford's experiences suggest that, despite its progressive rhetoric, the socially conscious Group Theatre reproduced systems of power and privilege that devalued difference. Opportunities for career advancement were curtailed for women during the 1930s in order to prevent the economic displacement of men. It was not so much that women shouldn't work but that their labor should be confined to "women's jobs."[47] Women in powerful positions were regarded as suspiciously "unfeminine." The Group Theatre replicated these patterns, masking their operation through a liberal agenda grounded in a rationalist tradition in which the inappropriate expression of emotions and desires threatened its reasoned politic. The gendered paradigms operative at the time left Crawford in a difficult position to negotiate. On the one hand, her ambitions worked against the good of the Group Theatre because her "unchecked" emotions interfered with her capacity for sound judgment. In turn, if she denied her feelings (i.e., her womanliness), then her lesbianism became suspect and marked by her visible position of power. In the end, the only compromise available was to suppress her feelings and submit to the decisions of her male collaborators, allowing Crawford to find empowerment in the responsibilities assigned to her as the lone female cofounder. A sense of community based on freedom and equality would have to come later.

Crawford did not find immediate success as an independent producer following her resignation from the Group Theatre, producing five consecutive failures before finding a modicum of success at the Maplewood Theatre. The three seasons Crawford spent producing stock included touring productions and tryouts from New York, but they were most noted for productions of contemporary and classical plays that employed professional designers and actors from New York, including Ethel Barrymore, Tallulah Bankhead, Jane Cowl, Edna Ferber, José Ferrer, Walter Hampden, Canada Lee, Elsa Maxwell, Paul Robeson, and Gloria Swanson. Crawford's most successful production at Maplewood was also its last: a revival of *Porgy and Bess* that transferred to Broadway in 1942, marking the beginning of her career as a musical producer, as well as the beginning of her reputation as "the producer in skirts."

Crawford's career as an independent producer profited from the changing social attitudes regarding gender norms, but it ultimately was held in check by the politically reactionary period that followed the war. In *Communists, Cowboys, and Queers,* David Savran interrogates the politics of Cold War America by examining the dramaturgy of the two major American playwrights to emerge during the 1940s: Arthur Miller and Tennessee Williams. Miller's plays reinforced a rigid sex-gender system, staging anxieties about male and female sexuality so they could be socially purged. Williams, in contrast, sought to subvert traditional gender and sexual roles, suggesting that the possibility for revolution was always present even when not spoken.[48] As a producer, Crawford passed on opportunities to stage both Miller's *All My Sons* and *Death of a Salesman* but went on to produce Williams's *The Rose Tattoo* (1951), *Camino Real* (1953), *Sweet Bird of Youth* (1959), and *Period of Adjustment* (1960). It is tempting to suggest that the figure of Williams as a revolutionary poet appealed more to Crawford than the maverick politics of Miller's dramaturgy.

But the economic pressures of producing on Broadway during the 1940s suggest differently. The number of productions staged in New York had dramatically decreased since Crawford started her professional career in the theater. Brooks Atkinson estimates that 264 productions were staged during the 1927–28 season (approximately the time when Crawford began her association with the Theatre Guild). By 1930–31 (the season immediately proceeding the Group Theatre's first production), that number had decreased to 187. Only 72 productions were staged during the 1940–41 Broadway season.[49] Despite the intermittent success of a drama or classical revival like Crawford's 1945 production of Margaret Webster's *The Tempest,* musicals dominated the stage of the 1940s. The energy and spectacle of works like *Brigadoon* (1947), *Finian's Rainbow* (1948), *Kiss Me, Kate* (1948), *Oklahoma!* (1943), *One Touch of Venus* (1943), and *South Pacific* (1949) enabled the commercial theater to compete with the growing popularity of Hollywood films. Theater became a potentially lucrative but costly venture.

The business of Broadway functioned according to rules of conduct similar to those found in American corporations, whose upper levels of management characteristically lack structure. Because such organizations rely on individuals rather than structures for their maintenance, self-protective systems built on mutual trust are created to hold members to a set of common standards.

In examining the effect of gender on corporate experiences, Rosabeth Moss Kanter identifies tokenism as one of the means through which the dominant group marks its boundaries. Placed in highly visible positions, tokens are under constant pressure to assimilate.[50] The description of Crawford as "the producer in skirts," for example, visibly marked her difference from the male norm, at the same time that it subsumed her sexual difference. The rigid gender dichotomies that Stacy

Wolf sees operative in Mary Martin's negotiation of the closet in another essay in this collection were also at play for Crawford.[51] Both Martin and Crawford wrestled with received notions of femininity and domesticity, manipulating the public discourse surrounding their successful careers to cloak their rejection of normative heterosexuality.

At the same time that she navigated the world of commercial theater, Crawford played key roles in artistic enterprises like the Actors Studio, the American National Theatre and Academy, and the American Repertory Theatre that outright challenged Broadway commercialism. This seemingly queer contradiction allowed Crawford to work more intimately with many of the gay and lesbian artists with whom she collaborated throughout her professional career. Encouraged by their success with *The Tempest,* for instance, Crawford, Margaret Webster, and Eva Le Gallienne founded the American Repertory Theatre in 1945. The American Repertory Theatre was a classical repertory company that aspired to become the "American Old Vic."[52] Crawford, whom Webster and Le Gallienne sensed shared their artistic and sexual values, was excited to work with "two such towers." She experienced an enthusiasm that she hadn't felt "since [she] started in the theatre when everything was glittering."[53] The glow quickly faded, however, as the company encountered unprecedented demands from theater unions, followed by a lukewarm reception from reviewers. It was as if "too much fuss had been made over [them] and [that they] had better be warned."[54] Crawford resigned from the company in 1947, unfulfilled by a season plagued with artistic and managerial compromises. She feared the worst: "perhaps [she] was not *strong* enough to work with partners."[55] With the demise of the American National Theatre and Academy shortly thereafter, Crawford "became again that naked individual [she] had tried to avoid."[56]

In 1942, the *New York Herald Tribune* printed a full-page article on Crawford in its magazine section, which included some of her favorite recipes. The article featured two photographs. The first shows Crawford sitting alone in a dark, empty theater, taking notes. The second reveals her in a well-lit, fully equipped kitchen, tossing a salad. "In food, as in drama," reads the text, "Cheryl Crawford has what it takes."[57] The contrast between the images of Crawford as a producer and homemaker illustrates the extent to which women, despite the social and economic opportunities made available through the war effort, remained valued according to their relationship to domesticity. Crawford's success as a woman producer was explained in highly gendered terms. Her record as a producer of musicals was so impressive, Flanner writes, "that on

Cheryl Crawford in her kitchen

(Courtesy Billy Rose Theatre Collection, Lincoln Center Library for the Performing Arts, New York Public Library.)

Broadway she [was] almost superstitiously credited with having some
special feminine touch for making them pay," including "the elimination
of a lot of customary, costly, masculine waste."[58]

Whereas the performance of femininity during the 1940s represented
an acceptability through which Crawford could "pass," it was viewed as
dangerously excessive during the reactionary 1950s. The theater was
regarded by some at the time as a matriarchy. Norris Houghton attributed the theater's "femininization" to the earning capacity of its actresses
and the dominant characters they portrayed on stage.

> If our stage has become more and more a woman's world, it is
> because we have withdrawn too much from the world of men, be-
> cause we have become content to reflect the trivialities of domestic-
> ity and to enjoy the safe sentimentality of our relations with Mom or
> the girl-friend rather than face up to the sinewy and exacting life of
> our time.[59]

Houghton assumes a direct correlation between visibility and power. In
arguing that the increased presence of women contributed to the femini-
zation of the American theater, he fails to mark the economic power of
men in labor unions and as reviewers that, in the case of the American
Repertory Theatre, enabled the "little band of men" to protect themselves from the "Amazonian hordes."[60] The identification of the problem as peculiar to the American theater of the Cold War era, moreover,
points to the operations of domestic containment through which feminism and homosexuality became demonized. Houghton's is a theatrical
version of "momism," according to which, the reliance on overly maternal women breeds an "effeminacy" (i.e., homosexuality) among men
that stifles rationalism and independence. Feminism in turn became
synonymous with lesbianism insofar as the economic and social independence of women undermined the institutions of marriage and
motherhood that characterized national identity.

Crawford's enactment of femininity mocked these "family values,"
offering a site where the contradictions of compulsory heterosexuality
were played out. Flanner concludes,

> In her studious, ungarrulous way, Crawford seems quite content to go
> on, if possible, producing successful, high-class, not too costly musi-
> cal comedies, but some of her friends feel that this is not good enough
> for her. "In the musical-comedy business," one of them said not long
> ago, "she's a painted horse on a merry-go-round. In the old days, it
> was different. She was a war horse. She looked more natural then."[61]

Crawford's "unnatural" performance of heterosexuality was indeed marked by appearances. The postwar medical profession maintained that lesbians only appeared happy; beneath the surface, they were sad and lonely but afraid to admit it.[62] While such narratives pathologized lesbianism, physical appearance became one of the primary means through which lesbianism was encoded. Crawford boasted that her suits were made by Marlene Dietrich's tailor and that, unlike Veronica Lake, she never wore plunging necklines. After all, she was a producer.[63] Crawford's manner of dress not only was appropriate professional attire, it signified her sexual identification to others in the know. Crawford's "manly womanliness" in the end was an ironic performance, one that positioned her outside the heterosexual norm in a space where lesbian and gay communities were imagined.

For the artistic and cultural elite of gay New York, whose everyday lives were preoccupied with passing as "normal," Fire Island became a place during the late 1940s and 1950s where they could openly express their sexual identities. Economic power bought them tolerance. Many of Crawford's professional and personal acquaintances, including Flanner, Williams, Jane Bowles, Carson McCullers, and Oliver White (to name a few), summered in Cherry Grove. Esther Newton also points out in her ethnographic history that "several old timers said they heard of the Grove through [Crawford] or wanted to come because they knew through theatrical grapevines that she was there."[64] Crawford herself makes no mention of her summers at the Grove, except that she read the script for *Brigadoon* on a beach on Fire Island.[65] She frequently rented Pride House with Ruth Norman, a caterer and cookbook author with whom she had a lasting relationship during the 1940s and 1950s. Crawford, more significantly, played a part in the development of the Grove's cultural community, serving on the advisory board for the Cherry Grove Community Playhouse with other theater professionals, including Frank Carrington and Hallye Cannon, the wardrobe mistress at the Theatre Guild during Crawford's tenure. The playhouse hoped to become "the Provincetown of the next decade" by forming a lesbian and gay community adjacent to but outside the theater.[66] "Cherry Grove is brimful of artistic talent," explained the program notes for the *Cherry Grove Follies* of 1948. "We won't have to import performers or artisans from the Mainland to have ourselves a theatre to enhance both the fame of Fire Island and our own *joie de vivre*."[67]

As the Grove became more class-diversified, its bourgeois lifestyle found itself threatened. Fearful of the openness represented by butch-femme couples, the Grove's more discreet "ladies" moved to the Connecticut countryside, making it the third point on what became known as the "bermuda shorts triangle" that also included the Grove and the Upper East Side of Manhattan.[68] Crawford and Norman were among those who migrated to Connecticut, purchasing the five-acre estate of Eastham near the country home of their friends Mary Martin and Richard Halliday. Eastham became a sanctuary for Crawford: "I think this retreat saved my sanity and health. I relaxed under transparent summer skies and stalked through the white snows of winter. Ruth Norman planted vegetables, and I picked them."[69]

For the last thirty years of her career, when artistic and commercial success as a producer proved more difficult, Eastham represented a place where Crawford "belonged." Elspeth Probyn, in describing the geography of lesbian desire, remarks,

> Belonging . . . conjures up a deep insecurity about the possibility of really belonging, truly fitting it. But then, the term "belongings" also forefronts the ways in which these yearnings to fit in will always be diverse: at times joyous, at times painful, at times destined to fail.[70]

Indeed, when Eastham burned on February 5, 1969, Crawford called Norman (then living in Westport, Connecticut), asking her to save whatever charred remnants she could (i.e., to salvage the belongings of Crawford's life as one naked individual). Her desire to belong was at times fulfilled and unfulfilled, at times painful and joyous. It was rather like drowning: not bad when she stopped struggling.

NOTES

I would like to thank the members of the "Reading Group" for their comments and discussions and to acknowledge my debt especially to Jill Dolan, Erin Hurley, and Stacy Wolf.

   1. Cheryl Crawford, *One Naked Individual: My Fifty Years in the Theatre* (Indianapolis: Bobbs-Merrill, 1977), ix.

   2. Bruce A. McConachie, "New Historicism and American Theater History: Toward an Interdisciplinary Paradigm for Scholarship," in *The Performance of Power: Theatrical Discourse and Politics,* ed. Sue-Ellen Case and Janelle Reinelt (Iowa City: University of Iowa Press, 1991), 267.

   3. Sidonie Smith, "Who's Talking/Who's Talking Back? The Subject of Personal Narrative," *Signs* 18 (winter 1993): 404.

   4. Christopher Lehmann-Haupt, "Books of the Times," *New York Times,* April 26, 1977, 37.

5. Crawford, *One Naked Individual,* ix.

6. Eve Kosofsky Sedgwick, *Epistemology of the Closet* (Berkeley and Los Angeles: University of California Press, 1990), 80.

7. Martha Vicinus, " 'They Wonder to Which Sex I Belong': The Historical Roots of Modern Lesbian Identity," in *The Lesbian and Gay Studies Reader,* ed. Henry Abelove, Michèle Aina Barale, and David M. Halperin (New York: Routledge, 1993), 433.

8. Joan W. Scott, "The Evidence of Experience," in Abelove, Barale, and Halperin, *Lesbian and Gay Studies,* 399–400.

9. I am using the term *queer* to interrogate "the open mesh of possibilities, gaps, overlaps, dissonances and resonances, lapses and excesses of meaning when the constituent elements of anyone's gender, of anyone's sexuality are made (or *can't be* made) to signify monolithically." See Eve Kosofsky Sedgwick, *Tendencies* (Durham, NC: Duke University Press, 1993), 8.

10. Crawford, *One Naked Individual,* 6.

11. Ibid.

12. Judy Michaelson, "Our Town's Leading Business Women," *New York Post Magazine,* September 1, 1964, 25.

13. Grace Turner, "She Knows What We Like," *New York Herald Tribune Magazine,* May 24, 1942, 39.

14. Crawford, *One Naked Individual,* 10.

15. Ibid., 8.

16. Lynne Yamaguchi and Karen Barber, eds., *Tomboys! Tales of Dyke Derring-Do* (Los Angeles: Allyson Publications, 1995), 13.

17. Harold Clurman, *The Fervent Years: The Group Theatre and the Thirties* (New York: Harcourt Brace Jovanovich, 1975; reprint, New York: Da Capo Press, 1983), 97.

18. Richard von Krafft-Ebing, *Psychopathia Sexualis,* trans. Franklin S. Klaf (1886; New York: Bell Publishing, 1965), 278, quoted in Esther Newton, "The Mythic Mannish Lesbian: Radclyffe Hall and the New Woman," in *Hidden from History: Reclaiming the Gay and Lesbian Past,* ed. Martin Duberman, Martha Vicinus, and George Chauncey Jr. (New York: Penguin, 1989), 287.

19. Cheryl Crawford; quoted in Mary Anderson, "Kudos for Three Hits Go to Two Women," *New York World-Telegram,* February 11, 1944, 28.

20. Crawford, *One Naked Individual,* 244.

21. Esther Newton suggests just this in *Cherry Grove, Fire Island: Sixty Years in America's First Gay and Lesbian Town* (Boston: Beacon Press, 1993), 85.

22. Crawford, *One Naked Individual,* 7.

23. Janet Flanner, "A Woman in the House," *New Yorker,* May 8, 1948, 35.

24. Florence Ramon, "Cheryl's Chock Full of Stage Ideas," *Morning Telegraph,* May 30, 1941, 1.

25. Judith Butler, *Gender Trouble: Feminism and the Subversion of Identity* (New York: Routledge, 1990), 143.

26. Crawford, *One Naked Individual,* 15.

27. For a more detailed discussion, see Pamela S. Haag, "In Search of 'The Real Thing': Ideologies of Love, Modern Romance, and Women's Sexual Subjec-

tivity in the United States, 1920–1940," in *American Sexual Politics: Sex, Gender, and Race since the Civil War*, ed. John C. Fout and Maura Shaw Tantillo (Chicago: University of Chicago Press, 1993), 171.

28. Crawford, *One Naked Individual*, 30.

29. Ibid., 39.

30. More detailed discussions about the bohemian cultures of Greenwich Village, Harlem, and their relationships to one another can be found in Lillian Faderman, *Odd Girls and Twilight Lovers: A History of Lesbian Life in Twentieth-Century America* (New York: Penguin, 1991), 62–92; and David Levering Lewis, *When Harlem Was in Vogue* (New York: Knopf, 1981; reprint, New York: Oxford University Press, 1989).

31. Crawford, *One Naked Individual*, 29.

32. Michaelson, "Town's Leading Business Women," 25; Flanner, "Woman in the House," 37.

33. "Maplewood Summer Theater is Success," unmarked clipping, Clippings File, Billy Rose Theatre Collection, Lincoln Center Library for the Performing Arts, New York Public Library.

34. Flanner, "Woman in the House," 38.

35. Crawford, *One Naked Individual*, 63.

36. The details about Crawford's affair with Patten come from John Wilson, *From Chattanooga to Broadway: The Dorothy Patten Story* (Chattanooga, TN: Chattanooga News–Free Press, 1986). Wilson does not characterize their relationship as sexual, nor is there any discussion of Patten's breakdown. For this, see Wendy Smith, *Real Life Drama: The Group Theatre and America, 1931–1940* (New York: Knopf, 1990).

37. Crawford, *One Naked Individual*, 60.

38. Ibid., 109–10.

39. Ibid., 45 and 46–47.

40. Sedgwick, *Epistemology of the Closet*, 81.

41. Patricia Meyer Spacks, *Gossip* (Chicago: University of Chicago Press, 1986), 19.

42. Mel Gussow, "First Things First: An Interview with Robert Lewis (1909–1997)," *American Theatre* 15 (January 1998): 27.

43. Andrew Parker, Mary Russo, Doris Sommer, and Patricia Yaeger, introduction to *Nationalisms and Sexualities* (New York: Routledge, 1992), 1.

44. Lawrence Langner, *The Magic Curtain: The Story of a Life in Two Fields, Theatre and Invention* (New York: Dutton, 1951), 118.

45. Crawford, *One Naked Individual*, 52.

46. Crawford directed three productions for the Group Theatre, all failures: *Big Night* (1933), *Till the Day I Die* (1935), and *Weep for the Virgins* (1935).

47. Elaine Tyler May, *Homeward Bound: American Families in the Cold War Era* (New York: Basic Books, 1988), 48–49.

48. David Savran, *Communists, Cowboys, and Queers: The Politics of Masculinity in the Work of Arthur Miller and Tennessee Williams* (Minneapolis: University of Minnesota Press, 1992), 9.

49. Brooks Atkinson, *Broadway*, rev. ed. (New York: Macmillan, 1974; reprint, New York: Limelight, 1985), 424.

50. Rosabeth Moss Kanter, *Men and Women of the Corporation* (New York: Basic Books, 1977), 210–11.

51. See her article in this volume, "Mary Martin: Washin' That Man Right Outta Her Hair," as well as "The Queer Performances of Mary Martin as Woman and as Star," *Women and Performance* 8, no. 2 (1996): 225–40.

52. Margaret Webster, Eva Le Gallienne, and Cheryl Crawford, "Plans for the American Repertory Theatre, Inc.," Margaret Webster Collection, Manuscript Division, Library of Congress, Washington, D.C.

53. Cheryl Crawford, letter to Margaret Webster, July 4, 1946, Margaret Webster Collection.

54. Margaret Webster, *Don't Put Your Daughter on the Stage* (New York: Knopf, 1972), 161.

55. Cheryl Crawford, Letter to Eva Le Gallienne and Margaret Webster, June 10, 1947, Margaret Webster Collection. Economic pressures are traditionally cited as reasons for the failure of the ART. For a discussion of the impact of gender on the company's demise, see Robert A. Schanke, *Shattered Applause: The Lives of Eva Le Gallienne* (Carbondale: Southern Illinois University Press, 1992), 173–80.

56. Crawford, *One Naked Individual*, 162.

57. Turner, "She Knows."

58. Flanner, "Woman in the House," 34.

59. Norris Houghton, "It's a Woman's World," *Theatre Arts Monthly*, January 1947, 34.

60. Ibid. Houghton's expressed misogyny serves as an affirmation of his masculinity, one that detracts attention away from his own homosexuality.

61. Flanner, "Woman in the House," 47.

62. Faderman, *Odd Girls*, 131.

63. Ramon, "Cheryl's Chock Full," 1.

64. Newton, *Cherry Grove, Fire Island*, 337 n. 8.

65. Crawford, *One Naked Individual*, 164.

66. "Cherry Grove Follies of 1949," unmarked clipping, Clippings File, Billy Rose Theatre Collection.

67. Program for the *Cherry Grove Follies of 1948*, Clippings File, Billy Rose Theatre Collection.

68. Newton, *Cherry Grove, Fire Island* 220.

69. Crawford, *One Naked Individual*, 170.

70. Elspeth Probyn, "Queer Belongings: The Politics of Departure," in *Sexy Bodies: The Strange Carnalities of Feminism*, ed. Elizabeth Grosz and Elspeth Probyn (New York: Routledge, 1995), 2.

Monty Woolley

The Public and Private Man
from Saratoga Springs

Billy J. Harbin

Monty (Edgar Montillion) Woolley (1888–1963), who had begun his professional career in the theater as a director, gained the role of his life in 1939 when Moss Hart and George S. Kaufman asked him to portray Sheridan Whiteside in their play *The Man Who Came to Dinner*. Whiteside was based upon Alexander Woollcott (1887–1943), a celebrated, temperamental theater critic, radio personality, and member of the Algonquin Round Table crowd. Woollcott had a considerable reputation as a stinging wit and master of the insult. His bitchy behavior could be cruel, and his egocentric demands for attention could be maddening, but those who were fond of him (Kaufman's wife was one of his closest friends) could perceive beyond his tantrums a gentle and lonely man. Presumably, an illness at the age of twenty-two had rendered Woollcott impotent, and he remained all of his life a repressed homosexual who never found a mate.[1] Naturally, Kaufman and Hart believed that Woollcott himself would be the perfect Whiteside, but Woollcott turned it down (although he later did the role on the West Coast). After offering the role to Robert Morley and Adolphe Menjou, both of whom in turn rejected it, Hart then had the idea of casting Monty Woolley, whom he had known for several years. Early in 1935, Woolley, Hart, Cole and Linda Porter, and Howard Sturges had sailed around the world on the *Franconia* for the major purpose of putting together the musical *Jubilee,* with Porter creating the music and lyrics, Hart, the book, and Woolley as director.[2]

Hart had long known that Porter and Woolley were homosexuals. Within the world of the theater, one's sexual orientation rarely was any more controversial than one's religious preference, although disclosure to colleagues called for discretion, and disclosure to the public (especially during Woolley's lifetime) called for silence. George Chauncey's history of homosexuality in New York (from 1890 to 1940) clearly reveals that "the policing of the gay world before Stonewall [1969] was even more extensive and draconian than is generally realized." Extant laws criminalized not only the sexual relationships of gay men but their social relationships with each other as well.³ Court records of the early twentieth century show that homosexuals caught in sexual interaction during police raids upon taverns, public baths, or even private homes could receive "more than seven years in the state penitentiary. The severity of the punishment reminds us," Chauncey states, "why men went to [great] lengths to hide their involvement in the gay world from their nongay associates."⁴

Certainly, Woolley and Porter all of their lives publicly disguised their homosexuality and privately revealed it within their circle of trusted friends. With Moss Hart, Woolley and Porter maintained no disguises. Indeed, "apparently feeling that Hart was straddling the sexual fence and a potential convert," Cole and Monty in good humor "would often" tease Hart to join their lifestyle. But Hart never acknowledged any leanings in that direction.⁵ During the four and a half months of the journey around the world, the group ate, socialized, and worked together, becoming as knowledgeable and understanding of each other's virtues and faults as any close-knit family. Hart's familiarity with the actor undoubtedly influenced his decision four years later to cast Woolley as Whiteside. Monty seemed to possess many of the fictional character's traits: the gruff bark and flashing wit, even the sophisticated charm that could turn impishly vulgar. Furthermore, Woolley seemed to have within him something of the tension that makes Whiteside dramatic: an external bravado that perhaps masked an inner, secret self.

One night in Hollywood, after Woolley had finished what he later derisively called a "cheesy" role in the film *Dancing Co-ed* (1939), he celebrated with a few martinis and had gone to bed "cockeyed," when Moss Hart called from New York, offering him the role of Whiteside. "Moss, are you drunk?" Monty barked into the phone. Monty quickly sobered and did "some fast thinking. Here was a Kaufman and Hart play and I was being offered the leading part. It was the chance of a lifetime [and] I grabbed [it]."⁶

By 1939 Alexander Woollcott had become known throughout the country for his radio broadcasts, in which (much to the surprise of those who knew him privately) he succeeded in endearing himself to the nation's listeners as "the Town Crier." He presented (not insincerely, although it was a seldom-shown facet of his character) the image of a genial, erudite uncle whose abundant enthusiasm for literature, theater, storytelling, and charitable causes enlightened and entertained millions of Americans. Kaufman and Hart knew both the public and private Woollcott as well as anyone (Kaufman had coauthored two plays with him, both flops), and the idea of using for a play the celebrated Woollcott, who was welcomed into the nation's homes as "the idol of the air-waves" and at the same time was often persona non grata to his friends, became irresistible. Besides, Woollcott, who loved acting on the stage, had pestered the authors for two years to create a vehicle for him. Little did he realize that the eventual play would be not merely *for* him, but *about* him.[7]

The play's plot fell into place for the authors after a disastrous week-end visit by Woollcott to Hart's home, during which Woollcott's incessant demands for personal attention and comfort threw Hart and his household into turmoil (he wrote in Hart's guest book, "I wish to say that on my first visit to Moss Hart's [home] I had one of the most unpleasant evenings I can ever recall having spent").[8] Hart said to Kaufman, "What if he had broken his leg . . . and I had to keep him there?"[9] It was the plot device they needed to imprison Whiteside within a morally and socially self-righteous, middle-class family home, which Whiteside would then for three acts subvert and shake to the foundation.

Kaufman and Hart permitted Whiteside little chance to display the sentimentality and geniality of "the Town Crier." Rather, Whiteside's public celebrity empowers his egocentric, dictatorial authority in his host's home and community, enabling him to become a privileged outsider who ridicules their inflexible, conservative mentality. For Monty Woolley, Whiteside as iconoclastic alien and savage wit was a familiar, comfortable role. As Kaufman told Hart, after Woollcott and others had refused to act the role, "There is this drama professor I met up at Yale. . . . He's been playing Alec [Woollcott] for years in New Haven."[10] Indeed, Woolley, erudite wit, homosexual celebrant, and cynical critic of social convention, seized the opportunity, like Whiteside in the play, to realize publicly on stage a role that fulfilled the fantasy of his own gay membership: an outsider who challenges "the legitimacy of bourgeois morality."[11] As the sexually ambiguous Whiteside, Woolley could not only publicly flaunt convention and get away with it, but be applauded for it. Whiteside's gleeful demolition of his host's rigidly observed decorum, accomplished merely through weapons of wit and shameless effrontery, represented for gay and liberal audiences a subversive minority that defies traditional social codes and wins. Kaufman and Hart's ingenious device of anchoring the deviant Whiteside in a wheelchair not only prevents his escaping the premises he deplores, but at the same time renders him physically impotent, confining his artillery to verbal assault and diminishing to some degree the seriousness of his threat.

Woolley's mastery of the role was evident at the first public preview in Boston, when his presentation of Whiteside won admiration not only for his technical proficiency but because he was utterly convincing as the character. Woolley said later of his performance that it was "more Woolley than Woollcott,"[12] which supports both Kaufman and Hart's earlier perceptions of Woolley's offstage persona. Monty's success as Whiteside was so pervasive and pronounced that the public thereafter identified him (and not Woollcott) with the role.

Monty Woolley was born in New York City, in the old Hotel Bristol (Fifth Avenue and Forty-second Street), one of several owned or managed by his father, William Edgar Woolley. When Monty was three, his father gained the lease of the legendary Grand Union Hotel in Saratoga Springs and moved his family to the proprietor's house on the hotel grounds.[13] At a testimonial dinner in his honor at Saratoga in 1949, Woolley recalled his childhood there, especially during the race season, when the prominent and wealthy came with their horses and servants and stayed for three months. His father introduced him to Lillian Russell, "with her broad black hat and full bosomed dress," and Diamond Jim Brady, "who showed me his cane, the top of which was an immense diamond." Victor Herbert came every season to conduct his orchestra in morning and afternoon concerts, and Monty saw his first theatrical performance when DeWolf Hopper played in *Midsummer Night's Dream* in the hotel's courtyard.[14] It was a heady, worldly environment for a boy growing up.

Monty's stern father and indulgent mother (Jessie M. Arms Woolley) provided the boy and his only sibling, James (1882–1958), a privileged upbringing. A rigid disciplinarian, William Edgar Woolley (who looked "like a miniature of a Roman senator") kept a tight hold on the purse strings, not permitting the boys to "waste" their allowances on "foolishness." Nevertheless, he "saw to it that his sons had the best clothes to be made in New York" and "the best rooms at school and college."[15] Monty, in adolescence, toured Europe with his parents, prepared for college at the Mackenzie School, in Dobbs Ferry, and entered Yale (in 1907) with the class of 1911.

At Yale, Woolley "fell in with the set which owned pianos [and] studied wine lists, and . . . he soon became the leader of a clique which dabbled in dramatics and profligacy."[16] His privileged background was not unlike that of Cole Porter, whose wealthy, authoritarian, maternal

**Monty Woolley signing the register at the Grand Union Hotel
on "Monty Woolley Day," July 9, 1949, Saratoga Springs**

*(Courtesy of the George S. Bolster Collection of the Historical Society
of Saratoga Springs.)*

grandfather (in Peru, Indiana) controlled the purse strings, and whose
devoted mother, acting as liaison between the two, nearly always managed to satisfy Cole's every financial need.[17] Porter entered Yale in 1909
(class of 1913), by which time Woolley had become a dominant figure in
Yale's social fraternities and the Dramatic Association (of which he became president in his last year).

In many ways, Cole, Monty, and their friends were "cut from the
same cloth. They were invariably bright and personable and came from
good, well-to-do families."[18] They were drawn together as homosexuals,

too, although not all in their circle were gay. A fellow classmate described Leonard Hanna, wealthy son of a Cleveland industrialist, and Monty Woolley as "both clearly homosexual," although the signs that so obviously identified the two are not recorded.[19] Woolley, older by a couple of years than most of those active in the Yale Dramatic Association, had gained an acknowledged leadership role, not only artistically but socially, and probably influenced Porter and others in their theater work, in their wit and humor, and in liberating their views of themselves as homosexuals. Literate, inventive, and clever, he had a remarkable command of language, including fluency in Old English.[20] Furthermore, Woolley, unlike Porter, was an exceptional student, and his intellectual prowess enabled him soon to gain graduate degrees from both Yale and Harvard.[21]

Although within his own social and theatrical circles at the university Woolley never disguised his homosexuality, he realized the necessity for public discretion, especially on campus, where he maintained not only a visible leadership role among undergraduates in his student years, but, also, later, a prominent faculty position. His intelligence and intuitive sense of performance allowed him to construct a public Woolley whose inventive wit and robust humor could invert what tradition held dear and at the same time disarm critics through laughter. Cole Porter and other gay Yale companions were drawn to Woolley in part because of his irresistible, campy sense of humor. Charles Ludlum, in attempting to define camp, notes that "Proust describes [it] as an outsider's view of things other people take . . . for granted. Because of the inversion, everything that everyone else had taken for granted isn't true for [the outsider and] things become funny because [one is] seeing . . . a reverse image." In the hands of the witty and clever, camp becomes "a rigorous revaluing of everything. What people think is valuable [is not] valuable. Admiring what people hold in contempt, holding in contempt things other people think are so valuable" are remarkable standards of camp.[22]

In any event, within a short time of their meeting, Woolley became Porter's confidant and intimate friend and remained so throughout both their lives. Both were homosexuals (although never lovers), precocious, and socially sophisticated; both had an infectious, even outrageous sense of humor. They shared a love of gossip, cafe society, costume parties, practical jokes and pranks, drinks and cigarettes, handsome young men, and, above all, anything to do with the theater. Charles Schwartz's biography, *Cole Porter*, reveals the pleasure they took in each other's company, talents, and humor over a period of half a century, and it provides as well candid accounts of their homosexuality and pursuits of partners.[23]

Woolley graduated with the bachelor of arts in 1911, but he stayed on at Yale to gain a graduate degree (M.A., 1912), and then went to Harvard, where he earned another advanced degree (M.A., 1913), under George Lyman Kittredge, the Shakespearean scholar.[24] Woolley returned to Yale that fall to teach English and act as coach to the Yale Dramatic Association.[25] Meanwhile, Cole Porter, under pressure from his grandfather, enrolled in the Harvard Law School in 1913. Soon, however, he pushed aside law studies and responded to Woolley's request for a show for the Yale Dramatic Association, creating *Paranoia* (April 1914), and *We're All Dressed Up and We Don't Know Huerto Go,* which Woolley and Porter took to an annual reunion of Yale clubs in Cincinnati in May 1914.[26]

During the Mexican expedition of 1916, Woolley enlisted in the army, soon received a lieutenant's commission, and in 1918 spent eight months in France. Cole Porter had moved to Paris in 1917, and he soon had a large circle of friends. Some were Yale graduates (Archibald MacLeish, Howard Sturges), and others were wealthy Americans living abroad (Elsa Maxwell, Elsie de Wolfe, and the socialite divorcée, Linda Lee Thomas, whom he married in 1919). Woolley joined the group for partying, gossiping, and carousing whenever he could obtain military leave.[27]

After the Armistice, Woolley settled in New York to forge a career as a director. He gained some experience as stage manager for Brock Pemberton and Arthur Hopkins, but directing jobs proved hard to secure.[28] After a few years of erratic employment, Woolley in 1923 gratefully accepted a faculty position at his beloved alma mater, where for the next four years he lectured on drama and directed undergraduate productions in the Dramatic Association.[29] Among his students were Stephen Vincent Benet, Thornton Wilder, Philip Barry, and Dwight Deere Wiman.[30]

In the summer of 1923 Woolley had visited the Porters in Venice at their splendid Palazzo Barbaro on the Grand Canal, and in the following year Cole suffered a career crisis. He had created several songs (including "Two Little Girls in a Wood") for the Greenwich Village Follies; when they attracted little public notice, Porter became despondent, believing his musical career had come to a dead end. H. C. Potter (Yale 1926) recalls that it was Monty Woolley, who, concerned about Cole's depression, used "every bit of the exuberant enthusiasm and persuasion that was so wonderfully his" to nudge "Cole out of . . . virtual retirement." Urged by Monty to compose a show for the Yale Dramatic Association, Cole created *Out O' Luck* (1925), which Woolley directed, and "the success of the songs undoubtedly played a part in getting [Cole] out of the doldrums" and back on the track of his musical career.[31]

But Woolley himself soon faced a career crisis at Yale. In 1927 he resigned in response to what he considered Yale's lack of confidence in his work. Edward Harkness had recently given Yale a million dollars to establish an experimental theater program; when Yale chose George Pierce Baker, rather·than Woolley, to direct it, Monty left Yale for New York to pursue once again a professional career.[32]

Meanwhile, Woolley maintained his close relationship with Cole Porter, and after Monty returned to New York, they shared many adventures and sexual pursuits. Sometimes, in the thirties, they drove around Manhattan in an open convertible, cruising for "action."[33] Schwartz records that Porter and Woolley used "procurers to supply them with the physical types that appealed to them." They devised a scheme for getting the male prostitutes into their fancy hotels without arousing suspicion: disguised delivery men arrived, bearing fake packages.[34]

In 1929 Cole had asked Monty to direct *Fifty Million Frenchmen* (book by Herbert Fields); the show (which opened on November 14) became Porter's first Broadway triumph. Its success reflected upon Woolley, too, and he thereafter directed several productions in New York, including Howard Dietz's *The Second Little Show* (1930); Porter's *The New Yorkers* (1930); Herbert Fields's *America's Sweetheart* (1931); Vernon Duke's *Walk a Little Faster* (1932); Laurence Langner's *Champagne Sec* (an adaptation of *Die Fledermaus*) (1933); and Porter's *Jubilee* (1935).

Although *Jubilee* contained some of Porter's most memorable songs ("Begin the Beguine," "Just One of Those Things"), the $150,000 production failed, "without coming close to recouping the money invested in it."[35] The show's failure may in part account for Woolley's decision to go to Hollywood in 1936 to seek work as a director. Once there, however, he hit "a low point of his career," failing to obtain any kind of job. While Woolley "was languishing in Hollywood," his former student, Dwight Deere Wiman, who was now producing *On Your Toes* in New York, offered him a major supporting role in the show. Although he had not acted since his years at Yale, he was desperate enough to accept the challenge.[36] *On Your Toes* (1936) became a smash hit, and Woolley, in the role of the flamboyant ballet impresario, caught the attention of the critics and public. His confidential display of pomposity, brashness, and bitchiness attracted offers from film studios, and, giving up his ambitions as a director, he devoted himself to acting.

Woolley soon signed a contract with Metro-Goldwyn-Mayer and went again to Hollywood. He had been impressive in *On Your Toes* because of his originality, a startling, spontaneous, larger-than-life presence. Impressive, too, was his offstage appearance: his neatly trimmed red beard and mustache (which within a few years turned white) imparted a certain aloof dignity to the man, and his thunderous voice, which he could lower to a booming bass, raise to a raspy contralto, or plummet to a hissing whisper, conveyed a distinct individuality. But, as Woolley was to discover, in Hollywood talent and distinctiveness do not necessarily lead to success.

When Woolley began his film career in 1937, the industry, reflecting the judgmental moral attitude of the nation as a whole, had become rampantly homophobic, especially after pressure from civil and religious organizations (such as the Legion of Decency) forced the establishment in 1934 of the Production Code (policed by the Hays Office). Although censorship of heterosexual relationships was absurd enough (a husband and wife could not be depicted as sleeping together in a double bed), the depiction of homosexuality was utterly forbidden, except as an object of ridicule, contempt, or ludicrous amusement.[37] Most actors were unwilling to be identified with such gay roles, but a few spent their careers specializing in them, especially Franklin Pangborn (1893–1958) and Grady Sutton (b. 1908), both of whom made innumerable films playing harassed clerks, swishing tailors, or put-upon floor managers.[38]

Although MGM had hired Woolley as a stage actor of original talent, once in Hollywood he was given no opportunity to display his wit and distinctive individuality and became a target of ridicule. In his first film, *Live, Love, and Learn* (1937), Woolley was required to lose his trousers as he was simultaneously doused with a bucket of water.[39] Casting offices regarded him "as that guy with the muff, whose dignity made him the natural object of cruel comedy," which evoked the image of a sexual pervert.[40] Woolley later remembered that he "faced the cameras trembling, frightened of Hollywood and all its works." During the two years of his MGM contract (1937–39), Woolley acted minor roles in fifteen films (four of them at Paramount), becoming increasingly "humiliated, disgusted, and desperate." He confessed a few years later, "The nearer I used to get to the studio of a morning, the more I'd wish a tire would blow out and leave me suffering no pain, but moaning softly in a ditch."[41] His future seemed to promise little variation from the incessant grind of doing another minor role in yet another film, every six weeks. But his fortunes changed when Kaufman and Hart dropped into his lap the role of Sheridan Whiteside.

The Man Who Came to Dinner began its out-of-town tryout in Boston on September 25, 1939, and word spread quickly that the production would be the hit of the season in New York. And indeed it was. The premiere at the Music Box Theatre on October 16 brought out an audience dressed to the nines. Brooks Atkinson called it "an evening of astringent merry-making," with Monty Woolley "presiding over the comedy with wonderful aplomb and his own whiskers," playing Whiteside/Woollcott "in the grand manner with dignity and knavery." The role, among other things, is "a literary part, and the Woolley as well as the Woollcott knows how to speak lines."[42] Atkinson followed up his review on Tuesday with a longer essay in the Sunday edition, assessing the authors' fictionalization of the "White Owl of Lake Bomoseen" (Woollcott), and Woolley's portrayal.

Some controversy had emerged among members of the Round Table about the authors' exploitation of their friend, Woollcott. Dorothy Parker, for example, thought Kaufman and Hart "distorted" Woollcott's personality in their "nasty little play."[43] Atkinson asked, "Is it ethical to make game and capital out of your personal friends in public?" He answered his question with an emphatic yes, especially, he added, if one travels in the "blistering circle" of literary and show business wits in which Woollcott, Hart, and Kaufman moved. But their circle provided "no banquet of flattery"; rather it conducted "its affairs with the retort discourteous, no holds barred and the rules for fouls permanently suspended." Atkinson, aware that the authors had initially attempted to cast Woollcott in the role, recognized the immeasurable contribution of Woolley, "who would be hard to improve upon," and who had no need "to imitate the illustrious model his part represents," possessing himself ample sophistication and humor "to offer his own style of attack."[44]

Woolley's achievement in the role elevated him to stardom as a performer and to celebrity as a personality. Columnists such as Lucius Beebe, Walter Winchell, and Cholly Knickerbocker sought him for interviews and news items, and popular national publications (including the *Saturday Evening Post*, the *New Yorker*, and *Time*) made Woolley's name and face familiar across the country: photographs show him in a neatly trimmed Vandyke beard and mustache, an eyebrow slightly lifted, the lips slyly about to smile. He looks like a mischievous professor, and, indeed, the "hook" of the many stories on him centered upon the phenomenon of an erudite Yale professor who had moved from the hallowed halls of ivy to the glitter of Broadway.

During his two seasons with *The Man Who Came to Dinner,* Woolley lived for a while at the Ritz Hotel and most of the time at the Astor, where he occupied a single room. Russell Maloney, who interviewed Woolley in late 1939 for the *New Yorker* "Profile" that was to appear in January, claimed, "Woolley's life is simplified by the fact that he has no possessive instinct: he owns an old Cadillac touring car, the usual amount of clothing, and nothing else." Woolley's room at the Astor was "usually a horrid welter of letters, linen, and empty bottles." His only needs, Woolley told Maloney, are "a bed, a bathroom, and a telephone."[45]

None of the interviews printed in the months following the show's success mentioned that Woolley was living with a homosexual companion, Cary Abbott (1890–1948) (Yale, 1911), who joined him sometime in 1939. Two years later, however, Lucius Beebe, a popular columnist, observer and elbow-rubbing member of the cafe society crowd, and himself a homosexual, interviewed Woolley at the Astor (after the actor's return from the Hollywood filming of *The Man Who Came to Dinner*) and slipped the name of the actor's companion into the story. Woolley's "principal adventure in his transcontinental travels [from the West Coast]," Beebe wrote, "befell him in . . . Cheyenne, Wyoming, where he stopped off for a few days so that his courier-secretary-traveling companion, Carey [*sic*] Abbott, could visit his family."[46]

Although Beebe presumably knew very well that Abbott and Woolley were sexual partners, it is a sign of the times that Beebe disguised it for his readers and that Woolley felt compelled to disguise it for his public. The press in general maintained silence on homosexual relationships as well as on heterosexual infidelities. But the press could *hint,* as Beebe did with Woolley and Abbott. The conventional labels used to disguise sexual partnerships, such as "secretary," "traveling companion," or "valet," did not fool sophisticates, but they apparently were accepted by the general public.[47]

Cary Abbott, two years younger than Woolley, was the son of a distinguished Cheyenne family. His father, George, longtime vice president of the First National Bank, had been treasurer for the state of Wyoming in 1900. After Cary's graduation from Yale in 1911, he returned to Cheyenne, took a position in his father's bank, and resided with his parents until about 1916, when he entered the army.[48] After the war, Cary resumed his bank position and residency with his parents. Thereafter, his record is difficult to trace until he became Woolley's partner in 1939. Abbott remained Woolley's companion and lover for the rest of his life; he died prematurely of lung cancer in the actor's home at Saratoga Springs in 1948 at the age of fifty-eight.⁴⁹

Meanwhile, Warner Brothers had bought the screen rights to *The Man Who Came to Dinner* for $350,000. Then, in characteristic Hollywood fashion, the studio had the script rewritten so that Cary Grant could play Whiteside as a younger man. When Bette Davis agreed to play Whiteside's secretary, Maggie, she had the good sense and sufficient clout to insist that the script be restored to the original, and, consequently, Woolley was cast as Whiteside.⁵⁰ The film became a popular success, and Woolley's bellowing, wasp-tongued, literate, and strangely appealing depiction of Whiteside established him as a movie star. The film, as had the play, further established for the public the image of Woolley, not Woollcott, as the crotchety celebrity, whose impudent wit punctures pretention and subverts social rule, and who emerges with dignity intact, grinning like a Cheshire cat.

After the film's success, Woolley received many subsequent movie offers and never returned to the stage. He was nominated for an Academy Award as best actor in *The Pied Piper* (1943) and for best supporting actor in *Since You Went Away* (1944). In 1946 he had the unique distinction of playing himself in the Warner Brothers' fictionalized version of Cole Porter's life, *Night and Day*. The scripted characters and their relationships had little resemblance to truth. The film became a story about love and success; the emphasis was upon the romance of Cole and Linda, and upon Cole's extraordinary musical career. Woolley played Woolley as an asexual Yale professor and supportive chum to Cole, as the script demanded. No hint of the homosexuality of Porter or Woolley was permitted to emerge. In life, of course, Linda had always been fully aware that Cole and Monty were gay. After *Night and Day,* Woolley played character roles in only four films: *The Bishop's Wife* (1947), *Miss Tatlock's Millions* (1948), *As Young as You Feel* (1951), and *Kismet* (1955). He completed his last film at the age of sixty-seven.

By 1943 Monty was being paid "$3,750 for every six days" before the camera, and "$1,000 each week for thirty minutes on the radio."⁵¹ After the completion of *Life Begins at 8:30* in late 1942, Woolley had bought a "modest new home" in Saratoga Springs, at 2 North Circular Street, a few blocks from his brother's home on North Broadway; it had only five rooms, no swimming pool, and no tennis or badminton courts. "The house is inexpensive and just what I want," said Woolley at the time.⁵² Woolley, then fifty-four, and Abbott, fifty-two, made it their permanent home. After many years of living in hotel rooms and in the public eye, the domestic retreat in Saratoga represented the long-sought private sanctuary where Woolley and Abbott could spend the rest of their lives, among friends, family, and a community that had known Monty since childhood.

Sometimes, in the midforties, Monty and Cary drove out to the only gay tavern in the area, the Little Club, in the Fish Creek Marina, at the north end of Saratoga Lake.[53] They commuted to Hollywood when a film project emerged, and upon its completion, they hurried home to Saratoga Springs. Although their Saratoga retreat provided them an escape from the celebrity-seeking press and public, their "private sanctuary" did not actually permit them to abandon the disguise of their homosexual partnership. Saratoga townspeople treated them like good community citizens, as indeed they were; nevertheless, Cary was still identified publicly as Monty's secretary, and only among their inner circle of friends and family was their sexual partnership known. Their closest friends in the community included Frank Sullivan, native Saratogian, member of the Algonquin Round Table, humorist and columnist for the old *New York World* and longtime contributor to the *New Yorker;* Clarence H. Knapp, former mayor of Saratoga; Monty's brother James; and his cousin Myron Woolley, a lifelong bachelor, who ran the Gideon Putnam Hotel.

At the time of his death, on October 5, 1948, Cary Abbott had become "widely known in Saratoga Springs and had many friends," reported the local newspaper. Abbott had unassumingly integrated himself into the community that actually knew little about him. Educated, literate, sophisticated, and, in earlier years a man of considerable means, Abbott carried to his grave the public label that had disguised his true relationship to Woolley for so many years: the *Saratogian* announced, "Cary Abbott, Secretary to Woolley, Dies."[54]

Joe Deuel, a Saratoga friend of Woolley and Abbott, spent "considerable time in their presence" and even visited them in Hollywood while Monty was making a film. Yet Joe Deuel never knew that Woolley and Abbott were homosexual partners.[55] While Monty had many friends in Saratoga in whom he did not fully confide, his inner circle of friends (Sullivan, Knapp, Myron Woolley, and James Woolley) knew of his sexual partnership with Cary Abbott. After Abbott died, Sullivan and Knapp spent "many relaxing hours" with Monty, aware of his "loss," and trying "to cheer their friend."[56]

In about 1958 Woolley met Nathan Goldsmith, owner of the Country Gentleman Restaurant in Saratoga Springs. Curiously, they had never met before but soon developed a close, platonic friendship, and Woolley began coming into the restaurant every evening for drinks and dinner, a ritual that he continued until he died. For Goldsmith, who had no knowledge of Monty's homosexuality, Woolley was "a generous and sweet man who was fun to be with." Woolley's drink was always a martini, or several martinis. "He drank a lot," Goldsmith recalls, "but he was not a drunk, and he was always delightful company." Sometimes "a little old lady would come up to him at the bar and ask for his autograph. He would howl, 'Don't be silly! What earthly good will it do you?' He would fuss a bit and then sign his name. And the lady could see that he was putting on a Monty Woolley act."[57]

On the night of April 6, 1963, Monty Woolley called Joe Deuel on the telephone, saying that he was ill and needed help. Deuel drove him to the emergency room of the Saratoga Hospital, "not realizing that Monty was so ill that he would not return."[58] Woolley was transferred on April 8 to the Albany (New York) Hospital, where he died on Monday, May 6. At Woolley's death, his family (surviving sister-in-law Dorothy Woolley) received telegrams from Cole Porter (who was to die in the following year), Isabelle Wilder (sister of the playwright), and Gerald Murphy, a former Yale classmate and longtime friend of Cole Porter and Monty. Perhaps most poignant of all was a message from the Yale Dramatic Association, which read, "With fond memories . . . for the man who was so rich a part of our theatrical heritage."[59]

For posterity, Woolley's achievements as a director and actor are minor but indelible. The *New Yorker* stated that if he had done nothing else in life, "the delight and solace" he brought to Cole Porter would justify his existence.[60] But to give Woolley his due, one should grant that he achieved exceptional critical and public recognition for his work on stage and in films, entertaining millions of people at the end of the Great Depression and throughout World War II. That his peers in the film industry nominated him for an Academy Award as best actor in 1943, and for best supporting actor in the following year, testifies to the artistic distinction he had been able to gain in an industry that initially had treated him without respect. After the success of *The Man Who Came to Dinner* at Warner Brothers, Twentieth Century Fox signed Monty to a long-term contract and aggressively pursued screen properties for him. *The Pied Piper* (1942), *Life Begins at 8:30* (1942), *Holy Matrimony* (1943), and *Molly and Me* (1944), were not only popular but critical successes; in the latter two he was teamed with Gracie Fields, retaining the witty, acerbic, and undeniably charming Woolley/Whiteside persona. One critic noted that although

Woolley had in several pictures,played virtually the same character, "he remains as freshly comical as ever."[61]

Woolley's homosexuality undoubtedly affected his public career as well as his personal life. His earliest success on Broadway as the ballet impresario in *On Your Toes* stemmed from his gay sensibility and humor, as well as his innate talent. Moreover, Kaufman and Hart's awareness of Monty's homosexuality, penetrating wit, and skillful role-playing influenced their casting him as Whiteside, a role that became inseparable from Woolley's own persona throughout his career. Certainly, Woolley publicly played variations upon the essential Whiteside, on screen and off, as long as he lived. Further, Woolley's lifetime need to disguise his private sexual lifestyle from the public surely sensitized his understanding of like individuals, real or fictional, accounting in part for his perceptive and appealing depictions of irascible wits, always outsiders, who wage verbal assault upon the petty thinkers who dominate the landscape.

In his hometown of Saratoga Springs, although his homosexual relationship with his lover Cary Abbott remained secret to the community at large, Monty Woolley clearly was respected by the townspeople. In 1945, Woolley was elected mayor of Saratoga by a write-in vote. Gratified and touched by the tribute, he initially accepted and then declined, because he feared that he could not do justice to the demands of the job. For the community, he gave a special performance of *The Man Who Came to Dinner* in 1948, and in the following year, Saratoga Springs awarded him an elaborate testimonial dinner, the pageantry for which lasted the full day leading up to the evening banquet, the largest event ever staged by the town for one of its own citizens.[62]

"My heart lies in Saratoga Springs," Woolley once said. "In Saratoga there [are friends], and there is a good way of life, and more than anything else, in Saratoga, I'm not Monty. I'm Edgar and that makes me very happy indeed."[63] Actually, such were the times that even in his beloved heartland, aside from a few childhood friends, Monty was compelled to disguise the private Edgar until death.

NOTES

1. Marion Meade, *Dorothy Parker* (New York: Villard Books, 1988), 58–59.

2. Robert Kimball, ed., *Cole* (New York: Holt, Rinehart and Winston, 1971), 130–31.

3. George Chauncey Jr., *Gay New York: Gender, Urban Culture, and the Making of the Gay Male World, 1890–1940* (New York: Basic Books, 1994), 2. Chauncey's history demonstrates that social and legal condemnation of homosexuality was present in all periods of American history, although some eras were more repressive than others, with the era following World War II being the most homophobic.

4. Chauncey, *Gay New York*, 135–36.

5. Charles Schwartz, *Cole Porter* (New York: Dial Press, 1977), 38.

6. Frederick C. Othman, "The Beard That Talks Like a Man," *Saturday Evening Post*, September 4, 1943, 46.

7. Howard Teichmann, *Smart Aleck: The Wit, World, and Life of Alexander Woollcott* (New York: Morrow, 1976), 256. Kaufman collaborated with Woollcott on *The Channel Road* (1929) and *The Dark Tower* (1934).

8. Ibid., 253–54.

9. Ibid., 257.

10. Ibid., 262.

11. The phrase comes from an essay on camp: Thomas A. King, "Performing 'Akimbo': Queer Pride and Epistemological Prejudice," in *Politics and Poetics of Camp*, ed. Moe Meyer (New York: Routledge, 1994), 28.

12. Unidentified newspaper clipping, Monty Woolley File, Billy Rose Theatre Collection, Lincoln Center Library for the Performing Arts, New York Public Library.

13. For a history of the Grand Union Hotel in the late nineteenth century see Hugh Bradley, *Such Was Saratoga* (New York: Doubleday, Duran, 1940).

14. *Saratogian*, August 2, 1949.

15. Russell Maloney, "Profiles," *New Yorker*, January 20, 1940, 26.

16. Ibid., 26.

17. Schwartz, *Cole Porter*, 31.

18. Ibid., 29.

19. Ibid., 30.

20. In the thirties, when Woolley came to Saratoga Springs he and Frank Sullivan often met at the Worden Hotel for drinks. After a few martinis, they would create pornographic verse in Shakespearean style, which Monty then gleefully recited aloud in Old English to the lounge patrons (Michael Noonan, Saratoga Springs, telephone interview by author, February 12, 1996).

21. Schwartz (*Cole Porter*, 23) reports on Cole's modest grades during his Yale career and notes that although he entered the Harvard Law School in 1913, he soon abandoned his studies.

22. Charles Ludlum, *Ridiculous Theatre: Scourge of Human Folly: The Essays and Opinions of Charles Ludlum*, ed. Steven Samuels (New York: Theatre Communications Group, 1992), 225–26.

23. Schwartz, *Cole Porter*, 112–15.

24. *Historical Register of Yale University, 1701–1937* (New Haven, CT: Yale University Press, 1939), 554.

25. Schwartz, *Cole Porter*, 36; Maloney, "Profiles," 27.

26. Schwartz, *Cole Porter*, 36–37.

27. *Saratogian,* May 6, 1963; Schwartz, *Cole Porter,* 49.

28. Irving Drutman, "The Town Crier Plus Whiskers," *New York Herald Tribune,* October 15, 1939.

29. *Historical Register of Yale,* 554.

30. *Saratogian,* May 6, 1963.

31. Potter, quoted in Kimball, *Cole,* 72.

32. The decision to hire Baker, which was unpopular with Yale undergraduates, who favored Woolley, resulted in "numerous demonstrations on the campus, climaxed by an attempt to burn Baker in effigy" (Maloney, "Profiles," 28).

33. Schwartz, *Cole Porter,* 114.

34. Ibid., 114–15.

35. Ibid., 145.

36. *Saratogian,* May 6, 1963.

37. Chauncey, *Gay New York,* 353.

38. Alfred E. Twomey and Arthur F. McClure, *The Versatiles* (New York: A. S. Barnes, 1969), 180, 219.

39. Othman, "Beard That Talks," 46.

40. Unidentified newspaper clipping, Monty Woolley File, Billy Rose Theatre Collection.

41. Othman, "Beard That Talks," 44.

42. Brooks Atkinson, *New York Times,* October 17, 1939.

43. Meade, *Dorothy Parker,* 318.

44. Atkinson, *New York Times,* October 22, 1939, sec. 9, p. 1.

45. Maloney, "Profiles," 25–29.

46. Lucius Beebe, *New York Herald Tribune,* November 9, 1941.

47. George Kelly (1887–1974), the American playwright, contemporary with Woolley, lived with his male lover, William Weagly, for nearly fifty years; Weagly was always publicly identified (even to Kelly's Philadelphia family) as George's valet.

48. 1910 Federal Census for Cheyenne, Laramie County, Wyoming; Cheyenne City Directory (1910–11); Cheyenne City Directory (1913–14); Ruth Messick, Saratoga Springs, telephone interview by author, February 11, 1996.

49. *Saratogian,* October 5, 1948; 1920 Federal Census, Cheyenne, Laramie County, Wyoming.

50. Unidentified newspaper clipping, Monty Woolley File, Billy Rose Theatre Collection; *Saratogian,* May 6, 1963; Othman, "Beard That Talks," 12–13.

51. Othman, "Beard That Talks," 12. Woolley appeared as guest on many radio programs and costarred briefly on the *Al Jolson–Monty Woolley Show.* In 1950, he starred in a weekly radio series, *The Magnificent Montague* (with Anne Seymour as his wife and Pert Kelton as the maid), which relied upon the Whiteside/Woolley persona. The show, composed "almost exclusively of insults," contained merely enough plot to move Woolley from scene to scene (John Crosby, "The Art of the Insult," *New York Herald Tribune,* December 20, 1950).

52. Unidentified newspaper clipping, "Modest Home for Woolley," December 19, 1942, Monty Woolley File, Billy Rose Theatre Collection.

53. Interview of anonymous resident, February 11, 1996, by Ruth Messick, and conveyed to the author by telephone.

54. *Saratogian,* October 5, 1948.

55. Interview of Joe Deuel, February 11, 1996, by Ruth Messick.

56. Bruce E. Ingmire, "Edgar Montillion 'Monty' Woolley," *Poor Richard's Saratoga Journal,* January 1993.

57. Telephone interviews, by the author, of Nathan Goldsmith, January 16, 1996; Ellen de Lalla, January 10, 1996.

58. Interview of Joe Deuel, February 11, 1996, by Ruth Messick and conveyed by correspondence with the author.

59. *Saratogian,* May 9, 1963.

60. Maloney, "Profiles," 25.

61. Alton Cook, unidentified newspaper clipping, Monty Woolley File, Billy Rose Theatre Collection.

62. *Saratogian,* May 6, 1963.

63. Norman Poirer, *New York Post,* April 9, 1963.

Cold War Maneuvers

Mary Martin

Washin' That Man Right Outta Her Hair

Stacy Wolf

Mary Martin (1913–90) occupies a singular, almost legendary place in American musical theater history. She created some of the best-known and best-loved roles on Broadway, including Maria in *The Sound of Music* (1959), Nellie Forbush in *South Pacific* (1949), and her signature role—*Peter Pan* (1954). Martin also had a successful touring career, which included extended runs of *Annie, Get Your Gun* (1947), and *Hello, Dolly!* (1965). She performed on radio, on television, and in films, and continues to be associated with the era in Broadway history of lavish musicals with outstanding female characters.

Martin's performances, fame, and life, when read in the context of that moment in political and social history—the Cold War—provide a more complex subject than her sincere, sweet persona and her charismatic, powerful, star quality may suggest. Martin's public, onstage performances, and her "private" offstage ones worked simultaneously and cooperatively to enable her life as a (closeted) bisexual. Her professional choices permitted certain performances of heterosexuality while avoiding others. In the 1940s and 1950s when, as Lillian Faderman writes, "every aspect of same-sex love . . . came to be defined as sick," reading Martin as a lesbian explains many of her personal and professional interests, desires, preoccupations, and practices.[1]

Gossip, Rumor, Innuendo, and Desire

Fall 1994. I'm on a mission. Mary Martin was a lesbian, I've been told. I've never heard this before. I begin to ask around. Gay men nod appreciatively, or maybe condescendingly. "Of course," they say. Straight people look confused. A friend asks, "But wasn't she married?" Lesbians raise an eyebrow. Some say, "What? Are you kidding?" surprised that there is one they didn't know. More often, though, a lesbian friend or acquaintance will grin, and say, "Now, that's juicy." They chuckle. While gender or sexual orientation doesn't guarantee knowledge, particular social positions do enable the acquisition of certain knowledges. White gay men's fascination for musical theater is well documented in autobiography, history, and criticism. For example, in *Love! Valor! Compassion!* (1994) and *Party!* (1995), the central white gay male character quotes and performs bits from Broadway musicals. In the film *Clueless* (1995) and the television sitcom *The Nanny* (CBS, July 24, 1995), a character's knowledge of musicals actually signifies his gayness. Michael Warner notes that gay culture is often practiced at material sites—high art, popular culture, the home, places to shop, and so on—through consumption of theater, film, museums, food, household items, and clothing.[2] Musical theater qualifies as such a material site for many white gay men. Their knowledge of musical theater lore, facts, and trivia serves as both cultural capital and a marker of identity.[3]

On the other hand, straight-thinking positions unproblematically align social practices with visible, naturalized heterosexual identity. If Mary Martin was married (and she was, twice), if she had children (which she did, two of them), then she must have been straight. Or rather, she could not have been a lesbian. And she must have been one or the other. And the existence of her husbands and children is irrefutable. While one might relegate the facts of Martin's personal life to the realm of the private, that displacement would unproductively reinforce false binaries: of public/ private, truth/fiction, authenticity/performance, history/gossip. I hope that this essay, written from my own identity position with its vexed access to "knowledge," will productively dismantle those binaries. My interpretation of Martin's life and work and her personal and professional choices is instigated by the "rumor and gossip [that] constitute the unrecorded history of the gay subculture."[4] I'm interested in the use value of Mary Martin, in the usefulness in both knowing her as, and reading her as, a lesbian. I want to mark the differences between these two approaches. As one succeeds when it secures proof or the facts, the other succeeds by persuasion, but its proof is as real, its effects as palpable, as truth. As W. J. T. Mitchell asserts, "Evidence is a set of facts that have been mustered and put into an interpretive context and are no longer raw material. Of course, then there's a question of whether the facts are raw material."[5] Martin's life "facts" construct her as a literal and performative text whose meanings are struggled over. Her life has been written, her performances sometimes recorded, and all that we know is representation. As all texts are mediated through their public performedness, through language, and through the assumptive operations of heterosexualized narratives, there is nothing transparent about Martin or about sexuality. The facts of her life, her own writing, writing about her, interviews with her, her correspondences, her performances, reviews of those performances, and histories of musical theater in America become elements that can be made to mean differently.

My readings of Martin's self-performances, on and offstage, in her autobiography and interviews, are necessarily fueled by desire, too. My desire encourages and requires active, transgressive readings that always happen in historical work but that are denied, masked, or naturalized. My desire produces this biographical/critical/spectatorial reading of Martin, her career, and her life.

Martin and Halliday: A Passing Marriage

Scholars of gender identity and gender relations in mid-twentieth-century America frequently describe the 1940s as a time when gender relations were disrupted and the 1950s as an era of rigidly defined gender roles. Historian Mary Ryan notes that during and after World War II, "Gender dichotomies assumed a larger role in American culture than in decades past. . . . All in all, the war brought male and female into sharper ideological relief."[6] The marriage of Martin and Richard Halliday and their performances of gender in "private" (that is, offstage, for Martin) at once affirm and confound the stereotypical roles that historians document.

Martin had been married once before, at age sixteen to Benjamin Hagman, with whom she had a son, the actor Larry Hagman. Martin and Hagman divorced several years later, and Martin's mother raised Larry. Interestingly, Martin's first marriage was not publicly revealed until she married Halliday in 1941.

Martin and Halliday met and married quickly in Hollywood, while she was under contract at Paramount and he was a story editor there. Martin and Halliday's brief courtship was not atypical for the early 1940s. They had a daughter, Heller, within a year, and, like many other young families, moved to a smaller, simpler house during the war.

Because of Martin's "starlet" status, their elopement and the events of the early days of their marriage were detailed in the press. The "reality" of their married life, then, is inseparable from its media representation; the facts are within the context of Hollywood studios who could and did fabricate family histories, personality quirks, and stars' tastes and preferences. Still, Martin's later portrayal of her marriage in her autobiography and letters between Martin and Richard Rodgers reveal consistencies introduced by the press in the early 1940s.

Interviews with the newly married Martin follow two overlapping narratives. In the first, she chooses Halliday carefully and rationally, identifying him as an appropriate husband who, like her, is serious and dedicated to his work. In the second version, she finds him irresistible. In one interview, she exclaims: "Everybody said not to marry until I was more firmly established and had the advantage of a romantic publicity campaign—seeing my name coupled with all of the smart men-about-town in Hollywood. Marriage deglamourizes a girl is the Hollywood theory."[7] She adds, "But I'm the kind of girl who's just stubborn enough that when I want something, everything else seems of minor importance. And Dick and I wanted each other."[8] By seeming to reject the pressures of the studio's publicity office, Martin constructs herself as stubborn but also as sincere, two key elements of her enduring star persona. The story that locates her as most interested in her career is tempered by another in which she is unable to resist the man of her dreams, her masculine individuality softened by feminine emotions. While the marriage may "deglamourize" her, it also publicly displays her (and his) heterosexuality.

After their marriage, Martin plays the adoring wife, but these interviews, too, can be read against the grain. During a lunch, one reporter describes "a strange expression [that] lingered for a moment on her mobile face" when Halliday enters the room, "but it changed quickly to one of joy as he rushed over to her, gave her a big kiss."[9] The reporter asks Martin about "the queer look she had worn when she saw her husband": " 'He doesn't object to your lunching with another man for business, does he?' . . . 'Oh, no, of course not,' Mary protested. 'When I saw him standing there I just thought how AWFUL it would be if I weren't married to him.' " Her "strange" and "queer" expressions suggest the "awful" prospect of not being safely married. Lillian Faderman argues that "the 1950s mandated that women learn to lead a double existence if they wanted to live as lesbians and yet maintain the advantages of middle-class American life."[10]

Through the 1940s and 1950s, Martin and Halliday reversed stereotypical gender roles. Ryan comments that "the feminine side of the gender dichotomy . . . was infused with especially potent images of domesticity." Halliday, though, who had a penchant for food and flowers, ran the household. Martin was not interested in cooking or decorating or other domestic activities. Halliday made less then one-tenth as much as Martin at Paramount during an era when a wife's work could add to the family's economic status "as long as she achieved only 'moderate success,' that is, did not challenge the superiority of the male breadwinner."[11] Jonathan Katz, linking such gendered divisions to sexuality, points out "the re-association of women with the home, motherhood, and childcare, men with fatherhood and wage-work outside the home—[this] was an era in which the predominance of the heteronorm went almost unchallenged."[12]

Halliday's becoming Martin's manager masculinized him by legitimating his "feminine" interest in clothing, food, and style, and by providing him with a high-status, business-oriented substitution for "masculine" work outside the home. Midcentury journalists and later biographers downplayed the unusual division of labor in their marriage and emphasized the management aspect of Halliday's activities. Barry Rivadue, author of Martin's bio-bibliography, writes, "Richard's dominance extended to deciding how Martin should look, what she would wear, and how their various homes would be furnished—even mundane aspects of living were sharply redefined for her."[13] She becomes the flighty star and he the reasonable controlling force of the household and of her career.

Still, those who knew Halliday well described him frequently as hysterical and feminine. He was, apparently, not only protective but fiercely overprotective. According to Rivadue, "Halliday had a sensitive, driven nature that often caused him to be acutely defensive and argumentative with Mary's creative colleagues, which, during various stage productions over the years, caused a stream of damaged egos."[14] Noël Coward, with whom Martin and Halliday spent considerable time, portrays Halliday as moody and temperamental, "neurotic, hysterical, noisy and a bad drinker."[15] Martin dedicates her autobiography to Halliday, and she unceasingly thanks him throughout for taking care of her personally and professionally. Martin's excessive professed gratitude to Halliday in her autobiography is at once sincere, as he did enable her to focus solely on work, and also an effort to avoid his being characterized as feminine.

Martin and Halliday's partnership can be read as a passing marriage: They married quickly and had a child soon after that which secured a heterosexual, public front. Halliday became Martin's manager, allowing the public and private to blur, making the public believe that it knew something about the lives of the Martin-Hallidays. Comfortably monied and closeted, they bought a ranch in Brazil near Martin's lifelong best friend Janet Gaynor and her husband (Gilbert) Adrian's property, both for Martin and Gaynor to spend time together, and to escape the glare of

Hollywood and New York publicity. Martin and Halliday's marriage was long and productive, founded on friendship, a business partnership, and a mutual understanding of their bisexuality—an understanding that usefully enabled both of their lives and careers.

Whatever their personal orientation, the gay-baiting of the 1950s assured that Martin and Halliday would maintain a stable marriage. There were political implications as well. As Stephanie Coontz explains, "A 'normal' family and vigilant mother became the 'front line' of defense against treason; anticommunists linked deviant family or sexual behavior to sedition."[16]

Martin achieved fame in the late 1940s and 1950s, during an era in which homosexuality was equated with moral weakness and conflated with Communism. Although there is no indication that Martin was in any way directly involved in the McCarthy hearings, no doubt they had a chilling effect on any person who would engage in homosexual relationships or practices. Martin's money, her well-publicized marriage to Halliday, her child, and her visibility in one of theater's most popular forms could both protect her and insulate her.

Friends

In " 'They Wonder to Which Sex I Belong': The Historical Roots of the Modern Lesbian Identity," Martha Vicinus compellingly tracks an elusive lesbian history while theorizing lesbian historiography. She both praises and critiques Blanche Wiesen Cook's frequently cited assertion, "Women who love women, who choose women to nurture and support and to create a living environment in which to work creatively and independently, are lesbians."[17] As Vicinus notes, this definition both broadens the notion of lesbian identity and lessens the significance of actual sexual practices. In the case of Martin, even Wiesen Cook's concept is problematic, as Martin also relied on many men "to work creatively" and to some observers, was anything but "independent."

Leila J. Rupp, in her essay on relationships between women in mid-twentieth-century America, uses Wiesen Cook's work to distinguish self-identified lesbians who may (or may not) have participated in a lesbian subculture from "a broader category of women-committed women who would not identify as lesbians but whose primary commitment, in emotional and practical terms, was to other women." She adds that "sexual behavior—something about which we rarely have historical evidence anyway—is only one of a number of significant factors in a relationship."[18] Unlike the women in Rupp's study, Martin eschewed politics, feminist or otherwise. When pressed, her politics were extremely conservative, perhaps explicitly racist. She was happily married for many years, to a man whom she most certainly loved. She enjoyed the privileges of money and fame.

Throughout her life, though, Martin had close working and personal relationships with many women, including Cheryl Crawford, Jean Arthur (the Peter Pan who preceded Martin), and Janet Gaynor. She professes her love for these women in her autobiography, beginning with Mildred Woods, her "friend, companion, chaperone, boss, [and] secretary," who accompanied her to California to begin her career. Martin later explains that she and "close friend" Arthur were both obsessed with Peter Pan. Arthur, the godmother of Martin and Halliday's daughter and an outspoken feminist, also "adored" the role, writes Martin, and they took turns dressing as Peter Pan at costume parties. With perhaps unintentional double entendre, she writes that "it got so bad we would call each other up and declare our intentions." They "had endless discussions about how Maude Adams played the role, and Eva Le Gallienne, and we mourned that we had never seen them in it."[19] While Martin's prose always tends toward the hyperbolic, the chapter on *Peter Pan* is rife with passion and peopled with lesbians, including Arthur, Adams, and Le Gallienne.

While the exact nature of Martin's friendships with these women is unknown and unknowable, that the women provided Martin with love, support, and companionship is clear.[20] Martin's chapter on *The Sound of Music* in her autobiography, for example, creates a female world. There are no photographs of men, but rather a publicity photo of Martin as Maria and the mother abbess, and personal photographs of Martin and the real Maria von Trapp, and of Sister Gregory, another "close friend," holding Martin's grandson. Martin explains a particular closeness with the women in this chapter. She describes Sister Gregory, whom she met during rehearsals for *South Pacific*, as "tall, strong, vital," and Martin identifies with her: "She came straight in and boomed, 'Mary . . .' in the kind of voice you would expect from—well, me, but not from a nun." Martin also bonded and blurred with the real-life Maria von Trapp (on whose autobiography the play is based), who told her, "Mary, you were born in Texas and I was born in Austria, but underneath we are the same Maria." Martin studied with Maria von Trapp before rehearsals, and she explains, "After I learned to know her, I could see what she meant. We both have the same drive, the same determination. We are alike." All three reject passive and traditional femininity and insist on closeness between women.

For most of her life, Martin's best friend was film actress Janet Gaynor. After Halliday died, Martin sold the Brazilian ranch and moved to southern California, close to Gaynor, and the two women traveled frequently together. In 1982, they were in a car accident in San Francisco, after filming a segment of Martin's television show for seniors, *Over Easy*. Gaynor sustained injuries in the accident from which she died two years later. Nevertheless, the intimacy and interdependence of their friendship was extraordinary and is necessary to a rethinking of Martin's married life. In a fascinating disclosure, Martin recounts an occasion in which she thought she saw herself on television, but it was actually Janet Gaynor.[21]

The Tomboy, the Star Persona

Martin's relationships with both men and women—her marriage and friendships that sustained her personally and privately—point to a bisexual identity. But even Martin on her own, in the spotlight of interviews and performances, performs an unconventional femininity that signifies "lesbian."

I find Martin's undeniable tomboyishness evidence of her bisexuality. I am also persuaded by Eve Sedgwick, who argues (following Gayle Rubin) that questions of gender and of sexuality are "not the same question," yet that "every issue of gender would necessarily be embodied through the specificity of a particular sexuality, and vice versa."[22] Because of the rigid notions of femininity that prevailed during the postwar years, a nonconventional performance of gender—that is, the active, aggressive, physical tomboy—translates into nonconventional sexuality—that is, lesbianism.

From the beginning of her autobiography (which Martin wrote in the early 1970s, another period of struggle over the meanings of femininity), Martin characterizes herself as a tomboy and portrays her childhood as one full of adventures and promise. She writes that, according to her mother, she was supposed to be a boy. She had a gift for dancing (the physical), was unable to read music (the mental), and refused to wear dresses.

Martin also depicts herself as not conventionally heterosexual. She notes that she read *The Well of Loneliness,* "the quintessential lesbian

novel,"²³ at age eleven. Although she writes that "I didn't have the re-
motest idea what [it was] all about," her reading it at such a young age
and noting it as one of the few books she read as a child is remarkable.²⁴
She emphasizes that her marriage to Hagman at sixteen came from her
desire to get out of a girls' finishing school. After their precipitous divorce, she ran what became a lucrative dancing school in Texas before
heading to California to become an actress.

When Jerome Kern heard her sing, he purportedly urged her not to be
prima donna but to "find and perfect" her own style. Laurence Schwab
helped her land a small part in Cole Porter's *Leave It to Me* (1938) and
sent her to New York. Martin made one of the most stunning debuts in
Broadway history with "My Heart Belongs to Daddy." The lyrics played
on the double entendre of a "daddy," and Martin removed a fur coat, hat,
skirt, jacket, gloves, and beads to reveal a lace chemise and slip while
singing the song sweetly, innocently, "straight." She made several films in
the 1940s but did not become a film star, in part because Paramount
could not successfully mold her into a glamour girl.

The tomboy image dominates Martin's public self, emanating from
her physical and "personal" presence that rejects typical femininity but
relies on it for meaning. Significantly, Martin's body was not "mannish,"
and her personality was "charming and friendly"; thus her boyish qualities were not threatening but rather noted throughout her career and life
without comment. Sometimes described as "tomboy" or "butch," or as a
negation of appropriate femininity ("not pretty," "not seductive"), Martin established her boyishness through her hair, her body, and her behavior. Physicality transmutes into "personality," as boyishness often gets
written as sincerity, implying that Martin lacks feminine wiles and coy-
ness, although such traits are invariably complimentary. In the early
1940s, journalist John Rosenfield dubs her "a friendly, gabby West Texas
girl with an entirely universal enthusiasm for a new and pretty (her word)
husband and a new and very pretty Bel Air house."²⁵ Irving Stone writes
in 1956, "She has no mask to take off. She is enchanted with life."²⁶

Over time, Martin's image mellows; she attains gracefulness, but her
boyishness sustains youthfulness. With "pixie poise unparalleled" and
"unflagging youth," she becomes an adult tomboy: "a curious combination of the great lady and the imp. She is an elegant tomboy." While
tomboyishness does not guarantee lesbian identity, it representationally
signifies it. Models of inversion persisted in the 1940s and 1950s, as the
lesbian was seen as a man trapped in a woman's body. Barbara Creed
writes, "The tomboy who refuses to travel Freud's path, who clings to her

active, virile pleasures, who rejects the man and keeps the horse, is stigmatized as a lésbian."²⁷ In relation to other prevalent images of women in the media, films, and theater of the 1940s and 1950s—glamour girl, sex kitten, wife, mother, ingenue, and even the belting bravado of Ethel Merman—Martin clearly embodies the tomboy.

Throughout her career, Martin's extremely short hair drew attention and became a site of struggle in her performance of femininity. Although she may have originally cut it for the repeated hair-washings of *South Pacific* (and for which she advertised shampoo), and cut it even shorter in a "butch" cut for *Peter Pan,* she kept short hair her entire life. Martin hated beauty parlors: "A waste of time; women sit there and gossip," and she was "one of two women 'permitted' to have their hair cut in the Plaza's barber shop" in the 1950s.²⁸ Martin's hair signifies hetero-femininity when she plays Maria in *The Sound of Music.* A journalist notes in an interview, "The first thing she did was pat her hair appreciatively and exclaim: 'Thank heavens I'm not playing boys' parts any more or hillbillies. I'm being a mature woman again and I like it.' "²⁹ The writer and Martin rely on European traditional notions of long hair as marker of true femininity and of women's (hetero)sexuality.³⁰

Martin's lifelong attachment to the role of Peter Pan also suggests a perception of her own boyishness. She writes, "I cannot even remember a day when I didn't want to be Peter." Martin's overidentification with the role of Peter Pan, more than anything else in her career, underlines a nonheteronormative identity. In her autobiography, she not only repeatedly notes the role's significance in her career, but also connects it to her emotional development and her fantasies. For example, she writes, "I wish I could express in words the joy I felt in flying. I loved it so. The freedom of spirit—the thing Peter always felt—was suddenly there for me. I discovered I was happier in the air than on the ground. I probably always will be."³¹ In a text that underlines, perhaps excessively, her love of everyone, her luck in the theater, and her simple, unassuming entitlement to money and mobility, the passages about Peter Pan convey an underlying unhappiness, a discordance.

Martin's cross-gendering is made textual in a memo from one television executive to another in the 1950s. The memo attempts to sell the "Music with Mary Martin" show for television, explaining why it will get high ratings. One section, called "Fashion," explains how Martin "has a tremendous reputation for favorite fashion" with girls' clothes. "She is likely to set a new fashion in men's clothes because in one number she is to wear 'high hat, black tie and tails.' This should be a sock."³²

**Mary Martin washin' that man right outta her hair
in *South Pacific***

(Photograph courtesy of The Rodgers and Hammerstein Organization.)

That Martin could influence men's clothing implies that she could be seen as a boy.

Martin on Stage

The 1950s are known as the golden age of Broadway musicals, and Martin is known as one of the leading ladies of that golden age. Composers and lyricists like Rodgers and Hammerstein, Lerner and Lowe, Jule Styne, and even the young Stephen Sondheim wrote vehicles with memorable melodies and words. Choreographers like Agnes de Mille and Jerome Robbins worked on Broadway to create dances that were integrated with a musical's book and that charged performers with new skills of movement and dance. While Rodgers and Hammerstein, one of the most prolific and successful musical theater teams, are often criticized for their predictable plots, overly romantic values, and sentimentalized characters, their work answered a cultural desire for optimism, stability, predictability, and an assurance that the (white, heterosexual, Christian) American way was best.

In stark contrast to *South Pacific* and *The Sound of Music,* Broadway also saw the politically, ideologically, and dramatically challenging work of playwrights such as Arthur Miller and Tennessee Williams in the 1950s. Musicals, on the other hand, provided unabashed entertainment that seldom challenged the status quo. Musicals also began to attract a wider audience. *Oklahoma* and *South Pacific,* two of the most popular musicals of the mid-to-late 1940s, as well as *Annie Get Your Gun,* were set outside of New York and featured rural characters. The *Sound of Music, The King and I,* and *Peter Pan* featured children. By representing a broader picture of America, these plays guaranteed their long-term success, and musicals of the 1940s and 1950s continue to be performed in a variety of theatrical venues across the country today. Their widespread popularity attests to their distinctly conservative content.

Although television became the most popular form of entertainment during the 1950s, surpassing film, which had long since eclipsed theater, Broadway musicals still functioned as popular culture available to the middle class. Economic prosperity after World War II insured financial support for Broadway musicals. Musicals' popularity guaranteed hegemonic representations and conservative ideological work; in other words, there were no representations that might denaturalize assumptions about sexuality.

On the other hand, women had much visibility on stage, the best roles were for women, and they dominated Broadway musicals in the 1940s and 1950s. Martin worked with a range of composers, lyricists, librettists, directors, designers, producers, and actors, many of whom were the most famous and powerful of the time. The form of musical theater, with its boldly constructed characters, its emphasis on broad emotions, and its direct performative style, capitalized on Martin's energy and vivacity. Her star power in the 1950s enabled her to choose roles that stressed performative energy and charisma over narrative romance. She could thus play the leading lady and fall in love but spend most of her performance singing solos or dancing with a group of women or children.

According to Martin's autobiography, stories about her, and interviews published during and after her life, she always wanted to be a performer. She was a dancer from a young age and taught dance as well. She was physical, a tomboy, high-spirited, and friendly.

As an actress, Martin's job was to be someone other than herself. Her boyish star persona gave her the latitude to evade stereotypically feminine roles. Because she worked primarily in theater and not in film, she had an unconventional range of opportunities. Her work as an actor in some ways protected her. It shielded her private life, enabling her to create roles that she performed and embodied. At the same time, she was an object of affection and admiration, observed and watched.

In *Womanhood in America,* Mary Ryan cites Helen Deutsch's 1945 *Psychology of Women: A Psychoanalytic Interpretation,* an extremely popular "multi–volume catechism of female psychology" that describes "true woman" as "normal, vaginal, and maternal." Interestingly and tellingly, Martin never played a "true woman." Despite popular culture's glorification of maternity in ladies' magazines and ad campaigns, Martin never played a mother.[33] As Ethan Mordden writes, Martin forcefully remade the Broadway musical to accommodate her own talents, skills, and appearance, with a "goofy verve, a rural gaucheness, not before encountered in a heroine."[34]

Martin also exhibited an unconventional athleticism. She reveled in her flying escapades in *Peter Pan,* despite many injuries. *Peter Pan*'s setting in a world of make-believe gave Martin a freedom to play gender, bound only by the lengthy and complex (although always played by a woman) history of the role. There was no heterosexual romance to play. Heller, Martin's daughter, played Liza the maid in the first production and provided the extratextual proof of Martin's appropriate motherhood-femininity.

The Sound of Music, another play that Martin actively pursued, allowed her to play a particular kind of white femininity, simultaneously recuperating her performance as a woman and resisting traditional rigid gender roles of the Cold War. According to one reviewer, there was no "chemistry" between Martin and Theodore Bikel, who played the captain.[35] For the role of Maria, Martin focused on her physicality and love of music and avoided the heterosexual romance. In her autobiography, Martin describes the German version of the film, in which Maria is always late, "dashing madly" and running as fast as she can, and she appears in the first scene sliding down a long banister. "So off she goes down the banister and lands with a nice clunk—right at the feet of Mother Superior. I couldn't wait to do that. All through rehearsals I kept asking, 'Where's my banister?' "[36] When preparing for *The Sound of Music,* Martin took up boxing.

In one preview article, Martin says,

> I've played very young parts for so long. . . . Here, as Maria von Trapp, I start off young but have to grow up and mature, become a woman with a husband and seven children. Vinnie Donehue [the show's director] said, "Every time you sound young, like a little girl, I'm going to come back and tell you." And he does—and I like it. I'm delighted because I do want to play a woman.[37]

Unlike her performance as Peter Pan, in which she felt like she "was" Peter effortlessly, Martin knows that for her, playing a woman is acting. She writes, "I had to remember the character always, keep a tight rein on my emotions and my performance." She at once acknowledges that she has not played women before, and that women are not natural, are to be played with restraint: "You could never do a kidding thing, never play it broadly."[38]

Performing Lesbian

In all of her performances, Martin refused to feminize (that is, in 1950s aesthetic terms, to weaken) her body. Her taped-for-television performance as Peter Pan demonstrates a commitment to the role—and a joy in it—that surpasses any other. Other taped performances display her resisting a typical performance of heterosexual romance.

In a scene from *South Pacific* that was part of a 1954 televised "Tribute to Rodgers and Hammerstein," for example, Martin plays a female romantic lead unlike any of the other actresses in the scenes from other shows. Barefoot and wearing shorts, her body is strong, and she seems slightly embarrassed that she's been caught falling in love with a man.

Martin is host for the show, which is as much an extended commercial for General Foods as it is a tribute to the musicals of Rodgers and Hammerstein. Martin tells jokes, introduces a scene and song from each show, and performs in several numbers.

When she enters at the beginning as host, she wears a strapless, flowing gown, but she is spunky and unfeminine. She does a comic bit with Jack Benny, then exits. After a scene from *Oklahoma* and a commercial in which a group of women backstage uses General Foods products in preparation for the after-show party, she comes on stage, shaking her head and laughing. Martin seems entirely unlike the women who are preoccupied with cake mix and Sanka.[39] She is active and empowered; she sings, "I feel so gay in a melancholy way that it might as well be spring."

In the scene from *South Pacific* near the end of the show, she enters and sings, winking, "I'm Gonna Wash That Man Right Outta My Hair." The song, performed with other women, plays as female bonding. She strikes her trademark pose in publicity photographs for the show (besides the clownish one in sailor's drag): sitting with legs spread and her elbows on her knees. She sings with her chin up, looking straight out. She's not the ingenue at all.

When Ezio Pinza enters, she performs a gag with a towel over her head, facing the audience and looking quite silly. He sings "Some Enchanted Evening," and he looks big and dark standing behind her, but protective, not threatening, since we know that he's European, monied, and therefore "respectful" and respectable. After the song, they kiss, and one expects that she will come out of the kiss transformed (into a woman) and languid, as do the women in each of the other romantic scenes. Instead, she nods quickly, and puts her hand over her mouth, as if in shock. The song that follows is not sweet but a comic lilting piece, written for Martin. In the first part of the song, (Martin as) Nellie tries to convince the women that she is "normal as blueberry pie." She is very playful and sings with her arms extended and her body loose and gawky, not contained like the women in the other scenes. During the musical interlude she does a barefooted softshoe and puts her hat over her head to sing the second verse, partly hiding her face, again a silly pose. Compared to the dancing and singing styles of the women in the other scenes, Martin as a performer is aggressive, not graceful, not careful.[40]

A publicity photo from *The Sound of Music* also features Martin in an image of strength and independence. It shows her standing left with legs spread and head up—not unlike her Peter Pan pose—guitar in hand and smiling broadly. The seven children are gathered right in a group in sailor suits, all but one bent over, hands on knees, looking up at Martin and smiling. Lauri Peters, who played Liesl, stands behind the other children and eyes Martin/Maria suspiciously (or with curiosity? or with desire?). Despite the publicity about Martin growing her hair for *The Sound of Music,* it is very short, and she looks quite boyish next to Peters's softness and longer hair. The photograph pulls one's gaze toward Martin, confident and competitive, utterly uninvolved with the children. Martin looks up and out, not directly at the camera, but over the heads of the imagined audience in the orchestra. While Martin, the star, and the children were the show's great appeal, the photograph conveys not an image of nurture or interaction, but one of independence. The guitar serves both as a marker of power and as a physical barrier. Although she claimed to be delighted that she was "singing legato for a change," this image is typical Martin, the tomboy.[41] Martin's image resists the play's normalizing forces of heterosexual femininity; she stands apart.

Closets and Evidence

Martin's career extended into the 1980s, including performances in *Hello, Dolly! Legends, I Do! I Do!* and many television shows. But she is still known best for her signature role of Peter Pan, the boy who wouldn't grow up, and this image shadows the later part of Martin's offstage life. Halliday died in 1973 and Martin moved to Rancho Mirage, near Gaynor. The two, who had a "uniquely close relationship," traveled frequently together until the car accident in 1982.[42] Martin died in 1990.

" 'Closetedness' itself is a performance initiated as such by the speech act of a silence," writes Eve Sedgwick, "not a particular silence, but a silence that accrues particularity by fits and starts, in relation to the discourse that surrounds and differentially constitutes it."[43] Martin performed herself offstage as a singer and dancer; as a woman, a white woman, a heterosexual woman; as charming, sincere, sweet, and cooperative; and as a charismatic star. Her offstage performances resonated with and against her onstage performances as Peter Pan, Maria, Nellie, and in the host of numerous television specials. Her onstage and offstage performances are differentially formed in relation to hegemonic assumptions of femininity and heterosexuality of midcentury America. Because the very identity of a "star" is one that makes herself remarkable in relation, Martin's particular silences may be unheard.

But "evidence is rhetorical," as Antoine Compagnon asserts.[44] As scholars of gay and lesbian theater history, we must listen to silences and construct new sounds. Martin's performing herself as straight assured the success of her career. Her wealth and her authentic sincerity, kindness, and hardworking behavior consolidated her performance of heterosexuality. At the same time, the rigid gender roles of the 1950s provided a ground against which her unconventional performances of femininity can be read.

NOTES

1. Lillian Faderman, *Odd Girls and Twilight Lovers: A History of Lesbian Life in Twentieth-Century America* (New York: Columbia University Press, 1991), 133. I use the term *bisexual* to describe Martin's likely actual sexuality; certainly she had sexual relations with men, if only to produce two children. I use the term *lesbian* throughout to mark what I demonstrate to be her significant attachments to women. My use of *lesbian* is meant to suggest the blurriness of the distinction between the terms and its very usefulness in the case of Martin. See Marjorie Garber, *Vice Versa: Bisexuality and the Eroticism of Everyday Life* (New York: Simon and Schuster, 1995). Some of this "evidence" appears differently contextualized in my articles, "The Queer Pleasures of Mary Martin and Broadway: *The Sound of Music* as a Lesbian Musical," *Modern Drama* 39, no. 1 (spring 1996): 51–63, and "The Queer Performances of Mary Martin as Woman and as Star," *Women and Performance: A Journal of Feminist Theory* 8, no. 2 (1996): 225–39.

2. Michael Warner, ed., *Fear of a Queer Planet: Queer Politics and Social Theory* (Minneapolis: University of Minnesota Press, 1993), vi–vii.

3. For example, Boze Hadleigh, a gay music and film writer located in Hollywood, presumes Martin's lesbianism in several of his books. While his presumptive knowledge indicates the access to which I refer, his "evidence" exists. One might reject Hadleigh's texts as persuasive evidence because they exhibit a gossipy, "let's dish" style. On the other hand, Hadleigh's insider status and his ability to schedule interviews with numerous filmmakers, actors, and designers invites a second look at his books. Hadleigh may wish gayness onto some Hollywood figures, but certainly not all. In *The Vinyl Closet*, he describes Martin as a "feminine woman who despite more than one marriage (the second to a gay man) and more than one child, was a lifelong lesbian with once-famous girlfriends— among them Janet Gaynor, Oscar's first Best Actress—and a platonic friendship with Nancy Reagan, whose godmother was lesbian legend Alla Nazimova, once MGM's top-paid star" (*The Vinyl Closet: Gays in the Music World* [San Diego:

Los Hombres Press, 1991], 105). See also Hadleigh's *Hollywood Lesbians* (New York: Barricade Books, 1994), 62, 150. Martin's lesbianism is also mentioned in Donald Spoto's *Blue Angel: The Life of Marlene Dietrich* (New York: Doubleday, 1992), 105n.

4. Andrea Weiss, " 'A Queer Feeling When I Look at You': Hollywood Stars and Lesbian Spectatorship in the 1930s," in *Stardom: Industry of Desire,* ed. Christine Gledhill (New York: Routledge, 1991), 283.

5. "The Status of Evidence: A Roundtable," *PMLA* 111, no. 1 (1996): 22.

6. Mary Ryan, *Womanhood in America: From Colonial Times to the Present,* 3d ed. (New York: Franklin Watts, 1983), 259.

7. Mary Jane Manners, "Making the Honeymoon Last," *Silver Screen,* March 1941, 44.

8. Ibid.

9. Franc Dillon, "Trouble at Home," *Screen Life,* April 1941, 48.

10. Faderman, *Odd Girls,* 145.

11. Ryan, *Womanhood in America,* 259, 286. Martin's having only one child per marriage also underlined her difference from typical heterofemininity (see Ryan, 268). They also apparently had a very large bed—ten feet square (Dillon).

12. Jonathan Ned Katz, *The Invention of Heterosexuality* (New York: Dutton, 1995), 96.

13. Barry Rivadue, *Mary Martin: A Bio-Bibliography* (New York: Greenwood Press, 1991), 9.

14. Ibid.

15. Graham Payn and Sheridan Morley, eds., *The Noël Coward Diaries* (Boston: Little, Brown, 1982), 282.

16. Stephanie Coontz, *The Way We Never Were: American Families and the Nostalgia Trap* (New York: Basic Books, 1992), 33.

17. Martha Vicinus, " 'They Wonder to Which Sex I Belong': The Historical Roots of the Modern Lesbian Identity," in *The Lesbian and Gay Studies Reader,* ed. Henery Abelove, Michèle Aina Barale, David M. Halperin (New York: Routledge, 1993), 435.

18. Leila J. Rupp, " 'Imagine My Surprise': Women's Relationships in Mid-Twentieth Century America," in *Hidden From History: Reclaiming the Gay and Lesbian Past,* ed. Martin Duberman, Martha Vicinus, and George Chauncey Jr. (New York: Penguin, 1989), 408, 409.

19. Mary Martin, *My Heart Belongs* (New York: Morrow, 1976), 202.

20. I found hundreds of fan letters, many of which express crushes that girls had on her, with Martin's responses attached, in her scrapbooks at the Theatre Collection of the Museum of the City of New York.

21. Martin, *My Heart Belongs,* 241, 243, 245, 244, 243, 243, 89. Martin and Sister Gregory might have had more than a close friendship. In an amusing story open to multiple readings, Martin tells of Sister Gregory helping her to rehearse for *I Do! I Do!* by playing Robert Preston.

22. Eve Kosofsky Sedgwick, *Epistemology of the Closet* (Berkeley and Los Angeles: University of California Press, 1990), 30–31.

23. Faderman, *Odd Girls,* 173.

24. Martin, *My Heart Belongs,* 18.

25. John Rosenfield, " 'Howyah, Hon?' or Merely Mary Martin: The Studio Can't Understand It, But Her Heart Belongs to Daddy," August 24, (1940?), n.p., Martin's scrapbook, Theatre Collection of the Museum of the City of New York.

26. Irving Stone, "Mary Martin's Marriage," *Life,* January 8, 1956, n.p.

27. Roger Dettmer, "Review of *Annie Get Your Gun,*" *Chicago American,* October 1, 1957, n.p.; Robert Heilman, "Hello, Mary! Seattle Greets 'Dolly' Star. Aura of Youth Surrounds Miss Martin," *Seattle Sunday Times,* August 22, 1965, 1; Margaret McManus, "Mary Martin: Elegant Tomboy," *Baltimore Sun,* March 29, 1959, 9; Barbara Creed, "Lesbian Bodies: Tribades, Tomboys, and Tarts," in *Sexy Bodies: The Strange Carnalities of Feminism,* ed. Elizabeth Grosz and Elsbeth Probyn (New York: Routledge, 1995), 96. Interestingly, Martin is astride a horse on the back cover of her autobiography. For other recent essays that demonstrate the tomboy-as-lesbian, see Terry Brown, "The Butch Femme Fatale," in *The Lesbian Postmodern,* ed. Laura Doan (New York: Columbia University Press, 1994), 229–43; Paula Graham, "Girl's Camp? The Politics of Parody," in *Immortal Invisible: Lesbians and the Moving Image,* ed. Tamsin Wilton (New York: Routledge, 1995), 163–81.

28. Cited in Rivadue, *Mary Martin,* 166, 173.

29. T. H. Wenning, "The New Season: View from Backstage," *Newsweek,* September 28, 1959, 108. Contrary to what she says in this interview, Peter Pan supposedly remained her favorite part of all time. Martin also wore her hair short through her life as her preferred style.

30. Martin also tellingly parallels gender and class. Maria allows her to play "feminine" and "upper class."

31. Martin, *My Heart Belongs,* 202, 205.

32. Martin's scrapbook, Theatre Collection of the Museum of the City of New York.

33. Ryan, *Womanhood in America,* 264, 261.

34. Ethan Mordden, *Broadway Babies* (New York: Oxford University Press, 1983), 119.

35. Alvin Klein, "*Sound of Music* Sung Superbly," *New York Times,* August 22, 1982, sec. 11 (Long Island section), 21. Klein refers to the original production in his review of a 1982 revival.

36. Martin, *My Heart Belongs,* 242.

37. Seymour Peck, "They Made the Sound of Music," *New York Times,* November 15, 1959, 1, 3.

38. Martin, *My Heart Belongs,* 239.

39. Ryan points out that "the proliferation of automatic gadgets, miracle cleaning potions, and instant food products served primarily to clutter up the household and compound women's chores" and to increase the amount of time women spent doing housework from 1920 to 1960 (*Womanhood in America,* 271). Also see Elaine Tyler May, *Homeward Bound: American Families in the Cold War Era* (New York: Basic Books, 1988), 162–82.

40. Martin's performance of the "goofy heroine" is not unlike the World War I type played by Elsie Janis (see Lee Morrow's essay in this volume) and others.

Read in the context of typical performances of femininity in the 1950s and in relation to Martin's life, her heroine can be seen as resisting femininity and resisting a typical image of heterosexuality.

41. Wenning, "The New Season," 108.
42. Rivadue, *Mary Martin,* 17.
43. Sedgwick, *Epistemology of the Closet,* 3.
44. "The Status of Evidence," 22.

Joseph Cino and the First Off-Off-Broadway Theater

Douglas W. Gordy

In *The Reader's Guide to Periodical Literature* there is no listing for Caffe Cino or Joe Cino [1931–67]. In the Theatre Collection of the Library of the Performing Arts at Lincoln Center there is, in addition to an obituary file, one slim volume of written material that contains some notes on Caffe Cino . . . . It is impossible to do factual research on Joe Cino or his theatre. There are no written records for conventional documentation. One must depend upon personal remembrances. It is as if the details were made deliberately obscure.[1]

Such was written in 1972, five years after the suicide that ended Joe Cino's life, and four years after the seminal Off-Off-Broadway theater that he started, the Caffe Cino, closed its doors for good.

In the ensuing years, not much more has been written about this mysterious figure and his essential theater: a few mentions of the tiny Caffe in scholarly articles on Off-Off-Broadway, a random sentence or, at most, a paragraph in more mainstream sources. Although the Lincoln Center Library presented a retrospective display of some artifacts from the Caffe Cino in 1985, the written holdings remain woefully slight. Playwright Robert Patrick, who served an apprenticeship at the Cino, has fictionalized his experiences there in both his 1975 award-winning play, *Kennedy's Children,* and the 1994 roman à clef, *Temple Slave,* yet there remains no book-length history, dissertation, or, to my knowledge, even a major article, on either the man or his theater. With the deaths and dimming, sometimes drug-addled, memories of those who played major roles in the Cino's success, it becomes even harder to sift fact from myth. Cino's family, many of whom have also since died, have been loathe to provide pertinent personal information, apparently due to some embarrassment over Cino's sexual orientation.

Another problem in obtaining any concrete information on Cino himself is that, like many gay men and other theatrical characters, he created several alternative personae, embellishing and stretching the truth about his life when it suited his fancy to do so. Patrick, who knew him for as long and as well as anyone, says, "Joe told so many people so many different versions of every story."[2] There can be no doubt, however, that Joe Cino was not only the instigator and prime force behind what would eventually become known as Off-Off-Broadway, but was also the first, and for many years the only, entrepreneur to openly encourage the depiction of homosexuality, in all its myriad manifestations, upon the New York stage, at a time when it was still strictly illegal to do so.[3]

What can be established definitively is that Joseph Cino was born on November 20, 1931.[4] He sometimes professed to have been born in New York City's Little Italy, but it is far more likely that his nativity occurred in upstate Buffalo, where he spent most of his youth. His mother, Mary, was kept busy raising her four sons, while Joe led people to believe that his Sicilian father had some connection with the Mafia or Cosa Nostra (which may indeed have been true, and could also account for the family's reticence to discuss Joe's background).

Photos of the young Cino reveal a round, open face, with an olive complexion, bulbous nose, wide-set dark eyes, generous, thick-lipped mouth, and high forehead with curly dark hair; later photos show him with longer, straggly hair and a full beard. Though he felt he was overweight and too short (contemporaries estimate his adult height at 5' 9"),[5] Joe harbored dreams of becoming a professional dancer. He studied dance in Buffalo and made his first theatrical appearance at the age of twelve, singing "I'm Beginning to See the Light" on *Uncle Ben's Liberty Shoe Hour.* Dropping out of high school, Cino arrived in Manhattan by bus during a blizzard on February 7, 1948, barely sixteen years old, to pursue his career. Recalling those days for an interview in 1965, Cino said, "I didn't have a dime . . . and I don't have one now."[6]

The young Cino took a succession of menial positions at the YMCA in Penn Station, at Howard Johnson's, and at the Hotel Statler. "When I got the job at the Statler," Cino said, "I enrolled in the Henry Street Playhouse and took courses in everything—acting, dancing, speech, makeup, things like that. I was there for two years."[7] In the summer of 1953, he was given a dance scholarship to Jacob's Pillow. He also danced with Mary Anthony's company and in March 1957 toured with Alfred Brooks and Maxine Munt.

The heady, liberating atmosphere of the big city seemed to agree with Cino, and he felt free to express his homosexual orientation—an unusually brave move for anyone in the repressive Eisenhower years, when arrests of homosexuals were commonplace. Playwright Robert Heide recalls that the first time he met Joe in 1963, he was warned that Cino ran with a rather wild bunch; that Joe's idea of fun was to dress in drag with his friend, Charles Loubier, then walk the streets trying to pick fights with punks and beat them up.[8] Patrick says that he and Cino sometimes visited gay bathhouses together for furtive, anonymous sex, and that there were even occasional sex parties after closing time at the theater itself.[9] By the time the Caffe Cino was in full operation, however, Joe had become involved in a long-term, tempestuous relationship with a man named Johnny Torry (whose name has alternately been printed as Torrey, Torre, Tory, and even Torres), who worked as a professional theatrical electrician. Torry seems to have been everything Joe prized in a partner and felt lacking in himself: the proverbial tall, dark, and handsome, but also educated (Patrick recalls Torry had a Ph.D.), and strongly masculine.

Those who knew him best describe Cino in mostly glowing, if less idealized, terms; the words warm, gregarious, kind, tender, wise, paternal, honest, supportive, friendly, charitable, and outrageous are frequently used. He could also be stubborn, temperamental, and petty. One critic states: "Joe Cino was like his room: complex, dirty and brilliant. He kept a bottle of Florida Water in the back room which he used profusely when he did not want to wash."[10] Although he spoke perfect English, he would often adopt a comic Italian accent to delight his friends and make fun of his own ethnic background. He also invented a great many slang terms (*kukaya* meant "crazy") and pet names for his coterie: his nickname for himself was *la duchesa porchesa* (roughly, "the porky duchess"); while the highest praise he could give someone else would be to call them a "Rockette," as he adored the precision dancers and thought them the pinnacle of artistic achievement.[11]

As Joe realized his size, or perhaps lack of talent, precluded any chance for real success in the dance field, he opened a small coffeehouse in 1958, first on MacDougal Street, right next door to the legendary Provincetown Playhouse, in the bohemian Greenwich Village area. This initial location proved unsatisfactory, and in December of that same year Joe moved his establishment to its permanent residence at 31 Cornelia Street, on a block-long thoroughfare between Bleeker Street and West Fourth Street, near Washington and Sheridan Squares. The start-up funds for the Caffe (the Italian spelling) Cino were saved from Joe's weekend job working at the Playhouse Cafe, where he first learned the fine art of espresso making. Cino kept his dime and nickel tips in a drawer: "I emptied the drawer out into a paper bag and took it to the bank and it

was $400."¹² Patrick, however, says he was informed that Joe uncava-
lierly "had talked a lover into backing the Cino for him and then dumped
the lover and taken the lease."¹³ This gentleman was undoubtedly Ed
Franzen, a painter who was Cino's initial partner in the new venture.
Cino tells how the new location, the ground floor of a tenement building,
was discovered.

> Ed was working at NYU, in the printing department. He was look-
> ing for a studio to paint in and exhibit his work, and he knew I was
> looking for a place of some kind. He called me one day in Novem-
> ber, 1958, and said, "I just walked down Cornelia Street, and hang-
> ing on this piece of manila rope is a sign saying, For Rent." And I
> said, "What does it look like?" And he said, "It looks like a big
> storefront studio."
>
> When I got there, Ed was in conversation with Josie, the landlady,
> who was hanging out the upstairs window with blonde sausage
> curls. He said, "This is Mrs. Lemma." I said, "Oh, you're Italian."
> She says, "Yes, what are you?" I said, "Sicilian." So she said, "I
> don't even have to come down, I'll throw the keys." She threw the
> keys and we went in and viewed the ruins. The first thing you saw
> when you looked down the room was the toilet at the back. I
> thought, "There's a toilet, and there's a sink, and there's a fireplace.
> This will be a counter, a coffee machine here, a little private area." I
> turned around and looked and said, "This is the room. I have no
> idea what to do with it."¹⁴

Although the rent was fairly modest (less than one hundred dollars),
until 1960 Joe continued his day job as a typist with the American Laun-
dry Machinery Company to supplement the meager income he derived
from the sale of comestibles. The menu consisted of pastries (bought
around the corner at the Bleecker Street Bakery and marked up), eggs,
greasy sandwiches (provolone, peppers, and pimento), Italian sodas,
espresso, and cappuccino (sixty cents a cup and often given free to those
artists who couldn't afford to pay). When there was a shortfall, Joe often
told friends, his family, embarrassed by their gay offspring, sent supple-
mental funds to keep him far from Buffalo.

Cino envisioned his coffeehouse as a place where his friends could
relax, sip coffee, display their art and photography, read Beat poetry, and
discuss philosophy (particularly the new existentialism). In describing its
genesis, Cino stated,

> I started thinking about the cafe in 1954. It would just come and go.
> It would usually go when there were too many people trying to have

a part in it. I would talk about it with close friends and it would just dissolve away into nothing. My idea was always to start with a beautiful, intimate, warm, non-commercial, friendly atmosphere where people could come and not feel pressured or harassed. I also thought anything could happen. I knew a lot of painters, so my thought immediately was, I'll hang all their work. I was thinking of a cafe with poetry readings, with lectures, maybe with dance concerts. The one thing I never thought of was fully staged productions of plays. I thought of doing readings, but I never thought any of the technical things would be important. . . .

We opened on a Friday night in early December, 1958. There were 30 people in there, and they were friends. We had one of those old coffee machines, like a Vittorio Arduino, with the eagles on it. It turned out the machine had no gaskets in it, and at pressure the coffee gushed all over the place. So I borrowed coffee pots all over the neighborhood and set them under the counter and pretended I was getting the coffee out of the machine. I had never thought of having a waiter, so one of the friends took care of the other friends.[15]

The storefront location was a long and narrow space, about fourteen feet from wall to wall, but with a twelve-foot-high ceiling strung with fishnets. It was a dingy, smoky, dusty, cool, cluttered room, with a dozen tiny tables surrounded by bentwood chairs. The walls in time became adorned with paintings done by the clientele, as well as photos of movie and opera stars clipped from papers and magazines, twinkling Christmas tree lights, snapshots, posters, memorabilia, glitter stars, crunched tinfoil, Valentines, religious icons, and other ephemera, eventually accumulating to a depth of a dozen or more items in places. Periodically, everything would be taken down to paint in an effort to discourage the rampant cockroach population, with everything neatly replaced in precisely the same location.

At some point, Cino had actor Charles Stanley and Robert Patrick inscribe a motto above the Caffe's entrance: *Io son l'umile ancella* ("I am the humble handmaiden of the arts"), taken from the Cilea opera *Adrianna Lecouvreur*. Dominating the front counter was Joe's prized espresso machine, which accumulated a screen of bells, beads, knick-knacks and wind chimes in front of it, which Joe would ring to announce the start of a show. Cino presided over everything in his customary uniform of blue jeans, yellow construction boots, and an inside-out sweatshirt, augmented on special occasions by an exotic black thrift-shop cape. For most of the Caffe's existence, Joe slept on a mattress in the back room; occasionally friends would lend him keys to their apartments so that he could get a good night's rest on sofas or spare beds.

Cino's lover, electrical wizard Torry, along with John P. Dodd (who would become the Caffe's resident lighting designer-operator), illegally hooked the Cino into the city subway system's electrical lines; Con Edison had no idea that it was providing free electricity for the exterior, interior, and stage lighting of the first Off-Off-Broadway theater. On the constantly playing jukebox, Joe eschewed the folk and pop music of the day (Bob Dylan, for example, was strictly forbidden until Cino learned he was a nice Jewish boy living in Brooklyn), in favor of grand opera and the more traditional sounds of Rudy Vallee and his beloved Kate Smith.

Although there was no formal acknowledgment of such, most of the regulars were young men who had gravitated to New York in the closeted fifties and early sixties to express their first glimmerings of homosexual orientation. (Though several women—Helene Hanft, Magie Dominic, Lady Hope Stansbury, and Merrill Mushroom among them—made important contributions to the Cino, there appear to have been few, if any, overtly lesbian women in the Cino inner circle.) And though they considered themselves extremely avant-garde, most of the predominantly white customers were, by today's standards, rather clean-cut and mainstream; pictures from the time show them with short hair and wearing the requisite turtlenecks and chinos. The eclectic clientele would also come to include several ex cons; middle-aged, middle-class tourists who wandered in; and, after their own shows were over, the neighborhood strippers: the wall proudly displayed the garter belt of an ecdysiast named Stormy who would often demonstrate her technique to the crowds. Joe himself would occasionally essay a little dance step around the room, often in the nude after hours. Johnny Torry would also sporadically strip, kinkily drip hot candle wax over his torso, and enlist the help of the customers to peel it off after it hardened.[16]

Eventually, Joe began to allow folksingers to try out their material; impromptu poetry readings soon followed. There was initially no stage or designated playing space; performers would set up at the far end of the room or alternately range throughout the eating area. As the room had no license—indeed, at the time there was no licensing category for a coffeehouse-cum-performance space—all presentations were strictly illegal and therefore free. Consensus has it that the first theatrical offerings were initiated by an acting student named Phoebe Mooney; she and other aspiring thespians would try out monologues and short scenes before performing them for their classes, occasionally passing the hat for recompense. Cino recalls,

> We started doing poetry readings, and we had the Risa Corsin Chamber Theatre Group. It turned out to be a bunch of flaky poets. What a farce! They were given every second Sunday, a matinee and an evening. The first reading we had was Jean-Paul Sartre's "No Exit." They did it with three chairs and three scripts. The room was packed, but I didn't even think of doing it again. I thought there were people who didn't want to see this, and I didn't want to disturb the rhythm of the room. But that was a Sunday reading, and soon after that we added Monday. It was one performance a night, and before long we added Tuesday, and so on. The hardest thing was to avoid having performances on the weekend. It took almost two years to get from those Sunday readings to a full week. It was always something different every week. They went into staging right away. The biggest thing was two performances a night. It seemed very challenging to have an 11 o'clock performance. . . . We started doing two a night by January 1961.[17]

The first recorded "production," appropriately enough, was a cutting from Oscar Wilde's *The Importance of Being Earnest,* performed on February 7, 1959. The initial offerings tended to be from classics in the public domain (Aristophanes, Chekhov), or pirated one-acts and adapted short stories (Salinger was a favorite, as was Tennessee Williams, neither of whom ever received a dime in royalties from these underground productions). Almost everyone agrees that the first original script to have been produced at the Cino was an otherwise forgotten entity by James Howard entitled *Flyspray,* sometime during the summer of 1960; although the title provocatively seems to herald the artistic bent of the budding theater, no one now recalls what the play was about or how it was received. However, by 1963, nearly all productions at the Cino were of new, original scripts.

Approximately 250 productions were produced there during the Caffe's nine-year existence. Extra shows were often added at one o'clock in the morning on weekends, or when overflow crowds demanded (playwright Connie Clark remembers that Tom Eyen's one-hour play *Who Killed My Bald Sister Sophie?* had to be performed fourteen times in one weekend to accommodate the overflow crowds). Popular shows occasionally ran more than one week, or, once other venues began opening, would make the Off-Off-Broadway circuit, returning to the Cino for additional runs. Revivals of audience favorites, sometimes years later, were also frequent. At least four shows—the musical *Dames at Sea,* Heide's *The Bed,* Wilson's *The Madness of Lady Bright,* and Patrick's *The Haunted Host*—played over one hundred performances each. Patrick, who began at the Cino as the doorman, recalls, "Legal limit—if we'd been legal— was about 90. . . . I could squeeze in 250—literally—with people on the tables and the floor."[18]

Joe enjoyed introducing the shows with his trademark exclamation, "It's Magic Time!" He would then inform the audience of those Cino-ites and other celebrities who were celebrating birthdays, occasionally dedicating performances to his favorite opera and movie stars, or, on more than one occasion, dropping his trousers to playfully "moon" the audience. Although he would come to nominally direct, or more accurately, oversee, a few productions, Cino maintained a practical, laissez-faire attitude toward most of the shows. Playwright Daniel Haben Clark states,

> Attempts to canonize Joe Cino as a sort of Mother Cabrini of the theater leave me unconvinced, but there is one debt I owe him. He taught me to cut. Joe often referred to the Cino as "The Room," as if it were a nightclub. He was convinced that forty minutes was all the show "The Room" could take. He came to my dress rehearsal with a stopwatch set for forty minutes. He said the lightman had instructions to douse the lights when the alarm went off whether the show was over or not. My play was fifty-two minutes long. Every fourth word had to go. It did. I still use this method. When I get to Hell, I'll thank him.[19]

To realize the importance and lasting significance of the Cino, it is essential to understand the hierarchy of the theatrical venues then in operation. The big Broadway houses, then as now, catered to pleasing the mass audience with big-budgeted, commercially viable vehicles—largely musicals or dramas by established names like O'Neill, Miller, and Williams. Off Broadway, still a relatively recent development, was also primarily interested in proven vehicles by recognized talent; most of its productions were budgeted at an extravagant twenty thousand dollars or more. There were then no places for experimental work by unknown playwrights to try out on a shoestring budget, nor for material that would have proved shocking to the vast majority of the downtown audience. The necessity for such a testing ground was evident, but it was the inspiration of Joe Cino to facilitate its happening in a tawdry little coffeehouse in the Village. In providing such a venue, Cino was fulfilling not only his personal needs for artistic expression, but also, unwittingly, the communal needs of a fledgling homosexual community experiencing its own first steps toward recognition and validation.

According to almost everyone who worked there, Cino had no personal artistic agenda or criteria for what was presented. His dictate to his burgeoning flock of talent was "Do your own thing. Do what YOU have to do." Like La Mama's Ellen Stewart (who would model her own establishment on the Cino in 1962—three years after the Cino had begun presenting shows), Joe rarely read scripts, but rather relied on his own intuition about the people who came to ask for permission to present productions. Because his makeshift theater was never intended as a moneymaking enterprise, Cino's only real restrictions were of time and the imagination. As Patrick has written, the Cino

> was unique in that it presented plays without concern for profit, publicity, propaganda, posterity, propriety, prana, or particular esthetic principles. It was an asylum for rejects. . . . It was a fair pickup joint. It was a good time cheap. It was also what a prominent OOB producer called it: a "homosexual drug ring." . . . Joe let people put on plays because they seemed to need to, and he liked to fill people's needs.[20]

In 1966, for a short introduction he provided for an anthology of Off-Off-Broadway plays (the only published piece he ever wrote), Cino set out his idiosyncratic theatrical philosophy/credo.

> We try to change the feeling of the room as much as possible to go with the current production. When it works it's very rewarding. It's never really planned, but somehow we make it happen in that 24-hour changeover between productions.
>
> The best things happen when the entire company works together with concern for the entire production. The attitudes vary a great deal, but the best rhythm is when the entire company is involved with the production, on stage and off.
>
> I decide on everything that comes into the room. I talk to playwrights, I talk to directors. I work with people. I work by intuition much more than by reading scripts. . . . The thing I've been thinking about is how to be more selective. It's the most difficult thing of all. Sometimes I've let people do things here for no particular reason and their work has turned out to be very special. Certain people have had periods when they did things that were very high, but they're just not doing anything imaginative now. And there are

a few people who come in year after year wanting to work here and I always say no. I like to feel that we're open to everything, but I don't like to feel that the stage is being used simply for abuse or to be shocking. . . . But this is a theatre, a mirror of all the madness of everything else that is happening. . . . It's very small, but there's everything here, and it just keeps moving. Every day it keeps happening. And it's always different.[21]

Despite such moralizing, it is certainly not coincidental that most of the people that Cino allowed to work at his theater happened to be overtly homosexual men, and many of their productions would have been considered shocking to a bourgeois audience.

Because of the illegal nature of the entire enterprise, the shows could not initially be conventionally advertised, even had there been money to do so. Kenny Burgess, an artist who also washed dishes at the Cino, created handmade, one-of-a-kind posters (photocopy machines being nonexistent) that were hung out front or stapled to neighborhood poles and trees. These posters, done in what would become known as the "psychedelic" style, could be read by the cognoscenti or anyone who took the time to decipher them but looked abstract to the uninitiated and, hopefully, the authorities (Burgess went on to become one of the primary designers for Fillmore rock posters). As early as December 1960, however, the *Village Voice* began sending its critic down to review the shows. By spring of 1962, with the arrival of several other "illegal" Off-Off-Broadway venues, the Cino did begin advertising regularly in the *Voice*. However, when the too numerous "Off-Off Broadway Theater" listings were separated out from the "Cafe" listings in 1963, the Cino's ads steadfastly remained in the latter category.

Payola to the authorities to guarantee nonintervention was also commonplace; Patrick remembers, "I used to see Joe slip bills to some of the neighborhood cops. Others he'd take in the back and they'd come out red-eyed or zipping their flies. The cops never bothered us while Joe was alive."[22] The sexual favors to the cops became a problem between Cino and Torry, occasioning more than one breakup during their off-again, on-again relationship. Although today such a relationship might be viewed as dysfunctional or codependent, friends thought Joe and Johnny were a fairly typical, nonmonogamous gay couple for the era. Though their separations lasted anywhere from a few hours to several months, the pair would always eventually reconcile.

As time passed, the need for a more sturdy playing area at the Caffe became apparent; a semipermanent raised platform, eight feet by eight feet, was set in place. (Patrick recalls that it was playwright Lanford Wilson who helped to supply the stage.) Torry and John P. Dodd also installed a primitive light board. As there was little room for elaborate settings or properties on the minute stage, a bed or sofa and a long wicker table that Wilson recalls were in practically every show were typically the only settings. Casts were usually limited to the three or four performers who could fit comfortably on the tiny stage.

Despite the crude conditions, the list of neophyte talent who honed their craft at the Cino reads like a veritable Who's Who of the late-twentieth-century's theatrical elite. Among the recognizable award-winning names are playwrights Sam Shepard, John Guare, and Oliver Hailey, actress-director Tanya Berezin, and performers Al Pacino (whom Heide recalls would often recite Shakespeare at the Cino), Harvey Keitel, Bernadette Peters, Frederic Forrest, Paxton Whitehead, and Shirley Stoler.

What is more important, the Cino was also the breeding ground for an emerging group of more or less openly homosexual artists who would prove the front-runners in the new arena of gay theater. These included actors Charles Stanley and George Harris (who, under his drag name, "Hibiscus," would go on to found the radical drag troupes Angels of Light and San Francisco's Les Cockettes), actor-directors Neil Flanagan and Andy Milligan, directors Tom O'Horgan, Marshall Mason, Ron Link, Michael Smith, and Robert Dahdah, and a plethora of now-established playwrights: Tom Eyen, Paul Foster, William M. Hoffman, Robert Patrick, Jean-Claude van Itallie, Doric Wilson, and Lanford Wilson. Other less recognizable names equally vital to this initial flurry of gay-themed drama include Soren Agenoux, George Birimisa, Haal Borske, Alan Causey, Robert Heide, Allan James, H. M. Koutoukas, David Starkweather, Ronald Tavel, and Jeff Weiss.

Many early Cino offerings were also by well-known European homosexual playwrights: André Gide's *Philoctetes* and *David and Bathsheba* were performed in August 1961; according to Patrick, Genet's *Deathwatch* (October 19, 1961) was done near-nude, *The Maids* (July 1961) near-porno.[23] Although their homosexuality was perhaps less widely acknowledged or known, the works of other gay authors, such as Noël Coward, William Inge, Thornton Wilder, Truman Capote, Jean Cocteau, and Tennessee Williams were also frequently presented. And when the content itself was not blatantly homosexual, the plays were often presented in what could best be described as a "gay" style.[24]

Doric Wilson (no relation to Lanford) was the first playwright to regularly present original gay-themed scripts at the Cino. Though he has achieved some renown since for such plays as *The West Street Gang* (1979), *A Perfect Relationship* (1979), and his retelling of the Stonewall Riots, *Street Theatre* (1988), Wilson was writing openly about homosexuality as early as his first Cino show, *And He Made a Her*. Initially presented on March 23, 1961 (seven years before the oft-cited "first" modern gay play, Mart Crowley's *The Boys in the Band*, appeared in 1968), this examination of the drag scene would be followed by many others. Wilson recalls the typical Cino bedlam that accompanied one show.

> My play *Babel, Babel, Little Tower* (June 24–29, 1961) was written for the Cino and dedicated to Joe. It made use of the whole room, from behind the counter and the toilet in back (flushed on cue) to the tables which Ralph took away from the customers and piled on top of each other to build a tower he hoped would prove I-forget-what to Eppie. At the time, the NYPD were as happy as hornets preventing plays in coffee houses by handing out summonses when not actually physically stopping the performance. I incorporated this living history into the climax: a coppish-looking actor entered from Cornelia Street, ad-libbed a fracas with the waiter/doorman (Scotty), demanded the actors put the tables back where they belonged. The actors refused. Authority in blue destroyed the tower. Most of the audience thought it was for real.
>
> It was very convincing. Too convincing. Opening night a front table was occupied by strippers from Third Street. They were very protective of us innocents in theatre. As the actor playing the cop approached the stage, Sunny (her specialty was tassel twirling) kneed him in the groin. The actor has since taken up Scientology.
>
> The actors and Joe shared the same butcher block in the kitchen— they to make up; he to make sandwiches. There was the night Joanna Vischer . . . applied a slice of pepperoni to her cheek at the very moment Scotty delivered to a customer a rouge pad on a roll.[25]

Wilson followed this production with *Now She Dances* (September 1961), a highly stylized exposé of homophobia in which "Oscar Wilde's *Salome*, as played by some characters in *The Importance of Being Earnest*, turns into a comic and chilling nightmare trial of a liberated, contemporary gay man."[26] Wilson's final show at the Cino, *Pretty People*, was enjoying an extended three-week run (November 19–December 2, 1961), when Wilson and Cino got into an angry argument. Joe wanted to start charging a small admission, or setting a minimum food/drink limit, to reap additional profit from the popular show; Wilson argued that his actors could get into serious trouble with Equity if any form of admission was begun. The run was cut short and, sadly, Wilson and Cino remained on nonspeaking terms until the latter's death.

The quintessential Cino playwright, however, was H. M. (Haralimbus Medea) Koutoukas. Called Harry by his friends, Koutoukas is virtually unknown today, primarily because he refused to allow his extremely visual, crazily chaotic scripts to be published (*Invocations of a Haunted Mind*, a later script from 1969, is included in the out-of-print *The Off Off Broadway Book*). His first of a dozen productions at the Cino, *Only a Countess May Dance When She's Crazy* was the New Year's Eve extravaganza for 1965. Although they were rarely overtly homosexual in content, Koutoukas's stylized shows were high camp before there even was such a concept. Patrick writes that Koutoukas was

> a true poet who enshrined such Cino cult-objects as mirror-balls, cheap glitter, dyed feathers ("cobra feathers"), rhinestones . . . and all other forms of "tacky glamour." Lots of people wrote for the Cino, but only Harry wrote about it. In his feverish fantasies it became: a sewer where an immortal lived with a pearl-coated lobster; the basement of a mad scientist's tower; and the "Heaven of Broken Toys" in his lovely *All Day for a Dollar* (December 22, 1965). . . . He influenced many writers, directors and actors who needed a whiff of the grand manner to enliven their gravity.[27]

Koutoukas's magnum opus was undoubtedly *The Stars May Understand, or Medea in the Laundromat* (October 1965), in which the title character was portrayed by Charles Stanley in drag with a full beard. The playwright was eventually awarded a special career Obie award for his "outrageous assault on the theatre." Koutoukas's final show for the Cino, *Michael Touched Me*, was one of the last shows to play the Caffe before its closing in 1968.

Several other pivotal Cino plays were notable for their "ahead-of-its-time" gay content: Lanford Wilson's elegy for a lonely middle-aged drag queen, *The Madness of Lady Bright*, debuted at the Cino on May 14, 1964, and would play over two hundred performances in its frequent revivals. In Robert Patrick's first play, *The Haunted Host* (November 29, 1964), a gay playwright exorcizes the ghost of his dead lover when a straight boy, the lover's spitting image, invades his apartment. (Patrick claims that the opportunistic relationship depicted was intended to parallel Cino's own with one of the Caffe's hangers-on.) William M. Hoffman's *Thank You, Miss Victoria* (September 7–19, 1965) dealt with phone sex decades before it became a 1990s safe-sex staple, while his

Goodnight, I Love You (August 17–September 5, 1965) portrayed a gay man's fantasies of being impregnated by his lover. George Haimsohn's campy *Dames at Sea, or Golddiggers Afloat* was notable both for ushering in a craze for "nostalgia musicals" (e.g., *No, No, Nanette* and *42nd Street*), and introducing a chubby, unknown seventeen-year-old named Bernadette Peters in her first semiprofessional engagement.

Of course, with so many productions opening and closing so rapidly, quality varied widely—some shows were admittedly amateurishly awful— and numerous problems arose. Often, productions were not ready on time or had to be canceled due to actors not showing up or other unforeseen circumstances. Cino refused to deny his audience the entertainment they'd come for; when John Guare canceled a production at the last moment, the ingenious solution (Merrill Mushroom's inspiration) was to have Patrick run to the corner drugstore and purchase all the copies of whatever comic book they had most of in stock. Cino commandeered any actors he could find, dressed them in makeshift costumes, and made them perform with no rehearsals, the comic book scripts in hand. The actors, whose improvisational skills were already well honed by the campy "regular" Cino offerings, relished the opportunity; results were so popular that impromptu comic book theater became a Cino staple, with Archie and Wonder Woman particular favorites.

As a producer, Joe tended to be more diplomatic than despotic; Bob Dahdah remembers: "When there was a dispute between the writer or the director and the actors, Joe never took sides. He always canceled the show—the wisest thing to do."[28] Once a show opened, however, no matter how poor the production or small the audience, Cino refused to close a show. Michael Feingold recalls,

> It was one of Joe's strict principles that the show went on, audience or not; actors dismayed at facing an empty house were told to "do it for the room," a phrase that quickly became a Cino byword. "Joe regarded the room as a magical place," says Heide. "Things in the room as well as the plays there were somehow designated as sacred."[29]

Cino was certainly not motivated by greed in this regard; the take from the passing of the hat, according to Lanford Wilson, averaged sixteen dollars a week. Cino's close friend Charles Loubier has said, "Material things didn't mean a goddam thing to Joe. His waiters always made more money than he did."[30]

By the mid-1960s, the Caffe Cino was well established as Off-Off-Broadway's premier theater, now joined by Ellen Stewart's La Mama (whose first light board was generously installed by the Cino's Torry and Dodd), Al Carmines's Judson Poets' Theatre, Theatre Genesis, and at least a dozen other venues ranging from church basements to lofts; all modeled themselves after the original, the Caffe Cino. In recognition of their efforts, in 1965 Cino and Ellen Stewart were awarded special Obie awards "For creating opportunities for new playwrights to confront audiences and gain experience of the real theatre."

The Caffe also began attracting the attention of both the media and other notable theatrical celebrities. Besides the regular *Village Voice* coverage, Eleanor Lester wrote an influential article for *New York Times Magazine* on the Off-Off-Broadway phenomenon. Arthur Miller, never raising his eyes from his coffee cup, attended David Starkweather's *So Who's Afraid of Edward Albee?* while the titular character of that satire also frequented many Cino presentations. Even the once-banned Bob Dylan attended a show.

Just as things were running smoothly, tragedy struck the Caffe Cino in a fire that gutted the interior on March 5, 1965—appropriately enough, Ash Wednesday. Although officially blamed on a gas leak, Heide says the fire was set, accidentally or on purpose, during one of Torry's periodic drunken rages.[31] The fire's containment was attributed to a fireproof ceiling installed as part of a new lighting grid, the final payment for which, ironically, had been made two days before the blaze. Jean-Claude van Itallie's *War* had just opened, and the sets, costumes, and props were ruined. The productions scheduled for the following month were allowed to perform on the off nights at La Mama and other Off-Off-Broadway theaters, while director Ron Link and Ellen Stewart organized several benefit performances to help pay for the reconstruction.

Playwright Heide recalls that during that time Cino accosted him at a hamburger joint: " 'I think it's time you wrote that "existentialist" play,' he demanded. 'But make it a play for blond men. You know what I mean, Heide. It's time to get off your ass and write it. Now.' "[32] The result, initially performed for a major benefit held at the Sullivan Street Theater, was a play about two homosexuals dissecting their dead-end, drug-saturated relationship (the play featured Larry Burns, who was indeed blond, and the dark-haired James Jennings). Simply entitled *The Bed*, it became a succès de scandale. After the reopening of the Cino (on the following Good Friday), *The Bed* began a regular run. One night, FBI agents arrived to investigate and make sure the gay content wasn't "hardcore." Andy Warhol eventually filmed the production, which became part of his split-screen epic *Chelsea Girls*.

Joe Cino in lobby preceding benefit for burned-out Caffe Cino
(Courtesy of the photographer, James D. Gossage.)

This influx of the "Warhol crowd" inadvertently spelled the moment
of decline for the Caffe Cino. Although casual drug use had been a part of
the Cino scene almost from the beginning, Warhol's minions brought a
more frenzied, hard drug experience to the fore. Pot and pills gave way to
heroin, speed, and acid; life itself became precarious. Under the influence
of drugs, Cino-ite dancer Freddie Herko was performing an impromptu
nude dance to Mozart's *Coronation Mass* in lighting designer John Dodd's
apartment one evening and either intentionally or accidentally leaped out
the fifth-floor window to his death.

Heide recalls that on one fateful night, a distraught Cino asked him to check the Caffe's bathroom. Heide found Warhol "superstar" Pope Ondine, who was notorious for the size of his genitalia, watching himself masturbate in front of the mirror. Heide left and went to sit with Joe. Ondine came out of the bathroom with a syringe and gave Joe a shot of speed; Heide claims he had no idea until then of Joe's own drug habit. Heide continues the story:

> Robert Dahdah recently told me that Joe went to a doctor during this agitated period of his life and was advised to stop taking all drugs, that his heart could not stand the strain. He then flew home to Buffalo, to his mother, where he planned to stay two weeks and go cold turkey. He returned to Manhattan after three days, following a convulsion. Joe seemed to need drugs to assuage his intense emotional pain. But his friends were noticing that he was becoming more and more paranoid. He believed he was being followed and would jump at people's slightest moves.[33]

The "intense emotional pain" was due to a combination of ingredients, not least of which was the sudden death of Cino's longtime lover, John Torry. Toward the end of 1966, Torry took a trip to New Hampshire to work on the lights for a stock production. What happened there is a matter of conjecture. Perhaps also high on drugs, Torry, who surely knew better, was not wearing gloves as he hung the lights. Whether he intentionally touched a live wire, as some believe, or whether a wrench he wore on his belt accidentally brushed against one, Torry was electrocuted and died instantaneously. The death of his lover, combined with his own drug problems and his despondency over growing older and fatter (Joe often told friends that his unattractiveness precluded him finding another lover), proved too much for Cino.

Four months after Torry's death, on Friday, March 31, 1967, Cino began hallucinating while at the home of actor Neil Flanagan—someone had slipped him LSD earlier in the evening. Although Flanagan tried to keep Cino there, Joe insisted he was all right and wanted to return home to the theater. Later that evening, the upstairs landlady overhead an argument in the Caffe: someone screaming at Joe, daring him to kill himself and end it all. Cino took a kitchen knife and cut his wrists and arms and opened his flabby stomach. He maintained consciousness long enough to phone for help to his friend, director and *Village Voice* critic Michael Smith, who lived just down the street. Smith brought Thorazine, thinking that Cino was experiencing a "bad trip," but found him in a pool of his own blood.

Joe was rushed by ambulance to St. Vincent's Hospital, where he lingered. Word spread quickly throughout the theatrical community and over 130 people showed up to volunteer blood for him—the largest one-day contribution the hospital had seen since the end of World War II. News from the hospital that Cino was out of danger and would recover came almost simultaneously with the announcement of his death. He died April 2, 1967, at the age of thirty-five—on John Torry's birthday.

In another macabre coincidence, the production then playing at the Cino was a revival of Lanford Wilson's *The Madness of Lady Bright,* the story of a lonely, suicidal, aging gay man. Cino had tried to dissuade the production, feeling that it was too close to his own situation. Following Cino's death, the production was canceled; William Hoffman draped all the mirrors on the set in black. Cino's family came, took Joe's personal possessions, and beat a hasty departure back to Buffalo. A celebration of Cino's life was held at the Judson Poets' Theatre a week later; Patrick called it "a huge surrealistic extravaganza."34

The Cino regulars tried to make a go of running the Caffe without Joe, but the life, literally, had gone out of the place. Twenty-eight-year-old actor Charles Stanley ran the Caffe for a while, "using for operating capital an enormous cardboard box of moldy change we found under the coffee machine."35 He eventually negotiated a lease-to-buy from Joe's family, but when he succumbed to his own drug demons, Michael Smith and Wolfgang Zuckerman, a harpsichord manufacturer, bought the theater outright.

But without the protection that Joe's payola and supposed or real Mafia connections afforded, the authorities swooped down on the still illegal operation. 1,250 violations quickly accumulated on the place. According to Patrick,

> Michael Smith had to present three sets of photographs to the court in a precise order: One set showed the Cino without a stage to prove that it was just a coffeehouse and qualified for a restaurant license; the next showed it with a conventional proscenium stage at one end to prove it was a real theatre existing for many years and deserved a theatre license; and the third showed it with an uncurtained stage in the center to prove it was a culturally valuable experimental situation worthy of a club charter and special dispensations from the State.36

The attempts to save the Cino ultimately failed. The legal hassles, the continuing drug problems, and deficit and tax difficulties were too much to overcome. The last production, by one of the few women to write for the Cino, poet Diane Di Prima's *Monuments,* was performed March 5–17, 1968, after which the legendary Caffe Cino closed its doors for good. Now, 31 Cornelia Street is still an abandoned storefront.

Although, sadly, the Caffe Cino and its sprightly owner have faded into undeserved obscurity, their lasting legacy has received a few tributes. The now-defunct Village theater magazine *Other Stages* commissioned several Cino alumni to write up their memories for a special series of articles printed in 1979. As mentioned, the Performing Arts Library at Lincoln Center staged an elaborate exhibit of Cino memorabilia in the Vincent Astor Gallery from March 5–May 11, 1985. It was at the opening ceremonies that La Mama Ellen Stewart spoke eloquently of her mentor, the fringe theater's "Papa": "Joe Cino started Off-Off Broadway. I would like to ask everybody to remember that."[37] And Robert Heide relates that every year on the anniversary of Joe's death, a group of former Cino regulars still gathers on Cornelia Street to remember the good times they all shared there, and the man who made it all possible.

However, the impact that this tiny theater-coffeehouse and its proprietor had, and continues to have, on the American dramatic landscape is immeasurable. Without the Caffe Cino's seminal example, who's to say that there ever would have been an Off-Off-Broadway? The tremendous number of theater artists who honed their skills at the tacky storefront, and would go on to win Tonys, Obies, Academy Awards, and Pulitzer Prizes, is legion. But perhaps Joe Cino's most honorable accomplishment is that, despite the failure of his own artistic ambitions and the instability of his relationship with Torry, as an openly and unapologetically homosexual man in an incredibly repressive age and society, he put himself and his establishment on the line to foster the first accurate, literate, and compassionate portrayals of homosexuality to appear on the New York stage. Without the barriers breached by Joe Cino and his Caffe Cino, the 1980s and 1990s influx of gay-themed drama (*Angels in America, Jeffrey,* et al.) may still have been a long time coming.

NOTES

1. Albert Poland and Bruce Mailman, eds., *The Off Off Broadway Book* (New York: Bobbs-Merrill, 1972), xvii.
2. Robert Patrick, interview by author, November 1995.
3. The so-called Wales Padlock Law, enacted in New York in 1909 and not

formally rescinded by the U.S. Supreme Court until 1975, prohibited any depiction of "sex degeneracy or perversion" upon the stage. See Kaier Curtin, *"We Can Always Call Them Bulgarians": The Emergence of Lesbians and Gay Men on the American Stage* (Boston: Alyson, 1987), 100ff.

4. Robert Dahdah, interview by author, November 1995. See also Mary Henderson, *Theater in America* (New York: Abrams, 1986), 315.

5. Robert Heide, interview by author, December 1995.

6. Michael Smith, "Joe Cino's World Goes Up in Flames," *Village Voice,* March 11, 1965, 1.

7. Ibid., 14.

8. Heide, interview.

9. Patrick, interview.

10. Poland and Mailman, *Off Off Broadway Book,* xviii.

11. Michael Feingold, "Caffe Cino, 20 Years after Magic Time," *Village Voice,* May 14, 1985, 50, 117.

12. Smith, "Joe Cino's World," 15.

13. Patrick, interview.

14. Smith, "Joe Cino's World," 14.

15. Ibid.

16. Robert Patrick, "The Other Brick Road," *Other Stages,* February 8, 1979, 3.

17. Smith, "Joe Cino's World," 14.

18. Patrick, *Other Stages,* 10.

19. Robert Patrick, *Temple Slave* (New York: Masquerade Books, 1994), 21.

20. Patrick, *Other Stages,* 3.

21. Joe Cino, "Notes on the Caffe Cino," in Nick Orzel and Michael Smith, eds., *Eight Plays from Off-Off-Broadway* (Indianapolis: Bobbs-Merrill, 1966), 53–54.

22. Patrick, *Other Stages,* 3.

23. Ibid.

24. See William M. Hoffman, ed., *Gay Plays: The First Collection* (New York: Avon Books, 1979), ix–x, for an illuminating discussion of gay style. Hoffman states: "the manner in which a play is acted and directed will determine if a production is 'gay theater.' I define 'gay theater' as a production that implicitly or explicitly acknowledges that there are homosexuals on both sides of the footlights. Gay theater winks, flirts, and looks at its audience in a certain way, as two homosexual strangers might at a party or bar. . . . Gay theater will certainly 'camp,' that is, emphasize style to such a degree that the style will become the subject matter."

25. Quoted in Richard Buck and Magie Dominic, "Caffe Cino and Its Legacy," 1985 Exhibition Catalogue, p. 7, Billy Rose Theatre Collection, Lincoln Center Library for the Performing Arts, New York Public Library. Ralph and Eppie were performers in the play.

26. Ken Furtado and Nancy Hellner, *Gay and Lesbian American Plays: An Annotated Bibliography* (Metuchen, NJ: Scarecrow Press, 1993), 162–63.

27. Patrick, *Other Stages,* 3, 10.

28. Robert Patrick, "Caffe Cino: Memories by Those Who Worked There," *Los Angeles Theatres*, November 1994, 20.

29. Feingold, "Caffe Cino," 117.

30. Ibid., 51.

31. Heide, interview.

32. Robert Heide and John Gilman, *Greenwich Village* (New York: St. Martin's Press, 1995), 30.

33. Ibid., 31.

34. Patrick, *Other Stages*, 10.

35. Ibid.

36. Ibid.

37. Feingold, "Caffe Cino," 50.

Contributors

Robert A. Schanke is Professor of Theatre at Central College, Iowa. His articles on theater history appear in *Theatre Survey, Theatre Topics, Southern Theatre, Central States Speech Journal,* and *Nebraska History.* He has contributed to numerous reference books and anthologies, including *Women in American Theatre, Cambridge Guide to American Theatre, Cambridge Guide to World Theatre, American Theatre Companies, Shakespeare around the Globe,* and *The Oxford Companion to the Theatre.* He is author of *Ibsen in America: A Century of Change* and *Eva Le Gallienne: A Bio-Bibliography.* His *Shattered Applause: The Lives of Eva Le Gallienne* was a finalist for both the Lambda Literary Award and the Barnard Hewitt Award for theater research. He serves as editor of *Theatre History Studies.*

Kim Marra is Associate Professor of Theatre Arts at the University of Iowa. Her articles and reviews primarily on gender and sexuality in late-nineteenth- and early-twentieth-century theater history appear in *Theatre Survey, TDR, Theatre Annual, Journal of Dramatic Theory and Criticism, ATQ: Journal of Nineteenth-Century American Literature and Culture, Theatre Research International, August Wilson: A Casebook, Staging Difference: Cultural Pluralism in American Theatre and Drama,* and *Performing America: Cultural Nationalism in American Theater.* She has served as book review editor for *Theatre Survey* and as a member of the Executive Committee of the American Society for Theatre Research.

Sam Abel is Assistant Professor of Theater at the University of Vermont. He is the author of *Opera in the Flesh: Sexuality in Operatic Performance* (Westview Press) and has published in *Opera News, Theatre History Studies, Theatre Journal, Theatre Topics, Theatre Annual,* and *Journal of Popular Culture,* and is coeditor of *New England Theatre Journal.*

Noreen Barnes-McLain is Associate Professor of Theater History and Director of Graduate Studies at Southern Illinois University, Carbondale. She coedited with Nicholas Deutsch *Tough Acts to Follow: One-Act Plays of the Lesbian and Gay Experience.* She has published in *Gender* *and Performance: The Presentation of Difference in the Performing Arts* and in several periodicals, including *Performing Arts Resources, Outlook,* and *Callboard.*

Milly S. Barranger is Alumni Distinguished Professor and Chair of the Department of Dramatic Art at the University of North Carolina at Chapel Hill and a member of the College of Fellows of the American Theatre. Her publications include *Theatre: A Way of Seeing, Understanding Plays,* and *Margaret Webster: A Bio-Bibliography.* She is writing a biography of Webster entitled *"Peggy": The Theatrical Lives of Margaret Webster.*

Lesley Ferris is Chair of the Department of Theatre at Ohio State University. At the time she wrote this essay she chaired the department at Louisiana State University. She has published two books—*Acting Women: Images of Women in Theatre* (Macmillan, 1990) and *Crossing the Stage: Controversies on Cross-Dressing* (Routledge, 1993).

Douglas W. Gordy has a Ph.D. from the University of Colorado. As a freelance writer he has published on contemporary and gay theater for numerous publications, including *Theatre Journal* and *Onstage Studies.* He is the theater critic for the *Marin Slant* and served as Conference Planner for the Lesbian and Gay Focus Group of the Association for Theatre in Higher Education.

Billy J. Harbin is Professor and Chairman of the Department of Theatre at Louisiana State University. His essays appear in *Theatre Companies of the World, Contemporary Poets and Dramatists of the South, Theatre Survey, Theatre Journal, Theatre History Studies,* and *Theatre Notebook.* He is coeditor of *Inside the Royal Court Theatre: Artists Talk.*

Jennifer Jones is Assistant Professor of Theatre at the University of Denver. She received her doctorate in theater history and dramatic criticism from the University of Washington and her M.F.A. in Dramaturgy from Brooklyn College. She has published in *Theatre History Studies, Modern Drama, Theatre Notebook, Theatre Studies, American Drama,* and *New England Theatre Journal.*

Lee Alan Morrow has a Ph.D. in theater from Northwestern University. He is the author of *The Tony Award Book: Four Decades of Great American Theater* and *Mary Shannon: A Career in Design,* and coauthor of *Creating Theater: The Professionals' Approach to New Plays*. He is editor of *Missionary Bob Coleman, Mary Telling, Sally Kerlin: Recollections*, and *Mary Shannon: A Career*, and he has contributed articles to *BackStage* and *Playbill*.

Jay Plum is a doctoral candidate in theater at the City University of New York. He has published articles on American drama and theater in such journals as *Modern Drama, Theatre Survey*, and *African American Review*. His current research explores the relationship among contemporary gay male performance, politics, and history from the experimental productions of Reza Abdoh and Pomo Afro Homos to the musical stages of Broadway.

Ginger Strand is Behrman/Perkins Fellow in the Humanities at Princeton University. Her publications include articles in *Theatre Journal, European Romantic Review*, and *American Literary History* as well as contributions to the anthologies *Assessing the Achievement of J. M. Synge* and *Performing America: Cultural Nationalism in American Theater*.

Denise A. Walen is Assistant Professor at Vassar College, teaching theater history and dramatic literature. Her articles and reviews have appeared in *Text and Presentation, Theatre History Studies*, and *Theatre Journal*. Currently, she is writing an article on conceptions of Sappho for an anthology of nineteenth-century English women playwrights.

Stacy Wolf is Assistant Professor in the departments of English and Theatre and Dance at George Washington University. She has published articles in *Modern Drama, New Theatre Quarterly, Theatre Research International, Women and Performance*, and *Journal of Dramatic Theory and Criticism*. She is currently working on a book about lesbian spectators and musical theater.

Index